National Minorities in Putin's Russia

Using a human rights approach, the book analyses the dynamics in the application of minority policies for the preservation of cultural and linguistic diversity in Russia. Despite Russia's legacy of ethnocultural and linguistic pluralism, the book argues that the Putin leadership's overwhelming statism and promotion of Russian patriotism are inexorably leading to a reduction of Russia's diversity. Using scores of interviews with representatives of national minorities, civil society, public officials and academics, the book highlights the reasons why Russian law and policies, as well as international standards on minority rights, are ill-equipped to withstand the centralising drive toward ever greater uniformity. While minority policies are fragmented and feeble in contemporary Russia, they are also centrally conceived, which is exacerbated by a growing democratic deficit under Putin. Crucially, in today's Russia informal practices and networks are frequently utilised rather than formal channels in the sphere of diversity management. Informal practices, the book argues, can at times favour minorities, yet they more frequently disadvantage them and create the conditions for the co-optation of leaders of minority groups. A dilution of diversity, the book suggests, is not only resulting in the loss of Russia's rich cultural heritage but is also impairing the peaceful coexistence of the individuals and groups that make up Russian society.

Federica Prina is Research Associate at the School of Social and Political Sciences, University of Glasgow.

Routledge Contemporary Russia and Eastern Europe Series

National Minorities in Putin's Russia

Diversity and assimilation

Federica Prina

Routledge
Taylor & Francis Group

LONDON AND NEW YORK

First published 2016
by Routledge
2 Park Square, Milton Park, Abingdon, Oxon OX14 4RN

and by Routledge
711 Third Avenue, New York, NY 10017

Routledge is an imprint of the Taylor & Francis Group, an informa business

British Library Cataloguing in Publication Data
A catalogue record for this book is available from the British Library

Library of Congress Cataloging in Publication Data
Prina, Federica.
National minorities in Putin's Russia : diversity and assimilation / Federica Prina.
    pages cm. – (Routledge contemporary Russia and Eastern Europe series)
    Includes bibliographical references and index.
    1. Minorities–Russia (Federation) 2. Russia (Federation)–Ethnic relations. 3. Minorities–Political activity. 4. Regionalism–Russia (Federation) 5. Russia–Politics and government–21st century. I. Title.
    JN6693.5.M5P75 2016
    305.800947–dc23   2015014490

ISBN: 978-1-138-78082-8 (hbk)
ISBN: 978-1-315-77045-1 (ebk)

Typeset in Times New Roman
by Wearset Ltd, Boldon, Tyne and Wear

MIX
Paper from
responsible sources
FSC   FSC® C013056
www.fsc.org

Printed and bound in Great Britain by
TJ International Ltd, Padstow, Cornwall

Contents

Tables

Acknowledgements

As this book is based on my PhD dissertation, I am most of all indebted to my PhD supervisors, Professor Bill Bowring and Professor Alena Ledeneva, for their invaluable advice, support and encouragement throughout the research.

My fieldwork would hardly have been possible without the advice and information provided by Dr Alexander Osipov, who made available to me his substantial network of contacts and unmatched expertise.

I am very grateful to the respondents, who shared with me their experience and knowledge, finding time in their busy schedules to answer my (ever-increasing) questions. I am particularly grateful to those who volunteered logistical support, and made their contacts and resources available to me: among many, I wish to thank Vladimir Abramov, Galina Arapova, Marat Gibatdinov, Lyudmila Gromova, Gulnara Khasanova, Lilia Sagitova, Viktor Shnirelman, Sergey Sokolovski and Zinaida Strogalshikova.

I am extremely thankful to the scholars who took the time to read my work and provide advice and feedback, and particularly Professor Bill Bowring, Dr Alexander Osipov, Professor David Smith, Dr Hèctor Alòs i Font, Dr Konstantin Zamyatin, Dr Pete Duncan, Dr Sherrill Stroschein and Professor Rob Dunbar.

I am grateful to the Economic and Social Research Council, which funded my PhD, fieldwork and trips to conferences, out of the CEELBAS programme (Centre for East European Language Based Area Studies).

Some excerpts of Chapters 4 to 9 originally appeared in academic journals. I thank the publishers of the following journals for allowing me to include an updated version of these materials in this book: the *Cambrian Law Review*, the *European Yearbook of Minority Issues*, the *Journal on Ethnopolitics and Minority Issues in Europe* and the *Netherlands Quarterly of Human Rights*.

Last but not least, I am truly grateful to my extended family for their continuous support. Special thanks go to Neil, Roberta, Ines, Mario, Gino and Carla. I dedicate this book to my father, Giuseppe Prina, without whose love and encouragement I would not have been able to write it.

Abbreviations

ACFC	Advisory Committee on the Framework Convention for the Protection of National Minorities
ADC	Anti-Discrimination Centre
AFUN	Association of Finno-Ugric Peoples of Russia
AO	Autonomous Okrug
ASRT	Academy of Sciences of the Republic of Tatarstan
ASSR	Autonomous Soviet Socialist Republic
CERD	Convention on the Elimination of All Forms of Racial Discrimination
CIS	Commonwealth of Independent States
CSCE	Conference on Security and Co-operation in Europe
ECHR	European Convention on Human Rights
ECRML	European Charter of Regional or Minority Languages
EGE	Unified State Examination (*Edinyi Gosudarstvennyi Ekzamen*)
EU	European Union
FCNM	Framework Convention for the Protection of National Minorities
FNCA	Federal National Cultural Autonomy
FRCSE	Foundations of Religious Cultures and Secular Ethics
FSB	Federal Security Service
GRP	Gross Regional Product
HCNM	High Commissioner on National Minorities
ICCPR	International Covenant on Civil and Political Rights
ICERD	International Convention on the Elimination of All Forms of Racial Discrimination
ICESCR	International Covenant on Economic, Social and Cultural Rights
IEA	Institute of Ethnology and Anthropology
IGO	Inter-Governmental Organisation
ILO	International Labour Organisation
NCA	National Cultural Autonomy
NGO	Non-Governmental Organisation
OSCE	Organization for Security and Co-operation in Europe
PACE	Parliamentary Assembly of the Council of Europe
PC	Public Chamber

RAS	Russian Academy of Sciences
RCC	Russian Constitutional Court
RSC	Russian Supreme Court
RSFSR	Russian Soviet Federative Socialist Republic
SSR	Soviet Socialist Republic
UDHR	Universal Declaration of Human Rights
UN	United Nations
UN-DESA	United Nations Department of Economic and Social Affairs
UNESCO	United Nations Educational, Scientific and Cultural Organisation
UR	United Russia
USSR	Union of Soviet Socialist Republics

1 Introduction

This book is about Russia's unique cultural and linguistic diversity. A multiplicity of ethnic, religious and linguistic communities inhabit its territory – including Slavic, Finno-Ugric, Turkic and Asian groups. According to the 2010 census, ethnic Russians[1] amount to 80.9 per cent of the population, meaning that nearly one-fifth of the citizenry identify themselves as belonging to other ethnic groups. The 2010 census lists 193 ethnic groups and subgroups besides Russians: starting from the biggest minority, the Tatars (3.87 per cent of the population), followed by Ukrainians (1.40 per cent), Bashkirs (1.15 per cent), Chuvashes (1.05 per cent) and Chechens (1.04 per cent); the rest of the population is made up of a myriad of much smaller groups.[2] Multi-ethnicity is legally entrenched: the Russian Constitution states that 'the bearer of sovereignty and the only source of power in the Russian Federation shall be its *multinational* people'.[3] And, while the Russian language is spoken by nearly the entire population of Russia (99.49 per cent), another 169 languages were recorded in the census.[4] Of these, 39 were languages of instruction in schools and 50 were taught as subjects,[5] while the regional media also operate in the languages of minorities. Religious diversity is similarly considerable: while ethnic Russians tend to identify with the Russian Christian Orthodox faith, four religions are regarded as traditional religions of Russia (Christianity, Islam, Judaism and Buddhism).[6] Islam is the largest religion after Orthodox Christianity: in 2010 there were over 16.4 million Muslims in Russia.[7] Russian citizens are further affiliated to numerous other faiths.[8] Yet, despite these exceptional levels of diversity, the Russian language and culture dominate Russia's public life. The plurality of minority cultures and languages occupy only a marginal space in the cultural life of the Russian Federation.

Over the years, the 'national question' has been of great salience in the multi-ethnic Russian empire and Soviet Union. Challenges linked to inter-ethnic tensions have also been a characteristic of post-Soviet history – ranging from the re-assertion of forms of minority nationalism; to the Chechen conflicts (with the spill-over of violence to the wider North Caucasus); to the growth of Russian nationalism and 'migrantphobia'; to the recent belligerency of Russia in relation to former Soviet states. Russian foreign policy in the former Soviet Union has led to international concern at egregious violations of international law – including in the shape of military intervention (South Ossetia and Ukraine). Such major, attention-grabbing events cause the more mundane, day-to-day majority–minority relations within Russia to recede into the background. What this book highlights is not the much-researched ethnically motivated strife (the Chechen conflicts, militant Islamic fundamentalism), violent hate crime against specific ethnic groups (particularly Roma or persons originating from the Caucasus or Central Asia), or relations between the Russian government and former Soviet republics. Rather, the book investigates what happens *within* the borders of the Russian Federation among ethnic groups that rarely make the headlines, and their efforts to promote their cultural and linguistic rights. Nevertheless, Vladimir Putin's adoption of patriotism as a quasi-ideology, and its more 'banal' manifestations, described in this book, go a long way in explaining Russia's attitudes vis-à-vis former Soviet countries and Western actors alike.

This book explores Russia's patterns of diversity and assimilation. Ethnic, linguistic and cultural diversity have been crucial components of past and unfolding Russian history. In the construction of identities, (ethnic) Russians have become accustomed to 'imagining' themselves in relation to the many ethnic groups with whom they have coexisted, whether over decades or centuries (Opalski 2001: 299). Ethnicity has been embedded in the very organisation of society of the Soviet Union and Russian Federation. It is still entrenched in its federal structure (with 21 *ethnic* republics), and there are countless references to Russia's 'multinational' character in laws, policy documents and public statements. A history of diversity (and particularly Soviet-induced ethnic federalism) cannot be nullified even by the most militant Russian nationalist leaders. At the same time, strong countervailing tendencies inexorably advance the assimilation of ethnic minority communities into the Russian majority. These are partially the result of globalisation, by which non-dominant (and non-marketable) languages and cultures tend to disappear unless positive measures are adopted by states to actively preserve them; yet they are also the result of (domestic) homogenising tendencies diluting Russian citizens' diversity. They originate from impulses towards statism and Russian patriotism, and are accompanied by the frequent exclusion from the public sphere of persons belonging to minorities, along with the marginalisation of their concerns.

When examining the dynamics of minority policies in Russia, two systems come into play which are analysed in this book: the *domestic* legal environment and political scene; and *international* mechanisms for the protection of minorities, their languages and cultures, which are also applicable in Russia. Both systems intervene to impact upon the domestic sphere: they are intertwined and at times overlapping. International instruments carry with them the potential to enhance the welfare of minorities, given the substantial corpus of relevant standards – treaties and recommendations by international bodies, as well as international case-law – that has developed especially since the 1990s. Some of these standards can complement the (largely declarative and underdeveloped) Russian legislation in the area of cultural rights of minorities, yet they also generate difficulties linked to the phenomenon of 'legal transplantation'. Meanwhile, there are obstacles in the implementation of both domestic and international law, with informal practices playing a significant role in these dynamics. Thus, this book provides an analysis of the processes surrounding the application of minority policies, demonstrating how actual (informal) practices often contrast with formal standards. It further shows the complexities in the process of relevant international standards filtering down to domestic law and practice. Hence, the book does not focus on normative questions, but on the empirical dynamics at work in the implementation of minority policies. In particular, it examines the interplay of factors that contribute to ethnic, cultural and linguistic homogenisation in Russian society – including the reasons why international standards and domestic law remain, overall, unequipped to withstand the movement towards advancing uniformity.

Russia faces formidable challenges posed by its exceptional ethno-linguistic and cultural diversity, combined with its enormous size. It goes without saying that Russia is a significant player in the international arena, whose potential inter-ethnic conflicts can have destabilising effects well outside its borders.[9] At the same time, tensions in the 'near abroad' – former Union republics of the USSR – are, in turn, reflected internally within Russia. The ethnic groups that have been affected by conflicts since the Soviet Union's collapse have fellow nationals in Russia (i.e. Georgians, Armenians, Azerbaijanis, Abkhaz, Ossetians, Moldovans and Ukrainians): internal and external tensions can be mutually reinforcing. Thus, the limited effectiveness of Russia's minority policies in safeguarding the country's remarkable linguistic and cultural diversity – even when supplemented by international standards and monitoring – could not only result in the loss of its cultural heritage, but also impair the peaceful coexistence of the individuals and groups that make up Russian society.

Main findings

This book argues that informal practices – together with centralism in some spheres, and localism in others – lead, overall, to an advancing cultural homogenisation and a dilution of diversity in Russia. *Informal practices* relate both to the application of international standards, and minority-related Russian law and policy, as well as the functioning of Russian institutions. The form of *centralism* analysed here consists of a centre-driven discourse around patriotism, as well as a widening democratic deficit caused by restricting the devolution of powers and civil participation to the regions. Localism (primarily understood in the sense of *laissez-faire* attitudes) relates to the limited state support for minority languages and cultures to counteract the progressive disappearance of linguistic diversity that is common in a globalising world. The main factors at play are outlined below.

Homogenising Moves. Russia continues to display remarkable levels of diversity and a form of federalism that is partially ethnicity-based. However, general moves towards cultural homogenisation, including as part of an overarching discourse around patriotism, can be discerned. Such homogenising tendencies do not originate from a sort of Russian imperialism aiming at Russification for its own sake – rather, they are instrumental to the furtherance of statism, which is promoted by the political leadership. They manifest themselves in an exclusively *cultural* discourse around minority policies, stripped of a political component, and at times a dilution of the salience of (non-Russian) ethnicity, through the promotion of a 'civic' form of nationalism. However, such 'civic' nationalism often falls back on 'ethnic' (Russian) attributes to concretise otherwise largely abstract principles. In parallel to this, the combined effects of Russia's unique diversity and territorial vastness lead to a preoccupation with unity and cohesion. This, in turn, results in a drive to level difference, rather than in policies targeted to pursue unity and equality *in tandem with* the preservation of diversity.

An alternation of centralism and localism. Russia's policies for diversity management are predominantly centralised, with feeble mechanisms for the participation of minorities in their conceptualisation and implementation – in terms of consultation, political participation and local autonomy. This situation has been exacerbated by a deepening of the democratic deficit under the Putin leadership. On the other hand, alongside discernible moves towards centralisation and uniformity, a condition of *laissez-faire* often prevails at the regional and local levels: the implementation of relevant minority policies and standards are not part of a comprehensive plan complete with targets, while laws and programmes regulating them tend to be declarative. Thus, policies for the enhancement of linguistic and cultural diversity are generally dependent on the discretion and goodwill of public officials, and may be easily neglected.

A prevalence of informal practices. Soviet institutions and models, particularly ethnic federalism, have given an impulse to ethnic mobilisation from the *perestroika* onwards; in turn, ethnic mobilisation itself has employed, and has been moulded around, the existing ethnicity-based institutional framework (Gorenburg 2003). Such institutions are resilient, and have successfully made the transition into the post-Soviet period, with few – or just cosmetic – alterations. At the same time, interview data for this research and secondary sources point to the limited effectiveness of such institutions. Informal practices affect their impact, while also intervening to compensate some of their shortcomings. This results in informal practices and networks frequently being utilised in lieu of formal channels – in the sphere of diversity management, as well as in Russian politics and society more generally. The use of these informal channels produces a sort of dynamics in state–minority relations that can, in some instances, reflect a form of co-optation of leaders of minority groups and the development of *symbolic*, rather than instrumental, policies around ethnic diversity (Osipov 2010, 2012). Informal practices come into play not only in relations between the political leadership (particularly the ruling party, United Russia) and minorities, but also in the interaction between the members of minority groups themselves, through concurring and intertwining inter- and intra-group dynamics.

The complex interaction of domestic and international standards. Circumstances at the domestic level can impair the transfer and application of international standards for minority protection. Such circumstances include the (already emphasised) ubiquity of informal practices, and the projection of the view of Russia as a 'great power' promoted by the political leadership. These factors result in the *selective* implementation of the relevant international standards. This book then reconfirms findings of research on Europeanisation, showing that local factors tend to play a greater role than external ones in determining outcomes in norm diffusion (Hughes *et al.* 2004), with adaptational pressure interacting in variable ways with domestic circumstances in different countries (Green Cowles and Risse 2001). At the same time, in parallel to obstacles to the (top-down) transposition of norms, dynamics running horizontally can also be discerned, which link international non-governmental organisations and some categories of Russian civil society through what Keck and Sikking (1998, 1999) describe as 'transnational advocacy networks'. Indeed, some civil society actors, including minority associations, employ opportunities offered by international law (and contacts with the international community) to promote minority rights. Thus, one should approach cautiously the widely held view that Russia treats international institutions (including those promoting minority rights) with defiance and neglect. More complex dynamics are at play, which are grounded in the intricacies of Russian politics and history, and in the perceptions of such institutions and norms. The analysis of these perceptions reveals complex patterns that vary between different societal segments, and also between individual members of the same group.

Ethnicity and groups

In addressing the cultural rights of national minorities, one has to recognise the need to problematise 'groupness', including the acknowledgment of its constructed, ephemeral and fluctuating nature. Following Brubaker (1996), I move away from a realist understanding of nations as 'real entities', and treat them primarily as 'categories of practice'. As Brubaker clarifies, this shift in perspective does not signify rejecting the 'reality of nationhood' itself: he suggests that '[w]e should not ask "what is a nation" but rather: how is nationhood a political and cultural form institutionalised within and among states?' (ibid.: 16). Accordingly, this book follows a social constructivist approach, treating ethnic identities as socially constructed. It further relies on an institutionalist perspective, by acknowledging that state institutions and programmes have a strong (possibly deterministic) impact in the shaping of identity and human behaviour (Bunce 1999; Brubaker 1996; Gorenburg 2003; Suny 1993). In particular, this book takes into account the legacies of the Soviet institutionalisation of ethnicity (Brubaker 1996), and the crucial role played by ethnic institutions in shaping self-identification and ethnic mobilisation. The research findings point to a lesser role for human agency in shaping inter-ethnic relations and a greater role for evolving socio-political circumstances. And indeed, following a period of ethnic mobilisation in the late 1980s and early 1990s, ethnicity has had, overall, only a marginal role in Russian politics (Giuliano and Gorenburg 2012), as new post-Soviet realities have unfolded. Institutional constraints often precede actors' choices, and this tends to imply institutional continuity and the fact that when institutions do evolve, they commonly to do so incrementally rather than radically (Agarin 2013). At the same time, this book is informed by the view that institutions may not only constrain action, but also have a potential 'constitutive' function, by shaping interests and actors alike (Brubaker 1996: 24). Thus, the study subscribes to the perspective that institutions can lead to the development of cognitive frames, anchoring specific understandings of ethnicity. As we will see later, institutions in Russia have impacted upon the development of particular forms of ethnic consciousness, perceptions and political outlooks, as well as providing a frame for public narratives.[10]

Around institutions per se, as well as government policies on minorities, one can discern ever-changing and ever-developing informal practices in Russian politics and society. Thus, the study examines the processual dynamics of interaction of ethnic institutions with informal practices, particularly drawing on Ledeneva's work on the latter (1998, 2006b, 2013). Formal institutions and informal practices create intertwining patterns that are at times complementary and reinforcing, and at times working in opposition to each other. Finally, I adopt a human rights approach: the cultural rights of minorities analysed here are located within the broader human rights context, and are treated as one of the 'dimensions of human rights' (Mannens 1999: 187); this is in recognition of the fact that an individual's cultural identity is bound up with his/her dignity (Packer 1999: 247; Mannens 1999: 186).[11] As Manners (1999: 186) puts it: ' "culture" constitutes the platform for the intended continuation of the (group) identity and from this it follows that words such as "culture", "existence", "identity", and even "dignity" are very much intertwined'. Cultural rights are examined in relation to participatory rights, as only through effective participation in decision-making and policy implementation can persons belonging to minorities be empowered to exercise their cultural rights.

Structure of the book

Following this chapter's outline of the research methods and focus, Chapter 2 introduces the notions of 'national minorities', 'minority rights' and 'cultural rights'. The chapter further outlines historical legacies in diversity management and the main characteristics of Putin's Russia that are of relevance to the book's findings. The main features of the case studies – three national minorities: Tatars, Mordovians and Karelians – are subsequently introduced.

The remainder of the book is divided into three parts: the application of relevant law and standards in Russia (Chapters 3 and 4); cultural pluralism versus homogenising processes (Chapters 5 and 6); and participation versus the exclusion of minorities in decision-making on cultural matters (Chapters 7, 8 and 9). Chapters 3 and 4 analyse how informal practices affect both domestic and international standards of minority protection. Chapter 3 shows that informal practices frequently prevail over a literal application of the law. The chapter further argues that features of Russia's approach to diversity are frequently at odds with international standards for minority protection – without however implying the international standards' a priori exclusion from the Russian sphere. Chapter 4 elaborates on the theme of selectivity of legal implementation, this time with a focus on legal and judicial practice. This chapter outlines the jurisprudence on linguistic rights of minorities by the Russian higher courts, highlighting the linkages between these judgements and Russia's specificities in majority–minority (and centre–regions) relations. Chapters 3 and 4 combined point to an (often informal) practice that can weigh more significantly than the law – with detrimental effects on the enjoyment of cultural rights by minorities.

Chapters 5 and 6 examine Russia's culturally homogenising tendencies since the 2000s. Chapter 5 outlines the promotion of a *civic* Russian identity under Putin's leadership, and the partial re-structuring of the Russian Federation in order to reduce the salience of ethnicity – processes that ultimately act as homogenising forces. Chapter 6 analyses the standardisation of minority education through legal reform particularly since 2007, and the emergence of a public discourse around patriotism. The resulting scenario is one where cultural distinctiveness tends to be gradually diluted.

Chapters 7, 8 and 9 analyse the obstacles to effective participation of persons belonging to minorities in the area of decision- and policy-making on their cultural rights. Chapter 7 focuses on consultation and cooperation between the authorities and civil society (primarily minority organisations); Chapter 8 examines the consultative mechanism championed by the Russian authorities – 'national cultural autonomy' (NCA); and Chapter 9 analyses the remaining forms of participation: non-NCA mechanisms of consultation and elected bodies. Combined, the three chapters show that minorities do not tend to impact, or even inform, policy-making that affects their cultural rights.

The book concludes that the practical application of minority policies contradicts formal standards, both international and at times domestic, resulting in a movement towards uniformity. Two issues are of particular relevance to minorities in Putin's Russia: an emphasis on the *Russian* language and culture along with the marginalisation of languages and cultures of national minorities; and a 'power vertical' that *inter alia* impacts upon minorities' cultural rights, with patron–client relationships being at times reproduced in the relations between the state and minority institutions.

Methods and fieldwork

The research focuses on the period 2000–2014. The timing offers insights into Putin's leadership, which started in 2000, and the introduction of the 'power vertical' with its centralising measures – prolonged through the joint leadership with President/Prime Minister Dmitrii Medvedev.[12] This period also saw the introduction of amendments, in 2007, to the Federal Law 'On Education', with potentially wide-ranging repercussions for minorities in Russia. The years 2010–2011, when the interviews for this study took place, saw initial, tentative steps to implement these new provisions and education standards.

In the study I do not approach Russia as an unusual, wholly *sui generis* case differing from the norm (Shleifer and Treisman 2004). I acknowledge that Russia faces many of the challenges common to other countries that negotiate relations between a majority and multiple minorities. At the same time, one has to take into account the interplay of factors that influence both political processes and their outcomes: Russia's unique ethnic composition, the legacy of its imperial and Soviet past, and the characteristics of the Putin(–Medvedev) leadership. The implementation of minority law and policies, whether domestic or international, could not be fully comprehended without taking into account Russian history and contemporary political reality.

The study uses data from semi-structured interviews. The interviews aimed at shedding light on some of the intricacies in the application of minority policies, by examining how individuals involved in, or interacting with, relevant institutions perceive and relate to them. Interview data is complemented by the analysis of minority policies, legislation, Russian and international jurisprudence, as well as documents compiled by and submitted to inter-governmental organisations (IGOs) – primarily the Council of Europe.

Case studies

The book focuses on three of Russia's national minorities as case studies: Tatars, Mordovians and Karelians. Representatives of the three groups, as well as other respondents, were interviewed in the relevant ethnic republics: the Republics of Tatarstan, Mordovia and Karelia. The study uses inference and the comparison of the three ethnic groups as case studies, seeking to discern commonalities between them despite their differences with regard to factors such as numerical size and wealth.[13] By comparing ethnic groups that share few common features, I seek to identify outcomes of the application of minority policies and relevant international standards on the basis of common explanatory factors (Landman 2003: 29–30). The research follows a *collective* approach – from Stake's (1995) categorisation of intrinsic and collective case studies. I do not focus on individual idiosyncrasies of the case studies, but I develop more general conclusions where possible (Peters 1998: 29). This collective approach aims at identifying regularities across the case studies that can apply to a broader context, while also recognising that each case study is unique, complex and multidimensional. The three case studies are compared primarily with reference to levels of preservation of cultural distinctiveness, as well as degrees of activism and participation.

Of the three case studies, the ethnic group that is in the strongest position politically, economically, demographically and culturally is the Tatar minority. Tatars speak a Turkic language and predominantly embrace Islam as a religion. Mordovians and Karelians have cultural and religious similarities (Finno-Ugric languages and generally Orthodox Christianity), but Karelians are in a particularly vulnerable position in terms of numbers and the use of the Karelian language, which is virtually disappearing as urbanisation advances in the Republic of Karelia. The Mordovian minority can be placed at an intermediate position between the Tatars and the

Karelians in terms of preservation of its cultural distinctiveness. An additional reason for selecting Mordovians as a case study was the inclusion of the Republic of Mordovia, with the Republics of Dagestan and Altai, in a joint European Union and Council of Europe programme 'Minorities in Russia: Developing Culture, Language, Media and Civil Society'. The two-year programme was launched in mid-2009 and was implemented together with the Russian Ministry of Regional Development – the ministry (then) responsible for minority issues.[14] It aimed to enhance the preparatory process towards the ratification of the Council of Europe's 1992 European Charter for Regional or Minority Languages.[15]

Fieldwork

The fieldwork was carried out in May–June 2010, in October 2010, and in February 2011. The cities visited were:

In ethnic republics: Petrozavodsk (Republic of Karelia), Saransk (Republic of Mordovia), Kazan (Republic of Tatarstan).
Outside ethnic republics: Moscow, St Petersburg, Voronezh, Tver.

Table 1.1 Case studies and fieldwork

Ethnic group	Fieldwork location
Tatars	Kazan, Moscow, Saransk
Mordovians	Saransk
Karelians	Petrozavodsk, Tver

Of the cities outside the ethnic republics, Moscow and St Petersburg were visited primarily to ensure access to scholars at relevant academic institutions and non-governmental organisations (NGOs), which provided valuable insights into the dynamics of majority–minority relations. Voronezh was chosen as an (overall) ethnically homogeneous city, although not devoid of ethnic tensions.[16]

Interviews

Interviews were principally aimed at providing insight into how institutions concerned with minority issues are navigated by people on the ground. More specifically, interviews were used to capture: the complexities in the application of international standards on the protection of minorities' cultural rights, and the respondents' perceptions of such standards; the difficulties in promoting minority languages and cultures through the education system; the dynamics of minority rights activism, cooperation with the authorities or patterns of loyalty, in their intersection with informal practices.

In total 92 people were interviewed – 49 women and 43 men. The respondents who are referred to in the book as belonging to specific minorities (whether the case studies or other) self-identified as such. At the same time, the data show a very frequent convergence of being 'born into a group' and perceptions of ethnic belonging in the respondents. The interviewees were guaranteed anonymity; as a result, interview data is not accompanied by respondents' names, but only by general information on their profession, ethnicity, gender and location of the interview. The majority of interviews were conducted in Russian, unless respondents were fluent in English and indicated that they were fully comfortable in speaking English. The excerpts from interviews in Russian that are reported in the book were translated from Russian by the author. The persons belonging to minorities interviewed were, in nearly all cases, more fluent in Russian than in their minority languages, while a few were bilingual. Media outputs were accessed in English and Russian. Laws, including the republics' (regional) legislation, were accessed in Russian.[17]

While I make no claims of full representativeness, I strove to reflect in the sample the internal diversity of persons belonging to the focus ethnic groups, as well as civil society and public officials involved in the implementation of minority policies. Although respondents displayed remarkable diversity – with regard to ethnicity, gender, place of residence, age, political affiliation, education levels, etc. – the research recorded some significant trends in the way various categories of respondents related to minority policies and their implementation, and in patterns of diversity and assimilation.

In cities not located in the three ethnic republics, I interviewed not only representatives of the focus ethnic groups, but, more generally, representatives of minorities active in the promotion of their languages and cultures. This was for two reasons. First, there were logistical considerations, such as the absence of representatives of one or more of the three focus ethnic groups and their institutions in some of the cities, or the fact that some of the individuals approached declined to take part in the study. Second, I wished to develop a broader view of the processes and institutions studied, and how a region may accommodate its minority population as a collectivity. Indeed, in numerous localities advisory bodies have been established to address minority issues jointly by the various minority communities residing in those areas; the members of these institutions did not always include representatives of the three case studies, while they at times encompassed other minority groups. The supplementary interviews resulted in triangulation and revealed commonalities in concerns across groups, including non-titular ones.

Different questions were put to different categories of respondents, depending on their specialisation and profession. The respondents were divided into the categories reported below. The codes correspond to the coding system used to identify respondents in the book (see the Appendix for full codes, a list of respondents and basic information on them):

1.1 civil society – national cultural autonomy (six respondents)
1.2 civil society – minority NGO (11 respondents)
1.3 civil society – cultural association (seven respondents)
1.4 civil society – peoples' congress (three respondents)
1.5 civil society – human rights NGO (11 respondents)
2   academia (23 respondents)
3   media (11 respondents)[18]
4   public official (18 respondents)
5   school employee (two respondents)

Each respondent is coded in the text: first with regard to their category – from 1.1 (civil society) to 5 (school employee); and second, in order of cities visited and interview date. In this way each respondent has a distinct code, through which the reader can find basic information on him/her in the Appendix (see Tables A1.1–A5.1). There is no full symmetry between the three case studies with regards to categories of respondents, as some of the institutions working on nationality issues slightly differed between regions: for example, Karelia and Mordovia had a specialised Ministry of Nationality Policy, while in Tatarstan the relevant competences have been divided between various state organs. Five different subgroups were identified for civil society respondents. Besides national cultural autonomies, analysed in Chapter 8, I differentiate between minority NGOs and human rights NGOs: although partially overlapping, minority NGOs focus on minority concerns and the preservation of minority cultures, while the human rights NGOs included in the study have a wider spectrum of activity which also encompasses minority rights. I refer to 'cultural associations' to indicate those semi-official organisations, sponsored by the state, that promote minority cultures – such as Houses of Nationalities – and can act as focal points for minority groups in their regions. Finally, Peoples' Congresses are structures established by minorities themselves for internal decision-making and administration. Civil society respondents interviewed included both persons affiliated to 'traditional' organisations (various reincarnations of Soviet ethnic institutions) and persons involved with institutions seeking to embrace new approaches, including through international cooperation. The academics interviewed were primarily employed in state institutions (the Russian Academy of Sciences in Moscow; the Academy of Sciences of the Republic of Tatarstan in Kazan; and state universities in the cities visited). As for the public officials interviewed, their professional activities related, directly or indirectly, to minority issues.

Given my focus on political processes and institutions, I chose not to interview 'ordinary' persons belonging to national minorities – meaning persons not active in promoting their cultures and languages. I concentrated instead on 'active' minority respondents correspond with one or more of the categories listed above. Among the respondents were also several ethnic Russians whose professional activities related to minority issues. Some respondents belonged to more than one category (e.g. academics who were also activists involved with minority associations). I classified the respondents according to their main profession at the time of the interview, but also indicated a possible overlap in categories in the list of respondents.[19]

Data from interviews, like the information on respondents, was coded, using the following categories:

* participation and civil society
* education
* nationalities policy (minority language programmes etc.)
* international standards
* legislation, courts and the judiciary
* media
* federal arrangements

Within these core areas, I looked for the respondents' main messages. I based my classification on the 'framework analysis' developed by Ritchie and Spencer (1994).[20] The commonalities that were distilled from the data analysis related to overarching themes on: informal practices; varied attitudes to the application of international standards on Russia; the alternation of centralism and localism; cultural homogenisation (including in the sphere of education); and minority participation.

Lastly, one should note that some of the issues analysed, such as the workings of Russian bureaucracy and informal networks, are very difficult to penetrate as an outsider. The complexity and the size of the subject studied were too great to allow sweeping deductions based on individual accounts. As a result, I followed the documentary flow and traced the information that was publicly available, while acknowledging the difficulties in gaining a full understanding of the forces behind events. For example, a delay in the implementation of a law could be linked to resistance to it, or to bureaucratic hurdles. I therefore combined factual data with information from interviews, and offered qualified interpretations of events. So as to minimise instances of anecdotalism – a frequent problem with qualitative methods (Silverman 2000, 2005) – I noted in the text instances in which information was provided by the respondents, but could not be otherwise corroborated. If different sources presented different interpretations, this was also explained. When reliable information on particular facts was unavailable, I either refrained from drawing conclusions or indicated that what I offered was my own interpretation.

Research focus

The book focuses on minorities with a historical presence in Russia, rather than 'new minorities',[21] as the latter would necessitate different conceptual tools and methods.[22] I also chose not to analyse a possible discrepancy in the enjoyment of cultural rights between representatives of titular nationalities residing inside 'their' titular republics and others outside them. Some general observations are drawn from interview data for Karelians outside Karelia (in Tver), and Tatars outside Tatarstan (in Moscow and Saransk). Generally, one may hypothesise that the problems affecting titular nationalities outside titular republics are similar to, but more pronounced than, those of minority representatives benefiting from territoriality; however, this hypothesis has to be buttressed by additional research. I also exclude from the analysis Russia's 'small-in-number' indigenous peoples of the North, Siberia and Far East:[23] in both Russian and international law indigenous peoples are subject to a separate rights regime from national minorities, which calls for targeted analysis.

As the research progressed, and particularly during the fieldwork, education and participation emerged as primary concerns for many respondents. These are the aspects of minority rights that feature most prominently in this book. Linguistic and cultural heritage can hardly be preserved without education through the medium of minority languages, or, at a minimum, the study of minority languages as subjects in schools. Additionally, adequate and targeted measures for the preservation and development of minority cultures and languages cannot be effectively formulated without the involvement of the interested parties: persons belonging to national minorities themselves.

Given the very broad scope of minorities' cultural rights,[24] and on the basis of interview data, I further restricted the analysis to the following areas:

- linguistic rights of minorities: the right of minorities to preserve and develop their own language;
- cultural rights in their intersection with the right to education: the right of minorities to be instructed through the medium of their own language – or to be taught their language, history and culture as subjects;
- cultural rights in their intersection with the right to participation: the right of minorities to participate in decision-making and to be consulted on issues that directly affect them, their languages and cultures.

In examining international standards on cultural rights of minorities, I focused on Council of Europe standards. This is for two principal reasons. First, respondents who were asked general questions relating to international standards on minority rights tended to gravitate towards Council of Europe standards, rather than referring to instruments developed by the UN or the Organization for Security and Co-operation in Europe (OSCE). Indeed, membership of the Council of Europe gives everyone in Russia access to the European Court of Human Rights, and the European Convention on Human Rights (ECHR) has penetrated Russia's judicial sphere to a significant degree.[25] Although the ECHR has a limited role in advancing minority rights – not being a minority rights instrument per se – it continuously reasserts the role of the Council of Europe as a supranational institution with the authority to issue binding judgements on human rights in Russia. Second, the Council of Europe's Framework Convention for the Protection of National Minorities (FCNM) is legally binding in Russia. The activity of its monitoring body, the Advisory Committee on the FCNM, has encompassed matters of relevance to minorities in Russia, including the themes found in this book: education in minority languages, political representation and consultative mechanisms. Where needed, I make reference to UN and OSCE standards on minority rights.

Notes on terminology

I use the terms 'nationality' and 'ethnicity' interchangeably, in the sense of the Russian *natsional'nost'*.[26]

I use the expression 'cultural rights', in conjunction with 'minority rights', to designate a set of rights that enables persons belonging to minorities to preserve their cultural distinctiveness and identity.[27]

The term 'minority' is always used with reference to *ethnic* minorities rather than sexual (or other) minorities. Hence, 'minority cultures' is employed in the sense of 'cultures of ethnic minorities'.

Notes

1 Those who declared themselves 'Russians' in the 2010 census.
2 2010 Census. See www.perepis-2010.ru/results_of_the_census/results-inform.php (accessed 3 December 2014).
3 Article 3(1), 1993 Constitution of the Russian Federation (emphasis added).
4 This number does not only comprise languages of national minorities, as the census gathered data generally on 'Knowledge of Languages by the Population of the Russian Federation.' See the 2010 census, Part IV, Item 5. Official figures refer to 130–160 minority languages in Russia. These data were provided by the Russian government for the 2009–2011 joint project (with the EU and Council of Europe) 'Minorities in Russia' (figures cited in Oeter 2013: 38).
5 'Comments of the Government of the Russian Federation on the Third Opinion of the Advisory Committee on the Implementation of the Framework Convention for the Protection of National Minorities by the Russian Federation', 25 July 2012, GVT/COM/III(2012)004, p. 6.
6 The preamble of the Law 'On Freedom of Conscience and on Religious Associations' (No. 125-FZ, 26 September 1997) refers to the four religions as 'an inalienable part of the historical heritage of the peoples of Russia'.

7 According to the Pew Forum, Muslims in Russia were projected to increase from approximately 16.4 million (2010) to 18.6 million (2030), and their share of the population from 11.7 per cent (2010) to 14.4 per cent (2030), http://pewforum.org/future-of-the-global-muslim-population-russia.aspx (accessed 5 October 2014).

8 These include: Roman Catholicism, various other Christian denominations (such as Jehovah's Witnesses and Protestants), Hinduism and neo-pagan religions.

9 There have been instances of ethnically-motivated conflict in post-Soviet Russia, namely the Chechen wars, followed by a spill-over of violence to other North Caucasus republics. Outside Russia, with reference to the Transnistrian conflict, the European Court of Human Rights has acknowledged Russia's responsibility in the perpetration of human rights violations in Transnistria (in the judgement *Ilaşcu and Others* v. *Moldova and Russia*, Application No. 48787/99, 8 July 2004; see also Chapter 3). In August 2008, Russia became involved in a conflict between the Georgian government and separatists in the breakaway region in South Ossetia, ostensibly to protect Russian citizens in the region; although a ceasefire was swiftly negotiated, Russia again went on the offensive by recognising the independence from Georgia of both South Ossetia and Abkhazia. At the time of writing, in 2014, Russia and Ukraine were on the brink of war, following the annexation of Crimea by Russia and clashes between Ukrainian and pro-Russian forces in Eastern Ukraine. In the former Soviet republics other ethnic conflicts have unfolded (Abkhazia and Nagorno-Karabakh), and ethnic tensions exist in the multi-ethnic Fergana Valley (Central Asia). The 'nearness' of these territories, and Russia's former political supremacy therein, result in an interconnectedness of events.

10 Acknowledging these dynamics does not, however, imply the reification of those groups that have been influenced by such frames. Neither does it signify that institutions are fixed: they are simultaneously inherited and, to some extent, malleable – thereby subject to a degree of alteration through their continuous use (Offe 2006: 35).

11 See Chapter 2. On linguistic human rights, see Skutnabb-Kangas (1994).

12 Putin became acting president on 31 December 1999 upon former President Boris Yeltsin's resignation. Having won presidential elections in 2000 and in 2004, he was president until May 2008. He was succeeded by (former Prime Minister) Dmitrii Medvedev, while Putin himself became Prime Minister. In September 2011 Medvedev announced that he would not seek a second term but that Putin would run again for presidency in the March 2012 elections. Medvedev and Putin swapped positions again in 2012, becoming Prime Minister and President respectively. It has been argued that Medvedev has not merely been a powerless entity in the duumvirate with Putin. The opinions of the two leaders have not always converged, for example over gubernatorial elections (see for example *The Moscow Times*, 27 March 2013. 'Medvedev Calls Limiting Gubernatorial Elections "Counterproductive"'). However, under Medvedev's presidency there has been no significant departure from the direction given by Putin to Russia's reforms (Hahn 2010). Hence, in this book I refer primarily to Putin's (or Putin-Medvedev's) policies.

13 For the case studies' similarities and differences, see Chapter 2.

14 The author was involved in the project in 2010–2011.

15 However, the goal of ratification was not attained following the programme's completion.

16 See for example, SOVA, 2 October 2007. 'A High Profile Neo-Nazi Leader Currently under Investigation', www.sova-center.ru/en/xenophobia/news-releases/2007/10/d11682/ (accessed 10 September 2014).

17 Citations from Russian texts were translated into English by the author. Any imprecision in the translations is therefore to be attributed to the author.

18 These interviews were primarily with journalists working for minority-language media. Reference to these interviews is made here for the sake of completeness, although – due to space constraints – issues relating to minority media are excluded from this book.

19 See Appendix. In just one case, a former public official who worked for an academic institution at the time of the interview was classified as a 'public official' rather than an 'academic', given that for most of his professional life he had been a prominent public official [4.13].

20 It involves the identification of the thematic framework, indexing, charting, mapping and interpretation. The list of codes was developed in tandem with the analysis of the data. The data were then classified though a theme-based approach.

21 Medda-Windischer (2014) refers to 'new minorities' as:

> [G]roups formed by individuals and families, who have left their original home-land and emigrate to another country generally for economic and, sometimes, also for political reasons. Thus, they consist of migrants, refugees and their descend-ants who are living, on a more than merely transitional basis, in another country than that of their origin.
>
> (Medda-Windischer 2014: 3)

She further describes historical, traditional or autochthonous minorities ('old minor-ities') as:

> [C]ommunities whose members have a distinct language, culture or religion com-pared to the rest of the population, and became minorities as a consequence of a re-drawing of international borders and their settlement area changing from the sovereignty of one country to another or did not achieve, for various reasons, statehood of their own.
>
> (Medda-Windischer ibid.: 3; see also Medda-Windischer 2008)

22 Moreover, the Council of Europe's 1995 Framework Convention for the Protection of National Minorities was traditionally conceived for 'old minorities'. Similarly, the European Charter for Regional or Minority Languages states that the expression 'regional or minorities languages' does not encompass the languages of migrants (Article 1(a)).

23 On Russia's indigenous peoples, see Chapter 2.

24 See Chapter 2.

25 See Chapters 3 and 4.

26 'Ethnicity' is close to the meaning of *natsional'nost'*, although the two terms do not fully converge. See Shahin (1989: 409–10). See also Chapter 2.

27 For more on this, see Chapter 2. In this book I focus on minority cultures and lan-guages, while for the most part leaving aside considerations on the expression of iden-tity through religion.

2 Diversity, national minorities and cultural rights

Russia and beyond

Institutions that have pioneered minority rights – the UN, the Council of Europe and the OSCE – have refrained from providing a definition of 'minority'.[1] This has meant a lack of consensus, resulting in limited clarity, as to which groups exactly 'minority rights' ought to apply (Thornberry 1991: 164). In practice states can forge their own definitions, and thereby refrain from recognising specific minorities – or *any* minority – residing in their territories.[2] There are various reasons for resistance to a definition in international law, including: the difficulty in formulating an all-encompassing definition given the differing circumstances of minority groups, in terms of historical legacies and social conditions;[3] and the sense of urgency in developing solutions to guarantee minority rights, with or without a conclusive definition (Sigler 1983: 3). Even without an agreed definition, minority rights concerns have existed for centuries, and have been the subject of international agreements, treaties and declarations. These instruments have delineated a minority's core features, although their exact meanings (and the responsibilities of states vis-à-vis minorities) have been the subject of debate and varied interpretations.

This chapter provides an overview of the meaning of 'minority' and 'cultural rights', followed by a brief outline of current debates on diversity, internationally and in Russia. Subsequently, the chapter delineates approaches to the national question in imperial and Soviet Russia, before moving on to the post-Soviet period – and particularly Putin's leadership.

Minorities and cultural rights: definitions and categories

The most frequently cited working definition of 'minority' is that formulated by Francesco Capotorti, former UN Special Rapporteur on the Subcommission on Prevention of Discrimination and Protection of Minorities:

> A group numerically inferior to the rest of the population of a State, in a non-dominant position, whose members – being nationals of the State – possess ethnic, religious or linguistic characteristics differing from those of the rest of the population and show, if only implicitly, a sense of solidarity, directed towards preserving their culture, traditions, religion or language.
>
> (Capotorti 1979)

While no definition has been codified into a legal text, the same qualifying attributes – 'ethnic', 'religious' and 'linguistic' can be found in Article 27 of the 1966 UN International Covenant on Civil and Political Rights (ICCPR), which stipulates:

> In those States in which ethnic, religious or linguistic minorities exist, persons belonging to such minorities shall not be denied the right, in community with the other members of their group, to enjoy their own culture, to profess and practise their own religion, or to use their own language.

These adjectives are also included, *inter alia*, in the title of the 1992 UN Declaration on the Rights of Persons Belonging to National or Ethnic, Religious and Linguistic Minorities.[4]

The search for an ideal definition is a thorny issue in international minority rights law. This question is, however, only marginal to Russia. Unlike states that refrain from recognising some (or all) national minorities residing in their territories, the Russian authorities have acknowledged the presence of over 170 separate ethnic groups in the country.[5] More complex is the meaning of 'nationality' (*natsional'nost'*), which is loosely comparable to the meaning of 'ethnic group': the Russian (originally Soviet) anthropological tradition divides 'nationalities' into two categories: titular and non-titular. A third category is represented by the 'small-in-number' indigenous peoples of the North, Siberia and the Far East.[6] Starting from this last category, one should note that the distinction between indigenous peoples and national minorities is clearly not unique to Russia: indigenous peoples worldwide have insisted on their being distinct from 'simple' minorities, not least because international mechanisms provide greater protection to indigenous peoples.[7] While there is some overlap between indigenous peoples and national minorities, in some cases one group will indisputably fall into one or the other category (Aukerman 2000). As for 'minority', there is no generally agreed definition of 'indigenous peoples',[8] yet a key factor is a close connection with the land a group inhabits as an autochthonous population, and on which the group depends for its livelihood. In Russia a total of 46 indigenous peoples is officially listed;[9] Russian legislation affords these groups special rights with regard to the use of land and natural resources, as well as some autonomy arrangements in the spheres of education, self-government and participation.[10]

For those groups that are not categorised as 'small-in-number' indigenous peoples, a supplementary distinction is made between titular and non-titular nationalities. Titular nationalities are those that were granted territorial autonomy during the Soviet period, and 'assigned' a territory generally named after the group. Given that these nationalities could benefit from territoriality, and that the Soviet nationalities policy enforced affirmative measures for their representation in their territories' administrative bodies, these groups do not tend to be perceived in Russia as 'minorities' – an expression that has been associated with vulnerability and low prestige. These groups have instead been regarded as 'titular nationalities'.[11] In this book I use the term 'minority' (or 'national minority') according to the meaning of the expression in international law. Although Capotorti's is only a working definition, it suffices to classify the nationalities considered in the book, including titular nationalities, as 'minorities'. The three case studies – Tatars, Mordovians and Karelians – are 'numerically inferior to the rest of the population of the state'; they are 'in a non-dominant position'; they are distinct from the rest of the population by the 'ethnic, religious or linguistic characteristics' they possess; and interview data indicate that they have a 'sense of solidarity' combined with a desire to preserve their cultures. Numerical factors are relative: although a minority is (by Capotorti's definition) numerically smaller than the majority, in some regions of a state its members might be more numerous than the majority population (Thornberry 1991: 169). Of the three case studies, only Tatars have a population more numerous than the Russians' within their republic;[12] still, international law approaches the condition of 'national minority' in relation to a country in its entirety. In fact a bigger population does not in itself imply dominance: some groups, though numerically superior, might be in a disadvantaged position.[13] A 'need for protection', then, has to be added to the equation (Ramaga 1992a: 119). It can be argued that Tatars are also in need of such protection in Russia: more than half of Russia's Tatars reside outside Tatarstan, and, even within Tatarstan, the Russian culture and language are, overall, dominant in the public sphere.[14]

Cultural rights

As in the case of 'minority', international instruments do not provide a conclusive definition of 'cultural rights'. Thus, one has to start by unpacking the meaning of 'culture'. The 2001 UNESCO Universal Declaration on Cultural Diversity states in its preamble:

> [C]ulture should be regarded as the set of distinctive spiritual, material, intellectual and emotional features of society or a social group ... it encompasses, in addition to art and literature, lifestyles, ways of living together, value systems, traditions and beliefs.[15]

Reidel (2010: 66) suggests the following definition: 'A set of shared meanings, norms, and practices that form a comprehensive world view that serves to unite a group and contribute to the identity of its members.' Kymlicka (1995: 76) refers to a 'societal culture', as one that: 'provides its members with meaningful ways of life across the full range of human activities, including social, educational, religious, recreational, and economic life, encompassing both public and private spheres.'

The broad range of notions included in the selection of definitions provided above bear witness to the complex, ephemeral nature of 'culture'. It can encompass lifestyles, value systems, shared meanings and various features that contribute to a group's collective identity. The link between culture and identity is

undisputed (Mannens 1999).[16] In Article 5(1) of the 1995 Framework Convention for the Protection of National Minorities (FCNM) both language and cultural heritage are defined as 'essential elements of ... identity' of persons
belonging to national minorities. Similarly, Reidel (2010: 68) lists as the primary
attributes of culture: shared history, shared belief, shared identity, language, traditions and practices. Cultural rights imply the opportunity for minority representatives to express their identity, through the practice of their distinct cultural
traditions and lifestyles, and the use of their language.[17] In light of this, I treat
language as a highly prominent group identity marker, at the heart of a minority's self-expression (Crystal 2000). As Estébanez (2005: 269) writes: '[L]inguis-
tic communication [is] possibly the most intangible and at the same time
fundamental of ... spaces [for the development of a group's identity], as language permeates almost every aspect of minority identity.'

Language encompasses all social spheres: the choice of language in the
media, the public sector, employment, Parliament and the courts has repercussions on a country's socio-political environment, as well as creating the potential
for multiple forms of linguistic discrimination. Language is also a symbol of
power (Bourdieu 1991); in the development of nations, the dominant group's
language crystallises and consolidates as the dominant language.[18] While cultural
rights do not benefit national minorities alone – they are included *both* in general
human rights international texts[19] and minority-specific documents such as the
FCNM – they are crucial to minorities given the menace to their identity represented by the majority within a (nation-)state, and globalising forces more generally. One can then speak of a 'right to identity' – or the right of a national
minority to protect its cultural destiny in an environment that can be hostile to
diversity (Thornberry 1991: 141–142; Pentassuglia 2002: 133).

Diversity and current debates

On 31 May 2011 Valerii Tishkov, an influential actor in the area of nationalities
policy in Russia, and who served as Minister of Nationalities under Yeltsin,
wrote in *Russkii Zhurnal*:

> If the 20th century was the century of minorities, the 21st century will be
> the century of the majority in the sense of recognising its interests, demands
> and rights.... Minorities today have international protection, they know how
> to self-organise, to promote themselves and make demands before Stras-
> bourg judges.[20]

In short, Tishkov argues that minorities have been *empowered*: they are in a
position akin to that of the majority, in terms of power and access to resources,
either at the level of the state, or at the level of specific regions within countries.
Far from being hapless victims, members of minorities can abuse their powers,
and even 'organise a genocide or terror against the majority'.[21] Tishkov's article
came after several much-publicised statements on multiculturalism by the

leaders of three Western European countries in 2010–2011: Germany's Angela Merkel, the United Kingdom's David Cameron and France's Nicolas Sarkozy. These pronouncements fuelled debate within and beyond the three countries. Merkel stated in October 2010: 'The approach [to build] a multicultural [society] and to live side-by-side and to enjoy each other … has failed, utterly failed.'[22]

Defeat was also said to be the end-result in Britain:

> Under the doctrine of state multiculturalism, we have encouraged different cultures to live separate lives, apart from each other and apart from the mainstream. We've failed to provide a vision of society to which they feel they want to belong.[23]

In France, in 2011, a law was introduced banning the wearing of the full-face veil (*niqab*) in public places.[24] (Then) President Sarkozy said: 'If you come to France, you accept to melt into a single community, which is the national community, and if you do not want to accept that, you cannot be welcome.'[25] Even the Council of Europe's Secretary General Thorbjørn Jagland argued that forms of multiculturalism that lead to the formation of 'parallel societies' within states, and generate 'radical ideas', have to come to an end, in the interests of containing terrorism.[26]

These statements speak of a struggle to find working solutions enabling the peaceful coexistence of different cultures and ethnicities in the same country. With the threat of terrorism often invoked (both in Russia and globally), the prevention of mini-clashes of civilisations in one's backyard seems pressing. In Russia, the Chechen conflicts and episodes of Islamic fundamentalism within its own borders could easily lead to the North Caucasus being perceived as incubating the 'enemy within'. Another layer of complexity is added when one needs to reconcile the integration of minorities with the preservation of linguistic and cultural pluralism as societal wealth. In fact, the forces of globalisation in today's world might have generated a new quest for identity – a desire for self-definition resulting from the dislocation and homogenising tendencies created by modernity.[27]

At the same time, the extent to which cultural pluralism ought to be actively encouraged, and if so to what extent and through what means, remains a disputed issue. The aforementioned statements by Western leaders have provided food for thought not only to Western audiences, but also to Russian ones. For example, two of the Russian public officials interviewed (in St Petersburg and Saransk) argued that Russia has been displaying 'too much tolerance' to difference [4.11; 4.18]. These respondents, whose interviews took place shortly after Merkel's public critique of multiculturalism, referred to her statements on the supposed failure of this approach to suggest that multiculturalism might not be the best course of action to manage internal differences in Russia and Germany alike. Similarly, Tishkov argued that concerns over potential cultural and religious clashes have led to 'panic' in Russia, resulting in the feeling that 'multiculturalism is to blame, that it was a mistake', thus echoing Merkel.[28]

To such doubts, the international human rights system asserts the contrasting view that linguistic and cultural pluralism ought to be preserved as societal wealth, as well as contributing to peace and security. This is in line with an emerging consensus that a plurality of minority cultures and identities 'enrich[es] the fabric of society as a whole'.[29] Indeed, states have endorsed multicultural approaches, through signatures and ratifications of relevant declarations and conventions. For example, the 2005 UNESCO Convention on the Protection and Promotion of the Diversity of Cultural Expressions had 133 state parties by 2014. Xanthaki (2010) argues that, although international human rights law does not refer directly to 'multiculturalism', its basic notions are reflected in international legal provisions. Minority rights law further implies a strong correlation between the acceptance of diversity, with the recognition of its intrinsic value, and stability. Indeed, the modern international minority rights system emerged from a drive to prevent gross human rights abuses against vulnerable minorities – abuses which could escalate into conflict.[30] Thus, ideals of unity and stability *and* the accommodation of minorities have not been treated as mutually exclusive by IGOs. Rather, one can argue that it is the societal marginalisation of particular groups that can lead to radicalisation. By contrast, international minority rights law places a strong emphasis on integration and social cohesion. For example, the FCNM's Explanatory Report clarifies that: '[Article 5 FCNM] acknowledges the importance of social cohesion and reflects the desire expressed in the preamble that cultural diversity be a source and a factor, not of division, but of enrichment to each society.'[31]

The international minority rights system implicitly recognises that diversity cannot simply be eliminated: it is a fact that the majority of states are, and have been, multi-ethnic. The attempt to transcend difference, with the (unrealistic) objective of creating a colour- and difference-blind society is not a viable option (Phillips 2002). The denial of difference does not solve its complexities, but merely removes them from the public discourse. Thus, Phillips (ibid.: 5) refers to a form of 'democracy *through* difference' [italics in original]; Packer places pluralism, and the rejection of an assimilationist nation-state, in the context of human rights and freedoms:

> In contradistinction from the exclusivist, coercive and assimilating nature of the putative 'nation-State' which values 'purity', we must think in terms of securing and expanding opportunities for multiple, open and evolving cultures and identities: we must value *freedom* [italics in original].
>
> (Packer 1999: 270)[32]

The principal challenge of the minority rights regime is the creation of a form of integration that does not tip the balance over to assimilation. In the words of the UN Working Group on Minorities: 'Integration differs from assimilation in that while it develops and maintains a common domain where equal treatment and a common rule of law prevail, it also allows for pluralism ... [in the spheres of] culture, language and religion.'[33]

In the case of Russia, Opalski (2001) argues that the attributes of its nationality discourse are not conducive to an approach to diversity in line with liberal pluralism. The legacies of Soviet and pre-Soviet policies are still present in the twenty-first century – visible in the continuation of such policies or in the repercussions that may ensue when breaking with them. Meanwhile, as will be seen below, Putin has promoted the view that Russia ought to follow its own models of accommodation of diversity, consolidated throughout its history. He has criticised the Western model of multiculturalism, which, he has argued, is a form of 'compensation for a colonial past';[34] one should not be surprised, he stated, that 'politicians and public figures in Europe increasingly talk about the collapse of multiculturalism, and about the fact that it is unable to guarantee integration into society of persons with other languages and cultures' (again, a clear reference to Merkel and Cameron).[35] By contrast, Russia has naturally developed as a 'poli-ethnic and poli-cultural' society. Reliance on Russia's way of accommodating diversity has been linked by Putin to Russia's sovereignty and its resistance to (Western) globalising moves; it has been further associated with the promotion of Russian values, including spiritual ones, which, instead the West has repressed, leading to its own 'degradation' and 'moral crisis'.[36] While one might set aside the populist rhetoric of Putin's pronouncements, in order to understand Russia's response to the challenges created by its diversity one needs to examine the historical trajectory of its nationalities policy.

The national question in Russia: from imperial to post-Soviet models

In Sergei Eisenstein's 1944 film *Ivan the Terrible*, the 1552 defeat of the Kazan khanate at the hands of the Russians is portrayed as the assertion of Russian power and a humiliation for the Tatars. After victoriously chanting 'to Kazan!', the city is swiftly and effortlessly taken by the Russians. In reality, the conquest of Kazan had been preceded by a combination of military and economic pressure – including a trade boycott – and efforts to co-opt the Tatar elite (Kappeler 2001: 25–6). Yet the military venture is depicted in the film as a reaction to the boldness of an envoy from the Kazan khanate, who had challenged Ivan the Terrible with a declaration of war, adding that 'Kazan is big' and 'Muscovy is small'. Ivan decides to himself march to Kazan with his troops and 'strike down those who have lifted their hand against Muscovy'.

This is an example of a culturally insensitive approach to Russia's multi-national character. Gibatdinov (2010) points out that, throughout Russia's history, Islam was portrayed in publications as a 'fake' religion, while Shnirelman (1999, 2006b, 2009b) presents evidence of textbooks being employed to support particular versions of history.[37] At the same time, the Soviet Union promoted what has been defined as 'the most ambitious affirmative action programme in history' (Martin 2001: 2). Nationality issues were accorded considerable attention, yet they rested on contradictory foundations, oscillating between the two poles of promotion of cultural distinctiveness and its hindrance.

Imperial Russia: partial autonomy, incoherent policies

While imperial Russia tends to be known for its absolutist, centralised policies, it also saw instances of local autonomy: the *zemstva* (local councils) and the *mir* (peasants' communities). Hosking (1990: 26) thus argues that the success of the soviets (workers' councils) in 1905 and 1917 primarily derived from 'the long experience of both peasants and workers in creating and running their own grass-roots institutions'. Bowring (2013a: 120ff.) traces the legacy of regional autonomy back to Russia's imperial past, as in the case of the granting of autonomy to Finland in 1809.[38] Moreover, from the sixteenth century onwards, according to a mutual agreement between Moscow and the Kazan and Astrakhan khanates, Tatars were able to retain their language and religion, as well as their lands, in exchange for loyalty to the tsar (Kutafin 2006). In the religious sphere, Catherine the Great (1762–1796) refrained from commanding religious uniformity and instead intro-duced a 'policy of toleration' for the many faiths present in Russia (Crews 2006: 2). Opportunities to self-manage in the area of education also existed: for example, Kokko and Kon'kova (2009) relate how the nineteenth-century reforms of Alexan-der II, with the establishment of *zemstva*, enabled Ingrian Finns to organise their education in the Finnish language, including, as of 1863, a three-year course for Finnish teachers, taught in both Finnish and Russian. In 1888 there were already 38 Finnish-language schools in Ingria, and, in 1913, 229 schools (ibid.: 18).

At the same time, from the mid-nineteenth century until the 1917 revolution the Russian language was promoted as a means towards enhanced unity within the empire. Russification policies involved the introduction of Russian in primary and secondary education, and the replacement of print media in local languages with Russian-language media. However, such Russification policies were selectively applied: they targeted primarily Slavic, Christian Orthodox groups, and the European regions of the Russian empire (Pavlenko 2008: 4–5). Moreover, the Russian empire aimed at, and largely succeeded in, ensuring pro-ficiency in Russian of titular elites, while most non-Russians continued princip-ally to employ local languages (Laitin 1998; Pavlenko 2008: 5). Thus, alongside Russification measures, (some) ethnic groups enjoyed a degree of local or regional autonomy that enabled the preservation of their cultures and languages.

The Soviet Union: diversity management

Elaborate and far-reaching policies for diversity management were introduced during the Soviet period. Two aspects of these policies are particularly relevant here: the institutionalisation of nationhood, accompanied by an essentialist con-ceptualisation of ethnicity; and a top-down form of diversity management.

Institutionalisation of nationhood

The Soviet era saw what Brubaker (1994) calls the 'institutionalization of nation-hood', which manifested itself in two forms: the 'territorial and political', *and* the 'ethnocultural and personal' (Brubaker 1994: 47). As part of the territorial/ political institutionalisation of nationhood, the Soviet Union (including Russia's predecessor, the Russian Soviet Federative Socialist Republic – or RSFSR) was divided into territories, several of which were 'assigned' to particular ethnicities. This created a form of asymmetric *ethnic* federalism: a hierarchy ranging from union republics, to autonomous republics down to smaller units. With some adjustments,[39] the structure of Russia's federalism was preserved in post-Soviet Russia. In 2014 Russia had 83 *subiekty*[40] (subjects, or territorial units), comprising: 21 ethnic republics,[41] 46 oblasts, nine krai, four autonomous okrugs, two federal cities (Moscow and St Petersburg) and one autonomous oblast (Jewish).[42] Ethnic federalism was based on the link between ethnicity and territory, encapsulated in Stalin's definition of a nation, as a historically evolved, stable community based on a common language, *territory*, economic life and psychological make-up manifested in a community of culture' [italics added] (Stalin 1950 [1913]: 239).

The 'ethnocultural and personal' form of nationhood, instead, related to the ethnicity of an individual regardless of place of residence. Ethnicity was recorded in Soviet passports and all official documents, forcing individuals to continue to restate their nationality. It caused nationality to become an '*obligatory ascribed status*' [italics in original] (Brubaker 1996: 18), and a primary form of self-identification throughout the Soviet Union (Brubaker 1996; Gorenburg 2003; Slezkine 1994; Suny 1993).

Institutionalised nationhood was an aspect of Soviet nationalities policy. It provided mechanisms to support linguistic and cultural diversity, including through the development of elaborate language policies (Anderson and Silver 1984; Grenoble 2003; Kirkwood 1989; Lewis 1972).[43] The state established an education system in multiple languages, as well as issuing newspapers in numerous non-Russian languages (Slezkine 1994). Linguistic policies further involved the codification and standardisation of languages, as well as the development of written forms of those languages that had until then been exclusively oral (Martin 2001; Grenoble 2003). Meanwhile, the administration of regions was ostensibly transferred to local leaders through the process of *korenizatsiya* (indigenisation): local leaders filled positions in the local administration, the local Communist Party, the judiciary and industry. Overall, titular groups were overrepresented in local government, and, while *korenizatsiya* policies were reduced from the 1930s onwards, affirmative action policies continued up to the *perestroika* (Gorenburg 2003; Slezkine 1994).

The institutionalisation of ethnicity pursued the goal of containing nationalist movements, by permitting the expression of national identity only within the rigid confines of the Soviet system of ethnic institutions. The post-revolutionary phase also brought a pressing need to communicate the Communist doctrine to a plurilingual population (Pavlenko 2008: 5–6; see also Liber 1991; M.G. Smith 1998). Thus, early language policies aimed at furthering the understanding, and thus the acceptance, of the new regime (Pavlenko 2008: 6). Stalin's view on this matter was that only the mother tongue could enable 'a full development of the intellectual faculties of the Tatar or of the Jewish worker' (Stalin 1950 [1913]: 21).[44] Finally, the identification of specific traits ascribed to individual ethnic groups – reflecting an essentialist approach to ethnicity – paved the way for the codification and subdivision of ethnic groups during the Soviet period (Tishkov 1997), so as to start unravelling, and coming to terms with, the ethno-linguistic complexity of the Soviet Union.[45] The institutionalisation of nationhood was meant to be a temporary solution, to be ultimately replaced by the forging of the *Soviet* people. Brubaker (1994: 54) calls it an 'irony of history' that in fact it became embedded in Soviet society.

Ethnic federalism, *korenizatsiya* and ethnic institutions[46] had the effect of heightening ethnic consciousness among representatives of titular nationalities, as well as creating, or promoting, national elites (Bunce 1999; Brubaker 1996; Gorenburg 2003; Suny 1993). This paved the way for ethnic mobilisation starting with the *perestroika* period, with ethnic institutions playing a role in establishing social networks and harnessing resources for national movements. In the late 1980s and early 1990s, nationalist leaders framed their messages around Soviet models for the accommodation of diversity, which resonated among co-ethnics as their identities and perceptions had moulded around them. What ethnic mobilisation aimed at was not the introduction of new models for majority–minority relations, but rather addressing the gap between the benefits that should in principle stem from titularity, and the reality of restricted autonomy at regional and local levels (Gorenburg 2003).

The Soviet treatment of nationality was not devoid of ambiguity. On the one hand, despite its emphasis on nationality, Soviet ideology rejected the biological determinism and race theories of Nazism (Hirsch 2005: 231ff.). The Soviets did not believe that ethnic identities were immutable, but that ethnicities would ultimately be transcended, through a new emphasis on the *homo sovieticus* (Connor 1984). On the other hand, despite Soviet ideology ostensibly distancing itself from racialism (Shahin 1989: 412),[47] the Soviet interpretation of ethnicity (at the basis of the Soviet theory of *ethnos*)[48] effectively embraced it. One of the fundamental sources of Soviet theory on ethnicity was Sergei Shirokogorov, who in 1920s laid the foundations of a primordialist approach to the interpretation of ethnicity, stressing its role as a 'biological category',[49] as well as developing a model for the 'classification of ethnoses' (Shnirelman 2009a: 138; Tishkov 1997: 1–2). It is this racialism that infused the theories of ethnologist Lev Gumilev, who saw ethnic groups as regulated by natural rather than social processes – as self-contained entities with a permanent identity transferred from generation to generation: an ethnos was believed by Gumilev to undergo a life cycle – from its origins, to development, to decline – in the same manner as a living organism (Bassin 2007; Gumilev 2007 [1978]). While Gumilev was marginalised in the Soviet period – his books being banned until the 1980s – the Soviet theory of ethnos was clearly influenced by the same primordialism, which implies a 'biologization of ethnicity' (Shnirelman 2009a: 138; see also Opalski 2001). Another scholar who substantially contributed to the Soviet theory of ethnos, Yulian Bromley, similarly conceived an ethnos as an 'ethno-social organism', with a specific 'psyche'[50] and exclusive group membership (Tishkov 1997: 3). While (in line with Marxist ideology) Bromley saw human societies as destined to go through various social formations (ultimately reaching Communism), he also believed that an ethnicity had stable, intrinsic features – an immutable essence (Banks 1996: 18). Thus, through exposure to these theories, the citizens of the Soviet Union imbibed primordialism and essentialism, reinforced through indoctrination via frequent ethnographic exhibitions (Hirsch 2005). Stereotypes of ethnicities abounded, and coexisted – sitting uncomfortably – with attempts at instilling a *Soviet* consciousness in citizens of all ethnic backgrounds. Moreover, Gumilev's theories were enthusiastically welcomed into mainstream narratives of Russian nationalism in the post-Soviet period.

Contributing to essentialising tendencies is the fact that the Soviet tradition implies a strong association between language and ethnicity. The expression 'native language' (*rodnoy yazyk*) has commonly been interpreted as the language of one's nationality (Arel 2002), which did not necessarily coincide with the language in which the speaker was most fluent. In the past, when census-takers asked about a person's native language, respondents often cited the language of their ethnic group, even when they were more fluent in, or used more commonly, Russian.[51] Meanwhile, ethnicity was generally seen during the Soviet period as inherited from parents[52] – stressing again the role of biological functions in ethnic identification. Ethnicity being so deeply entrenched in the fabric of society, it is unsurprising that the transcendence of ethnic difference, through the forging of a Soviet consciousness, never occurred. Instead, persons belonging to various nationalities learned to operate, and at times mobilise, within the (ethnicity-based) institutional framework of the Soviet period – using it as a platform from which to articulate their claims (Gorenburg 2003; Hirsch 2005). Thus, ethnicity became part of the organisation of Soviet society – from republics established 'for' titular nationalities to a range of ad hoc institutions – as a means towards the 'management' of diversity.

Diversity management

Russia's diversity management has relied on centralism. In Lenin's opinion (1972 [1913]), Marxism had to make use of centralising measures in order 'to sweep away the old, medieval, caste, parochial, petty-national, religious and other barriers'. This, however, had to be a form of 'democratic centralism', which would not preclude local self-government or autonomy: 'Obviously, one cannot conceive of a modern, truly democratic state that did not grant such autonomy to every region having any appreciably distinct economic and social features, populations of a specific national composition' (Lenin 1972 [1913]).

Although what ensued deviated significantly from the originally-conceived notion of 'democratic centralism', Soviet hypercentralism also displayed a degree of localism: local self-government constituted a mechanism for control but also provided some level of representation, involving individuals in the life of the community (Bowring 2010a: 665–666; Tiskhov and Filippova 2002). A degree of autonomy, albeit limited, was further created through *korenizatsiya*. The advent of Communism itself was portrayed by its leaders as the end of the oppression of the Russian Empire's peoples: the 1917 'Declaration of the Rights of the Peoples of Russia' contained guarantees of self-determination and equality. The Soviet Union, then, counted anti-imperialism and self-determination among its founding principles.[53]

At the same time, Soviet nationalities policy was incoherent, with an alternation of liberal and illiberal practices, and top-down decision-making. During the Stalin period some nationalities were subjected to repressive and deeply traumatic measures, including mass deportations.[54] Those Karelians and Mordovians interviewed who could remember the Soviet period described social attitudes that eroded their dignity as members of their ethnic groups, leading to feelings of shame about their origins. An aspect of identity – religious expression – was also repressed, in the case of minorities and ethnic Russians alike, with the killing of priests and the closure of churches and mosques, in the belief that religious institutions might hamper the process of collectivisation (Duncan 1999).[55] At a minimum there was a lack of real autonomy from Moscow, as regional leaders were required to signal their loyalty to the Communist Party apparatus (Duncan 1999; Roeder 1992). Ultimately, whether the regions and localities could exercise any autonomy in decision-making depended on the centre.

The Soviet Union was further characterised by a sharp linguistic asymmetry. As Pavlenko puts it:

> Russian speakers could afford to be monolingual, speakers of titular languages aspiring to social advancement had to be bilingual, and minority language speakers had to be either bilingual (with Russian or the titular language as a second language) or multilingual.
>
> (Pavlenko 2008: 8)

Moreover, *korenizatsiya*, and the promotion of minority languages, was reduced from the 1930s onwards. This shift coincided with the intensification of fears of 'bourgeois nationalism', accompanied by concerns about the limited proficiency in Russian of many non-Russians. The difficulties of 'presiding over 192 languages and potentially 192 bureaucracies' became apparent (Slezkine 1994: 445). In parallel to this, internal migration within the Soviet Union, boosted by the processes of industrialisation and collectivisation, led to ethnic mixing, with a concurrent enhancement of the role of Russian as the language of inter-ethnic communication. Thus, from the 1930s, the pendulum swung back to the promotion of Russian, with state programmes designed to strengthen the belief in the special role of the Russian language in the unification of the Soviet people and in advancing industrialisation (Pavlenko 2008). In 1938, the study of Russian was made compulsory by decree in non-Russian schools, and the overall amount of hours devoted to the study of Russian increased. Although the new regulations were unevenly implemented in different regions, this process, and the introduction of unified education standards, effectively consolidated the role of the

Russian language as the de facto official language of the Soviet Union (ibid.). In the 1930s, language planners further required a shift to Cyrillic for those languages that employed the Latin alphabet,[56] which in practice simplified the learning of Russian (Grenoble 2003: 48–51; M.G. Smith 1998: 121–142).

Thus, the Soviet Union moved from Lenin's original notion of 'democratic centralism' to top-down decision-making, including in the regulation of inter-ethnic relations. Given that Soviet leaders considered various non-Russian nationalities as 'backwards', the state adopted a paternalistic attitude towards them. The Soviets effectively repressed the cultural traditions of numerous ethnic groups by forcing them to work in collectives (Hirsch 2005: 251). And, while nationhood and nationality were actively promoted, *nationalism* itself (whether real or perceived) was repressed as a destabilising force. This approach points to a legacy of *management* of diversity rather than its respect or engagement with it. This form of 'managed diversity' further signals a policy based on assumptions about the meanings of diversity, guided by essentialist notions of minority groups, which were treated as internally homogeneous collectives.

Sovietisation affected not only ethnic minorities, but it also interacted with *Russian* national identity in complex ways. A conscious choice was made not to forge a Russian nation-state during Soviet period (Hosking 2005), as each citizen was ultimately to morph into the *homo sovieticus*. Thus, ethnic Russians were not privileged in all senses: the RSFSR had fewer titular institutions than other Union republics (with no *Russian* Academy of Science, or *Russian* Communist Party), while Russian nationalism could hardly flourish under Stalin's terror (Vujačič 2009). Slezkine provides an illustrative analogy to describe the situation of ethnic Russians in the Soviet Union: he takes Vareikis' 1924 comparison of the USSR to a communal apartment (Vareikis and Zelenskii 1924: 59, cited in Slezkine 1994: 415), in which each room is occupied by a national unit, except for the Russians. Instead, the Russians are allocated, in the centre of the apartment, 'a large and amorphous space not clearly defined as a room, unmarked by national paraphernalia, unclaimed by "its own" nation' (Slezkine 1994: 415). Thus, although the Russians were de facto the dominant group in the Soviet Union, they did not have a 'room of their own'.

At the same time, some (ethnic) Russian attributes coloured Soviet patriotism. While the establishment of the Soviet Union should have marked a break with Russia's imperial past, under Stalin a form of 'Soviet-Russian national identity' soon developed (Vujačič 2009). Increasingly distancing himself from the outright rejection of the Great Russian Chauvinism advocated by Lenin (1972 [1913]), Stalin reintroduced into the public discourse selected elements of Russian nationalism, particularly in the shape of love for the motherland, and the myth of quintessentially Russian historical figures such as Alexander Nevsky. Such themes were embellished through messianistic overtones,[57] with the affirmation that *Russia* was to guide the socialist revolution. In the same vein, Stalin (1954 [1926]) referred to Leninism as the 'highest achievement' of *Russian* culture. After Stalin's death a cult form of Russian nationalism continued. This encompassed the controversial literary movement known as village prose and the Russian peasant way of life, together with a rediscovery of some of the themes of the Slavophiles (Laruelle 2009c: 16–17). Although some nationalist undercurrents were promoted by dissidents, much of Russian nationalism was effectively part of the official Soviet ideology – if not explicitly incorporated into it, used alongside it and entrusted with a complementary function (Laruelle 2009c). The presence of a multitude of ethnicities in the Soviet Union, resulting in potentially conflicting forms of nationalism, generated a clear incentive for the Soviet authorities to blur the boundaries between Soviet and Russian nationalism. There is but a short step between the superimposition of 'Soviet' and 'Russian'.

Putin's Russia

Following the Soviet Union's collapse – and the turbulent Yeltsin years, characterised by state fragility and fragmentation[58] – Putin's Russia has crystallised around the idea of a strong state where Russian nationalism (under the guise of *patriotism*) is celebrated. This does not mean a repressive form of assimilation: rather the situation is characterised by diversity and pluralism, albeit accompanied by an overall movement towards uniformity and homogeneity. Thus, ethnicity continues to occupy a special place in Putin's Russia. The tradition of teaching minority languages in schools, as well as teaching through the medium of such languages, has made the transition from Soviet to post-Soviet Russia.[59] In addition, while theories explaining human behaviour through biology rather than through socio-economic factors effectively clashed with Soviet ideology, with the end of the Soviet Union the public discourse on class struggle was effectively replaced by one on ethno-national tensions. Once Marxism was discarded, socio-economic upheavals following the Soviet Union's collapse were seen through the lenses of inter-ethnic strife, with a concurrent expansion of ethnic terminology and rhetoric (Shnirelman 2006a: 187). The theory of ethnos was enthusiastically incorporated into mainstream public discourse – embraced by public officials, politicians, journalists and persons in charge of education policies alike. They employed themes of Soviet ethnology as foundations for emerging public narratives – which in practice much resembled Gumilev's view of the primacy of ethnicity in human evolution (Shnirelman 2006a, 2009a: 139). Fertile ground for these views was provided by the Soviet nationalities policy, through which individuals had become accustomed to perceiving themselves as belonging to separate ethnic groups (Brubaker 1994). This led to a revival of ethnic identity, including Russian nationalism.

Russian nationalism

As Russianness had receded into the background during the Soviet period, the USSR's collapse left not only an ideological, but also an identity, vacuum. The concept of *russkii* (belonging to the Russian nation) had by then become ephemeral, supplanted by vague notions of a 'Soviet people'. At the same time, there was a (at least partial) conflation of *russkii* and *rossiiskii* elements – loosely comparable to *ethnic* and *civic* attributes of Russianness respectively – particularly through the creation of the aforementioned 'Russian Soviet nationalism' (Vujačič 2009). Meanwhile, the post-Soviet period has generated the *russkii vopros* – the 'Russian question', or doubts as to Russians' self-definition vis-à-vis other nationalities sharing the same territory (Simonsen 1996: 91). Russians have historically perceived themselves to be at the centre of a multinational empire, or the *Staatsvolk* – the dominant group within a multi-ethnic state (Opalski 2001: 299); the post-Soviet period has, then, implied a need for Russians to re-position themselves, and re-shape their identity, following the loss of much of the 'empire' as the USSR fragmented (Hosking 1998). Post-Soviet Russia has thus seen a renewed effort – from critics, politicians and others – to 'forge the nation' (Tolz 1998; 2001). Chebankova (2012: 326–327) argues that Russians have still not developed a systematic multicultural policy, with different interpretations on the national question being championed by three main groups: the liberals, (Russian) nationalists and traditionalists. The complexity of the Russians' self-perception is exacerbated by the fact that the RSFSR, as noted, institutionally underdeveloped, meaning that Russians' self-understanding was not embedded in its territory. As a result, Brubaker (1996: 51–52) explains, 'the core institutional parameters of the emerging Russian state ... are in even greater flux, and even more vigorously contested, than those of the most incipient non-Russian successor states.' Among possible (re)interpretations of Russianness is the idea of Russia as a 'unique civilisation' – a view that places an emphasis on Russia's imperial past but also on its position 'in-between' East and West (Shnirelman 2009a), both geographically and conceptually. This 'in-betweenness' suggests an undefined, amorphous entity. Such abstract notion of Russian identity can be concretised through the 'Russian culture' in the sense of its language, symbols and history – as tangible, concrete references, which act to fill with meaning otherwise nebulous concepts.[60]

The reassertion of Russianness since the Soviet Union's collapse has fuelled Russian nationalism. Contemporary Russian nationalism is kaleidoscopic: numerous and varied groups espouse it, despite their displaying a vast range of ideological perspectives. Verkhovsky (2009: 100) divides these multiple approaches into two main types of nationalism: moderate and radical. The two effectively coexist, despite the Russian government's having attempted, with limited success, to suppress the more extreme, de-stabilising forms of nationalism (Verkhovsky 2009). Strong Russian nationalist sentiments are not confined to groupuscules of extremists, but have spread throughout Russian society (Laruelle 2009b; Verkhovsky 2009). According to a Levada Center[61] survey, conducted in 2013 in various regions of Russia, many Russians have feelings of dislike (30 per cent), anger (25 per cent), or fear (6 per cent) vis-à-vis persons from Russia's Southern republics residing in their cities (these percentages can be contrasted with those from surveys carried out in 2008: 14 per cent, 14 per cent and 2 per cent respectively).[62] Some neo-fascist views have reached the mainstream media, government institutions and academia through ideologues such as that of Aleksandr Dugin, founder, in 2002, of the Eurasia Party[63] – a party of Russian patriots (Umland 2009). Extremist attitudes have additionally spread through youth movements, such as the skinhead subculture (Pilkington *et al.* 2010). Extreme nationalism has generated instances of hate crime, including physical attacks against persons (often migrant workers) originating from Central Asia and the Caucasus.[64]

While the dangers of extremism are acknowledged by the Russian authorities,[65] a moderate form of nationalism (referred to as *patriotism*) is seen as a benign, positive force. Putin-endorsed patriotism is (at least nominally) apolitical and non-militant,[66] while 'nationalism' per se is seen as an exaggerated manifestation of the same tendencies (Daucé *et al.* 2010: Laruelle 2009a: 5). Thus, Russian nationalism has been treated as an apolitical (and controlled) phenomenon, the more extremist layers of nationalism being separated from 'healthy' patriotism, with a view to forging an overall *civic* unity.

Patriotism coming to the rescue of Russian society

As we will see in the following chapters, patriotism is an essential feature of the contemporary Russian education system and public discourse. Patriotism brings together elements of Russia's imperial and Soviet history whose threads have been laboriously pulled together: Putin has been at pains to trace a continuum throughout Russian history, and to find positive outcomes in all eras (Sakwa 2004: 241). Thus, Putin has promoted a perception of Russian history based on a *longue durée* approach (Laruelle 2009c) – by which there is no rupture between various historical junctions (whether imperial, Soviet or post-Soviet). This approach avoids the compartamentalisation of history as a series of false starts and mistakes for which younger generations of Russians need to pay the price. The emphasis on a long (overall positive) history of Russia contributes to restoring pride in one's country, by connecting a glorious past to the present. Putin's choice of a *longue durée* approach further reinforces an essentialist reading of ethnicity, as it suggests that the 'essence' of Russianness has been preserved in the course of the Russians' tumultuous history.

Existing Russian patriotism/nationalism is not aimed at resurrecting old (and largely obsolete) Russian imperial themes that had lain dormant during the entire Soviet period. It has already been noted how Russian and Soviet nationalism/ patriotism had become interconnected. This trend continued in post-Soviet Russia and thus precedes Putin. With the political instability of 1993 – so acute as to result in the Parliament's dissolution by Yeltsin, amid fears of the country's fragmentation along political lines – the political elite concocted a repackaged version of 'patriotic centrism' as a political idea to bring about cohesion (Laruelle 2009c). In 1994–1995 there were already attempts to breathe new life into patriotic rallies, and into a patriotic rhetoric around the motherland. By the 1999 Parliamentary elections, a new consensus had been reached among political actors as to the pressing need for stability and control of Russia's development. The strengthening of the state seemed critical when Putin came to power: the country had been led by a sick president; corruption was widespread and the power of the oligarchs seemingly unshakable; the federal centre had lost much of its control over the regions[67] (including through the first Chechen war); last but not least, there had been a significant drop in Russia's prestige in the international community, with the loss of its superpower status (Laruelle 2009c: 23–24).

In the following decade, Putin made ample use of 'patriotic centrism', as a unifying factor that could bridge ideological divisions among the political elite's members. A discourse built around nationalistic concepts has been sustained, to help cure the social ills that Russia has suffered since the 1990s. Stabilisation has been pursued by summoning political conservatism around the presidential party, United Russia, while Putin has offered to build a 'Great Russia' (with a strong economy, stability, and status in the international arena) through centralisation. A vestige of a social contract was thus created,[68] with citizens being guaranteed a strong and more prosperous state in exchange for acquiescing to its centralisation – effectively accepting limitations of their individual freedoms (Laruelle 2009a: 127ff., 2009c: 23–25).

Although various undercurrents exist, Russian patriotism has encompassed the country's political spectrum. It resonates with the Russian population,[69] which responds to the notion of Russia's greatness, and satisfies a need for normality, particularly in the sense of stability following a phase of acute political turmoil (Laruelle 2009c: 26). The Russian patriotic idea acknowledges the implicit value of Russian ethnicity and civilisation: it recognises the Russians as a 'distinct culture', which serves as an antidote to the Russian identity crisis, as well as accommodating anti-Westernist tendencies. It advances the view of the Russians' greatness and cultural superiority, which is implicit in the notion of messianism. It further offers solace to the trauma of ethnic Russians in post-Soviet republics outside Russia, who were unexpectedly and suddenly transformed from the 'elder brother' ('civiliser' of 'backward peoples') into mere ethnic minorities (Shnirelman 2009a).

To conclude, Russia has not refrained from acknowledging its multi-ethnic character. In light of its internal diversity, it has sought to find solutions to possible inter-ethnic tensions, with a view to enhancing stability through a balance between cultural pluralism and cohesion. The criticism of multiculturalism in the West has not gone unnoticed in Russia: some have seized upon it to emphasise its (real or perceived) shortcomings, contrasting it to the Russian model of diversity management. The promotion of this model projects a view of a strong Russia, infused with messianism, as well as reasserting the country's own sovereignty vis-à-vis the West.[70] Yet Russia's model of diversity management is not devoid of ambiguities. First, the Soviet institutionalisation of nationhood supported an essentialist reading of ethnicity, with ethnic institutions contributing to shape cognitive frames around which notions of ethnicity developed. The Soviet approach to multinationality created a tendency for members of ethnic groups to perceive themselves as separate collectives, sealed off from each other, and possibly in antagonism to each other. Second, the Soviet approach meant that ethnic diversity was promoted in some instances but also simultaneously undermined, causing ethnic identities (including the Russian identity) to be truncated. Third, while the Russian Empire and Soviet Union permitted discreet forms of local autonomy, modalities of diversity management were primarily developed (and applied) in a top-down fashion. In post-Soviet Russia, Russian nationalism/ patriotism is similarly centrally conceived. The patriotic discourse weaves civic and ethnic elements – often with a blurring of the two – and a conflation of *russkii* and *rossiiskii*.[71] This creates a tension between a 'multinational Russia' and Russian nationalism/patriotism, as well as paving the way for homogenising tendencies. Post-Soviet Russia's approach to diversity prolongs a legacy of its *management* rather than engagement with it, while patriotic centrism is employed to bridge not only ethnic divisions but also ideological and political ones.

Tatars, Mordovians and Karelians

Before moving on to the application of domestic and international standards on the protection of cultural diversity in Russia, I take a closer look at the three case studies: Tatars, Mordovians and Karelians.[72] The groups were selected on account of their differences, and as such they bear witness to the remarkable diversity present in the Russian Federation, as well as illustrating the varied circumstances affecting different ethnic groups in the preservation of their cultural distinctiveness.

Tatars are numerically the second biggest ethnic group (after the Russians) in the Federation, with a population of 5.3 million, of which two million reside in the Republic of Tatarstan. Within the boundaries of the republic, Tatars (53.2 per cent) are a numerical majority, surpassing ethnic Russians (39.7 per cent) (2010 census data).[73] The area of present Tatarstan, where the Volga Bulgars had establihed a kingdom in the tenth century, was invaded by the Mongols in the thirteenth century, resulting in Tatars having a dual heritage: that of the original Volga Bulgar state, and that of the Golden Horde (Kappeler 2001: 24). Following the defeat of the Golden Horde at the end of fourteenth century, the Tatar khanates were established – most notably the Kazan and Crimean khanates. Islam was proclaimed the state religion (Bowring 2007: 423; Mirgaleev 2001), although Islamic civilisation in the central Volga goes back to the tenth century (Kappeler 2001: 24). Under imperial rule some Tatars – unlike Finno-Ugric peoples – accessed the Russian nobility (albeit following Russification), as well as the administration (Kappeler 2001). Hence, Tatars and Russians have a long common history; as Bowring (2007: 424) puts it: 'If Muscovy conquered the Tatars, the Tatars thoroughly penetrated their conquerors. The Tatar-Turkic heritage is found throughout the Russian language and Russia's cultural heritage.'

The Republic of Tatarstan's predecessor was the Tatar Autonomous Soviet Socialist Republic (ASSR), established in 1920. Tatarstan is not only the epicentre of Tatar culture in Russia, with 'diaspora' policies for Tatars residing outside Tatarstan, but also a rich, oil-producing and highly industrialised republic.

Mordovians are a numerical minority in the Republic of Mordovia (39.9 per cent compared to 53.2 per cent of Russians). Tatars are also represented in Mordovia (5.2 per cent). The area of present Mordovia experienced multiple invasions (Tatar and Mongol as well as Russian), before Russia's conquest in the sixteenth century, and the consolidation of Russian rule in the following two centuries (Taagepera 1999). The Mordovians, like the Mari and Udmurt nationalities, were subjected to acculturation through forcible Christianisation in the eighteenth century, having previously practiced animism.[74] Two versions of the Mordovian language exist: Moksha and Erzya. Their speakers are referred to in Russian as simply 'Mordovians' (*Mordva*), but the local languages do not have a term designating Moksha and Erzya-speaking peoples combined. In some cases the expression 'Moksherzians' has been used (and 'Moksherzia' to designate Mordovia) (Taagepera 1999: 149–151). Like other Finno-Ugric languages, Moksha and Erzya have absorbed elements of Russian syntax and grammar (Haarmann 1998: 236). Tendencies towards Russian assimilation were present both before and during the Soviet period (Kreindler 1985).

The Mordovian ASSR was established in 1934. In the years following the Soviet Union's dissolution, debates were held as to whether Mordovia ought to be divided into Moksha and Erzya regions, but the idea was ultimately set aside. The organisation *Erzyan Mastor* has continued to call for an Erzyan national district within Mordovia; it rejects the term 'Mordovian' to designate the two groups combined, placing an emphasis on Erzyan speakers' separate identity (Taagepera 1999: 189–191). The artificial merger of the two languages has been proposed, yet this has been rejected by many of their speakers.[75] Newspapers and magazines, as well as some broadcasts, are available in both languages. Mordovia, like Karelia, does not enjoy Tatarstan's economic strength.[76]

Karelians are a very small numerical minority in the Republic of Karelia (7.1 per cent versus 79.9 per cent Russians). Karelians also live in relatively significant numbers in the Tver, Novgorod and Leningrad oblasts. Karelia was first conquered by Russia in 1250, although wars with Sweden and Finland meant frequent shifts of borders. The Karelian ASSR was established in 1920; two decades later it was incorporated into the Karelo-Finnish SSR, before being re-established as the Karelian ASSR in 1956. In the Karelo-Finnish SSR, the Finnish language was actively promoted, including through the education system, to the detriment of the Karelian language (Zamyatin 2012b: 89; see also Ilyukha 2009). Even before its incorporation into the Karelo-Finnish SSR, the Finnish influence in the region was strong, with the majority of books published in Finnish, and newspapers, magazines and theatres operating in Finnish (Taagepera 1999: 112–113), Moreover, the Karelian language, of which three main versions exist (Karelian Proper, Livvi-Karelian and Ludic Karelian) has numerous borrowings from Russian. With the end of the Soviet Union, the depopulation of villages due to the paucity of employment opportunities has led to a sharp decrease in areas densely populated by Karelians and the progressive shrinking of Karelian-speaking oases.[77] Two other ethnic groups residing in the Republic of Karelia are afforded some protection of their linguistic diversity:

Table 2.1 Case studies: main characteristics[1]

Ethnic group	Type	Population in Russia	Population in own republic	Total population of the republic	Percentage of titular population in the republic	Main religion
Tatars	Turkic	5,310,649	2,012,571 (Tatarstan)[2]	3,786,488	53.2	Muslim
Mordovians	Finno-Ugric	744,237	333,112 (Mordovia)[3]	834,755	39.9	Russian Orthodox
Karelians	Finno-Ugric	60,815	45,570 (Karelia)[4]	643,548	7.1	Russian Orthodox

Notes
1 Data from the 2010 census are used.
2 Other ethnic groups in Tatarstan (with over 1,000 members according to the 2010 census) include: Azerbaijanis, Armenians, Bashkirs, Belarusians, Georgians, Kazakhs, Kyrgyz, Mari, Mordovians, Germans, Udmurts, Uzbeks, Ukrainians and Chuvashes.
3 Other ethnic groups (over 1,000 members) include: Tatars, Ukrainians and Armenians.
4 Other ethnic groups (over 1,000 members) include: Azerbaijanis, Armenians, Belarusians, Veps, Poles, Tatars, Ukrainians, Finns and Roma.

Finns and Veps. Like Karelians, these two groups are considered autochthonous to Karelia;[78] Veps are also recognised as one of the (small-in-number) indigenous peoples of Russia.

Separate interviews were carried out with Karelians outside the Republic of Karelia, in the city of Tver. The version of Karelian spoken in Tver slightly differs from that of the Republic of Karelia, and it has been more heavily influenced by the Russian language (Haarmann 1998: 234). Tver Karelians have initiated language and cultural programmes, particularly through the establishment of the national cultural autonomy (NCA) of Tver Karelians.[79] Yet opportunities to promote their language and culture are limited, as is commonly the case for Russia's numerically small minorities. Some support has been provided by the local Tver government and also by Finland.

The case studies: similarities and differences

The first striking difference between the three case studies is that of (titular) population density in the three republics: a (regional) numerical majority in the case of Tatarstan (53.2 per cent); less than half of the population in the case of Mordovia (39.9 per cent); and a small numerical minority in the case of Karelia (7.1 per cent). Census data from 2010 indicate that the proportion of the titular population increased in Tatarstan (52.9 per cent to 53.2 per cent) and Mordovia (31.9 per cent to 39.9 per cent) since the previous (2002) census, and has decreased in Karelia (9.2 per cent to 7.1 per cent). Mordovia is an exception among Russia's Finno-Ugric republics, given the significant increase in the ratio of the titular population between 2002 and 2010, whereas the general trend has been one of population decline. However, rather than a rise in actual birth rate, this change is to be attributed to an increase in the number of persons self-identifying as Mordovians in the censuses, possibly due to shifts in individual approaches to ethnic self-identification as a result of regional policies (Zamyatin 2012b: 79). Conversely, Karelia has seen a considerable decline of the titular nationality: the 2 per cent decrease (from 9.2 per cent to 7.1 per cent) corresponds to a decline from 65,651 persons self-identifying as Karelian in the 2002 census to 45,570 in 2010. It means that those who self-identified as in Karelia in 2010 were over ten times more numerous than Karelians. However, the decline in the ratio of Karelians in the republic is also due to the high number of persons who refrained from indicating their ethnicity in the 2010 census: 25,880 persons (or 4 per cent of the population), compared to 3,153 persons in Mordovia (0.4 per cent) and 6,052 persons in Tatarstan (0.2 per cent), indicating a more pronounced tendency to assimilation in Karelia compared to the other two republics.[80] Cultural assimilation takes place at an even faster pace outside the titular republics, given the much more sparse, or inexistent, options for minority-language education. The Tatar population in the Russian Federation as a whole went from 5,522,096 (1989 census), to 5,310,649 (2010 census). The population of Mordovians declined from 1,072,939 (1989 census) to 744,237 (2010 census), and that of Karelians from 124,921 (1989 census) to 60,815 (2010 census).

The three republics experienced an ethnic and linguistic revival in the late Soviet period and the first years of the Russian Federation, although the conditions between them differed markedly. While in Mordovia and Tatarstan the titular languages were declared as co-official alongside Russian, Karelian was never recognised as second state language of the Republic of Karelia, thereby prolonging a de jure lower status than Russian. The Karelian language in Karelia is also de facto in an extremely vulnerable position: it is only taught as an optional subject in schools in Karelia, while in Mordovia and Tatarstan, titular languages have been declared compulsory subjects and also employed as medium of instruction. Arrangements for instruction in the titular language are, however, more far-reaching in Tatarstan than in Finno-Ugric republics generally, resulting in more pronounced assimilation in the latter cases.[81] For the titular languages under consideration, the degrees of language elaboration and length of literary traditions similarly vary, and, in the case of Karelian, the codification of the standard language has been an additional challenge. In Karelia, the post-Soviet period saw efforts to expand the vocabulary of the Karelian language, and for it to be employed in sophisticated spheres of language use, such as in the print media. For this purpose, the Orthographic Commission for the Karelian Language was established, which effectively forged new words; yet a Karelian respondent who had been involved in this process expressed disappointment at its overall poor results, despite sustained attempts to reverse the language shift [2.2]. Generally, the Council of Europe's Advisory Committee on the FCNM has referred to the Finno-Ugric nationalities as 'vulnerable groups' within their republics, despite their titularity, due to decreasing state support for initiatives to promote minority languages and cultures.[82]

The three republics display varying levels of ethnic consciousness. Demographic factors and (titular) population density have played a role in national revival and mobilisation. In Tatarstan, the titular group could harness more resources for national revival in the 1980s and early 1990s, while in the Finno-Ugric republics nationalist movements have remained feeble (Beissinger 2002; Zamyatin 2014: 87–88). Demographic factors on their own are, however, insufficient to explain levels of ethnic consciousness and mobilisation: some titulars in ethnic republics have shown no interest, or opposition to, programmes for ethnic revival, while ethnic Russians have at times supported the promotion of titular languages in ethnic republics (Giuliano and Gorenburg 2012). Economic wealth on its own is similarly insufficient to explain nationalist impulses – particularly when one takes into account the wealth discrepancy between Tatarstan and Chechnya, but the high drive for separatism in both cases in the 1990s (Giuliano and Gorenburg 2012). Mobilisation has further been linked to grievances amplified by nationalist leaders' messages on ethnic inequality being responsible for financial precariousness and job insecurity (Giuliano 2011). Thus, mobilisation derives from a combination of factors, which, among those already mentioned, include levels of autonomy and strength of regional ethnic institutions (Gorenburg 2003). Lastly, historical factors can play an additional role in the development of ethnic consciousness. For example, the Kazan khanate

Table 2.2 Case studies: similarities and differences

Feature	Similarities	Differences
Territoriality	Karelia/Mordovia/Tatarstan: ethnic republics	N/A
Ethnicity	Karelians and Mordovians: Finno-Ugric	Tatars: Turkic
Language	Karelian and Mordovian: Finno-Ugric	Tatar: Turkic
State language of the republic	Mordovian languages and Tatar: recognised as state languages in the Republic of Mordovia and the Republic of Tatarstan	Karelian: not recognised as a state language in the Republic of Karelia
Religion	Karelians and Mordovians: traditionally Christian	Tatars: traditionally Muslim
Education in the titular language	Mordovia and Tatarstan: as a subject and medium of instruction	Karelia: only as a subject
Size of population in Russia as a whole		Karelians: small population (60,815) Mordovians: medium population (744,237) Tatars: large population (5,310,649)
Percentage of the population – ethnic republic		Karelians: low (7.1%) Mordovians: medium (39.9%) Tatars: high (53.2%)
Wealth in ethnic republic	Karelia: low gross regional product (GRP)[1] Mordovia: low GPR	Tatarstan: high GRP

Note
1 In 2007 Karelia had a GRP that was a third higher than Mordovia (104,623 roubles versus 77,003 roubles), while Tatarstan had ten times the GRP of Mordovia (770,729 roubles). Data from the Federal Service of State Statistics, www.gks.ru/bgd/free/b01_19/IssWWW.exe/Stg/d000/vrp98–07.htm.

was already a flourishing political community at the time of Russia's conquest in 1552: it was inhabited by merchants, craftsmen and scholars, and was a centre of Islamic civilisation with a literary and historiography tradition (Kappeler 2001: 25); as a result, the area of present Tatarstan experienced lower levels of Russification compared to Karelia and Mordovia.

Religious markers vary across the case studies. Karelia is more culturally and religiously homogeneous than the two other republics: in Tatarstan there is an almost even Christian/Muslim split,[83] and in Mordovia the third nationality by size (after Russians and Mordovians) is the (predominantly Muslim) Tatar minority (5.2 per cent of the republic's population). Karelia's autochthonous nationalities (Russians, Karelians, Finns and Veps) have been traditionally Orthodox Christians, and the republic's ethnic and religious composition has only very slightly been altered through minor post-Soviet migration. The Tatars' affiliation to the Muslim faith likely contributes to reinforcing a separate identity from the Orthodox Christians majority.

Both Finno-Ugric nationalities and Tatars have organised themselves in overarching Finno-Ugric and Tatar institutions in Russia (Peoples' Congresses), as well as international movements (the World Congress of Finno-Ugric Peoples and the World Congress of Tatars).[84] Another commonality between the three case studies is that none of them has a kin state outside Russia, meaning that their languages and cultures could vanish in the case of assimilation into the Russian majority.

Following the discussion of the concepts and context of the study, Chapters 3 and 4 will analyse domestic and international standards for the protection of cultural rights of minorities, and their potential role in providing a counterweight to Russia's homogenising tendencies.

Notes

1 For a recent discussion on this issue, see Jackson-Preece (2014).
2 For example, the position of France is that there are no minorities on its territory.
3 In relation to the Framework Convention for the Protection of National Minorities (FCNM), the Council of Europe recognised that 'at this stage, it is impossible to arrive at a definition capable of mustering general support of all Council of Europe member States' (FCNM, Explanatory Report, §12); therefore, a 'pragmatic approach' was followed, with the adoption of the FCNM despite the absence of a conclusive definition.
4 Packer (1993: 57) criticises the overuse of adjectives in the absence of a definition: '[E]mphasis on the adjectives becomes largely irrelevant since they too lose their meaning in the absence of the noun: to say that something is "green" is not very helpful if one has no idea to what it applies.' See also Gilbert (1996: 169).
5 In its First Report to the Advisory Committee on the Framework Convention for the Protection of National Minorities (ACFC), Russia stated that 'The Russian Federation is one of the largest multinational states in the world inhabited by more than 170 peoples'. ACFC, (First) Report submitted by the Russian Federation, 8 March 2000, ACFC/SR(1999)015, p. 4.
6 'Small-in-number' refers to the fact that each group counts less than 50,000 members.
7 On indigenous peoples and international law see, among others: Barsh (1996); Ghanea

and Xanthaki (2005); Pentassuglia (2003, 2009); Thornberry (1991, 2002). On indigenous peoples in Russia, see Kryazhkov (2010) and Xanthaki (2004).

8 The UN International Labour Organization (ILO), in Convention No. 169, refers to indigenous peoples as:

> [P]eoples in independent countries who are regarded as indigenous on account of their descent from the populations which inhabited the country, or a geographical region to which the country belongs, at the time of conquest or colonisation or the establishment of present state boundaries and who, irrespective of their legal status, retain some or all of their own social, economic, cultural and political institutions.
>
> (1989 ILO 'Indigenous and Tribal Peoples Convention' No. 169, Article 1(1)(b))

9 Resolution of the Government of the Russian Federation 'On the Unified List of Small-in-Number Indigenous Peoples of the Russian Federation' (No. 255, 24 March 2000).

10 See Article 69 of the Russian Constitution, and special laws: Law 'On Guarantees of the Rights of Small-in-Number Indigenous Peoples of the Russian Federation' (No. 82-FZ, 30 April 1999); Law 'On the Territories of Traditional Nature Use of the Small-in-Number Indigenous Peoples of the North, Siberia and the Far East of the Russian Federation' (No. 49-FZ, 7 May 2001); and Law 'On Basic Principles of Community Organization of Small-in-Number Indigenous Peoples of the North, Siberia and the Far East of the Russian Federation' (No. 104-FZ, 20 July 2000). See also the 'Concept Paper on the Sustainable Development of Small-in-Number Indigenous Peoples of the North, Siberia and the Far East of the Russian Federation' (No. 132-r, 4 February 2009).

11 The expression 'minority' has been linked to representatives of titular groups living outside the territories 'assigned' to them. In fact, the expression 'national minority' was mostly excluded from the Soviet discourse, and only seldom resurfaced (Malakhov and Osipov 2006: 509).

12 See Table 2.1 for population data.

13 For example, black South Africans in apartheid South Africa.

14 The same applies to the other ethnic republics in which the titular nationality is numerically superior, amounting to over half the republic's total population (Chechnya, Chuvashia, Ingushetia, Kabardino-Balkaria, Kalmykia, North Ossetia and Tyva).

15 See also the UNESCO Statement on Cultural Rights as Human Rights, where UNESCO referred to 'culture' as: '[T]he totality of ways by which men create a design for living. It is the process of communication between men; it is the essence of being human.' 1970 UNESCO Statement on Cultural Rights as Human Rights, http:// unesdoc.unesco.org/images/0000/000011/001194eo.pdf (accessed 12 December 2014).

16 See also Article 1(1) of the 1992 UN Declaration on the Rights of Persons Belonging to National or Ethnic, Religious and Linguistic Minorities: 'States shall protect the existence and the national or ethnic, cultural, religious and linguistic *identity* of minorities within their respective territories and shall encourage conditions for the promotion of that identity.' [italics added].

17 Mannens (1999: 185–6) considers 'cultural rights; as: 'those rights which assist in the preservation, maintenance and development of a culture – the specific elements of the social or cultural life of a group which contribute to the separate identity of the group'.

18 According to Anderson (1991), this process occurred through the development of the printing press.

19 Among these, three UN instruments: the 1948 Universal Declaration of Human Rights, the 1966 International Covenant on Civil and Political Rights and the 1966 International Covenant on Economic, Social and Cultural Rights.

20 Tishkov, V. 31 May 2011. 'XXI Vek Priznaet Prava Bol'shinstva' [The 21st Century Recognises the Rights of the Majority], *Russkii Zhurnal*, www.russ.ru/Mirovaya-povestka/XXI-vek-priznaet-prava-bol-shinstva (accessed 22 January 2015).

21 Ibid.

22 Cited in BBC News, 17 October 2010. 'Merkel Says German Multicultural Society has Failed', www.bbc.co.uk/news/world-europe-11559451 (accessed 13 October 2014).

23 'PM's speech at Munich Security Conference'. Transcript of the speech delivered on 5 February 2011, www.gov.uk/government/speeches/pms-speech-at-munich-security-conference (accessed 13 October 2014).

24 The law came into force on 11 April 2011.

25 Cited in *Agence France Press*, 10 February 2011. 'Multiculturalism has Failed, Says French President'.

26 In an interview with the *Financial Times*. Hollinger, P. 16 February 2011. 'Council of Europe Warns on Multiculturalism', *Financial Times*.

27 Hylland Eriksen, T. Autumn 1999. 'Globalization and the Politics of Identity', *UN Chronicle*, http://folk.uio.no/geirthe/UNChron.html (accessed 13 October 2014).

28 Tishkov, *Russkii Zhurnal* (see note 20 above). Criticism of multiculturalism has also come from other sources. Barry (2001) sees the differentiated treatment of various societal groups as a threat to equality. Hasan (2010) likens multiculturalism to segregation and ghettoisation. Others have noted a potential for illiberal practices harming vulnerable persons within a minority group (Okin 1999, 2002). Žižek (2011: 44) argues that multiculturalism as an ideology is in fact 'hegemonic', and conjures up an 'illusion of anti-racist multiculturalism'.

29 UN Human Rights Committee, 'CCPR General Comment No. 23: Article 27 (Rights of Minorities)', 8 April 1994, CCPR/C/21/Rev.1/Add 5, §9.

30 The Preamble of the 2001 UNESCO Universal Declaration on Cultural Diversity states that: '[R]espect for the diversity of cultures, tolerance, dialogue and cooperation, in a climate of mutual trust and understanding are among the best guarantees of international peace and security.'

31 FCNM, Explanatory Report, §46.

32 See also Article 1 FCNM, stating that minority rights are 'an integral part of the international protection of human rights'.

33 Working Group on Minorities, Commission on Human Rights, 'Commentary of the Working Group on Minorities to the United Nations Declaration on the Rights of Persons Belonging to National or Ethnic, Religious and Linguistic Minorities', 4 April 2005, E/CN.4/Sub.2/AC.5/2005/2, §22.

34 Speech by V. Putin, Meeting of the International Discussion Club 'Valdai', 19 September 2013, www.kremlin.ru/news/19243 (accessed 12 September 2014).

35 Ibid.

36 Ibid.

37 This has not only been the case with regard to the Russian majority. Shnirelman equally shows that, in the ethnic republics, there have been similarly ethnocentric representations of history.

38 Finland became an autonomous Grand Duchy in 1809, following the Finnish War between Russia and Sweden and the signing of the Treaty of Fredrikshamn. Allegiance to tsar Alexander I was pledged, in exchanges for guarantees that the laws and liberties of Finns be respected, including in the practice of their Protestantism.

39 See Chapter 5 on Russian federalism.

40 The number rose to 85 with the annexation of Crimea by Russia, and the adoption of Federal Constitutional Law 'On the Republic of Crimea's Accession to the Russian Federation and the Formation of New Subjects of the Russian Federation – the Republic of Crimea and Sevastopol, City of Federal Significance' (No. 6-FKZ, 21 March 2014). The annexation has increased the number of minority groups (de facto)

residing in Russia. On the possible consequences of the annexation of Crimea by Russia for Crimean Tatars, see Osipov (2014).

41 These are generally referred to as 'ethnic republics' (including in this book), given that they were established as part of the Soviet Union's ethno-federalist structure, and were named after titular nationalities. However, the 1993 Russian Constitution does not refer to them as ethnicity-based entities, but simply as 'republics'. See for example Articles 65(1), 66(1) and 68(2).

42 'Oblast', 'krai' and 'okrug' are expressions designating particular administrative units of the Federation ('districts' or 'regions').

43 Anderson and Silver (1984: 1019) have argued that the Soviet Union had a 'longer and more extensive experience with bi-lingual education than any other country in the world'.

44 However, while minority languages were promoted through education, the Russian language dominated in most spheres of language use, as it served as language of inter-ethnic communication across the Soviet Union.

45 Attention to the needs of non-dominant peoples has also had less pragmatic and more ideological foundations, with the proclamation of equality, sovereignty and free self-determination of all peoples, contained already in the 1917 'Declaration of the Rights of the Peoples of Russia.'

46 I rely on Gorenburg's definition of 'ethnic institutions', as:

> those institutions that are established to oversee a state's interaction with ethnic groups living on its territory. They include territorial administrative units for ethnic minorities, separate educational systems, language laws, official ethnic categories for censuses and identity papers, affirmative action programs for ethnic minorities, etc.
>
> (Gorenburg 2003: 3, fn 2)

47 Shahin (1989: 412) writes: 'Neither eternal nor genetic – racialism and ahistoricity were consistently rejected in Soviet views – ethnic particularity was treated as socially real.'

48 On the theory of ethnos, see Bromley and Kozlov (1989).

49 Even though Shirokogorov considered ethnicities to be in a constant state of flux (Shnirelman 2009a).

50 The definition of ethnos provided by Bromley is:

> a stable intergenerational community of people, historically formed on a certain territory, possessing common relatively stable features of culture (including language) and psyche, as well as a consciousness of their unity and of their difference from other similar entities (self-awareness), reflected in a self-name (ethnonym).
>
> (Bromley 1983: 57–58)

51 As Arel (2002) notes, in Soviet censuses, the question on one's native language immediately followed that on one's nationality, which could have led people to treat the two as effectively the same question (see also Grenoble 2003: 28–9, 45). Since the 2002 census the practice of asking about one's native language has been discontinued.

52 Although in the 1930s ethnicity was established on the basis of self-identification, this was soon changed, with one's nationality being made to coincide with that of one's parents (in the case of mixed marriages, one could choose the ethnicity of either parent). The system altered again in post-Soviet Russia: the 1993 Russian Constitution states that ethnicity is based on self-identification (Article 26(1)).

53 Ideologically the Communists were opposed to colonisation, although it has been pointed out that the Soviet Union could not have survived without the exploitation of the material resources of its constituent parts (Hirsch 2005: 78).

54 Some ethnicities were accused of collaboration with the Nazis, and deported to Siberia and Central Asia. Duncan (1999: 70) refers to the deportations as 'a demonstration of Russian firmness and a warning to other nationalities'. Among the ethnic groups whose members were (entirely or partially) subjected to forced relocation within the USSR were Germans, Crimean Tatars, Chechens, Kalmyks, Ingush, Karachay, Greeks, Meskhetian Turks, Koreans, Kurds, Ukrainians, Poles and Armenians (see Nekrich 1978; Pohl 1999).

55 Repression was reduced in1941, primarily for the pragmatic decision to involve religious institutions in the collective effort required by World War II. Repression intensified again in 1959, under Krushchev's leadership (Duncan 1999: 69–70).

56 Karelian remained an exception to this general rule.

57 On Russian messianism, see Duncan (2000).

58 The Yeltsin years are briefly examined in Chapter 5.

59 Although these opportunities have tended to decrease in the 2000s. See Chapter 6.

60 See Chapter 5.

61 The Levada Analytical Center is a Russian NGO that conducts sociological research. In 2003 it separated from the All-Union Center for the Study of Public Opinion (VTsIOM), established in 1987, to become a distinct institution under the management of Russian sociologist Yuri Levada.

62 See Levada Center, 5 December 2013. 'Rossiyane o Migratsii i Mezhnatsional'noi Napryazhennosti' [Russians on Migration and Inter-ethnic Tensions], www.levada. ru/05–11–2013/rossiyane-o-migratsii-i-mezhnatsionalnoi-napryazhennosti (accessed 12 September 2014).

63 The stated aims of the Eurasia Party include: 'reinforcing the strategic unity of Russia, her geopolitical homogeneity, the vertical line of authority … fighting separatism, extremism, localism'. See 'Theses of Dugin's Address to the Political Conference of the Pan-Russian Social-Political Movement Eurasia (1 March 2002)', http://eurasia. com.ru/dugin0103_eng.html (accessed 12 September 2014).

64 On this, see reports by the SOVA Center for Information and Analysis, www.sova-center.ru/en/xenophobia/reports-analyses/ (accessed 3 October 2014). Writing about developments in 2013, SOVA stated:

> The past year was characterized by a notable surge in ethnic violence…. A real persecution was unleashed against migrants from Central Asia and the Caucasus … 21 people died and 178 were injured as a result of racist and neo-Nazi violence, 9 people received credible murder threats.

SOVA, March 2014. 'The Ultra-Right Shrugged: Xenophobia and Radical Nationalism in Russia, and Efforts to Counteract Them in 2013', www.sova-center.ru/en/xenophobia/reports-analyses/2014/03/d29236/ (accessed 3 October 2014).

65 They have resulted in prosecutions (see SOVA, ibid.) and official pronouncements on the dangers of 'extremism'. See also Osipov (2013c: 66–67).

66 Despite this, at times the Russian authorities have used heavy-handed measures against certain ethnic groups, particularly those that suffer most from social exclusion, such migrants from Central Asia and Roma. For example, in October 2013, the Russian police rounded up and detained *en masse* migrant workers following large-scale and violent anti-immigrant protests that started in the Moscow district of Biryulevo. The protests were triggered by the murder of an ethnic Russian, of which an ethnic Azerbaijani became the primary suspect. On the treatment of Roma, see: Anti-Discrimination Centre (ADC) Memorial, 2012, 'Roma, Migrants, Activists: Victims of Police Abuse'; and ADC Memorial, 2011. 'Discrimination and Violation of Roma Children's Rights in Schools of the Russian Federation'.

67 See also Chapter 5 on this.

68 Positive electoral results seem to have been linked to Putin's ability to stop the decline in living standards experienced during the Yeltsin years (Colton and Hale 2009).

69 Primarily those who self-identify as ethnic Russians, but this type of narrative can also resonate with the Russian citizenry more broadly.

70 See Chapter 3.

71 See Chapter 5.

72 Persons who self-identify as such, primarily on the basis of cultural and linguistic affiliation.

73 Data from the 2010 census can be found at: www.gks.ru/free_doc/new_site/ perepis2010/croc/perepis_itogi1612.htm (accessed 3 December 2014).

74 An attack on animism began in 1750, as part of forcible Christianisation policies (Kreindler 1985: 46–47; Taagepera 1999: 162–163).

75 See ACFC, (Third) Opinion on the Russian Federation, 24 November 2011, ACFC/ OP/III(2011)010, §36.

76 See Table 2.2 on the republics' gross regional product (GRP).

77 Assimilation into the Russian linguistic sphere has been more pronounced in Karelia's urban centres than in rural areas (Grenoble 2003: 79).

78 In 2010 Karelia had 8,577 Finns (1.3 per cent of the population) and 3,423 Veps (0.5 per cent) (2010 census data).

79 On national cultural autonomy see Chapter 8.

80 The number of persons who did not state their nationality in Karelia in 2002 had been as low as 4,886, pointing to a sharp decrease in levels of ethnic consciousness in only eight years. On assimilation of Finno-Ugric peoples, see Strogal'shikova (2009a).

81 See Chapter 6.

82 ACFC, (Second) Opinion on the Russian Federation, 2 May 2007, ACFC/OP/ II(2006)004, §84. See also ACFC, (Third) Opinion on the Russian Federation (note 75); and Parliamentary Assembly of the Council of Europe (PACE), 'Recommendation 1775 (2006). Situation of Finno-Ugric and Samoyed Peoples', 26 October 2006, Doc. 11087.

83 On the basis that ethnic Russians (39.5 per cent) and the Chuvash minority (3.3 per cent) residing in Tatarstan tend to identify themselves as members of the Russian Orthodox Church, and Tatars (52.9 per cent) with the Muslim faith. The remainder of the population of Tatarstan is affiliated to various religious denominations.

84 See Chapters 8 and 9.

3 Minority rights standards

Domestic to international – and back to domestic

Chapter 2 has highlighted the Russian models of diversity accommodation originating from the Soviet period, and some of the challenges inherent in the sociopolitical environment of Putin's Russia. This chapter widens the discussion of minority rights standards to also incorporate international standards in their intersection with the Russian domestic environment. In Russia the dynamics of majority–minority relations have altered as, with the development of international law, they have come to be seen as part of a broader context. These formerly internal concerns have become internationalised, and international standards for minority protection, together with the inter-governmental organisations (IGOs) behind them, have become new instruments in the management of majority–minority relations. The controversial speeches of Western European leaders on multiculturalism, cited in Chapter 2, do not alter the fact that international mechanisms for the protection of minorities exist – under the auspices of the UN, the Council of Europe, the EU and the OSCE – and that minority rights have become subjects of international jurisdiction (Bowring 2015; Gilbert 2002; Henrard 2000; Moucheboeuf 2006; Pentassuglia 2003, 2009; Thornberry 1991, 2002; Weller 2007).

International standards on minority rights have the potential to influence the dynamics of diversity preservation or assimilation in Russia. They can play a role in furthering the promotion of cultural and linguistic wealth, *or* remain a mere appendage at the periphery of a more or less covert Russian nationalist discourse that marginalises other cultures. Thus, in examining minority policies in Russia from a human rights perspective, one cannot but incorporate the question as to whether participation in the international human rights system has enabled the Russian authorities to untangle some of the complexities linked to the country's diversity. It should be added that no state entirely fulfils its responsibilities under international human rights law. Moreover, an international body such as the Council of Europe grants its member states a margin of appreciation:[1] states are allowed relative flexibility in fulfilling their international human rights responsibilities, taking into account their political, historical and social circumstances. The degree of permitted flexibility is even more pronounced in the case of international minority rights law, so as to enable the devising of forms of implementation that match, as closely as possible, the specific needs of different minorities.

This chapter comprises two main sections. First, it illustrates the notion of legal transplantation, and theories on the role of cultural and socio-political factors in the relevant processes. Second, the dynamic interaction of Russian and Western European legal traditions is described. The chapter further outlines aspects of Russia's history that are relevant to the understanding of its present minority policies, and their interplay with international standards on minority rights, as well as the Russian leadership's attitudes vis-à-vis such standards.

Legal transplantation: from 'foreign' to 'domestic'

The expression 'legal transplantation' designates the transposition of a legal rule, or entire legal system, from one entity to another.[2] Watson (1974: 30) writes that: '[R]eceptions and transplants come in all shapes and sizes. One might think also of an imposed reception, solicited imposition, penetration, infiltration, crypto-reception, inoculation and so on ...'

Legal transplantation is common: Watson stresses the influence of foreign legal norms on most legislative systems: for example, Roman law has influenced the legal system in Scotland, Greek law in Germany, Swiss law in Turkey, and French law in Ethiopia (ibid.: 102). A particular form of transfer of norms that has been the subject of rich scholarly literature is Europeanisation.[3] The term refers to the integration of EU law and practices by the member states (EU-isation), although it can also be interpreted more widely to apply to European-level institutions generally, thus encompassing the Council of Europe.[4] With EU enlargement,[5] the scholarship on Europeanisation has shifted its focus from (old) member states to candidate states, later to become new member states – several of which are post-Communist – with reference to EU conditionality and post-accession compliance with EU norms (Bauer *et al.* 2007; Rechel 2009; Arias and Gurses 2012; Ram 2012). The influence exercised over the EU member and candidate states as part of Europeanisation processes is what Olsen calls the 'central penetration of national systems of governance'; this entails 'adapting national and sub-national systems of governance to a European political centre and European-wide norms' (Olsen 2002: 924). Europeanisation literature analyses the juxtaposition of one system over another, with the interplay of international and domestic models. Similarly, the literature on legal transplantation has generated theories on the transplantability of legal norms, which aim at identifying what particular conditions are necessary to bring about a successful transplant – one that is effectively integrated into an existing system. When integration takes place, the transplant becomes a functioning addition to the receiving system, rather than being subsequently 'rejected' or simply remaining unused.

One should note at this stage that the evaluation of the impact of legal transfers is fraught with difficulties. In the case of Europeanisation, authors have noted that its processes are not amenable to measurement through dependent and independent variables, as transformation takes place amidst mixed, co-evolving processes (Featherstone 2003: 4; Olsen 1996: 271). These dynamics, which can be more 'evolutionary than revolutionary' (Green Cowles and Risse 2001: 236), follow tortuous trajectories against a backdrop of ever-shifting circumstances. Thus, patterns of convergence and divergence of member and candidate states around the EU (or Council of Europe) 'core' can be difficult to explain (Green Cowles and Risse ibid.: 231). In some cases the effects of Europeanisation can be delayed, or not be immediately detectable (Martinsen 2012). Additional complexities are linked to the issue of causality, or the identification of possible causal links between domestic change and IGO activity (Exadaktylos and Radaelli 2012; Bache *et al.* 2012; Lynnggard 2012; Goetz 2000; Moravcik 1998). As a consequence, I do not attempt to measure a possible impact of legal transplantation; instead I highlight factors that complicate the implementation of international norms, including the perceptions of respondents who are (directly or indirectly) involved in the application of international standards on minority protection in Russia.[6]

Cultural and socio-political factors in legal transplantation

Factors influencing legal transplantation include legal and institutional cultures and practices. Powell and DiMaggio (1991) argue that the continuous interaction of institutions ultimately leads to convergence, even in the case of structures that have followed distinct historical trajectories. Others believe that the law develops to reflect, and mould around, specific socio-political, as well as cultural, contexts (Pulchalska-Tych and Salter 1996). Örücü (2002: 219) argues that a mismatch between legal systems is created when such systems are grounded (or not) on specific ideological or religious beliefs.[7] In the context of Europeanisation, Knill (1998: 24) sees the 'degree of embeddedness' of national institutional arrangements as a factor influencing domestic adaptation.[8] Green Cowles and Risse (2001) adopt a different perspective, by arguing that (partial) structural convergence can take place even in the presence of deep historical and cultural entrenchment of domestic institutions. In these cases, (EU) integration can be a pragmatic choice: 'actors evaluate existing models and determine which one is successful. They then adopt the model irrespective of its national origin' – although different degrees of convergence (or divergence), and varied responses to Europeanisation, are found in different countries (ibid.: 233). These two positions loosely reflect those of Watson and of Kahn-Freund on legal transplants, who by 1974 had developed diametrically opposed views on the matter.[9] Kahn-Freund's (1974) point of departure was the belief that legislation shapes around the people for whom it develops. The same concept is behind Ewald's (1995: 492) 'mirror theory of law', by which 'law is a mirror of society, and every aspect of the law is moulded by economy and society'. According to this view, the prerequisite for the transferability of legal principles closely resembles the socio-political environment of the donor and recipient states (Kahn-Freund 1974; Heim 1996: 196). Conversely, Watson (1974) stressed the facility with which norms may be transferred, travelling across borders, downplaying a possible resistance to 'foreign' legal norms, or the significance of local legal culture: his view was that there is not necessarily a link between the law of a country and its socio-political and economic conditions.

In relation to Europeanisation, an additional factor in domestic transformation is the pressure that can be applied by the EU, particularly in the shape of EU conditionality, previous to accession. Divergence between the EU and the candidate state results in a 'misfit'; in turn, a misfit leads to adaptational pressure (Green Cowles and Risse 2001: 222). Héritier (2001: 1) argues that, 'Where the established policy of a member state diverges from a clearly specified European policy mandate, there will be an expectation to adjust, which in turn constitutes a precondition for change.' At the same time, identifying clear patterns of fits or misfits is problematic (Green Cowles and Risse 2001: 223). Factors determining a possible 'goodness of fit' are not fixed, as both the EU and member or candidate states continue to evolve (Börzel and Risse 2003). Additionally, a misfit might produce pressure, yet pressure might not necessarily induce change. Even favourable conditions may not lead to convergence (Olsen 1996: 261–262).

One then needs to analyse the specific context of the transfer, as 'goodness of fit' approaches provide limited understanding of domestic change or lack of it. In the case of Europeanisation, studies have shown that local factors tend to be more important than external factors in determining outcomes of legal transfers (Hughes *et al.* 2004), and adaptation pressures interact in different ways with local circumstances (Green Cowles and Risse 2001). O'Dwyer (2006: 253) sees in these dynamics a 'combination of political opportunism and policy unpredictability'. If this is the case with EU-induced adaptation pressure, it is likely to be even more so in the case of the Council of Europe, which has not had at its disposal a 'gatekeeping' mechanism to regulate compliance with international obligations that is comparable to EU conditionality.

Thus, transformation is unpredictable. At the same time, what may at first sight appear to be a 'transfer' from a 'foreign' system might in reality not be so. The donating and the receiving systems do not tend to be completely separate entities, sealed off from each other until the transfer takes place. When a new treaty is ratified, the provisions it contains can often be already present in some shape or form in the ratifying state's legal system.[10] Then, comparative law does not amount to the 'comparison of two separate and unconnected entities, frozen in the present' (Bowring 2003: 180): most systems are mixed, originating from multiple legal sources, which commonly results in the blurring of the distinction between what is endogenous and what is exogenous. In order to understand the circumstances surrounding transfers, one has to examine the relations between the two polities in question, as well as the historical and political trajectory of the receiving state. In Russia, in addition to its history of interaction with the West, a significant role in the outcomes of transfers is played by a perception of such standards as 'double standards'.

International standards or double standards?

The international human rights system holds states to account for what happens *within* their borders.[11] In the case of the European Convention on Human Rights (ECHR), everyone in a Council of Europe member state is empowered to submit a case to the European Court of Human Rights. Thus, governments renounce their full sovereignty for an internationally-managed system, over which they have no direct control. Moravcsik (2000) refers to two reasons that could motivate this choice: coercion by great powers (realist approach) and altruistic reasons (ideational approach). Among the supporters of the realist theory there is a 'cynical strand' that sees liberal values and human rights as a tool in the hands of powerful governments to add a veneer of legitimacy to essentially selfish geopolitical pursuits. In line with this interpretation, Donnelly (1986) talks about the United States' 'hegemonic power' in relation to the inter-American human rights regime,[12] while Waltz (1979) denounces the imposition of the great powers' ideas over other countries (reminiscent of the old adage *cuius regio, eius religio*):

> Like some earlier great powers, we [the United States] can identify the presumed duty of the rich and powerful to help others with our own beliefs ... England claimed to bear the white man's burden; France had its *mission civilisatrice*.
>
> (Waltz 1979: 200)

This approach can lead to a perception that the international community is seeking to homogenise its members, by forcing domestic arrangements into convergence with pre-established frameworks. As a result, these dynamics may be perceived as a form of coercion exerted by the more powerful members of the international community to the detriment of the weaker members. Additional pressure to embrace human rights norms has been seen to originate from international institutions that are not human rights-based but carry substantial weight and can influence human rights regimes, such as the EU (Moravcsik 2000) and the World Bank (Brysk 1994). The ideational approach, instead, links the human rights system to ideals which not all governments necessarily share, but which are promoted by civil society organisations driven by altruistic sentiments. Moravcsik proposes a *third* approach: the 'republican liberal' theory, through which new democracies use international human rights mechanisms to 'lock in', and thereby solidify, democratic institutions – protecting themselves (through outside support and ready-made institutions) against internal non-democratic threats (Moravcsik 2000: 219–220). The realist and republican liberal approach see human rights as a pragmatic choice – to influence international and internal policies respectively.

Regardless of its genuine motivating factor(s), Russia has formally acceded to the international human rights regime. As a founding member of the UN, the Soviet Union participated in defining the scope of its human rights system, including early discussions on the 1948 Universal Declaration of Human Rights

(UDHR).[13] Russia, as the USSR's successor state, remains one of the five most influential players in the UN by virtue of being a permanent member, with the power of veto, of the 15-strong UN Security Council. The Soviet Union also participated in discussions, in the early 1970s, on the Conference on Security and Co-operation in Europe (CSCE), and signed the Helsinki Final Act in 1975. In 2014 Russia was one of the 57 OSCE participating states,[14] as well as a member of the Council of Europe, having joined the latter in 1996. Yet Russia has also accused IGOs of an anti-Russia political agenda, and of pursuing particularistic interests rather than human rights – somewhat in line with the 'cynical strand' of the realist theory. For example, with regard to the OSCE, President Vladimir Putin stated in 2007: 'They are trying to transform the OSCE into a vulgar instrument designed to promote the foreign policy interests of one or a group of countries. And this task is also being accomplished by the OSCE's bureaucratic apparatus.'[15]

What prompts such vehement criticism? Chandler (1999) argues that the OSCE system was primarily oriented towards the development of standards applicable to new Eastern European democracies, in order to create the conditions for peace in the new Europe following conflict in the former Yugoslavia. So as to avoid the post-World War I scenario – when treaties on minorities were forced solely upon Eastern Europe – OSCE standards were to be applied universally; at the same time, Western countries acted to reduce the scope of the OSCE's impact on *their* internal affairs. They insisted on strategic exclusions from the scope of international monitoring: Germany for 'new' minorities (to exclude its substantial immigrant population); the United States for 'indigenous peoples' (to exclude American Indians); the United Kingdom and Turkey (with Spain's support) in cases linked to terrorism (to exclude matters involving Northern Ireland and the Kurds respectively); and France for any national minorities in its territory, by claiming that none existed. Through these exclusions, and particularly those negotiated by the United Kingdom and Turkey, possible inter-ethnic conflicts in the West were left outside the scope of OSCE monitoring (ibid.: 67). In this way, 'universal' standards can rather be likened to 'double' standards.

Furthermore, Russia was not involved, prior to becoming a member in 1996, in the development of the Council of Europe as a regional human rights mechanism, including the formulation of its fundamental human rights treaty: the ECHR.[16] Neither did Russia participate in processes towards the adoption of the two main Council of Europe instruments on national minorities and minority languages: the 1995 Framework Convention for the Protection of National Minorities (FCNM) and the 1992 European Charter for Regional or Minority Languages (ECRML). For the late joiners, the Council of Europe required an accelerated route to full integration into its human rights system: in the case of Russia, it foresaw, *inter alia*, a commitment to ratify the ECRML. Russia signed the ECRML in 2001 but did not ratify it[17] – resulting in non-compliance with this obligation. Yet a country like France, which has also refrained from ratifying the ECRML (as well as the FCNM), has been under no obligation to do so, being one of the ten countries that ratified the Statute of the Council of Europe in

1949, thereby establishing the institution.[18] Meanwhile, in relation to EU criteria for Europeanisation (the Copenhagen criteria), countries of Central and Eastern Europe were faced by an invidious choice: either they conformed, or they renounced membership. Cordell (2013) argues that these conditions were informed by the Western powers' presumption that, without a progressive (Western) framework, inter-ethnic strife in Central and Eastern Europe would become the norm rather than the exception. These dynamics could easily further perceptions of unequal treatment, and thus double standards.

Russia, the West and 'legal transplantation'

Despite various sources of tensions with IGOs and some of their members, Russia is a party to numerous UN and Council of Europe instruments. In 1969, the Soviet Union ratified the UN International Convention on the Elimination of All Forms of Racial Discrimination (CERD) followed in 1973 by the UN's International Covenant on Civil and Political Rights (ICCPR), generating international obligations inherited by Russia as its successor state. In 1996, the Russian Federation became a member of the Council of Europe, and in 1998 it ratified both the ECHR and FCNM. As part of its implementation of the FCNM, the Russian government had, by 2010, submitted three reports to the Council of Europe,[19] detailing its activities to uphold the rights enshrined in the treaty. In its 2007 Second Opinion on the implementation of the FCNM by Russia, the Advisory Committee on the FCNM (ACFC) acknowledged that 'the Russian Federation has adopted a positive approach to the Framework Convention's monitoring process'.[20] This statement was echoed by the Committee of Ministers of the Council of Europe, which, also in 2007, observed that the Russian authorities had 'continued to pay attention to the protection of national minorities'.[21] There is indeed scope for minorities in Russia to benefit from accession to the FCNM (and ECHR), as Russian legislation on the protection of minorities and their cultural rights is predominantly declarative,[22] with provisions scattered in various pieces of legislation in the absence of a *lex specialis* on minority protection. International law, and the relevant international standards on the promotion of minorities' cultural rights, can crystallise obligations and make compliance more compelling by exposing Russian policies and jurisprudence to international scrutiny. Yet two factors complicate the implementation of international standards: the (aforementioned) scepticism of the Russian authorities vis-à-vis IGOs and their standards; and Russia's complex relationship with the West, along with the former's drive to assert its sovereignty and great power status.

The ambivalent reception reserved for 'imports' in Russia can be traced back to the old dispute between Westernisers and Slavophiles – or those who welcomed and emulated the West and its modernising influence, and those who wished to follow an inherently Russian path. This binary thinking has reflected a tension between two diametrically opposed positions: one favouring universalist values, and the other privileging what is indigenous (see also Figes 2003). The latter position espoused the notion that Peter the Great (1682–1725), by abruptly and radically introducing Western lifestyles and concepts, had weakened, rather than modernised, Russia, truncating its natural historical development. This interpretation was accompanied in the nineteenth century by the view that Russia ought not to be a cheap imitation of the West: new pride came with the defeat of Napoleon (1812), which was regarded as a manifestation of Russian superiority, and imbued with nationalistic messianism (Leatherbarrow 2010; see also Duncan 2000).

Elements of these narratives are still present in today's Russia. The comments voiced by Putin concerning the OSCE, reported above, reveal a suspicious attitude vis-à-vis international ('Western') institutions such as the OSCE, which have become locked in an 'us-and-them' discourse. Differences between Western Europe and Russia have been seized upon by some analysts to justify claims that a treaty such as the ECHR, as a 'Western' instrument, cannot be applied in Russia. For example, Kharlamova (2009) cites historical and psychological factors supposedly separating Russians from Western Europeans, such as Russian 'spirituality' and 'irrationality', as well as a presumed aversion to democratic reforms. Western authors similarly refer to differences that may not be reconciled. Solomon (2005: 341) describes Russia's judicial system as mirroring a political system characterised by a 'pluralistic form of authoritarianism'. Yet throughout its history Russia has borrowed from Western legal models: Russian law has a pre-Soviet grounding in the Roman-Germanic legal family (Ajani 1995), and Russia borrowed from the West – even during the Soviet Union – with regard to its civil law (ibid.: 94; Rudden 1994: 61). With the decline of Soviet models, the Soviet Union explored alternative socialist systems from Central and Eastern Europe, including Hungary and Poland, particularly during the *perestroika* period. This paved the way for reaching out further West for additional alternative models in later years: no longer required to be embedded in ideology, Russian legal scholarship was free to examine new normative solutions, including those from foreign sources (Ajani 1995: 101, 109–110).[23]

At the same time, it would be a mistake to assume that human rights principles have been transferred from the West onto a Russian *tabula rasa*. Concepts associated with human rights law were already present in pre-Soviet Russia. Jury trials presided over by independent judges operated in Russia from 1864 to 1917 (Bowring 2013a: 36ff.).[24] Thus, Bowring argues that Russia's accession to an instrument such as the ECHR is not so much a case of legal transplantation, but rather the restoration of principles and institutions that were already an integral part of the Russian legal tradition. Contacts with the West had resulted in a 'dynamic interplay of Russian and Western European … history and traditions' (Bowring 2003: 176). Equally, principles underlying Soviet and post-Soviet programmes for the promotion of minority languages and cultures, such as education in minority languages, closely resemble those contained in the FCNM and the ECRML. In post-Soviet Russia, international human rights law has been increasingly employed by Russian lawyers and judges;[25] and, as noted, the Soviet Union participated in the shaping of UN standards. Consequently, it becomes difficult to draw a neat demarcation line between Russian and international law. Despite this, international law has not fully shaken off the label of being 'alien' to Russia.

To counteract the 'excessive' penetration of foreign norms, the Putin leadership places an emphasis on the 'Russian idea', or the 'organic merger of universal, human values with primordial Russian values'.[26] Putin stated in 1999:

> The experience of the 1990s vividly shows that genuine and efficient revival of our Fatherland cannot be brought about on Russian soil simply through abstract models and schemes extracted from foreign textbooks. Mechanically copying the experiences of other states will not bring progress. Every country, Russia included, has a duty to search for its own path of renewal.
> [...]
> Russia will not soon, if ever, become a replica of, say, the United States or Britain, where liberal values have deep-seated traditions. For us, the state, with its institutions and structures, has always played an exclusively important role in the life of the country and its people. For a Russian, a strong state is not an anomaly, not something with which he has to struggle, but, on the contrary, a source and a guarantee of order.[27]

Hence, Russia seeks to access the international community, but on 'its own terms' and while simultaneously protecting its identity and geopolitical interests (Sakwa 2011a: 961). Through the media, and the manipulation of Soviet myths, Russians are encouraged to forge a Russian way to modernisation that does not reject, but integrates, elements of the Soviet past (Novikova 2010). Such a Russian path guarantees a strong statehood vis-à-vis Russia's external relations (i.e. Russia's status within the international system), internal policies (a strong federal centre) and the near abroad (the preservation of spheres of influence in the post-Soviet space).

A complicating factor in Russia's geopolitical orientation and self-perception is the existence of two parallel narratives of Russia as a *Eurasian* and *European* country. The first approach is a response to a quest for Russians' self-definition that is neo-imperial and aims at creating an 'Eurasian home' for the Russians and non-Russian nationalities residing in Russia and beyond (Opalski 2001: 301). Duncan (2004: 231) describes Eurasianism as a body of 'policies which give priority towards promoting the cooperation and unity of the post-Soviet states'. Eurasianism has pan-Slavic roots inasmuch as it defines itself in its opposition to Westernisation (Bonnett 2002: 444). At the same time, in the context of modernisation, official references are made to Russia's Europeanness. Despite multiple cases of Russian–Western tensions, Russia's foreign policy under Putin has been moderately pro-Western, which has positively impacted on his (and Medvedev's) popularity and electoral results (Colton and Hale 2009). Russian nationalism's references to Europeanness are evident in discourses promoted by the Kremlin and United Russia relating to Russia belonging to Europe (Laruelle 2009a: 202; Sakwa 2004: 168–169).[28] Yet efforts to incorporate international standards into Russian law and practice in post-Soviet Russia have coincided with a period characterised by internal uncertainty, not only linked to political instability but also to questions as to what it means to be 'Russian'. This can at least partially explain the rejection of (real or perceived) 'imports', and doubts over the Strasbourg law. Rather than the universality of human rights, Putin's position places an emphasis on cultural relativism, by pointing to the uniqueness of Russia's experience and attributes.

Russia: just another member state or great power?

The Russian leadership seeks to project an image of Russia not only as 'unique', but also as a 'great power'.[29] Putin has used self-aggrandising rhetoric: 'We should let the wealth of Russian culture guide us. Russia has always been among the nations that not only create their own cultural agenda, but also influence the entire global civilisation.'[30]

This approach implies the pursuit of an influential role for Russia within the international arena. Russia has sought to gain recognition and respect from the Western European powers over the centuries, even when its strength was withering domestically (Neumann 2005). This is an ongoing concern (Lynch 2001). Scholars have pointed to an asymmetrical relationship between Russia and the West: the values and ideologies of Western European and American powers have been imposed upon other countries, including Russia (Lieven 2003: ix), while Western powers have also developed the parameters of actorness (Haukkala 2008: 36). With some exceptions (such as the period following World War II), and particularly in relation to the formation of European institutions (the Council of Europe, the EU and OSCE), Russia has been a 'norm-taker' rather than a 'norm-maker' (ibid.: 2008: 53–54). It is these (West-to-East) tendencies that Russia is energetically resisting. As Sakwa (2011a: 957) puts it, Russia has sought to promote its 'self-identification as a great power ... as well as its implicit claim of equality with the dominant Western hegemonic order while retaining its autonomy in that order' (see also Baranovsky 2000). The Russian government has striven to either position itself as important ally of the West, or as a powerful opponent: thus, it aligned itself with the United States after 9/11, later shifting its alliance towards France and Germany, for example during the Iraq war (Neumann 2005). More recently Russia has positioned itself antagonistically to the West, in its competition with the EU over geopolitical influence in Eastern Europe,[31] and, even more crucially, through the 2014 annexation of Crimea and the support of separatists in Eastern Ukraine – developments that have triggered international condemnation. The fact that a view of Russia as a great power has been coupled with the reaffirmation of Russian identity and pride evidences how crucial this pursuit is to the Russian leadership (see also Sakwa 2011a).

In line with this, the Kremlin has referred to a monopoly of international institutions by Western powers, contrasting it to the protection of its own *sovereignty*.[32] The notion of Russia as a 'sovereign democracy' is generally attributed to Vladislav Surkov, Putin's main ideologist throughout the 2000s,[33] who defined it as:

> A form of the political life of society by which the authorities, their organs and actions are chosen, formed and managed exclusively by the Russian nation [*rossiiskaya natsiya*] ... for the pursuit of material well-being, freedoms and justice for all citizens.
>
> (Surkov 2006)

Sovereign democracy is multi-layered concept.[34] First, it is linked to a 'just world': this is intended as a 'community of free societies' (sovereign democracies) that cooperate and compete according to 'reasonable rules' – thereby resisting hegemonic forms of 'global dictatorship'. Supranational mechanisms should not develop to the detriment of the independence of their members (Surkov 2006). Putin has similarly criticised a perceived attempt by the West to 'reintroduce a unipolar, homogenising model of the world, to blur international law and national sovereignty. This ... world does not need sovereign states, it needs vassals'.[35] Former Advisor to the Presidential Administration Gleb Pavlovskii has further referred to 'Europe's paradox': in his opinion, Europe attempts to give lessons to Russia on the basis of 'common values', without however recognising Russia's role as 'co-author' of these same values.[36]

Second, sovereign democracy is not conceived as implying isolation from the international community: it is through the international scene that Russia can reassert its power (and sovereignty), as well as develop and flourish as a state. Sovereign democracy, Surkov argues, involves the 'expression of strength and dignity of the Russian people [*rossiiskii narod*], including economic powers' – by successfully competing with other powers – *and* the ability to influence world events (Surkov 2006). Putin has similarly reiterated the importance of Russia's role as a strong competitor, including in the spheres of economy and technology.[37] Two corollaries follow from this: the (already noted) view of Russia as a European country, and of its civilisation being part of European civilisation;[38] and the link between an outward-looking approach to foreign policy, and modernisation-cum-economic prosperity.[39] By developing the attributes of a sovereign democracy, Russia can promote its national interests, responding to problems such as corruption, economic stagnation, political isolation and technological backwardness (ibid.).

Thus, the Kremlin attempts to create a balance between its Europeanness, with participation in a global political and economic world order, and the preservation of its sovereignty (and cultural distinctiveness). The consolidation of a sovereign democracy, along with Russia's revival through a renewed, prominent international role, aims at overcoming both external and internal threats: globalising forces and possible Western hegemony in world politics, *and* potential extremism through mobilisation inside Russia's borders. The former implies Russia's efforts to assert itself in the international arena, and leads to virulent anti-Westernism often emanating from the Kremlin. The latter entails resistance to radicalisation that is ethnically or politically motivated, including in the shape of possible 'colour revolutions' (Laruelle 2009a: 124).

Russia's exceptionalism

The assertion of Russia's sovereignty has at times generated instances of clear avoidance of international responsibilities. Already in the early days of Russia's membership of the Council of Europe, the government refrained from fulfilling some of the commitments made at the time of joining. These included, in addition to the prompt ratification of the ECRML, the ratification of the ECHR's Protocol 6, on the abolition of the death penalty, which Russia only signed.[40] Additional sources of tension ensued, which included: Russia's blocking of the adoption of the ECHR's Protocol 14[41] for four years (this delayed a crucial reform of the European Court of Human Rights, which aimed to accelerate the adjudication of cases and reduce the Court's caseload)[42] the creation of obstacles to the investigation of cases against Russia, by refusing to cooperate with the European Court and hampering fact-finding missions in some instances; and the harassment of some applicants to the European Court.[43] Another point of contention has been Russia's insistence to retain *nadzor*, a supervisory review of judgements that are (and should be treated as) final, despite its incompatibility with the Strasbourg law (Koroteev and Golubok 2007; Pomeranz 2009). Political hostilities complete the picture: among other things, Putin has denounced the judgement *Ilaşcu and Others* v. *Moldova and Russia*,[44] as a 'purely political judgement', which 'undermines [Russia's] trust in the international judicial system'.[45] In the ruling the European Court had found Russia, together with Moldova, responsible for human rights violations in Moldova's breakaway region of Transnistria.

The Chairman of the Russian Constitutional Court, Valerii Zorkin, has similarly rejected some aspects of the European Court's jurisprudence, particularly with reference to the judgement *Konstantin Markin* v. *Russia*.[46] In this judgement the European Court had found Russia guilty of discrimination for denying a divorced male soldier a three-year parental leave to care for his children, which was routinely granted to women. Zorkin acknowledged that the ECHR law had, until then, contributed towards addressing some of the lacunae present in Russian legislation, yet the *Markin* case had changed the situation 'dramatically'. He referred to it as a 'direct invasion' of national sovereignty, beyond the scope of the ECHR.[47] Significantly, he added that, although the ECHR was an integral part of Russia's legal system, it was 'not above the Constitution'; thus, Russia could not display an 'infinite pliability': limitations to compliance had to be set, on the basis of Russia's sovereignty, Russian institutions and national interests. He added:

> [W]hen certain decisions of the Strasbourg Court are questionable in terms of the essence of the European Convention on Human Rights itself, and also directly affect our national sovereignty, the fundamental constitutional principles, Russia has the right to develop a defence mechanism against such decisions.[48]

There have been other instances in which the Russian authorities have denounced criticism emanating from international bodies as unfair and unsubstantiated. The

Russian government argued that the ACFC's views have been 'unreasonably negative', referring to a 'somewhat biased interpretation of the Russian legislation and law-enforcement practice'.[49] The Russian authorities further rejected the findings of a 2007 report on Russia by the UN Special Rapporteur on Contemporary Forms of Racism, Racial Discrimination, Xenophobia and Related Intolerance.[50] Referring to the report, the Permanent Representative of the Russian Federation at the UN, Valerii Loshchinin, complained that:

> [A] range of problems … was extrapolated which for our country either don't exist or aren't really that serious or systematic … unfortunately, there have been incidents of racist and ethnic intolerance. However, to make far-reaching conclusions … based on unproven data and falsifications … is absurd.[51]

A degree of protectionism of a country's sovereignty is certainly not a purely Russian phenomenon.[52] Trochev (2009: 146) adds that one should not assume, as is often done, that Russia's reception of international law is 'somewhere between defiance and quiet ignorance'. Russia is responding to the new challenges stemming from accession to international human rights mechanisms – whether through cooperation or resistance, or a mixture of both. Motivating factors for Russia's accession to the Council of Europe are likely to encompass opportunities for trade, the development of ties with Western Europe, and the maintenance of a connection with the former Soviet bloc – whose newly independent states located in Europe have also joined the Council of Europe (Bowring 2013a: 154; Jordan 2003). Indeed, debates in the Duma prior to joining referred to membership as enhancing Russia's ability to protect the interests of Russians (and Russian speakers) outside Russia, particularly in the Baltic states (Bowring 2013a: 152). Furthermore, membership of the Council of Europe in all likelihood has been seen as a stepping stone towards recognition as a fully-fledged and influential actor at the European (and global) level (Malfliet and Parmentier 2010). Finally, the Russian leadership might believe that 'locking in' (Moravcsik 2000) selected aspects of the international human rights system could be to its advantage. These factors point to a utilitarian approach by Russia in its interaction with international law, where a state interest has to be identified prior to the fulfilment of its commitments. In the case of the (aforementioned) report by the UN Special Rapporteur on Contemporary Forms of Racism, while Russia denounced the criticism therein, interestingly it also used it in a different context. In the case *Georgia* v. *Russia*[53] – an interstate application filed by Georgia against Russia on its large-scale deportations of Georgians in 2006[54] – Russia justified the deportations on the grounds of illegal immigration from Georgia, and noted that the Special Rapporteur had stated in his report that there was 'no State policy of racism or xenophobia in the Russian Federation'.[55] In fact, the Special Rapporteur had concluded that 'while there is no State policy of racism in the Russian Federation, the Russian society is facing a profound trend of racism and xenophobia'.[56] Thus, Russia alternatively dismissed and used the report in an opportunistic fashion to meet its needs, isolating one finding from its overall context.

Similarly, a respondent in Moscow, the representative of a human rights NGO and an academic, believed that Russia linked engagement with international standards to specific advantages, for example in the form of trade benefits. International cooperation was seen as promoting state interests and potentially the personal interests of public officials involved in international exchanges. These civil servants wish to have:

> opportunities to travel to get in touch with international experts, to bring these people to [Russia], to be included in official delegations. They are interested in projects. Because international contacts and opportunities to travel can be helpful for trade, for funds … and also for the international image of the country.
>
> [1.5.1]

More prosaically, the same respondent added that 'also travel is for pleasure'. Whatever their underlying motivation, these exchanges expose Russian public officials to international standards, and involve them in mechanisms for human rights and international cooperation, while the ECHR, albeit slowly and somewhat inconsistently, is increasingly penetrating Russian legal practice. But is it enough? Russia has advanced the idea of its own 'exceptionality' – of being a special case for which European institutions have only limited relevance (Medvedev 2008: 222). Presenting Russia as 'different' can justify a selective implementation that oversteps the commonly-accepted boundaries of the margin of appreciation envisaged by the European Court, and the adoption of an elastic approach to the FCNM in relation to the protection of minorities and their cultural distinctiveness. Russia has further resisted the obligation to place international law above domestic law at all times, reserving the right to comply only selectively with international standards.

Conclusion

In each case of legal transplantation, the legal tradition and culture of the receiving state, and its ideological foundations and ever-changing political circumstances, create intricate dynamics. In the case of Russia, one has to take into account its history, its complex relationship with the West – at times rejected as the 'other', at times used as a model – and its dual identification with European and Eurasianist traditions. At the same time, 'fits' and 'misfits' between international and domestic systems are also complex and multi-faceted, and cannot be easily placed into two distinct categories. The richness of Russia's history means that the same tradition can have *both* fits and misfits: thus, for example, although the Russian judiciary has seen a tradition of servility, precedents of judicial independence also exist. This chapter thus makes two primary arguments: first, drawing a dividing line between Russia and the 'West' would be an artificial exercise, as the two systems have not developed by following two distinct and mutually exclusive trajectories; second, the modality of application of international norms at the domestic level largely depends on domestic factors (including historical and institutional legacies), and with them prevailing attitudes to such norms. While I do not attempt to measure the impact of the actual transfer of norms from the supranational to the domestic level per se – given the difficulties in discerning driving forces behind transfers, and isolating them from other variables – perceptions of such norms influence their application. These include: a (not wholly unfounded) perception of double standards; and the notion that some international legal principles are alien to Russia (in some instances in conflict with it).

These attitudes are combined with a utilitarian approach to international norms. It goes without saying that the international human rights system is not always an undiluted force for good, behind which lie purely altruistic motives; pragmatic (realist) considerations might well be behind many member states' (including Russia's) decisions to develop and/or join these instruments. The republican liberal theory can also apply to Russia inasmuch as some aspects of human rights – such as the rule of law as opposed to its full disregard – can provide favourable foundations for the development of existing political, legal and economic regimes at the domestic level. To this has to be added Russia's goal to be recognised as an influential player at the international level. Its political leadership aims at following a 'Russian way', which however does not signify a rejection of Russia's Europeanness (even in the presence of a parallel Eurasianist narrative). Yet the assertion of its sovereignty results in partial resistance to international standards and tensions with IGOs, which have been accused of actions that are subject to politicisation and biases against Russia. Meanwhile, Russia's own exceptionalism can be employed to legitimise an 'elastic approach' to the implementation of international standards, including in the area of minority protection. Indeed, representatives of civil society interviewed pointed to the limited impact of international standards caused by this selectivity, particularly in relation to nebulous international obligations on minority rights. This is shown in the next chapter, which focuses on legal practice, further incorporating into the discussion selected jurisprudence on matters relating to the linguistic rights of national minorities.

Notes

1 This concept is used by the European Court of Human Rights in its case-law, in light of the cultural and historical differences between the Council of Europe member states that can lead to (slightly) differing interpretations of the European Convention on Human Rights and modes of implementation.

2 Other expressions are used interchangeably, including 'borrowing', 'transfer' or 'transposition' of norms. The expression 'legal transplant', or 'legal transplantation', is mostly used in this book.

3 Among others see: Bache *et al.* (2012); Bauer *et al.* (2007); Börzel and Risse (2003, 2012); Exadactylos and Radaelli (2012); Featherstone (2003); Grabbe (2001); Green Cowles and Risse (2001); Héritier (2001); Hughes *et al.* (2004); Lynnggard (2012); O'Dwyer (2006); Olsen (1996, 2002); Risse *et al.* (2001).

4 Risse *et al.* (2001 : 3) define Europeanisation as:

> [T]he emergence and development at the European level of distinct structures of governance, that is, of political, legal, and social institutions associated with political problem solving that formalize interactions among the actors, and of policy networks specializing in the creation of authoritative European rules.

5 The conditions for EU accession are listed in the Copenhagen criteria, and involve the development by the candidate states of the capacity to apply EU law and practice, by undergoing an institutional reconfiguration in line with the regulations contained in the *acquis communautaire*. The candidate countries' accession has been regulated through EU conditionality, which has acted as a 'gatekeeper', only allowing states complying with the *acquis communautaire* to advance along the path to accession.

6 See Chapter 4 on this.

7 Orücü (2002: 219) sees as key in overcoming a possible mismatch between the donor and the recipient states what she calls the process of 'tuning' – a form of adaptation of norms to accommodate local conditions.

8 Scholars have also stressed the importance of additional factors, such as domestic capacity for reform (Goetz 2000; Knill 1998).

9 For a comparison of the two theories, see Heim (1996).

10 For example, Watson (1974: 97) argues that, 'Often the host system had a similar rule and little of importance was received apart from the terminology.'

11 Or in areas under the de facto control of states.

12 The Inter-American Court of Human Rights and Inter-American Commission on Human Rights of the Organization of American States (OAS).

13 However, the Soviet Union abstained from voting on the UDHR on 10 December 1948.

14 The CSCE became the OSCE in 1994.

15 Cited in Kolesnikov, A. 12 February 2007. 'The Munich Speech. Vladimir Putin Tells Off the United States', *Kommersant*, www.kommersant.com/p741749/r_527/Munich_Speech_Vladimir_Putin/ (accessed 14 March 2014).

16 The treaty dates from 1950, while Russia joined the Council of Europe in 1996.

17 It still had not been ratified at the time of writing (2014).

18 Together with Belgium, Denmark, Ireland, Italy, Luxembourg, the Netherlands, Norway, Sweden and the United Kingdom. In 2014 France removed obstacles to the ECRML's ratification. See for example *EurActiv.com*, 3 February 2014. 'France One Step Closer to Ratifying Regional Languages Charter', www.euractiv.com/culture/france-gets-closer-ratifying-reg-news-533181 (accessed 13 December 2014). Yet by 2014 France had neither signed nor ratified the FCNM.

19 Pursuant to Article 25(1) FCNM. Russia submitted state reports, which are due at five years intervals, in 2000, 2005 and 2010.

20 ACFC, (Second) Opinion on the Russian Federation, 2 May 2007, ACFC/OP/II(2006)004, §6. The same point was made in the Third Opinion on the Russian Federation, 24 November 2011, ACFC/OP/III(2011)010, §6.

21 Resolution 'On the Implementation of the Framework Convention for the Protection of National Minorities by the Russian Federation', 2 May 2007, CM/ResCMN(2007)7, Point 1(a). See also the 2013 Resolution (same title), 30 April 2013, CM/ResCMN(2013)1, Point 1(a). The resolutions also list issues of concern.

22 See Chapter 4.

23 In tandem with this, Russia also displays a long history of opposition to the West (Heim 1996: 210; Riasanovsky 1985).

24 Bowring refers to the fact that Semyon Desnitskiy (1740–1789), who laid the foundations of law as an academic discipline in Russia, studied at the University of Glasgow under Adam Smith. He was influenced by the Scottish Enlightenment, as well as

introducing Russian readers to it. Moreover, in 1864, Russia introduced, following the English model, trials by jury and justices of the peace (Bowring 2013a: 21–43).

25 See Chapter 4.

26 Putin, V. 30 December 1999. 'Vladimir Putin: Rossiya na Rubezhe Tysyacheletii' [Russia on the Eve of the Millenium], *Nezavisimaya Gazeta*, www.ng.ru/ politics/1999–12–30/4_millenium.html (accessed 12 November 2014). In this statement Putin used the adjective *rossiiskii* (civic Russian) rather than *russkii* (ethnic Russian), thereby employing an expression inclusive of non-Russian nationalities.

27 Ibid.

28 This approach was also reflected in the statement of a former high-ranking public official interviewed, who said that Russia 'is part of Europe', and thus cannot ignore Europe's legal standards [4.13].

29 See also Chapter 5 and Sakwa (2011a).

30 President of Russia, Address to the National Assembly of the Russian Federation, 12 December 2012, http://eng.kremlin.ru/transcripts/4739 (accessed 24 September 2014).

31 With its opposition to former Soviet states signing association agreements with the EU. See for example Prina (2014).

32 Neumann (2011) links Russia's continuous preoccupation with 'sovereignty', and its role in Russian identity formation, to the 'Mongol yoke'.

33 Deputy Head of the Presidential Administration from 1999 to 2011; Deputy Prime Minister of the Russian Federation from 2011 to 2013.

34 According to Bowring (2013a), the concept of 'sovereign democracy' has been heavily influenced by Carl Schmitt and his 'decisionism'.

35 Speech by V. Putin, Meeting of the International Discussion Club 'Valdai', 19 September 2013, www.kremlin.ru/news/19243 (accessed 12 September 2014).

36 Pavlovskii, G. 31 May 2004. 'Rossiya Vsyo Eshche Ishchet Svoyu Rol' v Mire' [Russia is Still Looking for its Place in the World], *Nezavisimaya Gazeta*, www.ng. ru/courier/2004–05–31/9_role.html (accessed 7 November 2014).

37 Speech by V. Putin (see note 35).

38 Speech by V. Surkov, 'Suverenitet – Eto Politicheskii Sinonim Konkurentosposobnosti' [Sovereignty – The Political Synonym of Competitiveness], at the United Russia Training Centre, 7 February 2006. www.rosbalt.ru/main/2006/03/09/246302. html (accessed 5 May 2014).

39 Speech by V. Putin (note 35).

40 Since 1996 there has been a moratorium on the death penalty, although it has not been formally abolished (see Bowring 2013a: 174–192). Bowring further shows that Russia has regarded obligations arising from Russia's membership of the Council of Europe simply as 'recommendations' rather than commitments (Bowring 2013a: 152–154).

41 2004 'Protocol 14 to the Convention for the Protection of Human Rights and Fundamental Freedoms, Amending the Control System of the Convention'.

42 All Council of Europe member states ratified Protocol 14 between 2004 and 2006, with the exception of Russia, which ratified only in February 2010.

43 Russia has at times refused to provide documents to the ECHR, particularly on Chechen cases (see Koroteev, K. 26 June 2008, 'The European Factor in Russian Justice', *openDemocracy*, https://www.opendemocracy.net/article/russia-theme/the-european-factor-in-russian-justice, accessed 2 September 2014). Moreover, Russia did not cooperate with the European Court of Human Rights (ECtHR) in the preparation of a numbers of cases, such as *Klyakhin* v. *Russia* (Application No. 46082/99, 30 November 2004) and *Poleshchuk* v. *Russia*. (Application No. 60776/00, 7 October 2004) (Solvang 2008; Trochev 2009). A fact-finding mission was refused in the cases *Shameyev and 12 Others* v. *Georgia and Russia* (Application No. 36378/02, 12 April 2005), *Trubnikov* v. *Russia* (Application No. 49790/99, 5 July 2005) and *Mikheyev* v. *Russia* (Application No. 77617/01, 26 January 2006). There have been instances of

harassment of applicants to the ECtHR: for example, in the case *Fedotova* v. *Russia* (Application No. 73225/01, 13 April 2006) a tax inspection against the applicant's representative was used as a means of harassment, and was considered by the ECtHR to be a form of interference with the right to individual petition.

44 Application No. 48787/99, 8 July 2004.
45 Speech by V. Putin, Meeting of Members of the Council for Civil Society Institutions and Human Rights, 11 January 2007.
46 Application No. 30078/06, 7 October 2010.
47 Zorkin, V. 29 October 2010. 'Predel Ustupchivosti' [The Limits of Compliance], *Rossiiskaya Gazeta*, www.rg.ru/2010/10/29/zorkin.html (accessed 10 December 2014).
48 Ibid. In November 2010 Zorkin went further, stating that 'Russia, if it wishes, may withdraw from the jurisdiction of the European Court of Human Rights.' Cited in Pushkarskaya, A. 22 November 2010. 'Valerii Zor'kin Gotov k Oborone Natsional'nogo Pravovogo Suverniteta' [Valerii Zorkin is Ready to Defend National Legal Supremacy], *Kommersant*. Moreover, in 2013 the Russian Constitution Court confirmed the constitutionality of the provisions applied by the Russian courts in the *Markin* case (RCC, Judgement No. 27-P, 6 December 2013). See also Golubkova, M. 7 December 2013. 'KS Postavil Svoi Resheniya Vyshe Mezhdunarodnykh' [The Constitutional Court Placed its Judgements Above International Ones], *Rossiiskaya Gazeta*, www.rg.ru/2013/12/07/reg-szfo/sud.html (accessed 2 September 2014).
49 'Comments of the Government of the Russian Federation on the Second Opinion of the Advisory Committee on the Implementation of the Framework Convention for the Protection of National Minorities by the Russian Federation', 11 October 2006, GVT/COM/II(2006)006, p. 11.
50 Report by the Special Rapporteur on Contemporary Forms of Racism, Racial Discrimination, Xenophobia and Related Intolerance, Doudou Diène, 'Mission to the Russian Federation', 20 May 2007, A/HRC/4/19/Add.3.
51 Statement by Ambassador Valerii Loshchinin, reported in: 'Open Letter to the UN High Commissioner for Human Rights Louise Arbour', 10 September 2007, www.sova-center.ru/en/xenophobia/news-releases/2007/09/d11531/ (accessed 22 October 2014). The letter was signed by numerous Russian NGOs.
52 See for example the reaction of the United Kingdom to *Greens and M.T.* v. *The United Kingdom* (Application Nos. 60041/08 and 60054/08, 23 November 2010), described in BBC News, 10 February 2011, 'MPs Reject Prisoner Votes Plan', www.bbc.co.uk/news/uk-politics-12409426 (accessed 2 May 2014); or the reaction of the Italian authorities to *Lautsi and Others* v. *Italy* (Application No. 30814/06, 18 March 2011), outlined in *The Guardian*, 3 November 2009. 'Human Rights Ruling against Classroom Crucifixes Angers Italy', www.guardian.co.uk/world/2009/nov/03/italy-classroom-crucifixes-human-rights?INTCMP=ILCNETTXT3487 (accessed 2 May 2014)
53 *Georgia* v. *Russia* (admissibility decision), Application No. 13255/07, 30 June 2001, §22.
54 Hundreds of Georgian citizens were deported from Russia in 2006, at the time of tense Russian–Georgian relations. In the case *Georgia* v. *Russia*, the Georgian authorities asserted that the Russian government had won public support for anti-Georgian policies through the widespread use of xenophobic messages in the Russian media, referring to data contained in the UN Special Rapporteur's report to substantiate the argument.
55 *Georgia* v. *Russia* (note 53), §23.
56 Report by the UN Special Rapporteur on Contemporary Forms of Racism (note 50), §69.

4   Law, informal practices and minorities' cultural rights[1]

Chapter 3 has highlighted that domestic factors can determine the fortunes of legal transplantation. In some instances Russia has refrained from applying international norms, often justifying its actions by invoking the need to protect its sovereignty. Mindful of the dynamics between (powerful) norm-makers and (malleable) norm-takers, in its foreign policy Russia aims at conveying the image of a 'great power' – or a 'constitutive member' of international society, potentially through a neo-revisionist approach to its norms (Sakwa 2011a). At the same time, many of the principles on minority protection, and on the promotion of cultural rights, are far from alien to Russia's traditions; it is hardly possible to draw a clear demarcating line between Russian and 'Western' legal and ideological approaches.

This chapter moves on to the actual implementation of both international standards and Russian law with reference to cultural rights of national minorities. It is argued that both international and domestic law are affected by informal practices and an elastic approach to legal regulation. To show this, I first focus on the modes of implementation of international law in Russia, linking these to minority rights; second, I examine the Russian higher courts' application of the Russian legislation on matters relating to minority languages.[2] I suggest that the letter of the law is frequently not followed in the case of either relevant international or domestic law; and, in the case of international law, a self-perception as a great (and sovereign) power, and as 'different' from other Council of Europe member states, results in the selective application of international norms. With regard to the regulation of minority language use, this chapter further argues that the Russian higher courts have been preoccupied with the issue of the country's *unity*, through a balance between the powers of federal and regional authorities.

Formal versus informal practices

Ledeneva (1998, 2006a, 2006b) has documented the presence of a myriad of ad hoc, informal practices throughout Russian society. They radiate from centrally developed policies and are employed in lieu of, or in addition to, formal rules. Informal practices are (often illegal) methods based on an 'opportunistic logic' that involves the use of unofficial channels to achieve particular ends (Ledeneva 1998), including through an alternative application of the law (Ledeneva 2006a, 2006b). The use of these practices does not signify an utter absence of formal regulations and the rule of law in Russia. However, a web of informal, non-transparent practices, existing alongside formal structures, can be traced. As Ledeneva puts it:

> [I]nformal practices were an integral part of the postsocialist transformation … they were beneficial for certain individuals but also made them hostage to the system. These practices were not simply illegal but integrated the law into political, media, and business technologies, often manipulatively. Similarly, they did not simply follow or contradict informal norms but relied on some of them and played one set of norms against the other.
>
> (Ledeneva 2006b: 190)[3]

Informal practices spread in Russia as a means to survive the hypercentralisation of the Soviet system. Similarly, post-Soviet Russia has generated novel ways of circumventing official channels, which sustain a vast corruption 'market' and perpetuate a political system that feeds on practices such as 'black PR'[4] and media manipulation. Informal channels are resilient and malleable, as well as contradictory: they adjust to new circumstances but can also act to resist change; they can use legal institutions while also undermining the rule of law; they are simultaneously an impediment and a resource for the Russian economy, government and society (Ledeneva 2006b). In the sphere of law and judicial practice, informal practices have a dual function: they enable an elastic application of the law, by permitting the bending of formal rules; and they have a compensatory function, by offering practical solutions to address lacunae found in formal institutions and their regulations. In this chapter I focus on the first dimension: the distortion of formal rules. In later chapters,[5] I develop another related argument, by showing that informal practices and networks are a double-edged sword for minorities: they can benefit their members, and even contribute to preserving, or furthering, the country's cultural pluralism; but also, and more commonly, they can have perverse effects.

International law: Russia's selective implementation

Informal practices affect the application of both international and domestic law. International law penetrates the Russian legal sphere in continuously novel ways, as it evolves through the expansion of international legal instruments and international jurisprudence. However, obstacles to implementation sharply reduce the guarantees that national minorities will receive protection through international mechanisms. While constitutionally endorsing the supremacy of international law over domestic law,[6] Russia reserves the right, in practice and in selected cases, not to honour its commitments.[7] It has developed what can be described as a form of 'selective implementation'. Sakwa (2011a: 962; 2005) refers to a 'dual and partial adaptation', by which 'Putin's leadership sought to negotiate a new balance, if not a third way, between adaptation to existing international norms and affirmation of what were seen to be essential elements of national identity (*samobytnost'*).'

Despite these reservations, the application of the ECHR, has, overall, increased in Russia since ratification – yet the ECHR is not an instrument specifically aiming at protecting minority rights,[8] although it provides basic guarantees for vulnerable individuals which can of course encompass members of minority groups. In the case of legal instruments specifically promoting minority rights, and particularly the FCNM, the impact of international standards is further reduced by the flexible nature of their application in Russia, itself facilitated by the standards' *own* fluidity.

Russia has engaged in substantial legal reform since its accession to the Council of Europe. It needed to remedy the fact that, following the collapse of the Soviet Union, it was ill-fitted to join the IGO. This was highlighted by the Parliamentary Assembly of the Council of Europe (PACE);[9] in 1994 it stated: 'the legal order of the Russian Federation does not, at the present moment, meet the Council of Europe standards as enshrined in the statute of the Council and developed by the organs of the European Convention on Human Rights.'[10]

There were even fears that Russia, by acceding to the Council of Europe, would lower the institution's human rights standards, with a consequent drop of status of the Strasbourg law (Janis 1997: 94). Russia's admittance to the Council of Europe was therefore made conditional upon institutional and legal reform, to harmonise its law and practice to Council of Europe principles.[11] Thus, Russia embarked on a legal reform programme, with the reforming of its codes of criminal and civil procedure (albeit with some reservations) (Nussberger 2008). However, the adoption of new legislation – as a form of norm diffusion resulting from access to a supranational body – and its *implementation* are two distinct processes: 'formal legislative engineering' has to be followed by a process of 'normative adaptation' (Hughes *et al.* 2004: 165). The specific form of implementation largely depends on the type of 'reception' of international law in each state.

The views of public officials: international law as foreign

Throughout Russian history exogenous ideas and practices have tended either to be welcomed and embraced as positive forces, or rejected as alien and pernicious (Figes 2003). This polarisation is reflected in the interview data from two categories of respondents (public officials and civil society), on the issue of the applicability of international law in Russia with reference to the protection of minorities and their cultural rights.[12] Public officials' responses tended to diverge from those of civil society, in that the former centred around the theme of Russia as 'different' from the rest of Europe – and, thus, from other Council of Europe member states. These respondents did not link Russia's 'difference' to a great power status,[13] but rather to its distinct historical and political traditions, and in particular Russia's unique pluri-ethnic make-up. This, in their opinion, made Council of Europe mechanisms ill-suited to accommodate Russia's needs. Conversely, civil society respondents predominantly saw international standards as an opportunity to advance their objectives – a perception often accompanied by a regret that the impact of international mechanisms did not have more far-reaching impact. Both public officials and civil society referred to the ECRML as well as the FCNM in the interviews, given the resonance of the Council of Europe programme 'Minorities in Russia',[14] and the resulting debate on the ECRML's possible ratification.[15]

A former high-ranking public official described the FCNM and ECRML as 'supplementary instruments' to the (domestic) mechanisms already employed in Russia to accommodate minority interests – an essentially superfluous additional layer [4.13]. He believed that 'the objectives of international standards are already realised [in Russia]', referring to the fact that the Republic of Dagestan officially recognises as many as 14 languages. An analogous view is expressed in Russia's Second Report to the ACFC, which states that 'basically all provisions of the Framework Convention have been respected'.[16] The same respondent thought that Russia should still ratify the ECRML; as to the reason for ratification he argued: 'The position of Russia is useful for Europe. In Europe Islam is a new phenomenon and Russia instead has 1,000 years of coexistence with Islam' [4.13].

One public official from Tatarstan, and three more persons in quasi-official institutions – one in Tatarstan and two in Mordovia – saw international standards on minority protection as fundamentally irrelevant to their ethnic republics. This perception stemmed from the view that minority rights are exclusively for disadvantaged minorities, which, in their opinion, was not the case for those nationalities that enjoy titular status. For example: 'There is no problem in Tatarstan. [In Russia] there are issues with small-in-number indigenous peoples of the North and their way of life, but there are no small-in-number indigenous peoples in Tatarstan' [4.8].

A public official in Mordovia similarly doubted the usefulness of international standards but added that 'perhaps there are some prospects' [4.11]. With regard to the ECRML, a public official from Tatarstan said:

> I am in favour of the ratification of the Charter [ECRML] and its application in Tatarstan … [But] the focus of the Charter is the protection of the languages of the small-in-number indigenous peoples, and languages that are disappearing. In Tatarstan there isn't a problem with this, although it could happen [in the future].
>
> [4.10]

And in Mordovia: 'Mordovia is not very interested in the Charter because it doesn't protect Mordovians in Mordovia, only the diaspora [Mordovians outside the Republic of Mordovia]. The Mordovian languages are already the state [official] languages in Mordovia' [4.12].[17]

These statements reveal a misunderstanding of international standards and particularly the ECRML. Both the FCNM and the ECRML are applicable in ethnic republics. The public officials' views cited here originate from a discrepancy between the general understanding of 'minority' in Russia and in international law: international law considers a 'minority' to be a group in a disadvantaged position in a country as a whole,[18] while titular nationalities in Russia are commonly not perceived as 'minorities'.[19] Traditional expressions to designate non-Russians employed during the Soviet period did not generally include 'minority'[20] but rather 'nation' and 'nationality' (*natsiya, natsional'nost'*) and 'ethnos' (*etnos, etnonarod*) (Sokolovskii 2004).

The statements of public officials interviewed suggest an underlying belief that Russia's titular nationalities might suffer a (unacceptable and possibly humiliating) drop in status if they were to be labelled as 'minorities'. This can reconfirm perceptions that international human rights mechanisms are based on Western countries' conceptualisation of nationality issues, and therefore unsuitable for Russia. Only two of the respondents cited above saw a potential benefit in the application of the ECRML in Mordovia or Tatarstan, but only in a possible future, should the use of titular languages be increasingly eroded. In fact the cultures and languages of titular nationalities in Russia are generally, albeit with variations, in a position of vulnerability. For example, in the case of the Republic of Mordovia, on the one hand the two Mordovian languages, Moksha and Erzya, are recognised as co-official alongside Russian;[21] on the other, equality in legal status is not translated into equality in practice, with Russian enjoying a dominant position in the public sphere, education and the media.[22] The interviewed public officials' position reveals a resilient perception of the importance of titularity as the source of special status, even when this might not result in tangible benefits. It supports an institutionalist reading of existing minority policies, inasmuch as (Soviet) ethnic institutions still appear to shape views around ethnicity and diversity management.

The public officials interviewed further elaborated on the framing of Russia as 'different' from Western Europe. The following extracts are from interviews with one public official in Tatarstan, three in Moscow and one in Mordovia:

> In Western Europe there is a very different situation from Russia. The people from Catalonia, America, Western Europe are different. Russia needs a strong hand [*sil'naya ruka*]. Somebody like Putin was needed. When there is no *sil'naya ruka* a Russian doesn't know what to do. It doesn't mean that the system in Russia is bad, just that it's different. But you can never tell, every generation changes.
>
> [4.10]

> There is a very different juridical understanding [in Russia], and harmonisation [with international law] is not easy.
>
> [4.15]

The situation in Russia is very different from that of the other member states; it's much bigger. Even the biggest member state [of the Council of Europe, after Russia] will have much fewer minorities and languages than Russia.

[4.13]

There are many nationalities in Russia. Ratifying the Charter in the United Kingdom, for example, is not the same as Russia ratifying it.

[4.16]

For Part III [of the ECRML][23] a lot of funds are needed, and it's difficult in Russia. It's not a country like Germany. There are much more languages.

[4.12]

Hence, the respondents presented several layers of 'difference', ranging from an idiosyncratic Russian 'psyche', to differing juridical interpretations, to more objective criteria such as the country's geographical size, number of ethnic groups and languages spoken in its territory. Civil society representatives interviewed commented on this form of dismissal of international standards by public officials. The director of a minority NGO in Moscow described a 'state policy' based on the Russian authorities' belief that 'Europe is not needed to fix problems in Russia' [1.2.3]. The director of a human rights organisation in St Petersburg said he had observed a resistance to the perceived need to shed Russia's distinctiveness from Europe in order to embrace international standards:

We had a project [which involved using Council of Europe standards] and there was a big resistance among some people. There is a big resistance from nationalists – they think that [using international standards] means assisting the West in influencing Russia, in making Russia a part of Europe.

[1.5.11]

No views on the superfluous nature of international standards, or their incompatibility with Russia's norms, were expressed in Karelia by either public officials or civil society. This might derive from the particularly vulnerable position of the Karelian language and culture within the republic, despite its titularity.[24] Finally, the views of two public officials – one in Kazan and one in Moscow [4.7; 4.14] – differed from those of the other public officials, in that they were supportive of international standards. These respondents were themselves representatives of minorities, and were committed to advancing minority interests. Therefore, their attitudes seemed more aligned to those of civil society respondents, rather than those of other public officials interviewed.

Respondents of the 'public official' category generally subscribed to the view that Russia should seek to re-affirm its sovereignty in its foreign policy. Russia's resolve to follow its 'own path' might explain why similar concerns are expressed by the ACFC in its first three Opinions on Russia,[25] with no significant progress made in the course of the monitoring cycles. The perception of Russia as a 'different' (non-Western) type of democracy, prevalent among the interviewed public officials, led them to voice the view that mechanisms such as the FCNM and the ECRML were effectively superfluous. Meanwhile, the Russian government's position, as stated in its reports to the ACFC, that it fully meets all FCNM requirements,[26] is facilitated by the fact that the FCNM is a flexible instrument. This flexibility allows for the development of tailored policies that can truly accommodate the specific needs of different groups – yet it is also a double-edged sword, as vague provisions may well generate vague policies.

The views of civil society: international law as weak

In stark contrast to the views of public officials, respondents from the 'civil society' category[27] tended to focus on what they perceived as flaws of the international minority rights system, which was regarded as ineffective given its flexibility. These respondents made no reference to international standards being alien or irrelevant to Russia. Rather, with few exceptions, they shared the view that international mechanisms ought to have been more far-reaching so as to directly influence Russia's law and practice. Concerns were raised as to the (already noted) intransigence of some public officials vis-à-vis the application of international standards. Exceptions were found in Mordovia and Karelia, where the respondents did not voice opinions relating to perceived flaws of the international minority rights system. In most cases, neither did these respondents list perceived benefits offered by the system. The absence of references to perceived flaws compared to their counterparts in other regions might be due to these respondents' lower awareness of the international minority rights system's potential impact in Russia, rather than to the belief of its flawlessness.

The statements of two civil society representatives, one in Moscow and one in St Petersburg, serve to illustrate the prevailing attitudes of the civil society representatives interviewed. The respondent in Moscow, director of an NGO working on inter-ethnic relations, believed that the flexibility of the FCNM was the primary reason for its lack of real impact. He noted that 'the FCNM does not state clearly that governments *have to* do specific things' [1.2.3], referring to the fact that ACFC Opinions only contain 'recommendations'. Similarly, the representative of a human rights NGO in St Petersburg, working on the protection of minorities, said:

> I would really like to see the FCNM implemented. It's a very good convention.... But the FCNM is only about principles. And if the Language Charter was ratified it would not really change things much. There is no mechanism for implementation; the [Council of Europe] monitoring is not very good. The Charter and FCNM only help at the moral level: they provide moral standards on which to orient oneself. Like the Russian Constitution, they are declarative, they do not provide details. But ideally what is in the FCNM should be realised, and all my work is directed towards this.

[1.5.7]

In fact, the FCNM, like the ECRLM,[28] *does* create legal obligations, but these have to be translated into practice by the state parties to the instrument – including through dialogue and negotiations between the government and minority groups. ACFC *Opinions*, whose very name suggests the absence of specific legal obligations, seem to be approached as loose recommendations which do not command remedial action. The Opinions are the basis of Committee of Ministers Resolutions – yet inasmuch as the FCNM is not enforced through binding judgements, it can be regarded as an instance of 'soft jurisprudence based upon hard law', as Hofmann puts it (2008: 173).[29] The absence of detailed obligations in the text of the FCNM minimises the impact of the 'hard law' part of the equation, with a resulting focus on 'soft law'.

Some respondents from civil society judged not only the FCNM, but international law generally, as inadequately equipped to withstand obstacles to its implementation in Russia. Among the reasons cited were: a possible conflict between domestic and international law; the fact that 'the interests of the authorities come before human rights' [1.5.3]; and a lack of a real commitment by the authorities to comprehensively implement international law. The last point was illustrated by the director of an NGO in Moscow: 'There were some important seminars of the Council of Europe [on the FCNM] in different towns of Russia …[30] There was some interest by public officials but then the years went by and there was no follow-up' [1.2.3].

Respondents from the 'civil society' category, as well as analysts ('academia'), referred to forms of opportunism by the state, or the appropriation of international standards to add a democratic veneer to what, in reality, had scarce democratic substance, with a view to promoting internationally a positive image of Russia. Despite these shortcomings, the exponential increase in applications to the European Court of Human Rights reflects the appeal of Strasbourg in defending human rights (and the concurrent distrust of Russian courts) (Trochev 2009). Civil society and minority representatives interviewed approached international standards in a pragmatic manner, as a tool that often accorded well with their own objectives in minority protection. They seized upon the opportunity to appeal to the Council of Europe as a supranational body that might rectify flaws at the domestic level. Far from fearing Western interference and the resulting loss of Russian sovereignty, they would have welcomed stronger international mechanisms to support their activities in Russia.

The views espoused by civil society respondents support Keck and Sikkink's (1998, 1999) argument that cooperation links between individuals and institutions are forged not (only) within a state, but through 'transnational advocacy networks'. Such networks are referred to as 'forms of organization characterized by voluntary, reciprocal and horizontal patters of communication' (Keck and Sikkink 1998: 8); the actors involved are bound by common objectives and various forms of cooperation, but also by *shared values*. These networks can act to promote the acceptance of international norms in the domestic sphere, including by shifting perceptions and influencing the behaviour of domestic actors vis-à-vis such international norms (Keck and Sikkink 1999: 89–90). In line with this,

Lipschutz (1992) and Peterson (1992) argue that states can no longer be considered unitary in the context of a growing 'global civil society'. Similarly, Mertus (1999: 1387) asserts that, with globalisation and the formation of a transnational civil society, non-state actors, particularly NGOs, have contributed to building a (global) human rights culture. These developments may further contribute to the construction of a national identity that does not place Russia in opposition to the 'West' (and the Council of Europe), but perceives it as being encompassed by the latter. While the East–West dichotomy is still present in the public discourse,[31] some of the respondents' statements point to networks that, from Russia, reach out to external, powerful actors to gain leverage so as to better enable the pursuit of their own goals (also known as the 'boomerang' effect – Keck and Sikkink 1999: 93).

Tatar activists have created another form of international network: the World Congress of Tatars. The Congress was established in 1992 in Tatarstan, with the participation of Tatar groups from other parts of Russia, CIS countries and beyond. According to the data of the Congress (retrieved in 2014), the institution comprises 352 national cultural organisations, 230 located in Russia and 122 abroad, in 34 countries.[32] Similarly, Mordovian and Karelian organisations participate in the World Congress of Finno-Ugric Peoples, coordinated by a Consultative Committee composed of the representatives of various Finno-Ugric groups; between 1992 and 2012, six sessions of the Congress were held – in Russia, Hungary, Finland and Estonia.[33] It is not only civil society that has established transborder cooperation: the republican authorities can also be involved in these endeavours. Thus, for example, Tatarstan has participated in the activities of the Congress of Local and Regional Authorities of the Council of Europe,[34] as well as establishing contacts with UN institutions such as UNESCO. Moreover, the Tatarstani authorities established a Ministry of Foreign Economic Relations in 1993, opened missions abroad, and signed agreements with foreign states (for cooperation in the area of trade, science and technology, culture and education) (Sharafutdinova 2003; Suleynamova 2011: 47–48). The aim of these initiatives has been to boost trade ties with Western countries, as well as special relations with Islamic countries such as Turkey, Egypt, the United Arab Emirates and Jordan – with a convergence of political, financial and cultural/religious factors motivating these international exchanges. Sharafutdinova (2003) argues that, through this form of paradiplomacy, Tatarstan has sought to assert its statehood by 'acting like a state', which has played a role in its identity formation. Whatever the motivation, new forms of interaction between individuals, groups and institutions transcend state borders, and are driven by personal, group and sub-state interests rather than exclusively state interests.[35]

Mixed outcomes

To what extent are efforts for the application of international standards on minority rights seen as effective? Given the differing views on such standards, and the varying conditions for their implementation, perceptions on the use and possible impact of such standards recorded in the interviews similarly varied. One should further note that the role of international standards is generally lessened due to the limited use made of instruments such as the FCNM. As noted, many of the respondents in all categories had little or no awareness of international standards on minority rights. The director of a minority organisation in Moscow summarised the situation thus: 'Since 2000 I've been working in this area [of minority rights] and I don't think that there are more than 100 professionals [in Russia] who know about or understand [international standards on minority rights]' [1.2.5].

The representatives of an organisation in Moscow [1.2.3] and one in St Petersburg [1.5.7] similarly held the view that minority organisations themselves had little or no knowledge of these standards. This was confirmed by the other interviews: it was the larger organisations, primarily in Moscow and St Petersburg, with international contacts, which possessed the specialised knowledge of Council of Europe mechanisms. They reported having used international standards in one or more of the following ways: by referring to them in their exchanges with the authorities, to add weight to their claims and campaigns; by participating in the compilation of shadow reports submitted to international bodies (particularly the shadow reports on the FCNM); or by attending international meetings and events, particularly as part of the programme 'Minorities in Russia'.[36]

In interviews, public officials in the three focus republics generally had very little to say on their encounters with international standards. For example, a representative of the Tatar Cabinet of Ministers said that he and his colleagues had not used the FCNM in their work, as they 'did not get to this' [4.10]. He added, with regard to Tatarstan, that 'Russia does not use confrontation' – perhaps linked to a perception that international standards and international mediation are used only in cases of severe ethnic tensions, which the republic had been fortunately spared. A high-ranking public official working on nationality issues in Moscow only noted that international standards are applicable mostly in the case of indigenous peoples [4.15]. Respondents from quasi-official institutions or well-connected minority associations displayed similar attitudes. A representative of the House of Nationalities in Moscow[37] said that: 'we don't deal with international standards, we work on cultural issues' [1.3.4]. In this case, international standards on minority rights were divorced from the preservation and promotion of cultural pluralism, despite the latter coinciding with the aims of these standards. One of the leaders of the Inter-Regional Social Movement of Mordovian (Moksha and Erzya) Peoples in Saransk rapidly dismissed the question of the possible application of the FCNM in Russia by saying that it is 'not really used' by the authorities – hinting at the complexities of its application [1.4.3].

In this environment, then, a compelling question is how, if at all, the federal authorities guarantee that international obligations arising from Russia's accession to the FCNM cascade down to regional and local state organs. The regional authorities were asked about possible mechanisms to coordinate FCNM implementation, through a three-level – local, regional and federal – framework.

Public officials in the regions noted that they did not operate within the scope of such a framework: they had received no specific guidelines besides the general principles of the Concept of State Nationalities Policy of the Russian Federation.[38] For example, a public official in Karelia stated: 'We didn't receive any instructions about how to implement international standards. We don't really have much information on the standards – although we do try to get and disseminate as much information as possible' [4.2].

A former Minister of Education of an ethnic republic – an academic at the time of the interview – stated that he had never been required to incorporate any aspect of international standards, including the FCNM provisions on education, in his work as a minister [2.12]. His personal opinion was that international obligations were not taken into account in shaping Russian domestic policies. He added that 'Russia is very good at writing reports [to international bodies]' – pointing to a greater attention to form than to practice on the part of the Russian authorities.

The question on the modality of implementation was then put to a representative of the former Ministry of Regional Development, the ministry (then) responsible for minority policies, and for FCNM implementation.[39] He confirmed the absence of guidelines: 'We don't give any instructions. There is already the federal legislation that is in compliance with international standards' [4.16].

The data strongly indicate that there is no clear implementation *plan* for the FCNM. Russian legislation provides a general framework for human and minority rights, but its implementation is hampered by a number of factors: the vagueness of the legislation; the large gap between what is de jure and what is de facto; and the overlooking of the state's *positive* responsibilities to engage in affirmative action to support minority cultures. The issue of vague legislation is captured in a statement by the director of a minority NGO in Karelia:

> International standards [on minority rights] should become the concrete basis of Russian law. If international law says that there should be minority education, it should actually happen. Now people see this just as a principle, as an ideal. We need to write everything in the [Russian] laws very clearly, that classes [for the study of minority languages] should be established etc. We need to have mechanisms for the realisation [of international standards].
>
> [1.2.1]

This statement reflects a perception of a need for the crystallisation of norms that can be easily pinned down rather than remaining as vague notions that are vaguely met. It echoes the view, reported above, that the FCNM only amounts to a set of principles [1.5.7]. Another respondent similarly emphasised the absence of *mechanisms* to realise the rights formally enshrined in Russian legislation, in the context of minority education [4.14]. The former Ministry of Regional Development's reliance on (vague) domestic legal norms has resulted in a lack of coordination between institutions at different levels and a generally passive approach to the implementation of international standards on cultural rights of national minorities. A respondent from Tatarstan complained about what he saw as Russia's disregard of its positive responsibilities with reference to the ECRML:

> The Charter has provisions on education in minority languages, for which the state has to create the conditions. Instead Russia's approach is that it should not go against the right to study [a minority language], rather than creating favourable conditions for it.
>
> [4.7]

In line with the point made by this respondent, public officials interviewed tended to view nationalities policy primarily as a form of 'benign neglect', or the negative obligation of the state *not to* interfere with the freedom of minorities to express their cultures and use their languages, without the concurrent positive obligation to create the conditions for their preservation.[40] Without the adoption of special measures, the same Tatar respondent argued, the authorities simply prolong their ongoing policies and activities, and perpetuate their shortcomings, rather than actively promoting minority cultures and languages [4.7]. The absence of a coordinated country-wide effort to enhance FCNM implementation, complete with targets that are periodically and centrally evaluated, points to an application of international standards characterised by a predominance of 'localism' in the sense of atomisation.[41] Russia's reports to the ACFC provide a list of individual programmes and events promoting minority cultures, without however supplying data that could enable the assessment of their overall impact.

The circumstances surrounding ECRML's non-ratification are another example of Russia's selective approach to international responsibilities. Russia has a clear obligation to ratify the treaty, given the commitment made at the time of its accession to the Council of Europe.[42] Despite this, interviews evidenced the perception among public officials and civil society alike that Russia has a choice to opt out and refrain from ratification.[43] As a respondent from a human rights NGO noted, the Russian government has an interest in international projects, and agreed to cooperate with the Council of Europe and the EU on the programme 'Minorities in Russia' [1.5.1]. Yet these efforts ultimately did not result in ECRML ratification, despite this being the programme's main objective. Instead, the programme seems to have consolidated the Russian authorities' resolve *not* to ratify the treaty: following the programme's completion, the Russian authorities argued that its findings 'demonstrate that the application of the Charter does not suit the specific multilingual situation seen in the Russian Federation'.[44] This might not only derive from a reluctance to take up new obligations, but also from a preoccupation with potential increased instability that may result from shifts in the status quo in majority–minority relations, in the event that ratification might embolden linguistic minorities and unleash a torrent of demands.

Every little helps: international standards as a tool for activists

Selective implementation implies some implementation nonetheless. The general conclusion of civil society respondents was not that international standards should be disregarded as irrelevant, but that what opportunities exist ought to be used. They managed to identify some benefits in the mass of flaws that they had enumerated. In particular, they welcomed the support from the Council of Europe (of a moral if not always practical kind), and the legal articulation of their convictions, framed as human *rights* and enshrined in legally-binding international documents. A respondent, an academic and Mordovian activist in Saransk, saw a symbolic significance in Russia's accession to international mechanisms that could ultimately have a practical impact on policy [2.14]. A public official from Karelia believed that the FCNM 'force[d] the [federal] authorities to think about [minority] issues and to think of solutions' [4.2]. Other respondents from both civil society and academia believed in a positive role for international standards in Russia, although they did not provide specific examples of what this role might be. Regional public officials reported invoking international standards on minority protection in centre–periphery exchanges. For example, a civil servant in Karelia had referred to Russia's international minority rights obligations to solicit the allocation of adequate (federal) funding to the republic for programmes on minority cultures, such as print media outlets in Karelian language. Moreover, Tatarstan's Parliament in May 2009 called on the Russian authorities to ratify the ECRML, to assist local efforts in upholding the right to access education in one's minority language – a right the regions saw as menaced by amendments to the Law 'On Education' introduced in 2007.[45] Minorities in Russia have started framing their claims by linking them to linguistic *rights*, rather than, more generally, to cultural programmes (Suleymanova 2010). The Council of Europe has acted as mediator, by facilitating exchanges between the Russian authorities and civil society at Council of Europe-sponsored events,[46] and by considering the claims and observations made by Russian civil society in shadow reports to the ACFC, which have contributed to the formulation of the ACFC's recommendations. An academic and activist from Tatarstan believed that the support of the Council of Europe and the OSCE might increase the chances of impact when civil society lobbied the Russian state in the area of minority rights. When, in 2009, a decree removed the option to take the final secondary school examination in Tatar,[47] in addition to addressing protest letters to the Russian authorities the respondent's pressure group had also contacted IGOs to request their support [2.6].[48]

The director of a minority NGO from Karelia had clearly identified international standards as an opportunity – something that could add substance to her claims as a minority representative [1.2.1]. She had noticed a growing interest in international standards among the regional government and courts in Karelia, although the actual 'application' of the standards was 'a different matter'. Her NGO's use of the new options afforded by international law can be contrasted with the position of the head of a national cultural autonomy (NCA)[49] in Moscow

[1.1.5]: in common with other NCA representatives, the respondent seemed to have very little knowledge of the FCNM. This suggests that NCAs, or other minority associations with close links to the authorities, might not look for supplementary lobbying opportunities other than those already offered by their own networks. The aforementioned NGO from Karelia had opted *not* to become an NCA. It did not engage in open criticism of the regional power structures – and instead sought to cooperate with the Karelian authorities wherever possible – yet it also pursued independent objectives. The Moscow NCA, instead, appeared to work in tandem with the authorities. Other respondents, leaders of NCAs or other minority organisations, had close contacts with the local authorities or the state (federal) or regional dumas.[50] The interviews thus point to a use of international standards inversely proportional to the overlapping of networks and interests between minority organisations and official institutions such as the state Duma. The data further indicate a preference for informal practices and networks rather than official channels, with some reliance on international standards when informal channels are seen as insufficient to address minority concerns.

In some instances international organisations have directly intervened to facilitate the defusing of majority–minority tensions. A civil society respondent from Karelia referred to the case of a representative of another Finno-Ugric group, the Mari. In 2005 Mari activist Vladimir Kuzlov was victim of an attack by unidentified individuals in the Republic of Mari El, which resulted in life-threatening injuries.[51] In the preceding years, relations between Mari organisations and Mari El's authorities had deteriorated, as 2000 saw the election of Moscow-born Leonid Markelov of the (right-wing) Liberal Democratic Party as the republic's president. Markelov refrained from collaborating with the existing Congress of Mari People and instead formed another organisation, the Mari Council, with hand-picked loyalists as its members.[52] The Mari minority had subsequently positioned themselves politically in opposition to Markelov. Following the deterioration of relations between the Mari minority and Mari El's authorities, and the incident involving Kuzlov, the Council of Europe issued a report expressing concern about the conditions of Russia's Finno-Ugric peoples.[53] The respondent believed that:

> The authorities [of Mari El] tried to change afterwards.... They don't want a big scandal. [After the Council of Europe report] they tried very hard to show that the situation is now fine. This was also reflected in Mordovia, [where] there have been a lot of events for Finno-Ugric peoples.
>
> [1.2.1][54]

Thus, Russian civil society has identified practical uses and benefits in the application of international standards on cultural rights of national minorities; yet a hindrance to their application is the fact that the FCNM is often (erroneously) treated as a 'soft law' instrument. The next section, then, deals with what is unambiguously viewed as 'hard law': the law of the ECHR and Russian domestic law.

Russian judicial practice and minority rights

In examining judicial practice in Russia, one should start by observing that the Russian judiciary is not fully independent (Hendley 2007; Ledeneva 2006a, 2006b, 2008; Trochev 2008),[55] with the interests of the executive often trickling down to the courts. Even Medvedev has admitted to the absence of an independent judiciary in Russia: shortly after becoming president, he called Russia a country of 'legal nihilism', adding that '[n]o European country can boast of such disregard of the law'.[56] Post-Soviet 'legal nihilism' finds its roots in Russian history (Pomeranz 2009: 15): in particular, in Soviet Russia courts operated according to unwritten, pliant rules and superiors' orders. The RSFSR and USSR Constitutions were rarely applied directly; rather, judges routinely prioritised secondary law, statutes as well as 'instructions' from above. These included 'resolutions' and 'letters' from higher courts, but also from non-judicial influential bodies such as ministries, thereby creating a 'culture of dependency' of the judiciary on the executive (Hendley 2007; see also Feldbrugge 1993). Instructions tended to be 'for internal use only': regulations were thus listed in unpublished documents, in the absence of judicial transparency (Burkov 2007: 26; Nussberger 2008: 635). In this climate, the impact of international law in the USSR remained insignificant, despite the country being a habitual ratifier of UN instruments.

As for other sectors, informal practices have infiltrated the judiciary (Ledeneva 2006a, 2006b; Solomon 2005, 2008a, 2008b). In politically controversial cases, the notorious phenomenon of 'telephone justice' may compel judges to issue rulings in line with the political imperatives of powerful individuals – following 'instructions' received over the telephone (Gel'man 2004; Krasnov 2004; Ledeneva 2006b, 2008).[57] Russian judges have experienced pressure from a multitude of actors: numerous organs can, or have tried to, exert their influence upon the judiciary. Solomon (2005: 340) cites, among these, the Ministry of Economic Development, the state Duma, the Federation Council, the *siloviki* (former military and security officials), and the government itself. Popova (2012) proposes the theory of 'strategic pressure' in the analysis of levels of judicial independence in Russia: she argues that in countries that are neither consolidated democracies nor consolidated autocracies, political competition hinders independent courts, as dependent courts are more useful to weak incumbents – a situation that gives way to the 'politicization of justice' (ibid.: 3). In some cases, Russian judges who have strived to remain independent when pressure was placed upon them have been discredited, isolated, and, ultimately, pushed out of the system.[58]

This is not to say that there are no, or very few, fair verdicts in Russia. Fair trials result from a combination of freedom from pressure and individual judges' own commitment to independence and fairness of proceedings. Hendley (2007: 267) argues that opportunities for judges to operate independently exist primarily in cases that do not touch upon the key interests of Russia's most powerful individuals, whether at the federal or regional level. In the case of protection of national minorities (and their cultural rights) through legal implementation and execution of judgements, courts have contributed to crystallising some relevant legal principles. However, obstacles to the application of both international and domestic standards persist: in the case of international standards, the primary stumbling block is the selective implementation of international law; in the case of domestic law, hurdles derive from the opacity of the relevant legislation – and the absence, for the most part, of self-executing legal principles – as well as the higher courts' approach to *unity* and *equality*, as will be seen below.

Russian courts and international law: 'application' without 'implementation'

Although there has been, overall, an increased application of the ECHR in Russian courts, this is contingent upon a combination of external circumstances, including possible political pressure and judges' own attitudes and commitment. Article 15(4) of the 1993 Constitution declares the supremacy of international law over Russian law:

> The universally-recognised norms of international law and international treaties and agreements of the Russian Federation shall be a component part of its legal system. If an international treaty of the Russian Federation establishes other rules than those envisaged by law, the *rules of the international agreement shall be applied.* [italics added].

The 1996 Constitutional Law 'On the Judicial System of the Russian Federation'[59] makes it compulsory for Russian courts to apply 'generally recognised principles and norms of international law and international treaties of the Russian Federation'. Similarly, the 1998 Law 'On the Ratification of the Convention on the Protection of Human Rights and Fundamental Freedoms'[60] obliges courts to apply the ECHR. Russia has a monist approach to international law – meaning that the treaties it enters into are immediately and directly applicable in the country, without the need for the adoption of supplementary domestic legislation.[61] A 2003 Supreme Court Resolution[62] states at Point 1 that:

> [T]he rights and liberties of the individual in conformity with commonly recognised principles and the norms of international law, as well as the international treaties of the Russian Federation, shall have direct effect within the jurisdiction of the Russian Federation.

However, there is a tension between Article 15's paragraph 4 (cited above) and paragraph 1 – the latter proclaiming the Russian Constitution, rather than international law, supreme: 'The *Constitution of the Russian Federation shall have supreme juridical force,* direct application and shall be used across the whole territory of the Russian Federation' [italics added].[63]

This tension is symptomatic of the complex relationship between Russian and international law. Russia is simultaneously proclaiming international law to be above Russian law and, effectively, the opposite, in the same constitutional provision. With reference to Article 15, Chairman of the Russian Constitutional Court Valerii Zorkin has insisted that the provision 'stipulates the priority of international treaties over [Russian] law, but *not over the provisions of the Constitution*'[64] [italics added] (see also Danilenko 1999; Burkov 2007).

The application of international law in Russian courts also presents logistical difficulties. It is not only a treaty such as ECHR, but also its body of jurisprudence, that requires incorporation into the Russian legal system. This is in line with the 'expansive meaning' of the Constitution's Article 15(4), which encompasses not only treaties themselves, but also their interpretation by international bodies (Danilenko 1999: 68). The volume of the European Court's jurisprudence grows with time, transforming the ECHR (a 'living instrument'), as well as developing the modes of its interpretation. It is no surprise that the application of the ECHR generates complexities and variance in judicial performance (Burkov 2007; Trochev 2009). Indeed, studies on the Russian judiciary have shown that, while application of the ECHR has tended to increase (Burkov 2007; Nussberger 2008; Trochev 2008), citations routinely relate to principles of law that complement or confirm the Russian Constitution, rather than their being used more creatively (perhaps controversially) to overcome contradictions or fill gaps in the Russian legal system (Burkov 2007: 40). Such gaps are numerous, as the Russian Constitution provides only vague provisions on human rights, meaning that the ECHR could serve the vitally important function of defining and crystallising Russian human rights legal principles (Danilenko 1999: 62). Moreover, Burkov (2007) and Trochev (2008) show that citations have often been superficial, lacking detailed references to, and analysis of, the ECHR jurisprudence. Danilenko argued already in 1999 that the Russian Constitutional Court had 'invented its own version of sources of international law for domestic consumption' (Danilenko 1999: 62). Hence, although the ECHR is used by Russian lawyers and judges, and concrete efforts have been made towards its incorporation into the Russian judicial sphere, one may say, as Burkov (2007) does, that the ECHR is 'applied' but is not 'implemented': 'implementation' can be interpreted as a coherent and comprehensive set of measures to progressively integrate international obligations into a country's domestic law and practice; and 'application' as a set of individual instances of judges or officials employing (selected) principles of international law. '*Selective* implementation' reflects a form of application that falls short of fully-fledged implementation. An additional, outstanding hindrance to a more substantial use of the ECHR to protect minorities is its limited application in cases relating to minority rights, given that it is not specifically an instrument for minority protection. Yet the ECHR jurisprudence has continued to grow in recent years[65] (Bowring 2015; Gilbert 2002; Medda-Windischer 2009; Pentassuglia 2003, 2009; Weller 2007), and has the potential to expand its scope to increasingly embrace minority issues.[66]

The Russian courts and the protection of linguistic rights

In parallel to moves towards enhanced ECHR application, the Russian higher courts have considered cases relating to minority language use. Yet the jurisprudence on the cultural and linguistic rights of national minorities in Russia is miniscule, for two main reasons. First, there is a weak – albeit growing (Trochev 2008; Trochev and Solomon 2005) – tradition of litigation in Russia. In addition to practical considerations such as the need for resources for litigation, lawsuits antagonise public officials when they become defendants in a case. As will be seen in Chapter 7, good relations with the authorities are often considered to be of paramount importance by minority representatives in their efforts to promote programmes for the preservation of their cultures and languages. The second reason is linked to the scarcity of instances that can be categorised as clear-cut minority rights violations. This stems from the fact that legislation on minority rights tends to be declarative, often referring generally to vague notions such as the 'development' of minority languages and cultures, as well as being devoid of mechanisms of implementation (Bowring 2013c: 33; Oeter 2013: 43). For example, Article 2(2) of the Law 'On the Languages of the Peoples of the Russian Federation'[67] states: 'The Russian Federation guarantees all its peoples regardless of their numbers equal rights on the conservation and development of the native language, freedom of choice and of use of the language for communication.'

This type of provision, despite being clearly in line with international standards on minority rights, does not generate specific responsibilities for state institutions.[68] Similarly, Osipov (2013c: 67) argues that references to 'national development' – in the sense of 'development of national groups'[69] – are effectively empty of practical significance, although they continue to abound in public discourses and official documents on inter-ethnic relations. A respondent, the director of a minority NGO in Petrozavodsk, pointed to multiple and severe shortcomings running through the Russian legislature and judiciary, concluding that:

> There is no structure to control the implementation of the legislation.... Since *perestroika* they [the authorities] have tried to build a new [legal] system; a lot of laws were adopted. But as they build this system they also undermine it, because when a law is adopted there can already be another law that [the law-makers] don't know about, and one law contradicts another. Instead, during the Soviet Union, when laws were passed everybody applied them. There was a strong mechanism of control.
>
> [1.2.1]

Thus, the respondent suggested that the post-Soviet judicial environment is still in a transitional phase, with a judicial vacuum left by the Soviet system that is still partly unfilled. In the post-Soviet legal climate, some elements of the 'old' system linger on, exerting residual control over the judiciary, without however assuring the coherence that could stem from a heavily centralised system.

Despite these complexities, the Russian Constitutional Court and the Russian Supreme Court have considered some cases on issues linked to linguistic rights of minorities, namely: requirements of proficiency in titular languages for regional leaders; minority-language education; and choice of script for minority languages. These cases show that language issues intersect centre–periphery relations: language is an area in which the regions have some autonomy in law-making and legal implementation, yet this form of devolution has to remain within the overarching legal framework of the Federation. Thus, the judgements evidence a tension between the centre and the regions, and an underlying preoccupation with the unity of the country. They further reveal a resistance to 'excessive' diversity across the regions, contrasted by a drive towards uniformity.

Centre–periphery relations and unity

The Russian Constitution states that all citizens of the Federation have equal rights (Article 6(2)), regardless of ethnicity and language (Article 19(2)). Citizens are further guaranteed the right to use their native language and freely choose their language of communication, education, training and work (Article 26(2)). Russian is declared the state language on the whole territory of the Federation (Article 68(1)), although republics have the authority to establish *their own* state languages – languages that are official within the territory of republics, and can be employed in the republics' state institutions alongside Russian (Article 68(2)).[70]

The Russian Constitutional Court (RCC) has ruled on republican legislation requiring heads of ethnic republics to have knowledge of both Russian and titular languages.[71] A case was submitted by the state Duma of the Federation in 1998, contesting the constitutionality of the Republic of Bashkortostan's provisions on the conditions for presidency of the republic, which included proficiency in both Bashkir and Russian.[72] The state Duma argued that it unduly restricted the constitutional right to equality, including on the grounds of linguistic affiliation. The RCC acknowledged that the Russian Constitution protects the right of the republics to establish their official languages (Article 68(2)): this assures the coexistence of Russian as a state language and the republics' own official languages, thereby creating the conditions for both unity and multilingualism.[73] However, it stated that:

> [Federal law] establishes the boundaries of the powers of the legislative organs [of the subjects]. If the law of the subject of the Russian Federation oversteps the boundaries of the powers delegated to it, and established in federal law, it violates Article 55(3)[74] of the Constitution of the Russian Federation.[75]

Although the RCC refrained from unambiguously ruling on the unconstitutionality of the requirement of knowledge of Bashkir for the republic's president, it left open the possibility for non-speakers of the language to be elected to the position. It held that: 'legal agencies are to ensure that citizens may exercise their rights during the electoral process *regardless of language requirements*' [italics added].[76] In a similar case on the Republic of Adygeya,[77] considered three years later, the RCC went further, and held that restrictions to passive electoral rights (the right to be elected to a position) may be imposed only by federal law, through uniform regulations applied across the Federation. The requirement of fluency in a titular language was then declared unconstitutional, thereby delimiting the ethnic republics' rights in this area.[78] Bashkortostan and Adygeya have since amended their legislation to eliminate the requirement of bilingualism.

In the sphere of minority-language education, in 2004 the RCC considered the case brought by an applicant – S.I. Khapugin,[79] residing in Tatarstan – who challenged the constitutionality of Tatarstan's legislation,[80] stipulating that the Tatar and Russian languages are to be studied 'in equal measure' in the republic's schools. The plaintiff argued that these provisions affected a constitutionally-entrenched right to equality, placing the citizens of Tatarstan in an 'unequal' position compared to residents of other territorial units through the obligation to study Tatar, thereby detracting from students' ability to master other school subjects. The RCC ruled that Tatarstan's arrangement was not unconstitutional: it facilitated the use of Tatar in all spheres of public life and in the education system, so as to enable the 'preservation and development of bilingualism (multilingualism) in the Russian Federation'. At the same time, the RCC stressed the authority of the federal centre in formulating language policies, including those affecting the republics' official languages. It added that the study of Tatar could *not* challenge the status of Russian as the only state language of the Federation in its entirety:

> The teaching of Tatar as a state language [of Tatarstan] … cannot occur to the detriment of the federal component of the basic federal curriculum … or be an obstacle to the realisation of the right of students to deepen their learning of other subjects of the curriculum, including Russian.

This meant that 'the status of the state languages of the republics within the Russian Federation … *cannot be entirely a matter of the subjects of the Russian Federation*' [italics added].[81]

In the same judgement, the RCC also considered a claim challenging amendments to federal legislation who in 2002,[82] stipulating that the alphabets of the Russian language, and those of the republics' official languages, 'shall be based on the Cyrillic graphic symbol'. The applicant – the Parliament of Tatarstan – argued that the amendments were unconstitutional, as they prevented the republics' choice of their own scripts, which, it submitted, could not be divorced from the constitutional right of Russia's republics to establish their own official languages.[83] The RCC held that the script of a language is linked to social, cultural and historical features of a country, as well as state interests; thus, decisions in this area may only be made at the federal level, so as to reflect 'the sovereign will of the state'. The choice of a common alphabet for all official languages of Russia, the RCC added, was instrumental to the preservation of 'national unity', along with the 'harmonisation and balancing' of Russian as the language of the Federation and the languages of the republics. While alphabets might be modified, the RCC concluded, this change could not be initiated 'arbitrarily' by the republics, as this would directly menace federal unity and the country's integrity. A possible change in regulations on scripts would have to be sanctioned by the federal centre, when it was convinced that 'it pursues constitutionally meaningful goals, meets historical, cultural, social and political realities, as well as the interests of the multinational people of the Russian Federation'.[84]

Equality and uniformity

The *Khapugin* judgement described above established that the republics' legislation cannot interfere with the compulsory study of Russian on the basis of federal educational standards. Variation in the requirements of the study of Russian in the republics, the RCC held, could lead to 'negative consequences in relation to the continuity of learning in a single federal educational environment', itself linked to *equality* in upholding the constitutional right to education.[85] The issue of equality was further considered by the Russian Supreme Court (RSC) in another case,[86] on students' inability, from 2009, to take to take the 'uniform state examination' (*Edinyi Gosudarstvennyi Ekzamen – EGE*), the final secondary school examination, in a minority language rather than in Russian. The case was filed by A.A. Kamalova, the mother of a student in a Tatar-language school in Kazan, who argued that the new language requirements placed her daughter in a disadvantaged position compared to students in Russian schools, having to take the final examination in a different language from that of instruction.[87] She further submitted that the right to take an examination in one's language was an extension of the right to receive an education in it, which was protected by Russian law. By contrast, the RSC's Appeals Chamber differentiated between the right to *receive* an education in a particular language and the language of the subsequent examination. Moreover, the study of Russian as a state language was linked by the RSC to the pre-emption of violations of the principle of equality, and to equal opportunities in accessing higher education as well as in professional life.[88]

This approach to equal opportunities in education is further exemplified in the Russian authorities' Third Report to the FCNM. In the report, the Russian government explained the motivating factors behind a refusal to allow some nurseries in the Republic of Karelia to operate exclusively in Karelian. The Karelian-language nurseries were the result of a civil society effort, following a methodology for the teaching of languages to small children already piloted in other countries, including Finland (known as 'language nest'), and involving full immersion in the language. The report states:

> The refusal of federal executive bodies to use in Russia [the] so called "language nest" technique applied in Finland … serve[s] as an example of efforts taken to ensure equal access to education for persons belonging to national minorities. The above technique is aimed at learning by the Finno-Ugric minorities of their native languages [*sic*]. However, its mechanism

creates [a] closed language environment within the frames of pre-school institutions where children plunge into native language from the early child-hood. In [the] multinational environment of Russia this would significantly reduce their socialization opportunities and, accordingly, would entail [a] *violation of the principle of equal opportunities* of education, further employment etc. and is considered as segregation of children on ethnic grounds.[89] [italics added]

This approach suggests an interpretation of equality that diverges from that of international minority rights law. An instrument such as the FCNM (like the ECRML) does uphold the principles of minority integration and national unity,[90] but it simultaneously envisages active measures on the part of the state to promote languages and cultures of minorities. What may be perceived as inequality (the different treatment of particular minorities) in fact amounts to special measures building concrete opportunities for substantial, rather than just formal, equality – akin to what Kymlicka (1995, 2007a) calls 'group-differentiated rights'. Special measures to support minorities are widely recognised as non-discriminatory, and as acting to elevate a minority to genuine equality with the majority.[91] The Russian authorities' approach, instead, indicates a perception of equality as akin to uniformity and sameness.[92] In their reporting to the ACFC, the Russian authorities have presented the closure of Karelian-only nurseries as an example of efforts to advance equality, while diversity has been associated with threats to unity and social cohesion. This sense of menace is aggravated by Russia's territorial vastness and high levels of heterogeneity, resulting in a preoccupation with unity, and with preventing the country's multiple parts from gravitating away from the centre. This objective seems to be linked to the levelling of difference, rather than the pursuit of unity and equal opportunities in tandem with the preservation of cultural pluralism. Conversely, the ACFC has argued in favour of increased regional autonomy in cultural matters, including by urging the Russian authorities to enable minorities' independent decision-making with regard to their alphabets.[93] It has stated that:

> [T]he choice of alphabet is intricately linked to the free choice of one's language, as contained in Article 10 [FCNM] … [T]he obligation to use Cyrillic script for languages that usually apply different alphabets, constitutes a disincentive to the use of these languages that contradicts also the principles contained in Article 10.[94]

To summarise, the Russian higher courts have crystallised some of the rights of minorities and protected their languages, particularly by ruling in favour of Tatarstan's right to require the study of Tatar and Russian in equal measure within the republic. At the same time, the RCC and RSC have reasserted the authority of the federal state with regard to centralised decision-making on school curricula, script and language of examinations, placing an emphasis on unity and uniformity. The cases examined in this chapter were filed by private citizens and, in two cases, by regional institutions: the Parliament of the Republic of Tatarstan (on the issue of the Latin script) and the State Council of the Republic of Adygeya (on bilingualism of the head of the republic). These last two cases serve as illustrations of regions' use of the higher courts in their battles against the federal centre. The incremental use of courts to defend the rights of minority groups and regions may, in turn, lead to a greater 'demand for law' (Hahn 2003: 133). This could expand the domestic jurisprudence on minority issues, and, concomitantly, the role of Russian courts in adjudicating on these cases.

Conclusion

The application of both international and domestic law in Russia is affected by informal practices and an elastic approach to legal regulation. In the case of international law, the Russian authorities' approach suggests a selectivity of implementation by which they seemingly seek to reap the benefits from adherence to an international system – for example through trade and international cooperation – while filtering what may be seen as an 'excessive' penetration of international principles into the Russian legal sphere. There are no guarantees that international standards will be applied comprehensively in Russia, which lessens the overall impact they may exert on domestic law and practice.

The prevailing perception among public officials interviewed was that international law is 'Western' and Russia is 'different' from other Council of Europe member states; in addition to objective criteria of 'difference', such as the member states' size and the number of recognised minorities, a self-perception of Russia as a 'sovereign democracy' seems widespread among public officials. Conversely, civil society institutions, including minority organisations, appear to be willing to take advantage of opportunities to further their objectives with the assistance of international standards. The predominant view among civil society respondents was removed from that of the Russian authorities, which instead favoured a measure of control over the application of international standards. The range of responses points to a web of links between Russian and international institutions in the shape of transnational advocacy networks, which comes into focus when we look beyond a state-centric approach to international relations.

International law has not been fully integrated into the Russian judicial system. Despite this, there are indications that the ECHR's scope of application in Russia is incremental. Yet in the case of minority rights, there are complicating factors influencing their execution via both international and Russian law. First, the European Court of Human Rights has devoted limited attention to minority rights: while generally upholding human rights and the rule of law, its jurisprudence does not encompass several issues of concern to minorities. This might alter through the widening of the ECHR's scope, although in 2014 the legal principles on minority rights arising from its jurisprudence were still limited. In the absence of precise judicial principles on the cultural rights of national minorities, crystallised through the European Court, the FCNM remains the main instrument, ratified by Russia, to uphold such rights. Yet its flexible, open-ended provisions tend to be perceived in Russia as more volatile than those contained in the ECHR: the interviews exposed the view among the respondents (public officials and civil society alike) that the FCNM merely amounts to a set of ephemeral notions. Meanwhile, there appears to be no coordinated country-wide effort to enhance FCNM implementation, with targets that are periodically and centrally evaluated, resulting in a gap between Russia's international commitments and practice on the ground. Thus, international standards for the protection of minority rights rest on shaky foundations; they are not well-placed to help Russia (and its minorities) resolve the challenges of inter-ethnic relations in post-Soviet Russia, or reverse an existing trend toward the homogenisation and exclusion of minorities from decision-making. At the same time, civil society has not shied away from attempts to benefit from the application of international standards where possible: opportunities are identified and pursued, although they are not buttressed by effective legal guarantees.

Second, the legal articulation of minority claims through Russian law is complex. The scarcity of concrete legal guarantees for minorities in Russian law stems from the absence of explicit regulations for the protection of the cultural rights of minorities – itself coupled with a weak tradition of using litigation to resolve disputes. Although the regions have used the courts to claim their rights vis-à-vis the centre – indicating a growing thirst for justice through litigation – these efforts are still relatively modest. At the other end of the spectrum, judges in Russia may be constrained in some of their actions: the fate of progressive judgements in controversial cases tends to depend more on political considerations than the rule of law. Indeed, the Russian judiciary cannot insulate itself from politicised institutions – themselves often at the mercy of informal practices. Despite these difficulties, the higher courts have begun to crystallise some of the principles relating to linguistic rights of minorities in ethnic republics. In its judgements, the Russian Constitutional Court has acknowledged the republics' right to establish their official languages and to require the intensive study of titular languages (in the case of Tatar in Tatarstan). At the same time, it has also delimited the republics' scope of action, by referring to, among other things, centre-driven federal policy on cultural matters, including on language policy. It has further emphasised that Russia's federal structure is based on the principle of integrity, a unified system of state power and a balance between the responsibilities of the federal centre and those of regional authorities. Some judgements reveal divergent understandings of equality between international human rights law and Russian legal practice, the former privileging substantial equality and the latter *formal* equality. Russia's approach paves the way for the pursuit of unity through uniformity.

Notes

1 Some of this chapter's sections were included in an article published in the *Netherlands Quarterly of Human Rights* ('Power, Politics and Participation: The Russian

Federation's National Minorities and their Participatory Rights', 30(1) 2012: 66–96), and in an article published in the *European Yearbook of Minority Issues* ('Linguistic Rights in a Former Empire: Minority Languages and the Russian Higher Courts', 10 2011: 61–89).

2 The focus on minority language use derives from the fact that this issue has featured repeatedly in the jurisprudence of the Russian higher courts.

3 Helmke and Levitsky refer more broadly to *informal institutions* as 'socially shared rules, usually unwritten, that are created, communicated, and enforced outside of officially sanctioned channels' (Helmke and Levitsky 2004: 727). Conversely, *formal institutions* are understood as:

> [R]ules and procedures that are created, communicated, and enforced through channels widely accepted as official. This includes state institutions (courts, legislatures, bureaucracies) and state-enforced rules (constitutions, laws, regulations), but also what Robert C. Ellickson [1991: 31] calls 'organization rules,' or the official rules that govern organizations such as corporations, political parties, and interest groups.
>
> (Ibid.: 727)

4 The practice of publicly discrediting political opponents.

5 Particularly Chapters 7 to 9.

6 Article 15(4) of the 1993 Constitution.

7 See also Chapter 3.

8 To date the ECHR has no provisions, nor is there yet a protocol, specifically relating to minority rights. Cases concerning minority rights must be based on provisions such as Article 3 (inhuman and degrading treatment), Article 8 (respect for family and private life) and Article 14 (discrimination in the enjoyment of specific rights).

9 PACE, 'Russia's Application for Membership of the Council of Europe', 18 January 1996, Doc. 7463.

10 PACE, 'Report on the Conformity of the Legal Order of the Russian Federation with Council of Europe Standards', 28 September 1994, Doc. AS/Bur/Russia (1994) 7.

11 In the Final Declaration of the Council of Europe's Vienna Summit of 9 October 1993, member states of the Council of Europe stated that they would 'welcome the democracies of Europe freed from the Communist oppression'; however: 'Such accession presupposes that the applicant country has brought its institutions and legal system into line with the basic principles of democracy, the rule of law and respect for human rights.' Russia was required to adopt various new laws, including a new criminal code, a new code of criminal procedure, a new civil code and a code of civil procedure (Nussberger 2008: 605).

12 The interviews that were particularly relevant to this and the next section were held with ten public officials and eight respondents from civil society. The latter comprised the following subcategories: minority association (1 respondent); minority NGO (2); cultural association (1); peoples' congress (1); and human rights NGO (4).

13 See Chapter 3.

14 See Chapter 1.

15 In the interviews, the respondents used the expression 'the Charter' (*Khartiya*) as short for the ECRML. 'The Charter' is used in their statements reproduced in this chapter.

16 ACFC, (Second) Report submitted by the Russian Federation, 26 April 2005, ACFC/SR/II(2005)003, p. 70. Similarly, the Third Report states: 'the Russian Federation consistently and systematically accounts in its law enforcement practices both the assumed obligations and the recommendations received following the previous FCNM monitoring cycles.' ACFC, (Third) Report submitted by the Russian Federation, 9 April 2010, ACFC/SR/III(2010)005, p. 4.

17 Russian is the only state language in the whole territory of the Russian Federation, as per Article 68(1) of the Russian Constitution, and Law 'On the State Language of the Russian Federation' (No. 53-FZ, 1 June 2005). The ethnic republics, with the exception of Karelia, have also officially recognised their own state languages – for example, the Tatar language in Tatarstan.

18 Regardless of whether a national minority is a numerical majority within a particular region (see Chapter 2). An alternative interpretation of the public officials' responses in the ethnic republics is that they were aware of the understanding of 'minority' under international law, but they did not wish to be regarded as such – due to a perceived link between minority status and inferior status – and preferred the expression 'titular nationality'. The rejection of their self-identification as members of a 'minority' was, however, not conveyed by the civil society respondents belonging to national minorities.

19 See Chapter 2.

20 With few exceptions (Malakhov and Osipov 2006: 509).

21 Article 3 of Law of the Republic of Mordovia 'On the State Languages of the Republic of Mordovia' (No. 4-Z, 24 April 1998) stipulates that 'the state languages of the Republic of Mordovia are Russian and Mordovian (Moksha and Erzya)'.

22 See also Chapters 5 and 6.

23 Part III of the ECRML includes specific undertakings for the promotion of minority or regional languages. Upon ratification, states are required, pursuant to Article 2(2) ECRML, to select and commit to a minimum of 35 undertakings from 68 options, in the spheres of: education and culture, judicial authorities, administrative authorities, media, and economic and social life.

24 It might also be explained by the fact that two of the four public officials interviewed in Karelia were themselves ethnic Karelians (one respondent displaying a particularly strong commitment to preserve Karelian identity); and by (what appeared as) scarce knowledge of international standards by the other two public officials interviewed.

25 Issued in 2002, 2006 and 2011.

26 See note 16.

27 The data included in this chapter are from interviews with representatives of organisations who were aware of international standards. The representatives of many organisations with limited resources and international exposure displayed no (or very limited) awareness of them.

28 The ECRLM requires its state parties to select, and commit to, a set of undertakings (see note 23).

29 Hofmann (2008: 173) differentiates between this system and that of the ECHR, which instead amounts to 'hard jurisprudence based upon hard law', inasmuch as cases on alleged violations are considered by an international court.

30 The respondent was referring to follow-up events in the final stages of the first cycle of FCNM monitoring, which aimed at promoting a three-way dialogue (between the Council of Europe, the Russian government and minority groups) to enhance FCNM implementation.

31 See, for example, Putin's criticism of the OSCE, reported in Chapter 3. See also instances of NGOs discredited for receiving funding from Western institutions, described in Chapter 7.

32 See the website of the World Congress of Tatars ('General Information'), http://tatar-congress.org/ru/about/obshaya-informatsiya/ (accessed 2 December 2014).

33 See www.fennougria.ee/index.php?id=10973 (accessed 15 January 2015).

34 A consultative body of the Council of Europe, aiming at assisting the member states in establishing effective local and regional self-government. See www.coe.int/t/congress/default_en.asp and https://wcd.coe.int/ViewDoc.jsp?id=1356917&Site=COE&BackColorInternet=DBDCF2&BackColorIntranet=FDC864&BackColorLogged=FDC864 (both accessed 2 December 2014).

35 Transborder cooperation has been more pronounced in the case of Tatarstan than for Mordovia and Karelia, given the numerous Tatar groups outside Russia, and the resources available to the Republic of Tatarstan.

36 At the time of the first set of interviews, in the summer of 2010, a series of public events had recently taken place in the programme's focus region of Mordovia, and also in Moscow. The interviews revealed an awareness of the ECRML that, presumably as a result of the programme, was more pronounced than that of the FCNM.

37 On Houses of Nationalities, see Chapter 7.

38 Presidential Decree No. 909, 15 June 1996. The Concept lists general principles, such as the right to equality for all citizens regardless of ethnic origin, the right to ethnic self-identification, indigenous peoples' rights, and the prohibition of ethnic hatred.

39 The Ministry of Regional Development was abolished in September 2014, with a view to 'improving state governance' (presidential Decree 'On the Abolition of the Ministry of Regional Development of the Russian Federation', No. 612, 8 September 2014). The responsibilities of the Ministry of Regional Development were divided among various ministries, with the Ministry of Culture being tasked with the 'realisation of the ethnocultural needs of citizens belonging to various ethnic groups' (Decree No. 612). The implications of this re-organisation were still unclear at the time of writing. The Ministry of Regional Development had been responsible for nationalities policy since its establishment in September 2004. Previously this had been the domain of the Ministry of Nationality Affairs, which was however abolished in October 2001.

40 With regard to positive obligations, Article 8 ECRML comprises provisions on the need 'to make available' different types of education. Article 7(1) states that:

> [T]he Parties shall base their policies, legislation and practice on the following objectives and principles: ...
> (c) the need for *resolute action* to promote regional or minority languages in order to safeguard them; [italics added] ...
> (f) the provision of appropriate forms and means for the teaching and study of regional or minority languages at all appropriate stages ...

41 'Localism' can be linked to both fragmentation and uncoordinated initiatives, or to local autonomy. See Chapter 6.

42 See Chapter 3.

43 Although this might admittedly originate from a lack of in-depth knowledge of Russia's international obligations.

44 'Comments of the Government of the Russian Federation on the Third Opinion of the Advisory Committee on the Implementation of the Framework Convention for the Protection of National Minorities by the Russian Federation', 25 July 2012, GVT/COM/II(2012)004, p. 12.

45 Gordeev, I. 19 May 2009. 'Tatarstan Gotov Prikrytsya Khartiei' [Tatarstan is Ready to Adopt the Charter], *Nezavisimaya Gazeta*. On amendments to the Law 'On Education', see Chapter 6.

46 For example, in the Council of Europe/EU programme 'Minorities in Russia' referred to above.

47 See p. 80 in this chapter ('The Russian courts and the protection of linguistic rights') and Chapter 6.

48 The appeals, however, ultimately had no practical outcome.

49 See Chapter 8 on NCA.

50 The state Duma is the lower house of the Russian Parliament. Regional dumas also exist in Russia's subjects.

51 Kuzlov was the head of the Mari organisation 'Mer Kanash' and editor-in-chief of the Finno-Ugric newspaper *Kudo+Kodu*. He was attacked on 7 February 2005. Criminal proceedings were also instigated against him for unpaid rent of the newspaper's premises. See International Helsinki Federation for Human Rights and Moscow Helsinki

Group, 2006. 'Russian Federation: The Human Rights Situation of the Mari Minority of the Republic of Mari El', pp. 51–53.

52 Ibid, p. 49.

53 PACE, 'Situation of Finno-Ugric and Samoyed Peoples', 26 October 2006, Doc.11087. PACE acknowledged 'anti-minority sentiment and actions' in Mari El under the Markelov presidency. Another ethnic group to which the Council of Europe has devoted considerable attention is the Meskhetian Turks. Deported from Georgia to Central Asia in the Soviet period, and having resettled in Russia (particularly in Krasnodar krai) in 1989, Meskhetian Turks were not granted Russian citizenship in large numbers following the Soviet Union's dissolution. See PACE's position on the matter: PACE Draft Resolution, 'The Situation of the Deported Meskhetian Population', 4 February 2005, Doc. 10451. See also ACFC, (Second) Opinion on the Russian Federation, 2 May 2007, ACFC/OP/II(2006)004, §278–9; and ACFC, (Third) Opinion on the Russian Federation, 24 November 2011, ACFC/OP/III(2011)010 §54; 174.

54 Another civil society representative (and academic) believed that the increased attention to the needs of Finno-Ugric people in Russia was in reality motivated by trade incentives with Finno-Ugric countries, such as Finland: stakeholders wished to remedy to the damage caused by the Council of Europe bringing to the attention of the international community the problems affecting Finno-Ugric peoples [1.5.1].

55 See also PACE, 'Allegations of Politically Motivated Abuses of the Criminal Justice System in Council of Europe Member States', 23 June 2009, Doc. 11993.

56 Cited in *Vedomosti*, 22 January 2008. 'D. Medvedev: Rossiya – Strana Pravovogo Nigilizma' [D. Medvedev: Russia – A Country of Legal Nihilism']. Putin has similarly referred to the need for a 'dictatorship of the law' in Russia. President of Russia, Address to the Federal Assembly of the Russian Federation, 8 July 2000, http:// archive.kremlin.ru/eng/speeches/2000/07/08/0000_type70029type82912_70658.shtml (accessed 22 November 2014).

57 See also PACE, Doc. 11993 (see note 55).

58 For example, in October 2010 Moscow City Court judge Sergey Pashin was dismissed after he criticised the conviction of a pacifist (and his subsequent ill-treatment in prison) for refusing to serve in the army during the Chechen conflict. In another case, a judge of the Russian Constitutional Court, Vladimir Yaroslavtsev, resigned from his position four months after complaining, in a 2008 interview to the Spanish newspaper *El País*, of intense political pressure on the Russian judiciary. The interview was used for the article: Bonet, P. 31 August 2008. 'En Rusia Mandan los Órganos de Seguridad, Como en la Época Soviética' [In Russia Security Forces are Used Like in Soviet Times], *El País*.

59 No. 1-FKZ, 31 December 1996.

60 No. 54-FZ, 30 March 1998.

61 With the technicality that they must be published in the official gazette (*Rossiiskaya Gazeta*). Instead, the Soviet Union had a dualist (rather than monist) approach, which did not envisage the direct application of international law in domestic courts.

62 Resolution of the Plenum of the Supreme Court of the Russian Federation 'On the Application by Courts of General Jurisdiction of the Commonly Recognised Principles and Norms of International Law and International Treaties of the Russian Federation' (No. 5, 10 October 2003).

63 Article 17(1) of the Constitution, instead, places international law and the Constitution at the same level: 'In the Russian Federation recognition and guarantees shall be provided for the rights and freedoms of the individual and citizen according to the universally recognised principles and norms of international law *and* according to the present Constitution' [italics added].

64 Zorkin, V. 29 October 2010. 'Predel Ustupchivosti' [The Limits of Compliance], *Rossiiskaya Gazeta*, www.rg.ru/2010/10/29/zorkin.html (accessed 15 January 2015). See also Chapter 3 on Zorkin.

65 For example, in 2013 the European Court referred to a state's 'specific positive obligations to avoid the perpetuation of past discrimination or discriminative practices' in a case on the Roma minority in Hungary (*Horváth and Kiss* v. *Hungary*, Application No. 11146/11, 29 January 2013, §116; see also Bowring 2015). Peroni and Timmer (2013) further point to the European Court's development of the concept of 'vulnerable groups', which provides new opportunities to address aspects of substantive equality.

66 For Russia the first relevant judgement was *Timishev* v *Russia* (Application Nos. 55762/00 and 55974/00, 13 December 2005), in which the European Court held that the Russian government had discriminated against the victim, a Chechen, on *ethnic* grounds. Since then, the European Court has also considered the cases *Makhashevy* v. *Russia* (Application No. 20546/07, 31 July 2012), *Antayev and Others* v. *Russia* (Application No. 37966/07, 3 July 2014) and *Amadayev* v. *Russia* (Application No. 18114/06, 3 July 2014), on the ill-treatment of persons of Chechen ethnic background.

67 Law No. 1807-I, 25 October 1991.

68 On this, see also the provisions on the financing of national cultural autonomies (Chapter 7).

69 See for example Article 71(f) of the Russian Constitution.

70 Article 68(2) states:

> The Republics shall have the right to establish *their own state languages*. In the bodies of state authority, local self-government and state institutions of the Republics they shall be used together with the state language of the Federation [italics added].

For simplicity, where possible I use the expression 'official languages' (in the context of the republics) to indicate those languages that are recognised as state languages of the republics.

71 This chapter does not aim to provide a comprehensive list of these cases, but only a range of illustrative judgements.

72 RCC, Judgement No. 12-P, 27 April 1998.

73 Ibid.

74 Article 55(3) states that '[t]he rights and freedoms of the individual and citizen may be restricted by *federal* law …' [italics added].

75 RCC, Judgement No. 12-P (note 72).

76 For RCC judges' dissenting opinions, see Prina (2011b). In this judgement the RCC also held that it could not rule specifically on the issue of language proficiency of Bashkortostan's president since the status of Bashkir as an official language of the republic was not enshrined in the republic's legislation. Indeed, a law on languages for the republic was adopted only in 1999, nearly a year after the judgement (Law of the Republic of Bashkortostan 'On the Languages of the Peoples of the Republic of Bashkortostan', No. 206-Z, 15 February 1999).

77 RCC, Judgement No. 260-O, 13 November 2001. The case was submitted by the State Council of the Republic of Adygeya ('Khase'), which requested the RCC to confirm the constitutionality of the legal requirement for the president of the republic to be proficient in both its official languages (Russian and Adyghe), as per Article 76(1) of the republic's constitution. Adygeya's State Council submitted that fluency in both official languages was a prerequisite for the fulfilment of the duties of the president of republic, and as such could not be regarded as discriminatory.

78 Ibid.

79 RCC, Judgement No. 16-P, 16 November 2004.

80 Article 9(2) of the Law 'On the State Languages of the Republic of Tatarstan and Other Languages in the Republic of Tatarstan' (No 560-XII, 8 July 1992).

81 RCC, Judgement No. 16-P (see note 79). Judgements of the Russian Supreme Court

(RSC) similarly held that the autonomy afforded to the republics in the teaching of their official languages has to be balanced against federal requirements for the study of Russian as the Federation's state language. See cases on the compulsive study of titular languages in the Republic of Karachay Cherkessia (RSC, Judgement No. 30-GO9–3, 15 April 2009) and the Republic of Dagestan (RSC, Judgement No. 20-GO9–6, 29 April 2009). Considerations were again based on the principles of legal fairness and equality.

82 Law 'On the Amending of Article 3 of Law of the Russian Federation "On the Languages of the Peoples of the Russian Federation" ' (No. 165-FZ, 11 December 2002). See also Chapter 5 on the amendments and the issue of script of the Tatar language.

83 In 1999, the Parliament of Tatarstan had legislated to re-introduce the use of the Latin alphabet for Tatar, through the Law of the Republic of Tatarstan 'On the Restoration of the Tatar Alphabet Based on the Latin Script' (No. 2352, 15 September 1999). The use of the Latin alphabet had been discontinued in 1939–40. See Chapter 5.

84 RCC, Judgement No. 16-P (note 79).

85 As well as to the following rights: to receive basic general education in one's native language; and freedom of movement and choice of place of residence. Ibid.

86 RSC, Appeals Chamber, Judgement No. KAS09–295, 2 July 2009.

87 Before 2009, students had been able to take the examination in either Tatar or Russian. See Chapter 6.

88 Similarly, in the Bashkortostan case referred to above (note 72), it was argued by the Russian Duma that the contested provisions contradicted the principle of equality enshrined in Articles 6(2) and 19(2) of the Russian Constitution. Article 6(2) states: 'Every citizen of the Russian Federation shall enjoy in its territory all the rights and freedoms and bear equal duties provided for by the Constitution of the Russian Federation.'

Article 19(2) reads:

> The State shall guarantee the equality of rights and freedoms of man and citizen, regardless of sex, race, nationality, language, origin, property and official status, place of residence, religion, convictions, membership of public associations, and also of other circumstances.

89 ACFC, (Third) Report submitted by the Russian Federation, 9 April 2010, ACFC/SR/III(2010)005, pp. 103–4.

90 See FCNM, Explanatory Report, with reference to 'social cohesion', §46.

91 Article1(4) of the 1966 UN International Convention on the Elimination of All Forms of Racial Discrimination (ICERD), ratified by Russia in 1969, states that:

> Special measures taken for the sole purpose of *securing adequate advancement* of certain racial or ethnic groups or individuals requiring such protection as may be necessary in order to ensure such groups or individuals equal enjoyment or exercise of human rights and fundamental freedoms *shall not be deemed racial discrimination*, provided, however, that such measures do not, as a consequence, lead to the maintenance of separate rights for different racial groups and that they shall not be continued after the objectives for which they were taken have been achieved. [italics added].

In the same vein, Article 4 (paragraphs 2–3) FCNM reads:

> 2. The Parties undertake to adopt, where necessary, adequate measures in order to promote, in all areas of economic, social, political and cultural life, full and effective equality between persons belonging to a national minority and those belonging to the majority.
> 3. The measures adopted in accordance with paragraph 2 shall not be considered to be an act of discrimination.

Similar provisions are found in Article 7(2) ECRML.
92 On this, see also Chapter 6, on the centralisation of the education system through uniform federal standards.
93 ACFC, (Third) Opinion on the Russian Federation (see note 53), §167–169.
94 Ibid, §168.

5   Strengthening the state through homogenising centralism[1]

Chapters 3 and 4 have shown that both Russian law and international standards are unequipped to effectively protect and promote the cultural rights of national minorities. In this and the next chapter, I examine minority policies in the context of unfolding socio-political circumstances in Russia. It is argued that the statism and centralism favoured by the Putin leadership result in homogenising tendencies, leading to enhanced uniformity and the downgrading of (minority) ethnicity. I outline the complexities deriving from Russia's diversity, which have resulted in a drive for a strong state and enhanced uniformity. Two main processes are identified and analysed in this chapter: the promotion of a 'civic' Russian identity to the detriment of minority identities; and the re-structuring of the Russian Federation to reduce the salience of (non-Russian) ethnicity. The next chapter focuses on homogenisation specifically in the sphere of education.

The complexities of diversity

The impulse towards homogenisation stems from the complexities posited by high levels of diversity in Russian society. As we have seen in Chapter 2, Soviet nationalities policy hinged on a link between ethnicity and territory, yet ethnic federalism did not help a large number of persons of non-Russian ethnicity. This was for two main reasons: first, smaller nationalities were not classified as 'titular' (and thus not 'assigned' a territory); and, second, clearly not all persons belonging to a titular nationality resided in 'their own' ethnic republic. In 1989 only 41 nationalities in the RSFSR benefited from territorial autonomy out of a total of 127 nationalities, and of the 41 titular nationalities only 55 per cent resided in 'their own' territory. In short, only ten million people of the 27 million non-Russians benefited from territoriality (Codagnone and Filippov 2000: 266). At the same time, ethnicity-based federalism led to a heightened ethnic consciousness in Soviet citizens, which ultimately triggered the ethnic mobilisation of the late 1980s and early 1990s (Gorenburg 2003).

The first President of Russia, Boris Yeltsin, inherited these unresolved difficulties. Following the Soviet Union's collapse, the regions started to gravitate away from the centre as they increasingly acquired autonomy through devolution (Stoner-Weiss 1999). In 1990, Yeltsin famously invited the regions to 'take as much sovereignty as [they] can swallow'. This is likely to have derived less from Yeltsin's liberal attitudes than from an inability of the federal authorities to fill the power vacuum left by the Communist Party's dethronement (Reddaway 2004: 6). The Yeltsin years were further characterised by statutory and political fragmentation, as evidenced by a plethora of ad hoc bilateral treaties with the subjects not regulated through a coherent federal legislative and administrative framework.[2] Asymmetry became the norm: from the 'unofficial asymmetry' of ad hoc measures and selective legal implementation (Hahn 2003: 115), to 'socio-economic asymmetry'[3] (Stepan 2000). Special arrangements to satisfy the par-ticularistic needs of regions (and their leaders) enabled the formation of virtual fiefdoms, ruled by assertive leaders engaging in 'regional warlordism' (Kirkow 1995; 1998: 139).[4] Far-reaching powers were enjoyed by prominent regional ethnic leaders in post-Soviet Russia, such as former President of Tatarstan, Min-timer Shaimiev (1991–2010), and former President of Bashkortostan, Murtaza Rakhimov (1993–2010). A republic like rich, oil-producing Tatarstan, with a high concentration of Tatars living in its territory, could defy the Russian author-ities and refuse to sign Yeltsin's Federation Treaty in 1992, insisting instead on a power-sharing treaty.[5] At the same time, the instability of the highly asymmet-ric system created by bilateral treaties was characterised by de-centralisation and state fragility; Russian federalism risked being transformed into a 'disintegrating confederal system' (Petrov 2004: 228).

Thus, at the end of Yeltsin's rule ethnic pluralism had become associated with instability and ineffective management. The Yeltsin presidency was further plagued by multiple social ills, due to the difficult transition to a market economy and large-scale privatisation, which resulted in economic precariousness, law-lessness and the rise of the oligarchs. In turn, newly found freedoms of the post-Communist period allowed forms of ethnic nationalisms to emerge, with calls for autonomy which could trigger further instability and fragmentation. It is these complexities that Putin attempted to resolve through the strengthening of the state, which involved, *inter alia*, homogenising processes, with new forms of uniformity and centralism.

Russia's homogenising efforts

Putin has pursued a process of re-centralisation by limiting the power of regional 'barons', including by depleting the financial resources at their disposal through a centralised fiscal system.[6] The chaos of the Yeltsin years convinced not only Putin, but members of the ruling elite more generally, of the need for a strong state. This is a belief which the various strands of the political leadership tend to share, despite diverging (more or less conservative) positions on issues such as nationali-ties policy and migration. It leads to a form of 'political centrism' in the pursuit of a strong state, which is also seen as instrumental for modernisation (Laruelle 2009a: 195–197). Centralism is further consistent with Russia's historic legacy of 'patriarchal monarchism' – as a state that crystallises around a strong leader, originally embodied by the tsar (Leatherbarrow 2010). The imperative of a strong state has been employed to justify, and then normalise, authoritarian tendencies, particularly by linking them the struggle against terrorism (Baev 2005: 323):[7] thus, centralisation processes have, among other things, been responsible for a growing democratic deficit.

In order to create a strong state, one needs the vestige of a national idea: this fundamental role is taken up by Russian patriotism. As we have seen in Chapter 2, *patriotism* is perceived differently from *nationalism* in that the latter is treated as potentially destructive, ultimately leading to secessionist tendencies. Instead, patriotism is viewed as a positive force embodying the overarching values through which any Russian citizen might find pride in his/her country and its achievements (Daucé *et al.* 2010).

Russian patriotism: overarching civic identity or pervasive Russianness?

Shortly after becoming president, Putin outlined Russia's principal values in the Millenium Manifesto: patriotism, power (*derzhavost'*) and statism (*gosudarst-vennichestvo*). Putin said about 'patriotism':

> This word is often used in an ironic and even vulgar sense. But for most Russians, it has retained its original, fully positive value. It is a sense of pride in their homeland and its history and accomplishments. It is a desire to make the country more beautiful, richer, stronger, happier. When these feelings are free of national arrogance and imperial ambitions, there is nothing reprehensible, bigoted. It is a source of courage, fortitude, strength of the nation. Having lost our patriotism, and with it our national pride and dignity, we lose ourselves as a nation capable of great achievements.[8]

Putin has built a patriotic discourse around 'values', while being generally cautious about using the expression 'ideology', given its negative Marxist connotations (Laruelle 2009a: 142). Yet in 2003, he went so far as to spell out that patriotism should serve as a 'unifying ideology of Russia'.[9] Frequent references to patriotism are made in the presidential Decree 'On the Strategy of State Nationality Policy of the Russian Federation until 2025',[10] signed by Putin in December 2012. At the same time, the Putin-supported patriotic discourse is non-militant and non-nationalistic (Daucé *et al.* 2010): it is an attempt to create what has been defined as 'multicultural constitutional patriotism' (Codagnone and Filippov 2000). The constituent themes that make up Russian patriotism have remained general: Russia as a great power within the international arena; its influence in the near abroad; and its strength as a state (Laruelle 2009a: 196). To highlight Russia's greatness, Putin has pointed to positive features in all periods of the country's history. For example, while he denounced the excessively 'bureaucratised' style of the old Communist Youth League (*Komsomol*), he upheld some of the principles behind it, such as 'the spirit of love of the homeland, of the fatherland'.[11] Soviet myths, following their rehabilitation, are further incorporated into what are essentially nation-building efforts on federal television (Hutchings and Rulyova 2009; Novikova 2010). Of crucial importance in these dynamics has been the balance between ethnic and civic attributes that Russian patriotism encompasses. Tolz (1998) argues that, following the end of the Soviet Union, Russia was faced with the need to create a post-Soviet state that reconciled two elements: '*civic* identities, based on inclusive citizenship, *and* ... exclusive *ethnic* identities, based on ... culture, religion, language, and common ancestry' [italics added] (ibid.: 993). Such a process would involve the forging of an overarching identity for the state's multiple ethnic groups, while at the same time enabling persons belonging to such groups to rediscover their own cultures, languages and/or religions that might have been marginalised (in some cases repressed) during the Soviet period. It would result in a combination of civic and ethnic attributes, to replace the vacuum left by the collapse of the Soviet Union and its ideological framework. Tishkov has also acknowledged the impossibility of a 'monoculture' in Russia. He argued:

> In Russia there is talk of Russian [*rossiiskii*] identity, of all-Russian [*obshcherossiiskii*] patriotism. The formula here should not be 'either-or' (either an ethnic Russian or a Russian citizen; either a Chechen or a Russian citizen) but 'both'. Democracy should be built in a way to reflect this complexity.[12]

Putin's Russia has, indeed, sought to promote overarching, non-ethnic values which supposedly unify nationalities residing in Russia, to act as a counterweight (or replace) potentially destabilising multiple forms of nationalism at the regional level. In 2006 the Russian government stated that it was pursuing a 'policy of de-ethnization of [the] domestic political scene', and that this choice of policy derived from the fact that 'national and ethnocultural issues blend perfectly in the concept of basic civil rights'.[13] In Russia's Third Report to the ACFC the expression 'unity in variety' is used.[14] Thus, *Russian* citizenship should replace forms of 'quasi-citizenship' in regions with strong national identities such as Tatarstan and Bashkortostan – ending their ability to forge an 'inner abroad' within Russia (Sakwa 2008: 234). In line with this, Tishkov (2011) has pointed out that, after the Soviet Union's collapse, all of the former 15 Union republics *except for Russia* effectively declared themselves 'nation-states'. Russia, instead, did not embark upon a journey to nation-statehood, but retained its multinational character, clearly stated in the 1993 Russian Constitution.[15] The post-Soviet period saw the creation of a new understanding of the Russian people (*rossiiskii narod*) as a civic nation (*grazhdanskaya natsiya*) – what can be referred to as 'Russian nation' (*rossiiskaya natsiya*) (Tishkov 2011: 15–16). This is a novel approach, as 'nation' has been more commonly perceived in ethnic terms; yet Tishkov argues that 'civic' and 'ethnic' understandings of a nation need not be mutually exclusive: a nation (in a civic sense) can include various nations (in an ethnic sense), like, he suggests, Britain includes Scotland within its borders (Tishkov 2011: 17). Thus, a new overarching

(Russia-wide) identity is supposedly being shaped, around a concept that I have called elsewhere the 'new Russian citizen' (Prina 2011a).

At the same time, Russia under Putin has experienced a reassertion of Russian *ethnic* identity, infused by messianism, patriotism and a notion of its own greatness, while also projecting the image of a strong state. Thus, the discourse around civic Russian nationalism can hide a superimposition of *russkii* and *rossiiskii* elements, by which the boundaries of the two tend to become blurred.[16] If de-ethnification is pursued to give space to civic values, yet they incorporate Russian ethnic attributes, the process can ultimately result in enhanced Russianness (and the concurrent dilution of minority pluralism) rather than the popularisation of a civic type of nationalism. Indeed, while a distinction is traditionally made between civic (liberal and inclusive) and ethnic (illiberal and exclusive) forms of nationalism (Kohn 1944), Anthony D. Smith (1998: 126) suggests that 'even the most "civic" and "political" nationalisms often turn out on closer inspection to be also "ethnic" and "linguistic"'. Others (Brubaker 1999, 2004; Kuzio 2002; Shulman 2002) have similarly argued that the distinction between the two forms of nationalism is overstated, and that attributes of the civic and ethnic spheres tend to converge. Thus, even in the presence of the most genuine intentions to promote exclusively civic values, civic nationalism might become coloured by ethnic attributes of the dominant group.

Another cluster of reasons for the blurring of ethnic and civic elements can be found in the specific features of the Soviet Union itself. The Soviet Union had employed 'institutionalized definitions of nationhood' (Brubaker 1994):[17] it divided the population into ethnic groups that were conceived as sealed off from each other and mutually exclusive. Consequently, the Soviet Union instilled, or heightened, ethnic consciousness in its population – while also consolidating perceptions of exclusive group membership. Moreover, nationality was institutionalised at the sub-state level (mostly the republics), rather than at the state level (ibid.: 50), and nationalism was equated with *ethnic* nationalism (Opalski 2001: 301). The post-Soviet world, then, has hardly a comprehensive set of civic principles that may become constituent parts of a new form of statehood. These factors complicate the forging of a state-wide, national – but overall civic – idea.

The emerging discourse is one that is often ethnically essentialising: it excludes notions of cultural hybridity or plural identities, while also consolidating perceived boundaries between groups (Shnirelman 2006a, 2009a). It results in the construction of a Russian (*rossiiskii*) identity which cannot be a hybrid one, as it is grounded on Russian (*russkii*) culture. A special role in Russian patriotism/nationalism is occupied by the 'civilisational' approach to the interpretation of Russian history and modern society, regarded as a unique civilisation, which, Shnirelman (2006a, 2009a) argues, is conceived primarily in ethnic terms.[18] Against this background it is difficult to escape ambiguity. Official pronouncements make reference alternatively to a 'Russian nation' (*rossiiskaya natsiya*) and to a 'multinational Russian state' (*russkoe mnogonatsional'noe gosudarstvo*). 'Russian' can have, in these discourses, both an ethnic and civic sense

(Laruelle 2009a: 148). Even the exact significance of *rossiiskaya natsiya* is far from clear: Shevel (2011) argues that the oscillation between a civic and ethnic approach to identity might be 'purposefully ambiguous', so as to enable an elastic (and opportunistic) approach to Russia's compatriots policy, giving it room for manoeuvre in the near abroad.[19] At the same time, Russianness tends to be conceived ethnocentrically within Russia. Already in 1996 the Concept of State Nationality Policy of the Russian Federation, while upholding the right of ethnic minorities to their national and cultural identities, also stressed the 'unifying role of the Russian [*russkii*] people in the territory of Russia'.[20] The 2012 presidential Decree 'On the Strategy of State Nationality Policy of the Russian Federation until 2025',[21] on the one hand contains references to the protection of minority languages and cultures, and to a 'Russian [*rossiiskii*] political nation'; on the other, it asserts that the Russian people (*russkii narod*) historically represent the 'backbone' of the union of peoples that constitute the present Russian state. This tension is also contained in Putin's 2012 state of the nation address:

> For centuries, Russia developed as a multi-ethnic nation … a civilisation-state bonded by the Russian people [*russkii narod*], Russian language and Russian [*russkii*] culture native for all of us, uniting us and preventing us from dissolving in this diverse world. To the rest of the planet, regardless of our ethnicity, we have been and continue to be one people.… We treat and will continue to treat with great care and respect every ethnic group, every nation in the Russian Federation. Our diversity has always been and remains the source of our beauty and our strength.[22]

This narrative simultaneously recognises Russia's multi-ethnicity and also treats (ethnic) Russians as the core nation of the Federation (its 'backbone')[23] (see also Shevel 2011). The same state of the nation address goes to great lengths to stress the importance of the Russian language, including a call for its promotion across the CIS (Commonwealth of Independent States) and beyond.

At the same time, the way forward has not been seen as Russification per se, but rather the validation of Russian identity, particularly though a leading role in global affairs (Laruelle 2009a: 148). In addition to seeking a prominent place in the international arena, this approach to Russia's revival encompasses an inward-looking quest for identity and its affirmation, which manifests itself through the promotion of Russianness within Russia, including through a curtailment of ethnic federalism.[24] Russia is increasingly being perceived by the Russians as an ethnic homeland – a novel approach to nation-statehood that is contrasted to the 'multinational' narratives of the Soviet Union (ibid.: 196). This new outlook resembles that which is found in other former Soviet republics, which Brubaker (1996, 2011) calls 'nationalizing states', or: 'states that are conceived by their dominant elites as nation-states, as the states of and for particular ethnocultural nations, yet as "incomplete" or "unrealized" nation-states, as insufficiently "national" in a variety of senses' (Brubaker 1996: 9).

Brubaker adds that nationalising dynamics bring about claims by the 'core nation' which, despite its titularity, 'is conceived as being in a weak cultural, economic, or demographic position within the state' (ibid.: 5). As a result:

> This weak position – seen as a legacy of discrimination against the nation before it attained its independence – is held to justify the 'remedial' or 'compensatory' project of using state power to promote the specific (and previously inadequately served) interests of the core nation.
>
> (Ibid.: 5)

The notion of 'nationalizing state' is normally applied to former Soviet Union republics (often the Baltic states) with the exclusion of the Russian Federation: the Russians of the Soviet Union treated the whole country as essentially 'their own' – Russian being the *lingua franca*, and the Russians effectively representing the Soviet Union's core nation. However, the fuzzy contours of Russian identity, and the paucity of ethnic institutions for ethnic Russians in the Soviet period,[25] have generated a yearning for a state that is conceived not only in civic, but also in ethnic, terms. The aspirations for unitary nation-statehood and an ethnic homeland are particularly evident in the popular slogans 'Russia for the Russians' and 'Stop Feeding the Caucasus'.[26]

In addition to identity validation, a Russo-centric approach serves several purposes. A purely civic nation has a very high degree of abstraction, and, as such, *rossiiskaya natsiya* can sound hollow. Something is needed to anchor it: thus, the (otherwise amorphous) notion of Russian patriotism is concretised through the Russian language, history and culture.[27] At the same time, patriotism is not fully exclusive, since minorities in Russia also have to be somehow accommodated to enable peaceful coexistence. Laruelle argues that what is presented is a 'concentric logic':

> [A]ll those who assert their 'Russianness' in one way or another are assured a place: ethnic Russians make up the inner core, followed by the national indigenous minorities (and here again there are more concentric circles: the Siberian peoples are for example closer to the core than those of the North Caucasus); the Russophone 'diaspora' settled in the former Soviet republics; communities of Russian emigres around the globe; and the citizens of CIS states who are invited to come and work in Russia and, by such migratory means, to preserve Moscow's role as the driver of Eurasian space.
>
> (Laruelle 2009a: 196)

Hence, the existing discourse combines ethnic attributes (and residual primordialism) with a form of loyalty to the state that can potentially transcend ethnicity, through a cohesive form of patriotism. Non-Russian groups can be accepted into a patriotic scheme, by adapting to a civic/ethnic form of nationalism, and directly or indirectly acquiescing to the reassertion of Russianness. As a result, a balance is somehow created even in the presence of a large number of minorities – those with a traditional presence in Russia as well as migrants, who have entered Russia in substantial numbers given the country's reliance on foreign labour.[28]

Meanwhile, a movement towards (non-Russian) de-ethnification serves to assuage fears of latent ethnic tensions that may result in inter-ethnic strife. Concern over 'excessive' diversity becomes a justification for uniformity and for a strong state. Indeed, the social upheavals following the end of the Soviet Union have been explained primarily through the lenses of ethnic difference. If an ethnicity is perceived as having specific traits, and its members an inherent 'mentality',[29] inter-ethnic differences can easily be seen as potentially leading to direct confrontation (Shnirelman 2006a: 189). These views conjure up a scenario that resembles Huntington's (1996) 'clash of civilisations'. Such a threat, whether real or perceived, can fuel xenophobia; thus, for example, one of the respondents from Tatarstan said: 'In Moscow there is a prejudice, a fear that if Russia has too many strong ethnicities and languages there will be problems' [4.7].

Similarly, a high-ranking public official working on nationality issues argued in an interview that state policies for the preservation of ethnic diversity were 'both good and bad' [4.18]. Although 'good' in promoting the preservation of Russia's cultural heritage, they were 'bad' inasmuch as they multiplied the potential triggers of disunity and conflict.[30] The movement towards de-ethnification of non-Russians can then constitute a route towards reducing those (ethnic minority) elements that can be in conflict with the majority, while also slowly assimilating them into the core nation.

Enhancing Russianness: practical steps

Practical steps towards enhanced Russianness encompass various efforts to promote the Russian language, culture and symbols. The motivations behind these dynamics do not originate exclusively from the Russian Federation itself, but are also a response to globalising forces. Globalising tendencies can not only lead to the disappearance of small languages through impulses towards cultural and linguistic uniformity, but they can also affect major languages used across regions of the world, such as Russian. Thus, the Russian linguistic environment is being modified by the ever-expanding use of English (a 'hypercentral language')[31] in mass culture and the media (Musina *et al.* 2011a: 5), which can trigger protectionist tendencies. Thus, Russian identity affirms itself in contraposition to both internal influences (from the country's own ethnic diversity) and external ones (globalisation).

The Russian language and the Cyrillic alphabet

The promotion of the Russian language, and corresponding demotion of minority languages, is the first step towards enhanced Russianness. Legal amendments and policy changes have been introduced since 2000 to modify the linguistic environment and reassert the primacy of Russian. In 2001 the federal programme

'Russian Language' for the years 2002–2005 was adopted, listing among its objectives:

> developing and spreading the Russian language as the state language of the Russian Federation; developing the Russian language as the national language of the Russian people [*russkii narod*]; strengthening the position of the Russian language as means of inter-ethnic communication between the peoples of Russia.[32]

Similar programmes were launched in the following years (for the periods 2006–2010 and 2011–2015). Additionally, the year 2005 saw the promulgation of the Law 'On the State Language of the Russian Federation',[33] which consolidates the status of Russian as the country's state language, while 2007 was declared the 'Year of Russian Language'. Parallel initiatives were introduced in the area of education, with legal reform introduced in 2007 to establish state educational standards at the federal level. As will be seen in Chapter 6, the study of and through the medium of minority languages has tended to decrease since 2000. The Decree 'On the Strategy of State Nationality Policy of the Russian Federation until 2025'[34] unambiguously states the primacy of the Russian language in the country, while Putin has dispelled any possible doubts on his position on the matter. In February 2013 he said:

> The foundation of the unity of the country is, of course, the Russian language: our state language and the language of inter-ethnic communication. It creates a common civic, cultural and educational space. And every citizen of the Russian Federation should know the language at a high level. In order to guarantee that people can learn Russian well, we need to create and continuously always improve conditions for it.[35]

On the same occasion, Putin referred to the federal programme 'Russian Language' for the years 2011–2015, which allocated 2.5 billion roubles to the support of the Russian language 'at the federal level and in all regions of the country without exceptions'. He noted that, in some parts of the country, Russian language skills were low, and this could 'ruin the country': residents of these regions would experience problems if they moved to other parts of Russia where the state language is needed for work and study. Putin further called for the Day of the Russian Language (the day of Pushkin's birthday) to be celebrated on a grander scale.[36]

Legal reform and a re-orientation of linguistic policy at the federal level have directly impacted upon the republics. For example, in Tatarstan, regional legislation was amended to re-define, and better clarify, relations between the centre and the republican authorities in the area of language and culture; and, following the adoption of the federal programme 'Russian Language', Tatarstan also launched the mirror programme 'Russian Language in Tatarstan' for the years 2001–2005[37] (Makarova 2011b: 14). In parallel to this, the early 2000s saw calls to drop the requirement in the republics' constitutions for their presidents to speak titular languages (Hahn 2003: 130),[38] and subsequently RCC decisions on the relaxation (and ultimately elimination) on the said language requirements.[39] This change has implied a lowering of the status of titular languages, despite the legal protection afforded to them in the 1993 Constitution, and the republics' own legislation, which in most cases has made the republics' titular languages co-official alongside Russian. It has been argued that these laws were never intended to be fully implemented, but rather to fulfil a symbolic function (Zamyatin 2014). And indeed, legal recognition of the official status of titular languages does not seem to have helped improve the dire conditions in which many of Russia's minority languages find themselves: the UNESCO Atlas of the World's Languages in Danger refers to 131 languages[40] of the Russian Federation under threat in 2010 (among these, Karelian, Moksha and Erzya are classified as 'definitely endangered').[41] The vulnerability of minority languages is not (only) a consequence of the Russian government's uniformising pressures: as noted in the Explanatory Report of the European Charter for Regional or Minority Languages (ECRML), the threats facing minority languages are also linked to broader, globalising tendencies: '[These threats] are often due at least as much to the inevitably standardising influence of modern civilisation and especially of the mass media as to an unfriendly environment or a government policy of assimilation.'[42] Such a 'standardising influence' forcefully implies that, if the dilution of diversity is to be prevented, a state needs not only to refrain from adopting assimilationist policies, but also to proactively promote multilingualism.

Another area in which Russia's homogenising tendencies can be discerned is the requirement that official languages of the republics employ the Cyrillic alphabet. Alphabets have been a contested issue in Russia since the Soviet period. In the 1930s a shift to Cyrillic was imposed for languages that used a Latin-based script. Some such languages, such as Turkic languages including Tatar, had only a few years earlier shifted from the Arabic to Latin alphabet (Grenoble 2003: 54).[43] In 2002, while Tatar organisations were calling for the re-Latinisation of their alphabet, the state Duma adopted an amendment to the 1991 Law 'On the Languages of the Peoples of the Russian Federation',[44] introducing the provision that the alphabet of both the Russian language and the republics' official languages 'shall be based on the Cyrillic graphic symbol'.[45] In 2004 the Russian Constitutional Court (RCC) turned down a claim submitted by Tatarstan's Parliament, denouncing the 2002 amendments as unconstitutional, inasmuch as they prevented the republics' choice of their own scripts.[46] Already in 1999 the Tatarstan had passed a law to restore the use of the Latin script,[47] abolished in 1939 (Suleymanova 2010); the RCC's decision, together with the 2002 amendments, resulted in Tatarstan having to set aside its project to reintroduce the Latin alphabet for its titular language. The 2002 amendments further mean that Karelian cannot be declared the state language of the Republic of Karelia as long as the traditional Latin script is used: as a consequence, Karelian is the only language of a republic's titular nationality not to be recognised as co-official alongside Russian. As a Karelian language expert noted during an interview,

Karelian 'needs to be a state language [within Karelia] but *also* it needs to keep the Latin alphabet' [2.2]: the respondent could not see the language being divorced from its traditional script.[48]

Russian symbols

The overarching civic values on which patriotism should rest are seemingly those by which any Russian citizen might find pride in his/her country. However, such common values, memories or symbols are rare – with the 'Great Patriotic War' perhaps remaining the last symbol, used in official discourse, of Russia's various ethnic groups uniting to pursue a joint goal by fighting a common enemy (Sperling 2009: 221).[49] As a result, Russian patriotism draws from elements of Russia's history (Tsarist, Soviet and post-Soviet), reproduced particularly through the Russian emblem, flag and anthem, following legislation adopted in December 2000.[50] The emblem includes the red flag (symbol of the Soviet period) and the double-headed eagle (symbol of the Russian, and Byzantine, empires); the tricolour flag, also used during the 1917 provisional government, was reintroduced in 1991. The old Soviet anthem was readopted in 2000, with the original music and only minor changes to the text.[51] The new symbolism, then, is a collage of the main junctures of Russian history. On this point, Putin has stated:

> In order to revive national consciousness, we need to link historical eras and get back to understanding the simple truth that Russia did not begin in 1917, or even in 1991, but rather, that we have a common, continuous history spanning over one thousand years, and we must rely on it to find inner strength and purpose in our national development.[52]

The Soviet period is rehabilitated as part of collective memory, common to the Federation's multiple groups. This approach, in addition to providing viable symbols, accommodates a residual Communist nostalgia[53] and a desire for stability through continuity. Putin's strategy is an example of 'syncretism', or 'the mixing and matching' of various approaches: he highlights (and associates himself with) the accomplishments of the Soviet past, while also presenting himself as an advocate for progressive change (Munro 2006: 307–308).

In order to stimulate patriotism, post-Soviet Russia has made use of various holidays and celebrations, including (slightly repackaged) Soviet ones. The 9th of May (Victory Day) has remained a holiday of significant symbolic value, incorporating notions of Russia's strength and military power. Celebrations are organised and promoted at the federal level but also at the local level, in cities and regions. For example, in 2012, Mordovia celebrated 1,000 years of union with the peoples of Russia.[54] New holidays have been introduced, often with a militaristic slant, commemorating victories of the imperial and Soviet Armies against Russia's enemies (Laruelle 2009a: 158–159). This phenomenon is part of a broader form of 'militarised patriotism' that celebrates military achievements, particularly the Great Patriotic War, with successive five-year programmes, reviving the Soviet tradition of military–patriotic narratives (Sperling 2009). This type of Russo-centric approach to language and symbolism brings into question whether the specific form of patriotism promoted by the Russian leadership is entirely 'civic'.

Effects of homogenisation

Various respondents belonging to national minorities, from both civil society and academia, voiced concerns vis-à-vis state policies on minority cultures and languages.[55] A recurring perception among these respondents was that the federal authorities, while to some extent accommodating diversity, prevented alternative ethnic identities from flourishing into something more than marginal.[56] A second group of (civil society) respondents believed that, given the finite resources available, existing efforts to promote minority cultures were still laudable. At the same time, this second group of respondents judged *local* public officials and their efforts positively, having established a working relationship with them, but had limited awareness of the measures adopted at the federal level to promote minority cultures. These respondents predominantly resided in Mordovia and Karelia, where ethnic issues feature less frequently in the public discourse than in Tatarstan. It is noteworthy that, even when not nurturing grievances towards the (local or federal) authorities, numerous respondents repeatedly expressed sadness that their languages were progressively losing prominence, and felt powerless to stop advancing Russification. These attitudes were particularly evident in the case of Karelian respondents in Petrozavodsk and Tver [1.1.2; 1.1.4; 1.4.1; 2.2; 2.5].

The use of Russian (*russkii*) attributes and symbolism can feed perceptions that the Russian leadership is primarily upholding the interests of the 'main group' – the Russians (Pain 2005).[57] The promotion of quintessentially Russian symbols and values creates an environment that is not conducive to a form of intercultural dialogue[58] based on the recognition of various cultures' equal worth, but rather one with a dominant Russian culture, alongside which other minority cultures are 'tolerated'. This 'tolerance' seems close to the meaning that Žižek (2011: 46) gives to the term, i.e. 'patronizing disrespect' camouflaged as 'respect':

> The very term 'tolerance' is here indicative: one 'tolerates' something one does not approve of, but cannot abolish, either because one is not strong enough to do so or because one is benevolent enough to allow the Other to retain its illusions – in this way, a secular liberal 'tolerates' religion, a permissive parent 'tolerates' his children's excesses, and so on.
>
> (Ibid.)

This type of 'tolerance' can be linked to 'benign neglect', by which minority languages and cultures are 'tolerated', without being necessarily actively and effectively promoted, despite the positive obligation to do so contained in international standards such as Article 5 FCNM.[59] In its Third Report to the ACFC, the Russian government provided a list of programmes under Article 5, centring around festivals and other cultural events.[60] Some respondents of the category 'civil society – minority NGO' argued that, although welcoming these programmes, they did not believe them to be substantially contributing to preserving elements of their cultural identity [1.2.1; 1.2.2; 1.2.5; 1.2.8; 1.2.9].[61] Equally, the ACFC has, on the one hand, commented positively on the abundance of cultural events across the Russian Federation, which 'generally promote the values of respect for diversity and tolerance in society';[62] on the other hand, it has argued that the emphasis placed by the Russian authorities on events such as festivals, which are 'expected from and provided by national minority communities and schools', can detract from other activities of relevance to minorities.[63] The ACFC further referred to criticism emanating from minority representatives and some of Russia's regions, including Tatarstan, on 'the heightened role … given to the Russian language and culture as the instrument for "consolidating" society'.[64] The ACFC stated on this point:

> While recognising the legitimacy of the aim to protect the state language, the Advisory Committee considers that this aim should not be given undue importance in this context and should be coupled with guarantees regarding the values of diversity and respect for the rights of persons belonging to national minorities.[65]

Shifts towards homogenisation are often incessant but subtle, and as such can easily remain undetected by much of Russia's population. These processes can be regarded as a form of 'banal nationalism' (Billig 2004) in the sense that they are largely imperceptible, despite being real. Some authors have further described insidious, covert means that might be used by the Russian authorities to contain diversity. Abramov (2010) describes what in Mordovia are, in his opinion, attempts to divide the Mordovian population along linguistic lines, by placing an emphasis on the distinction between Moskha and Erzya peoples, through 'propaganda' that started in the early 1990s. This was meant, Abramov suggests, to facilitate an ultimate shift toward a 'united and indivisible' Russia, by simultaneously weakening the overarching Mordovian identity (ibid.: 149–156).

De-federalisation as de-ethnification

Centralising measures affect Russia as a federation and contribute to its de-ethnification. As noted above, since the end of the Soviet Union there has been, first, a progressive relaxation of the central powers (under Yeltsin), followed by a subsequent reverse movement strengthening the federal centre (under Putin and Medvedev). Similarly, for much of its history, Russia has oscillated between the two diametrically opposed positions of localism (through devolution) and centralism. It has already been mentioned that, during the Soviet Union, powers were delegated to titular nationalities in 'their own' ethnic republics through the policy of *korenizatsiya*, yet local affairs were micro-managed by Communist Party institutions. In post-Soviet Russia, the 1993 Constitution simultaneously provides for the Russian Federation's sovereignty in all its territories (Article 4), *and* for the self-determination of Russia's peoples (preamble and Article 5(3)) (Varlamova 2001), along with the republics' right to their own constitutions and official languages (Articles 5(2) and 68(2)). The same tension is found in the constitutions of the republics themselves, simultaneously recognising the rights of titular nations (e.g. Tatars) *and* of all the republics' nationalities (e.g. Tatarstan's 'multinational people').

In 1993, Rafael Khakimov, an advisor on political affairs to Tatarstan's (former) President Mintimer Shaimiev, speculated that federalisation would prevail over centralism, ultimately leading to the disintegration of Russia as a country, as the regions became increasingly culturally assertive and financially autonomous (Khakimov 1993: 16). Sakwa (2008: 244) considered this unlikely, noting Russia's 'great power mentality', and the fact that its pluriculturalism had become one of Russia's intrinsic characteristics. Ethnic federalism has indeed been preserved to this day; it has, however, been weakened and, simultaneously, partially de-ethnified.

From ethnic federalism to civic centralism

Centralisation measures have reined in powerful regional leaders,[66] reducing their autonomy from Moscow. Putin has sought to establish the much-mentioned 'vertical of power', through a hierarchy with the Russian president and his administration at its apex. Federal reforms were elaborated by the Presidential Commission for the Demarcation of Powers between the Federal, Regional and Municipal Levels of Government, formed by Putin in 2001, under the management of (then) Deputy Head of the Presidential Administration Dmitrii Kozak. Some of the reforms were discussed with regional leaders, who secured their partial review;[67] nevertheless, ultimate responsibility for the reforms has rested on the highest echelons of the executive. I focus in this section on the ethnic (de-ethnifying) aspects of the reforms in relation to: a movement from election to appointment of officials, including leaders of ethnic republics; the creation of a dependency of the regions on the central authorities; and the merging of ethnic regions with predominantly Russian ones.

Before Putin's rise to power, Yeltsin's ad hoc bilateral treaties had resulted in the devolution of political and economic powers to the republics (Petrov and Slider 2010), with the creation of a complex web of agreements, and conflicting regional and federal legislation. The elimination of these contradictions was seen as necessary for the viability of the legal system. Putin referred to this process as an aspect of the 'dictatorship of the law', which commanded legal rigour as opposed to a general disregard of (federal) law.[68] Thus, centralisation measures aimed at the creation of uniform rules, transcending the mass of bilateral political negotiations and reconnecting the regions to the centre. Yet the package of measures introduced has also had a profound effect on ethnicity. Putin has moved towards a general, ethnicity-neutral bureaucratisation of the country, using opportunities offered by the super-presidential system foreseen by the 1993 Constitution: its provisions proclaim the president the 'guarantor of the Constitution' (Article 80(2)), with the authority to suspend regional laws contradicting federal legislation (Article 85(2)), and heading a unified executive that encompasses both centre and regions (Article 77(2)).

It should be noted here that dwindling ethnic mobilisation has not been caused exclusively by Putin's rise to power. The leaders of the republics themselves, already under Yeltsin, generally opted for a framework of loyalty – rather than ethnic nationalism – to gain or retain power (Gorenburg 2003). At the time of Yeltsin's bilateral arrangements, the heads of the republics, rather than nationalist leaders, held power; and, while national movements emerged in the early 1990s, in many cases they ultimately faded, or their leaders were co-opted by the regional authorities (Petrov 2004: 219).[69] Yet de-ethnification processes have intensified under Putin, together with other dynamics: the reaffirmation of a system based on patterns of loyalty and informal practices – especially through United Russia[70] – and the bureaucratisation of systems of representation and management, resulting in a deepening democratic deficit. The latter has manifested itself, in particular, through a shift in the concentration of power from the legislative to the executive branch – both at the federal and regional levels – with the consolidation of Putin's vertical structure of power. This type of political system marginalises all forms of political opposition and hampers mobilisation, including that which may be ethnically driven (Giuliano and Gorenburg 2012: 186–187).

A first de-ethnifying factor of centralisation has been the shift from elections to the appointment of regional leaders, with a view to creating a country primarily administered by appointed managers. This has been described by Filippov as: 'remov[ing] excessive politicisation elements from the Russian state system, to replace politicians, which hinder its effective operation, with managers and bureaucrats'.[71]

In 2005 the Russian presidency introduced controls over gubernatorial appointments. The new presidential powers followed an unconstitutional measure of September 2004, when Putin announced that the heads of the subjects of the Federation would be nominated by the president and confirmed in their position (nominally) by the legislature. The move was justified in light of the 2004 Beslan school siege[72] (Lemaître 2006), with Putin asserting that only the unity of the country could combat terrorism.[73] Although powerful leaders of ethnic regions, such as Tatarstan's Mintimer Shaimiev and Bashkortostan's Murtaza Rakhimov, were initially confirmed in their third term as presidents of their republics, in the absence of direct voting their powers became contingent upon the will and imperatives of the federal authorities. During his presidency Medvedev proved willing to remove governors: between May 2008 and October 2010 he replaced 34 regional leaders.[74] Shaimiev and Rakhimov eventually left their positions, in January and July 2010 respectively. One of the respondents, a scholar specialising in Tatar history, said in an interview:

> Shaimiev had political weight. He was independent, even with Putin. He had authority at the federal level, not only in Tatarstan. The current president is in a very different position. They can remove him very easily. He always has this Damocles' sword hanging over him.
>
> [2.7]

Shaimiev's successor, Rustam Minnikhanov, was seen by the respondent as a more pallid figure than the former president of Tatarstan, with a much-reduced level of freedom in representing Tatarstan's (and Tatar) interests.

Following large-scale public protests in late 2011 and early 2012, sparked by accusations of vote rigging during the 2011 Duma elections, the Russian authorities made some concessions, which included the reinstatement of gubernatorial elections in early 2012. Yet subsequent developments have chipped away at the new democratic gains: first, a 'municipal filter' was introduced,[75] and used for the first time in the October 2012 regional elections. The filter requires candidates to have the support of least 5 per cent of their subjects' deputies, and, in the case of independent candidates, to collect signatures of at least 0.5 per cent of the region's population. These regulations clearly reduce the opportunities for opposition candidates to run for elections. Second, legal reform in 2013 introduced the option for the president of Russia to appoint the governor of a particular subject if its legislature decides to cancel direct elections.[76] This measure was justified in light of the volatile political situation of the North Caucasus, by suggesting that gubernatorial elections in the region could exacerbate ethnic tensions.[77] An externally-appointed governor, it was argued, could rise above local inter-ethnic disputes; yet this measure also assures the federal authorities' control over appointments in regions where Kremlin-supported candidates are unpopular. When elections do take place, the Kremlin-backed candidates have tended to win, as, unlike other candidates, they benefit from administrative resources.[78] Third, democratic gains were undercut, in 2014, by a process of reshuffling governors.[79] In six instances between January and May 2014 the resignation of a governor led to the scheduling of early elections (for September 2014).[80] If these governors had completed their terms, elections would have been held in 2015 and 2016, when the federal authorities will be campaigning for the December 2016 Duma elections. As Putin accepted the resignations, he also reappointed the same persons as acting governors pending new elections. This process has been seen as a technique to boost incumbents' chances of victory – given the very short time available to opponents to prepare and conduct an electoral campaign – thereby also assuring loyal supporters in the regions ahead of the 2018 presidential elections.[81] And, when governors are appointed, the Kremlin does not tend to choose from the local political elite, but, as Petrov writes, 'it continues to bring in outsiders, shifting leaders from Yakutsk to Chita, from the Primorye region to Vladimir and from the more northerly Tyumen region to

Stavropol in the south.'[82] This implies a high likelihood that regional leaders will be detached from the needs of their constituency, including the concerns of local minorities.

Loyalty to the centre of power has been further increased through governors' incremental absorption into Putin's 'vertical' through United Russia, the 'party of power'. The opportunity for state officials to join political parties was introduced in 2005, when many governors joined the ranks of United Russia (Isaacs and Whitmore 2014: 705–708). Yet the past few years has seen a need to inject new vitality into the 'vertical': while in July 2013, 77 (out of a total of 83) governors were members of United Russia,[83] the party's control over the political orientation of governors had become more precarious.[84] The party's popularity was lower in the period 2011–2013 than in the second half of the preceding decade,[85] while the October 2012 gubernatorial elections resulted in some United Russia victories being disputed in court following accusations of falsification (in Bryansk and Ryazan regions).[86] Measures to strengthen the 'vertical' might further have been triggered by a desire to contain political dissent so as to avoid large-scale demonstrations and a political crisis such as that which shook the Ukrainian political leadership in 2013–2014. Thus, overall, the powers of the governors have been curtailed and subordinated to United Russia's own needs and priorities, while governors themselves have been increasingly incorporated into the party machinery (Slider 2010).

The most tangible manifestation of the regional leaders' lower status has been their exclusion from the Federation Council, the Russian Parliament's upper chamber. Since legal reform in 2000, regional leaders may only participate in the proceedings of the Federation Council indirectly through representatives.[87] The Federation Council comprises two representatives from each of the country's subjects: one from the legislature and one from the executive branch.[88] In the first case, the representative is a member of the regional duma, and is selected by the duma itself – although informal practices can infiltrate the system, when candidates are 'recommended' by the presidential administration (Remington 2003: 674). The second representative is selected by the governor,[89] who is generally Kremlin backed, if not directly appointed by the president of Russia. This creates a 'circular flow of power', continuously reinforcing the presidential power, in the Federation Council – a body that should act as counterweight to the executive (Sakwa 2008: 283).

The new Federation Council has been effectively de-ethnified as its members, in many cases, have no direct connection with the regions they represent; they have tended to come from Moscow or St Petersburg (Alexander 2004). Their background, connections and geographical location mean that they are, in principle, well placed to lobby central structures in favour of the regions. However, Alexander argues that the selection of non-titular representatives undermines the republics' distinct ethnic bases:

Not only will these representatives be personally removed from the issues of concerns to titular nationalities and thus less likely to fight for these issues, but their choice further indicates to the center that ethnic issues have become less potent in Russian politics. [This] threaten[s] to weaken the long-term viability of the ethnic republics as separate entities.

(Ibid.: 255–256)

The law prescribes, among the conditions for membership of the Federation Council, permanent residency in the relevant subject of the Federation for five years.[90] However, this requirement is waived when the candidate is already a member of the Federation Council, and when he/she is a member of the federal Duma, holds public office or a position in the civil service of the relevant subject, or did so in the five years preceding his/her nomination. Minority representatives have voiced the opinion that the appointment (rather than elections) of governors, and the absence of a direct connection between the governors and those they represent, have led to less attention being devoted to minority concerns in the Federation Council.[91]

In 2000, following their exclusion from the Federation Council, a new body was created for governors: the State Council.[92] The latter is essentially a consultative body, in which governors have been stripped of the veto power formerly enjoyed in the Federation Council. The change has reduced the governors' impact on decision-making, including on national issues and cultural choices. The resulting movement towards the de-ethnification of the regions was reiterated by Putin in his 2012 state of the nation address, when he said, with reference to the ethnic republics: 'We will not allow the emergence of closed ethnic enclaves in Russia, with their informal jurisdiction existing outside the country's common legal and cultural norms and disdainfully disregarding the accepted standards, laws and regulations.'[93]

The 'vertical' reaches down to localities within subjects of the Federation. The 2003 Law 'On Local Self-Government',[94] rather than empowering and enhancing the autonomy of localities, has primarily transferred their dependence from the regional authorities to the federal centre. Lankina described this as 'facilitating the extension of Putin's centralizing "power vertical" further down into the grass roots' (Lankina 2005: 146). Following the law's adoption, local government can be penalised by the federal centre for a multitude of reasons, including the accumulation of debts[95] and being a 'threat to Russia's territorial integrity, national security, [or] defence potential'.[96] Lankina adds: 'Ideas normally associated with decentralization, such as developing civil society, respecting the diversity of local contexts, and increasing popular participation and initiative in local decision making, receive little attention in the law' (ibid.: 165). Bowring (2010a) agrees that the Law 'On Local Self-Government' neglects the issue of representation of national minorities.[97] Hahn (2008) further stresses that the non-inclusive process of adoption of this law means that it could be appropriated by those networks that have an interest in strengthening the power vertical.

As for governors, the local administration has seen a movement from election to appointment. Regional leaders have continued to insist on the direct appointment of mayors so as to select politically-neutral 'professionals', effectively (pliant) managers, rather than politicians (Lankina 2005: 167).[98] The Kozak Commission, established in 2001 to formulate amendments to the Law 'On Local Self-Government', similarly stressed the need to eliminate the governor–mayor cleavage, in practice by appointing bureaucrats – whose activities are aligned with those of the head of a region, the presidential envoy and, ultimately, the presidential administration. Since 2003, various cities have introduced 'city managers', appointed civil servants who can marginalise, or in fact replace, mayors; many such cities have also directly abolished popular mayor elections. Along with political battles, these dynamics exclude systems of checks and balances, as well as minority representation (Lankina 2005: 169–170). The Kremlin's control, particularly in large urban areas, means that mayors and city managers are answerable to governors rather than their constituency.[99] Mayors and governors can also be removed – including under fabricated charges – for having run (and won) against United Russia candidates, or pressured into resignation for strategic reasons. Membership of United Russia is no guarantee of protection when the objective is, as Petrov puts it, 'shaking off unnecessary deadweight'.[100] Russia's power structure minimises options to create decentralised settings that could provide autonomy, through self-government, to minorities in decision-making on cultural matters. Those minority groups likely to be particularly affected by the paucity of opportunities for participation are non-titular minorities, or titular minority groups residing outside 'their' republics.

Dependency on the centre and regional mergers

A supplementary de-ethnifying factor has been the creation of forms of dependency of the regions on the centre. In May 2000 the subjects of the Russian Federation were grouped into seven (later eight) presidential okrugs,[101] and placed under the supervision of presidential envoys. The branches of the main federal agencies (the General Prosecutor's Office, the Federal Security Service, the Ministry of Interior and the Tax Inspectorate) were affiliated to the okrugs themselves rather than the regional authorities, thereby redirecting their loyalty to the centre (Melvin 2007: 209). Envoys and their 'super-regions' have created a new intermediary, bureaucratic layer in the communication flow between regions and the centre; and, despite claims of greater accountability, the new structure is excluded from public scrutiny, with the concentration of powers on regional matters being kept within the presidential administration via the envoys (Cashaback 2003: 8, 19; Baev 2005).

Meanwhile, new legislation has standardised the taxation system across the Federation. A form of 'fiscal federalism' was introduced under Putin, by which the majority of the regions' revenues have been claimed by the centre, to be later redistributed (Sakwa 2008: 274). Since the mid-2000s, Moscow has increased the collection of wealth from the regions, with 65 per cent of all revenues being allocated to the federal budget, and the remaining 35 per cent being shared by all subjects and municipalities. This, together with the regions' debt, causes widespread poverty and dependency on the centre;[102] as noted in the 2012 state of the nation address, only ten of Russia's 83 subjects are 'donors' that contribute to the federal budget, while the others are recipients of federal funds[103] – with Moscow the ultimate decision-maker in the redistribution of funds (Melvin 2007: 210; see also Hanson 2005). Not only are the poorer, heavily subsidised regions relying on the centre for funds, but so are the wealth-producing regions, as they await the re-allocation of some of that same wealth they have generated. Respondents in Tatarstan argued that the taxation system had reduced autonomy in respect of available choices to preserve their cultural distinctiveness [2.7; 4.7]. One respondent, a political analyst in Moscow, noted that, by contrast, poorer regions perceive the federal centre as a 'kind uncle' that assists them; at the same time, the absence of economic self-sufficiency disempowers them, by adversely affecting these regions' degree of assertiveness and autonomy [2.17].

Mergers of predominantly Russian regions with ethnicity-based autonomous okrugs are another example of homogenisation processes that involve the reduction of regional autonomy through top-down, non-consultative measures. Between 2005 and 2008 there were five mergers, which affected six small ethnic regions: Komi-Permyak autonomous okrug (AO), Evenk AO, Taimyr AO, Koryak AO, Ust-Orda Buryat AO and Agin Buryat AO.[104] The mergers, enabled by legislation adopted in 2001,[105] aimed at 'equalizing the levels of socio-economic development' and at the 'optimization of regional management, infrastructure and resources'.[106] The Russian government assured that the mergers 'did not affect the position of national minorities in the new administrative and territorial entities', as guarantees to the rights of minorities, including the preservation of their cultural and linguistic distinctiveness, were clearly stated in regional laws on the mergers.[107] The former 'autonomous okrugs', now just called 'okrugs', in principle retain a 'special status'; yet in practice this status is devoid of legal meaning under Russian law (Oracheva and Osipov 2010). The reduction in the number of subjects of the Federation seems to reflect a drive to resuscitate the (non-ethnic) administrative units of pre-revolutionary Russia.[108] Often dismissed as unrealistic, this idea has intermittently resurfaced. Preoccupied with the power of the governors elected in 1996–1997, many of whom were in opposition, Yeltsin also considered reducing the number of subjects from a total of 89 (in 1996) to 24 (Reddaway 2004: 11).[109] Similarly, a number of governors, presidential envoys and members of the state Duma have publicly stated that they were in favour of the reduction of administrative units of the Federation.[110] In late 2010, the newspaper *Vedomosti* reported on a possible plan to replace Russia's 83 regions with 20 large 'agglomerations' around Russia's main cities.[111] Even more radical proposals advocated the slashing of regions down to between eight and ten territories (Mitin 2008: 52).

Giving the level of entrenchment of ethnic federalism in Russia's society, the abolition of ethnic republics remains a remote possibility. In 1993 the (then) Minister of Nationalities Valerii Tishkov warned of the likelihood of violence if ethnic territorial units were eliminated (Tishkov 1993: 18). The regions' territorial arrangements are unlikely to be abandoned, as they are not only in the interest of the titular nationalities but also of ethnic Russians residing in the republics, who wish to retain some control over local resources (Hagendoom *et al.* 2008; see also Oversloot 2007; 2013). Yet the mergers are an uncomfortable precedent for many nationalities. Although referenda appear to have provided the democratic and legal bases for the mergers,[112] opposition to amalgamation has surfaced (Artobolevskii *et al.* 2010; Bowring 2010b).[113] One can take as an example the merger of Irkutsk oblast with (former) Ust-Orda Buryat AO. The central government strove to convince the okrug's residents of the financial gains to be reaped from the merger, while strongly hinting that the region could not survive without federal support. The Irkutsk administration committed to maintaining a special status for the post-merger okrug, along with cultural and social programmes for Buryats. The analysis of the impact of this and other amalgamations by the Institute of Contemporary Development revealed that these promises have, overall, not been kept (Artobolevskii *et al.* 2010), while the Moscow Helsinki Group documented voting irregularities during the 2006 referendum: these included strong incentives, and even threats, to induce voting in favour of the merger among the local population.[114] The effect of the 'vertical' was also discernible in the processes leading to the merger: the governor of Irkutsk oblast, Boris Govorin, who had promoted the union of Irkutsk oblast with Ust-Orda Buryat AO, was himself a product of Putin's 'vertical', having been appointed by the president (ibid.). His appointment, and his support for the project, enabled the merger to take place after a deadlock of three years.[115]

Although the Russian government has justified the restructuring of the Federation in terms of promotion of greater equality in socio-economic development,[116] standardisation through de-federalisation has not necessarily resolved the country's fragmentation and the utilitarian approach to its management (Sakwa 2004: 239). 'Selected co-operation' with regions of 'strategic importance' has continued (Chebankova 2007: 289). Meanwhile, the 'dictatorship of the law' did not prevent Putin (in 2004) unconstitutionally imposing a new form of presidential appointment of governors, which contradicts the principles of federalism and separation of powers enshrined in the Russian Constitution.[117] The prevalence of the federal centre in many spheres of public life in the regions, regulated by non-transparent processes, points to an absence of 'federal values' (ibid.: 295–299): Russia does not have the flexibility of a form of federalism that is 'dynamic' and in which 'separate political communities enter into arrangements for working out solutions, adopting joint policies, and making joint decisions on joint problems' (Friedrich 1968: 7). Rather, Petrov summarises the state of Russian federalism in this way:

> What is called federalism in Russia is a mixture of federal features along with a weak, centralized, unitary state, in which the central is opposed by quasi-democratic, semi-authoritarian, regional elites. Like Russian democracy, Russian federalism has many elements that are decorative rather than substantive and that appear similar to their Western analogues but have a different essence.
>
> (Petrov 2004: 213)

The 'spirit of federalism' is still missing, so that Russia resembles a centralised state rather than a federation; as argued by Artobolevskii *et al.* (2010: 174), it is 'de jure a federation (with independent local self-government), de facto a centralised state (with a vertical of power)'.

Conclusion

A patriotic discourse has reasserted Russianness, while the reformed federal structure has reduced opportunities for participation in decision-making at the regional and local level, marginalising local concerns – including those of ethnic republics and minority groups. The Russian government has spoken in favour of a policy of de-ethnification, with a view to promoting a civic form of nationalism; yet Russia's 'civic' identity has acquired an ethnic dimension by incorporating elements of Russianness – particularly in the shape of the Russian language, history and symbolism – leading to a blurring of the distinction between *rossiisskii* and *russkii*. Meanwhile, an essentialist approach to ethnicity complicates the transition to an all-inclusive (civic) identity that can both accommodate ethnic attributes and forge a civic consciousness for Russia's disparate groups. Exclusive identities, placed antagonistically to each other, further impede the development of overarching forms of identification, which may encompass *plural* identities.

Russia's pursuit of a 'civic' (Russian) identity can lead to its *replacing*, rather than *adding to*, minority identities. It results in an incremental devaluation of ethnic identities, with the exception of Russian culture, as well as being at odds with official pronouncements on Russia's multi-ethnicity. The motivating factor for increased uniformity is not necessarily the suppression of diversity with Russian neo-imperialistic undertones, but rather the strengthening of the state.[118] Still, this project could be interpreted as 'a disguised and embellished version of the old Soviet rhetoric of the fusion of all nations into a non-national Soviet nation' (Codagnone and Filippov 2000: 283). It further carries the risk of exacerbating the marginalisation of minority groups. Thus, in response to Russian nationalism, some persons belonging to minorities tend to place themselves antagonistically to it: those who wish to maintain their cultural distinctiveness often resort to a defensive approach inasmuch as it aims at self-preservation, particularly when facing homogenising forces or xenophobia – dynamics that can create or deepen multiple ruptures within Russian society.

In the area of federalism, the effect of the 'power vertical' has been a reduction of checks and balances, with the regions becoming part of a more rigid, technocratic state. Putin's *vertikal'* has eroded regional autonomy and weakened democratic processes through the convergence of powers at the centre. Undemocratic developments are particularly evident in the abolition of elections of regional leaders and voting irregularities in referenda. The reforms have excluded key actors, such as civil society, from decision-making (Hahn 2001; Taylor 2005), causing a dissonance between state institutions and the citizenry; they have further reduced opportunities for 'horizontal accountability' (Hashim

2005: 42–43), and deepened the democratic deficit. One could argue that some aspects of the federal reforms have become a force for good in Russia. The rule of law is hardly possible in a country with a mass of contradictory laws, where regional leaders may abuse their powers for personal gain. Yet reform processes have also caused a dilution of ethnic pluralism, together with a reduction of the democratic content of the Federation. They have further decreased the potential for the application of the domestic and international legal principles on minority rights, and their ability to prevent, or contain, homogenising dynamics.

The Russian leadership tends to justify a drive for the country's unity by referring to the imperative need for stability. Indeed, the Tatars who called for use of the Latin – rather than Cyrillic – alphabet in Tatar-language texts have been associated with separatism and described as a 'threat to national security'.[119] Perceptions of ethnic and cultural diversity, and ideas about the potential menace they pose, are much affected by the education system, which can contribute to instilling, or eroding, respect and appreciation of diversity. Thus it is Russia's education system that is examined in the next chapter, exposing similar tendencies towards uniformity and standardised cultural codes.

Notes

1 Some sections of this chapter were published in an article in the *Journal on Ethnopolitics and Minority Issues in Europe* ('Homogenisation and the 'New Russian Citizen': A Road to Stability or Ethnic Tensions?', 10(1), 2011: 59–93).

2 In 1990 and 1991 most of the republics of the RSFSR declared their sovereignty, in a phenomenon commonly known as the 'parade of sovereignties'.

3 With some regions enjoying greater economic power and control over resources than others.

4 Calls for devolution during this period were not only driven by ethnic motives, but also by political ones. Whatever the underlying reasons, ethnicity became a factor of mobilisation in multiple regions (Giuliano 2011; Gorenburg 2003).

5 A power-sharing treaty was signed two years later, in 1994. The only other republic that refused to sign the Federation Treaty was Chechnya.

6 Petrov, N. 17 December 2012. 'Putin and the Regions', *The Moscow Times*. On 'fiscal federalism' see also p. 113 in this chapter ('Dependency on the centre and regional mergers'). With reference to Tatarstan, see also Sharafutdinova (2003: 624–625).

7 Baev (2005: 336) further argues that the goal of counter-terrorism is not victory against terrorism, but rather enhanced statism: counter-terrorism thus becomes the means towards this objective.

8 *Nezavisimaya Gazeta*, 31 December 1999. 'Vladimir Putin: Rossiya na Rubezhe Tysyacheletiya' [Vladimir Putin: Russia on the Eve of the Millenium], www.ng.ru/politics/1999–12–30/4_millenium.html (accessed 13 October 2013). See also Duncan (2007).

9 *RIA Novosti*, 17 July 2003. 'Patriotism Dolzhen Stat' Ob'edinyayushchei Ideologiei Rossii – Vladimir Putin' [Patriotism Should Become Russia's Unifying Ideology – Vladimir Putin], http://ria.ru/politics/20030717/408317.html (accessed February 2015).

10 No. 1666, 19 December 2012.

11 *First Channel*, 19 December 2002. 'Razgovor s Rossiei: Stenogramma "Priamoi Linii s Prezidentom Rossiiskoi Federatsii V.V. Putinym"' [A Conversation with

Russia: Stenographic Report of "Direct Line with the President of the Russia Federation V.V. Putin"].

12 Tishkov, V. 31–5–2011. 'XXI Vek Priznaet Prava Bol'shinstva' [The 21st Century Recognises the Rights of the Majority], *Russkii Zhurnal*.

13 'Comments of the Government of the Russian Federation on the Second Opinion of the Advisory Committee on the Implementation of the Framework Convention for the Protection of National Minorities by the Russian Federation', GVT/COM/ II(2006)006, 11 October 2006, p. 2.

14 ACFC, (Third) Report submitted by the Russian Federation, 9 April 2010, ACFC/ SR/III(2010)005, pp. 6–7.

15 Preamble and Article 3(1).

16 See Chapter 2.

17 See Chapter 2.

18 Sakwa (2011a) has instead linked Russia's 'civilisational' approach primarily to cultural values, its self-representation as a great power and its positioning vis-à-vis 'the international'.

19 Particularly in 'trouble spots' such as South Ossetia, Abkhazia and Transnistria.

20 Presidential Decree No. 909, 15 June 1996.

21 See note 10.

22 President of Russia, Address to the National Assembly of the Russian Federation, 12 December 2012, http://eng.kremlin.ru/transcripts/4739 (accessed 24 September 2014).

23 Similarly, the Preamble of Law 'On Freedom of Conscience and on Religious Associations' (No. 125-FZ, 26 September 1997) on the one hand refers to four religions (Christianity, Islam, Judaism and Buddhism) as 'an inalienable part of the historical heritage of the peoples of Russia'; on the other, it states that the Federal Assembly of the Russian Federation 'recognis[es] the special role of Orthodox Christianity in the history of Russia, in the development of its spirituality and culture'.

24 See p. 107 in this chapter ('De-federalisation as de-ethnification').

25 See Chapter 2.

26 According to a 2013 survey by the Levada Center, 66 per cent of Russians overall agreed with the slogan 'Russia for the Russians', and 71 per cent with 'Stop Feeding the Caucasus'. See Levada Center, 'Rossiyane o Migratsii i Mezhnatsional'noi Napryazhennosti' [Russians about Migrations and Inter-ethnic Tensions], 5 November 2013, www.levada.ru/05–11–2013/rossiyane-o-migratsii-i-mezhnatsionalnoi-napryazhennosti (accessed 5 October 2014). The survey's participants were 1,603 persons from 45 regions of the country, from both urban and rural areas.

27 See p. 102 on this ('Enhancing Russianness').

28 According to the last census, in 2010 there were 11.2 million people in Russia who were born outside country, and 865,000 foreigners who were permanent residents. Data from 2013, compiled by the UN Department of Economic and Social Affairs (UN-DESA), show that Russia, with 11 million migrants, was the second recipient of international migrants worldwide after the United States (UN-DESA, '232 Million International Migrants Living Abroad Worldwide – New UN Global Migration Statistics Reveal', 11 September 2013, http://esa.un.org/unmigration/wall-chart2013.htm, accessed 15 January 2015). Russia's population decline (from 148.7 million recorded in 1991 to 142.9 million in the 2010 census) has created a reliance on foreign labour, although much of the workforce has not been legalised and resides in Russia in precarious conditions.

29 This is reminiscent of Bromley's definition of an *ethnos*, as possessing a particular 'psyche' (see Chapter 2).

30 See also Chapter 6 on the menace of instability as justification for uniformity in the education sphere.

31 From de Swaan's (2001) differentiation between: dominant languages within a region ('central languages'); dominant languages *across regions* ('supercentral languages'); and dominant language(s) at the *global* level ('hypercentral language') – currently the case of English.

32 Resolution of the Government of the Russian Federation 'On the Federal Programme "Russian Language" for the Years 2002–2005' (No. 483, 27 June 2001).

33 No. 53-FZ, 1 June 2005.

34 See note 10.

35 Speech by V. Putin, Meeting of the Council on Inter-ethnic Relations of the President of the Russian Federation, 19 February 2013, http://kremlin.ru/transcripts/17536/work (accessed 3 November 2014).

36 Ibid.

37 The programme was adopted on 22 February 2001 by the Collegium of the Ministry of Education of the Republic of Tatarstan. More recently, Tatarstan adopted the Law 'On the Use of the Tatar Language as State Language of the Republic of Tatarstan' (No. 1-ZRT, 12 January 2013). The law provides for the right of citizens to access education in Tatar language, and to receive information in Tatar from the state organs and the media (Article 2). Legal guarantees are also included Tatarstan's Law 'On the State Languages of the Republic of Tatarstan and Other Languages in the Republic of Tatarstan' (No. 1560-XII, 8 July 1992).

38 For example, in 2000, by Head of the Central Election Commission Aleksandr Veshnyakov. It is also indicative that in 2000 the Prosecutor of Khakassia argued that the Khakas Constitution should refer to 'Russian and Khakas languages' as the republic's official languages, rather than 'Khakas and Russian languages' (Hahn 2001: 513).

39 See Chapter 4.

40 These include multiple versions of a language: for example, four versions of Karelian, classified as separate languages.

41 Most of the languages recognised as co-official in the republics, together with Russian, have been found to be under threat: from 'vulnerable' (Adige, Avar, Bashkir, Chechen, Kabard-Cherkess, Chuvash, Dargwa, Ingush, Kumyk, Lak, Lezgian, Ossetian, Tabasaran, Tuvan, Yakut), to 'definitely endangered' (Abaza, Avar, Agul, Erzya, Kalmyk, Karelian, Khakas, Komi, Moksha, Nogai, Rutul, Tsakhur, Udmurt), to 'severely endangered' (Altai, Buryat, Mari). See Moseley (2010).

42 ECRML, Explanatory Report, Point 2.

43 The Latin alphabet was introduced for Tatar in 1927. A conversion to Cyrillic took place in 1939–1940 (Grenoble 2003: 70).

44 No. 1807-I, 25 October 1991. Amendments were introduced by Law No. 165-FZ, 11 December 2002.

45 Article 3(6) of the amended law.

46 See Chapter 4.

47 Law (Republic of Tatarstan) 'On the Restoration of the Tatar Alphabet on the Basis of the Latin Script' (No. 2352, 15 September 1999). This law was later repealed through Law No. 5-ZRT, 12 January 2013. That Tatar is written in the Cyrillic alphabet is further stated in another law, adopted on the same day: Law 'On the Use of the Tatar Language as State Language of the Republic of Tatarstan' (see note 37).

48 Indeed, commentators have argued that script is not only part of a language, but is itself linked to a group's identity (see for example Ramaga 1992b: 427).

49 On discourses around the 'Great Patriotic War', see Kangaspuro and Lassila (2012).

50 Three federal constitutional laws were adopted on 25 December 2000, on the Russian flag, anthem and emblem: Law 'On the State Flag of the Russian Federation' (No. 1-FKZ); Law 'On the State Emblem of the Russian Federation' (No. 2-FKZ); and Law 'On the State Anthem of the Russian Federation' (No. 3-FKZ).

51 So as to eliminate direct references to Communism (Laruelle 2009a: 156). The new version of the anthem was approved by presidential Decree 'On the Text of the State Anthem of the Russian Federation' (No. 2110, 30 December 2000).

52 Address to the National Assembly, 12 December 2012 (see note 22).

53 On this, see Munro (2006). At the same time, under Putin the section of the population subscribing to Communist political views has decreased (ibid.: 307).

54 A committee was established by presidential decree in 2009 to organise the celebrations through a series of events (Decree 'On the Celebration of 1000 Years of Unity of the Mordovian People with the Peoples of the Russian State', No. 46, 11 January 2009). See also www.mordva1000.ru/ (accessed 4 November 2014).

55 Many of the grievances were linked to new policies on minority education, examined in Chapter 6.

56 An example cited by some respondents was that of the 'language nest' nurseries, which provide full immersion into a minority language, and that have faced obstacles to their activities in Russia. On the 'language nest' pre-school education in Karelia, see Chapters 4 and 6.

57 For example, a Muslim respondent, a Tatar academic from Kazan, observed that (what he saw as) Putin's special relationship with the Russian Orthodox Patriarch had implicitly marginalised other religious denominations in the country. He further referred to what he perceived as Russia's 'institutionalised Islamophobia' [2.10].

58 In the sense of Article 6(1) FCNM, which reads:

> The Parties shall encourage a spirit of tolerance and *intercultural dialogue* and take effective measures to promote mutual respect and understanding and co-operation among all persons living on their territory, irrespective of those persons' ethnic, cultural, linguistic or religious identity, in particular in the fields of education, culture and the media [italics added].

59 Article 5(1) FCNM reads: 'The Parties undertake to promote the conditions necessary for persons belonging to national minorities to maintain and develop their culture, and to preserve the essential elements of their identity, namely their religion, language, traditions and cultural heritage.'

60 ACFC, (Third) Report submitted by the Russian Federation (see note 14), pp. 30–43.

61 Additionally, some academics and representatives of human rights NGOs referred to the superficiality of these programmes [1.5.1; 1.5.7; 1.5.9; 2.14; 2.16; 2.19]. See also Chapter 7 on the issue of 'folklorisation'.

62 ACFC, (Third) Opinion on the Russian Federation, 24 November 2011, ACFC/OP/III(2011)010, §66.

63 Ibid.

64 ACFC, (Second) Opinion on the Russian Federation, 2 May 2007, ACFC/OP/II(2006)004, §108.

65 Ibid, §108–110.

66 These are usually referred to as 'governors'. Leaders of ethnic republics have generally been called 'presidents' of republics; however, a 2010 law required the republics' leaders to discontinue the use of the title 'president' by 1 January 2015, to replace it with a generic title such as 'head' of republic (Law 'On the Amendment of Article 18 of the Federal Law "On General Principles of the Organisation of Legal (Representative) and Executive Organs of the State Power of the Subjects of the Russian Federation"', No. 406-FZ, 28 December 2010). Article 1 states that the title of a republic's leader 'cannot contain the same words or expressions that constitute the title of the head of state – the president of the Russian Federation'. In this book I use the expression 'governor', 'regional leader' or 'head' of republic; I use the term 'president' with reference to the period before the introduction of the obligation for regional leaders to switch to a different title.

67 Tsvetkova, M. and Shishkunova, E. 21 November 2002. 'Gubernatorov Budut Snimat' Izyashchno' [Governors Will Be Overthrown Delicately], *Gazeta.ru.*

68 The expression 'dictatorship of the law' was first used by Putin in his 2000 state of the nation address (President of Russia, Annual Address to the Federal Assembly of the Russian Federation, 8 July 2000. http://archive.kremlin.ru/eng/speeches/2000/07/08/0000_type70029type82912_70658.shtml, accessed 10 October 2014). The process of harmonisation of the regional and federal legislation aimed to address the fragmentation of the Russian legal space (Hyde 2001). By 2002, these efforts had brought nearly all 6,000 regional laws, which had been found to contradict federal legislation, into line with it. By April 2002, 22 of the 42 bilateral agreements between the centre and the subjects had been abolished, an additional 11 were abrogated in 2003, and the rest were declared null by 2005 (Mitin 2008: 58).

69 As Petrov (2004: 219) puts it: 'Many regional authorities came to power on the wave of nationalist movements, but then distanced themselves from national radicals and took control of national congresses.'

70 On United Russia, see Chapter 9.

71 Filippov, Y. 29 October 2004. 'State Duma Ponders Russia's Future', *RIA Novosti.*

72 On 1 September 2004 Islamic militants took hostage over 1,100 people in a school in Beslan (North Ossetia), demanding the withdrawal of Russian troops from Chechnya. The fighting between the militants and the Russian security forces led to the death of 334 people.

73 Speech at the Enlarged Government Meeting with the Government and Heads of the Regions, 13 September 2004, http://archive.kremlin.ru/eng/speeches/2004/09/13/0000_type82912type82913_76667.shtml (accessed 3 October 2014).

74 *Vedomosti*, 30 September 2010. 'Medvedev i Voevody' [Medvedev and Regional Leaders].

75 *RIA Novosti*, 29 June 2012. 'Stolichnaya Privilegiya: v Moskve Razresheno Samovydvizhenie Glavy Regiona' [Capital Privilege: Moscow Allows the Self-appointment of Heads of Regions], http://ria.ru/politics/20120629/688113748.html (accessed 24 October 2014).

76 In this case the president appoints one of up to three candidates selected by the regional legislature.

77 *Reuters*, 2 April 2013, 'Putin Signs Law to Allow Him to Pick Russian Governors'. www.reuters.com/article/2013/04/02/us-russia-elections-idUSBRE9310GR20130402 (accessed 22 October 2014); Winning, A. 24 March 2013. 'In Reversal, Duma Limits Gubernatorial Elections', *The Moscow Times.*

78 Petrov, N. 15 October 2013. 'Open Season on Governors', *The Moscow Times.*

79 Brennan, C. 23 April 2014. 'Tightening of Kremlin Control Seen in Governor Dismissals', *The Moscow Times.*

80 *The Moscow Times*, 5 May 2014. 'Putin Approves Murmansk Governor's Resignation in Lead Up to Early Elections'. Thirty governors ran in the regional elections of 14 September 2014, and all were reconfirmed in their posts.

81 Tétrault-Farber, G. 5 June 2014. 'St. Petersburg Governor Resignation Could Be Tactical Move, Analyst Says', *The Moscow Times.*

82 Petrov, *The Moscow Times* (note 78).

83 As reported in: *RIA Novosti*, 2 July 2012. 'Glavy Subektov Rossiiskoy Federatsii' [Heads of the Subjects of the Russian Federation], http://ria.ru/infografika/20120702/689874012.html (accessed 24 October 2014).

84 Earle, J. 23 January 2013. 'Bill to Limit Gubernatorial Elections Approved', *The Moscow Times.*

85 Standing at 64.3 per cent in 2007, and averaging 45 per cent in 2012–2013. Russian Public Opinion Research Center (VTsIOM), 27 March 2014. 'Reiting Putina: Novaya Vysota' [Putin's Ratings: A New Height], http://wciom.ru/index.php?id=268&uid=114759 (accessed 24 October 2014). See also Chapter 9.

86 Winning, A. 24 March 2013. 'In Reversal, Duma Limits Gubernatorial Elections', *The Moscow Times.*

87 Law 'On the Order of the Formation of the Federal Federation Council' (No. 113-FZ, 5 August 2000).

88 Article 95(2) of the Constitution.

89 See Articles 2(2), 3 and 4 of Law 'On the Order of Formation of the Council of the Federation of the Federal Assembly of the Russian Federation' (No. 229-FZ, 3 December 2012). This law repealed Law 113-FZ of 2000 (see note 87).

90 Ibid, Article 2(1) and (3).

91 ACFC, (Third) Opinion on the Russian Federation (see note 62), §208.

92 Presidential Decree 'On the State Council of the Russian Federation' (No. 1602, 1 September 2000).

93 Address to the National Assembly, 12 December 2012 (note 22).

94 The full name is Law 'On the General Principles of the Organisation of Local Self-Government in the Russian Federation' (No. 131-FZ, 6 October 2003). Provisions on local self-government are also found in Articles 12 and 130 of the Russian Constitution.

95 Article 75(1)(2) of the Law 'On Local Self-Government'. In this case the state can temporarily take over the functions of the institutions of local self-government.

96 Article 74(1)(2) of the Law 'On Local Self-Government'. In this case the law fore-sees the removal of the head of the municipality or the mayor from his/her position.

97 Despite the attempt by Russian officials to bring Russian legislation on local government into line with the European Charter of Local Self-Government, ratified by Russia in 1998.

98 For example, former governor of Sverdlovsk oblast (1995–2009) Eduard Rossel stated that elected mayors are 'engrossed in politics, rather than pursuing purely managerial activities' (cited in Lankina 2005: 162).

99 Ryzhkov, V. 3 March 2014. 'No Real Elections in Regions', *The Moscow Times*; Brennan, C. 19 May 2014. 'Russians Prefer Direct Mayoral Elections, Poll Says', *The Moscow Times.*

100 Petrov, N. 18 November 2013. 'Mayors Beware', *The Moscow Times.*

101 Seven districts were established by presidential Decree 'On the Envoy of the President of the Russian Federation in a Federal Okrug' (No. 849, 13 May 2000). The number of districts was increased to eight in January 2010, when the North Caucasus Federal Okrug was separated from the Southern Federal Okrug.

102 Other factors contributing to poverty in the regions are corruption, the costs of state bureaucracy, and the mismanagement of public funds. Ryzhkov, V. 12 August 2014. 'Why the Regions Hate Moscow', *The Moscow Times.*

103 Petrov, *The Moscow Times* (see note 6).

104 The new subjects are: Perm krai (resulting from the merger of Perm oblast and Komi-Permyak AO), Krasnoyarsk krai (Krasnoyarsk krai, Evenk AO and Taimyr AO), Kamchatka krai (Kamchatka oblast and Koryak AO), Irkutsk oblast (Irkutsk oblast and Ust-Orda Buryat AO), Zabaikalskii krai (Chita oblast and Agin Buryat AO).

105 Federal Constitutional Law 'On the Procedure of Introducing a New Subject in the Russian Federation' (No. 6-FKZ, 17 December 2001).

106 ACFC, (Third) Report submitted by the Russian Federation (see note 14), p. 98.

107 Ibid, p. 99.

108 Eight provinces under Peter the Great, 40 under Catherine the Great.

109 See also Netreba, T. and Tseplyaev, V. 12 April 2006. 'Natsional'nye Regiony – "Pod Nozh?"' [Are the National Regions "Under the Knife?"], *Argumenty i Fakty.*

110 Chirkin, D. 25 March 2002. 'Vladimir Putin – Russia's New Ivan Kalita. The Federation Subjects to Be Consolidated', *Pravda*, http://english.pravda.ru/news/russia/25–03–2002/36185–0/ (accessed 22 October 2014).

111 Pis'mennaya, Y. and Kostenko, N. 16 December 2010. 'Rossiyane Budut Zhit' ne v 83 Regionakh, kak Seichas, a v 20 Aglomeratsiyakh, gde Kontsentriruyutstya Resursy' [Russians will Live Not in 83 Regions, but in 20 Agglomerations, where Resources are Concentrated], *Vedomosti.*

112 Article 11 of Law No. 6-FKZ (note 105) states that the creation of a new subject has to follow a referendum.

113 See also Dmitriyev, I. 30 March 2007. 'Federal Misalliance Robbing Peter to Pay Paul', *The Moscow News.*

114 Moscow Helsinki Group, 'On Violations Committed in the Course of Organising and Carrying out Referendum on Merging Irkutsk Region and Ust-Ordynski Buryat-skyi Autonomous District', 2006.

115 Yasmann, V. 21 April 2006. 'Analysis: Is the Kremlin Looking to Dissolve Ethnic Republics?' *Radio Free Europe/Radio Liberty*, www.rferl.org/content/article/1067861.html (accessed 23 March 2014). An ethnic Buryat defined the merger of the two regions 'an unnecessary step towards Russian integration'. Private communication with the author, 24 February 2011.

116 ACFC, (Third) Report submitted by the Russian Federation (see note 14), p. 98.

117 See p. 108 ('From ethnic federalism to civic centralism').

118 In line with the principle of *gosudarstvennichestvo* (a strong Russian state).

119 For example, in a report presented before the Russian Parliament, cited in Saiga-nova, S. 8 February 2001. 'Turki Royut pod Russiyu cherez Tatarstan' [Turks Get into Russia through Tatarstan], *Vremya i Den'gi.*

6 Interculturalism or acculturation?

The education system[1]

Education has a pivotal role in the preservation or dilution of a country's cultural diversity. Minority-friendly policies in the education system include the teaching of minority languages, history, cultures and religions, and the use of minority languages as languages of instruction. Russia has a long tradition of education in minority languages, particularly through 'national schools' designed for non-Russian nationalities, established during the Soviet period. However, although Russia preserves high levels of diversity in its education system, homogenising trends are clearly detectable. These tendencies are caused by a combination of factors examined in this chapter: reform of the education system since the 2000s, which has affected the teaching of minority languages and cultures; and the incorporation of patriotic narratives into education programmes.

Russia is bound by the FCNM's Article 12 (on state parties' responsibility to foster the knowledge of cultures and languages of minorities and the majority) and Article 14 (on the right to learn one's minority language).[2] Where minority rights intersect education rights, there are two concomitant functions for the education system: providing minorities with the opportunity to receive a particular type of education (i.e. in a minority language) but also guaranteeing members of the *majority* an education that reflects society's pluralism. This form of inter-culturalism – promoting mutual knowledge and understanding – can only be achieved when states embrace their *positive* responsibilities, rather than remaining within the confines of their negative responsibilities, through simple non-interference in the cultural life of minorities. The active promotion of diversity[3] on the part of governments is often needed simply to prevent minority languages from disappearing from the linguistic landscape, by injecting new vitality into dwindling minority language use.

Reform of the Russian education system, particularly through the 2007 amendments of the Russian Law 'On Education',[4] impacts upon minority education[5] in two ways. On the one hand, the amendments enable an increased control by the federal centre over the regions in the sphere of education (a form of centralism). On the other, they aggravate the fractionalisation of the Russian educational space in the absence of a fully coherent, nationwide education policy (a form of localism). These two shifts seem to move in opposite directions but in fact they tend to simultaneously impact upon minority education. From the 2007 amendments I widen the discussion to incorporate other changes to the education system that affect minorities, with regard to language of examinations, and religious and patriotic education. This chapter shows that education policy since 2007 has led to shifts in the centre-periphery balance with regard to minority education, with repercussions at the three levels of the education system: regional, local and federal. These are analysed in this chapter following a brief outline of minority-language education in its transition from the Soviet to the post-Soviet period. Data from interviews[6] are examined, particularly with reference to the respondents' experience of education reform.[7]

From Soviet to post-Soviet minority-language education

As described in Chapter 2, the Soviet period saw the institutionalisation of education in minority languages (Anderson and Silver 1984; Kirkwood 1989; Lipset 1967; Slezkine 1994). In the 1920s, children of non-Russian families attended national schools providing minority-language education. However, teaching through the medium of non-Russian languages was progressively reduced: from primary and secondary education in 65 languages in the period 1934–1940, to 53 languages in 1976–1980 and to 43 languages in 1989 (Anderson and Silver 1984: 1027; Pavlenko 2008: 8). The decrease in minority-language education was accompanied by a growing emphasis on the Russian language and culture. Education reform in 1958–1959 (Bilinsky 1962) rapidly accelerated the decline of national schools: it lifted the obligation for students belonging to minorities to receive minority-language instruction, which led to a marked increase in enrolment in Russian-medium schools, as competence in Russian came to be seen as a prerequisite for social mobility (Pavlenko 2008: 7).[8] The only constituent units of the RSFSR to retain full secondary education in the titular languages following the reform were the Tatar and Bashkir ASSRs. The Finno-Ugric republics scored less well: in the Mordovian ASSR, schools operating in titular languages virtually disappeared from cities, and (primary) education continued to be provided only in rural areas (Zamyatin 2012b: 89). A tendency to confine the teaching of national languages to non-urban areas generally spread throughout the RSFSR. Even in Tatarstan, the use of the titular language in the education system was increasingly relegated to rural areas, while the use of Russian dominated in public settings (Gorenburg 2005: 3–6). Indeed, the presence of ethnically homogeneous Tatar villages in rural areas led to a higher proportion of national schools in these localities; Sagitova (2011: 72–73) further notes that the Tatar language remained at the periphery of processes of accelerated modernisation foreseen by Soviet planning – and implemented in the language of the dominant ethnic group – causing Tatar to be marginalised as a means of social interaction (see also Grenoble 2003: 71–72).

The situation changed again in the 1990s, with the revival of minority (particularly titular) languages as an integral aspect of the cultural renaissance of non-Russian groups. Access to titular-language education was substantially enhanced, especially in Turkic-language republics such as Tatarstan (Garipov and Faller 2003; Graney 1999; Gorenburg 2005: 9; Zamyatin 2012b). Post-Soviet Tatarstan is the republic of the Russian Federation with the highest degree of minority-language education among the three focus titular republics, followed by Mordovia and then by Karelia. According to data by the Russian government – included in the Third Report submitted to the ACFC in 2010[9] – in Russia there were: 2,166 schools in which Tatar was used as language of instruction, and 1,466 in which Tatar was studied as a subject; 200 schools where either of the two Mordovian languages (Moksha or Erzya) was used as language of instruction,[10] and 275 where either was studied as a subject; no schools where Karelian was the language of instruction, and 40 in which it could be studied as a subject.

In both Mordovia and Tatarstan the teaching of titular languages has been compulsory for all students, regardless of ethnicity – although this obligation was introduced in Tatarstan already in the early 1990s, and in Mordovia only in 2004. The two republics thus differ from Karelia, where the titular language has been taught only as an optional subject.[11] Much has been achieved particularly in Tatarstan, where there has been a significant expansion of the study of Tatar among students of Tatar and other ethnic backgrounds (Gorenburg 2005; Musina *et al.* 2011a: 4–5): tremendous efforts have been made to develop teaching through the medium of Tatar in secondary and tertiary education,[12] while in Mordovia the use of the titular languages as medium of instruction has been restricted mostly to primary school. In Karelia most students who opt to study Karelian only do so from the first to fourth grade (Kovaleva 2010: 313),[13] and courses only amount to one to three hours a week.[14] In those cases in which the Mordovian languages are studied as compulsory subjects, lessons are similarly held for only one to three hours a week (Zamyatin 2012b: 86). Additionally, respondents active in promoting the Mordovian languages in Saransk noted that the obligation to teach titular languages as subjects is not rigorously applied, in practice being contingent upon the personal inclinations of school directors and teachers [1.4.3; 2.14].

Hence, the three case studies had a very different starting point in the 1990s, and progress towards minority-language education has varied: Tatarstan has benefited from more substantial resources to promote titular-language education than Mordovia and, in particular, Karelia. What is even more significant for the purposes of this study is the fact that *all* three cases have been confronted by severe challenges to minority-language education, resulting in their being affected by homogenising, assimilationist tendencies. These dynamics are examined from the perspective of each of the three main actors in Russia's changing educational space – the regional, local and federal levels – with reference to both the repercussions of recent education reform and long-standing challenges.

The three players in the education system

Education reform was initiated in the 2000s,[15] as part of broader moves towards nation-building and national unity.[16] A drive for stability was the principal motivating factor: the Ministry of Education's 2001 draft Concept of State Ethno-National Education Policy refers to growing xenophobic sentiments in Russia and to 'problems of education in a multinational society', resulting in the need to create a 'unified education space'. An explanatory document accompanying the draft Concept justifies its proposed measures on the basis of conflicting interests between the 'dominant ethnic group', the Russians, who aim towards the consolidation of a unified state, and other groups, who seek to create separate 'cultural systems'. The idea of a menace to stability posited by ethnic diversity is captured in a statement by former Director of the Institute of Nationality Issues in Education of the Ministry of Education and Science, M.N. Kuz'min,[17] who argued: 'Compared to mono-ethnic countries, multi-ethnicity predestines a country to less stability, to the presence of additional areas of inner contradictions' (Kuz'min 2005: 16).

Although the draft Concept was subjected to criticism, particularly from the ethnic republics, and ultimately not adopted, it laid the foundations for the 2006 Concept of National Education Policy[18] (Zamyatin 2012c: 30). The 2006 Concept contains a set of principles and priorities of federal education policy, which, it states, are 'dictated' by the poli-ethnic character of Russian (*rossiiskii*) society: multi-ethnicity necessitates a coherent education system, by which schools accommodating various ethnic and cultural needs are integrated in the Russian (*rossiiskii*) educational space. The Concept declares that the experience of the preceding 15 years shows that, together with 'positive results' in the education system (i.e. the rise in the number of languages used therein), 'negative tendencies' have also developed: regional autonomy has led to a mismatch, and, at times, to contradictions between education policies implemented at the regional and federal levels. It has further caused regional objectives to take priority over federal ones, and a marginalisation of the Russian language and culture. Thus, according to the Concept, the education system of an ethnically diverse society must include, among its primary objectives, the 'spiritual consolidation of the multinational population of Russia into a unified political nation'. This is, again, linked to an imperative need to assure internal stability, cohesion through co-citizenship and common civic values. In light of this, the stated purpose of the Concept is to identify principles for a national education policy that is conducive to 'inter-ethnic harmony, unity and integrity', and that is based on the principle of 'unity of the federal cultural and educational space'.

The Concept was approved by the Ministry of Education virtually without public debate, paving the way for the adoption of amendments to the Law 'On Education'. These came in December 2007, with Law No. 309.[19] The new provisions introduced common Federal State Education Standards, with a myriad of small modifications interspersed throughout the law, adding the adjective 'federal' before 'state education standards'. In the context of the creation of a 'unified educational space',[20] Law 309 has effectively eliminated the 'national–regional component' – the most contentious aspect of the new provisions, which triggered vigorous protests from the republics. The pre-309 Law 'On Education' included three 'components': the federal level, the regional level and the individual school, each contributing to the curriculum. Regions devised the 'national–regional component' – approximately 15 per cent of teaching time of the standard school curriculum for all pupils – which could be employed *inter alia* to teach minority languages and cultures.[21] The school component – an additional 10 per cent – could be used at the school's discretion to further develop the teaching of minority languages. Since the amendments introduced by Law 309, the legislation makes no reference to such components. Yet the curriculum is still divided into parts: the 'obligatory' and 'variable' parts.[22] The former (70 per cent of total teaching time) is devised at the federal level, while the latter (30 per cent) is established by the 'participants in the education process' – meaning students, their parents and teachers.[23] Thus, the federal centre and local institutions have become the two principal actors in the Russian education system, while the role of the 'middle level' (i.e. the subjects of the Russian Federation) has been simultaneously diminished. The new (2012) Law 'On Education in the Russian Federation'[24] continues the same trend: Article 14 stipulates that education is guaranteed in the state language of the Federation, while the right to choose the language of instruction is provided 'within the opportunities offered by the education system'.[25] The same article states that, in schools situated in the republics, the teaching of, and instruction in, the state languages of the republics (the republics' official languages)[26] '*can* be introduced' [italics added]; this, however, has to be 'in accordance with the federal state education standards', and it 'should not be to the detriment of the teaching and learning of the state language of the Russian Federation'.[27]

Education reform has been justified in light of the need to raise education standards, by setting minimum requirements common to all schools. It was further argued that the amendments would bring regional legislation into line with the Russian Constitution: Kuz'min and Artemenko have advanced the view – along the lines of the aforementioned 2006 Concept – that language policies in several ethnic republics have not treated Russian as the state language of the entire Russian Federation, but as a state language of the *republics*, and have effectively placed it at a lower level than the titular languages (Kuz'min and Artemenko 2010: 44).[28] Similarly, the State Council of the Russian Federation has argued that the compulsory study of titular languages in the republics has led to schools' inability to satisfy the interests of students, while also lowering their knowledge of Russian, resulting in tensions at the regional level, and complaints from both parents and students.[29] The transfer of decision-making on minority-language education from the republican authorities to the 'participants in the education process' has been presented as a way of devising curricula on the basis of existing needs and individual preferences at the local level (ibid.: 46).

Indeed, in addition to enhancing the scope of application of *federal* standards in the regions, the new regulations have created a new form of localism, by dispensing a plethora of new rights and responsibilities to *local* institutions, particularly individual schools. Yet there are two sides to localism: a form of local autonomy that can accommodate the specific needs of minority communities; and the fragmentation of state policies into an uncoordinated mass of activities. In the first case, local autonomy serves to promote minority rights, as cultural diversity can be better enabled through decentralisation and flexible arrangements. For example,

Grin (2003) suggests that decentralisation is conducive to enhanced participation in policy-making, which can of course apply to local autonomy in the sphere of minority-language education:

> [I]t appears likely ... to be easier to implement [participatory democracy] in institutionally *decentralised settings*.... This multiplies the levels at which practical arrangements can be designed for individual citizens and grass-roots movements to make their concerns heard [italics added].
>
> (Ibid.: 152–153)[30]

In the second case, localism can lead to a *laissez-faire* approach that atomises efforts at the local level without their integration into a coherent state policy to safeguard the rights of national minorities, and with minimal support from the centre. A degree of centralism can provide an antidote to fragmentation, through a comprehensive framework within which local efforts can be situated; at the same time it can also entail the concentration of power by the central authorities (Wolman 1990), leading to the imposition of centrally-conceived policies without the involvement of civil society, including minorities.[31] The provisions introduced by Law 309 imply an oscillation between centralism (the federal centre and federal education standards) and localism (individual schools) in the management of minority education policies, with decreased guarantees for the regions.

The regions: decreased legal guarantees

Following the education reform, the division of responsibilities between the republics and the federal centre in the formulation and implementation of education policies has been replaced by a highly skewed asymmetry. Unsurprisingly, the adoption of Law 309 sparked centre–periphery tensions (Stepanov 2010: 5). The amendments were met with resistance and demonstrations[32] denouncing centralised decision-making on minority education as a violation of the constitutional right to freely choose their language of education.[33] Some regions reliant on Moscow for subsidies, normally timid in their claims to the centre, on this occasion acted in unison with other, more vocal and assertive republics articulating protests with 'one voice'.[34] An event in Kazan, in November 2008, saw the gathering of representatives of 21 regions, who jointly called for the restoration of regional autonomy in decision-making on the teaching of minority languages and cultures. The participants voiced concerns that the new regulations would cause the disappearance of national schools, and would also result in the youth of the regions becoming indifferent to cultural traditions, pointing to the falling rates of linguistic competence among young persons belonging to titular nationalities. Some participants went so far as to refer to a 'Russian [*russkii*] ethnocratic project' (Shnirelman 2010: 60).[35]

The reactions to Law 309 were recorded through interviews in the focus republics, as well as in Moscow and St Petersburg, where several national schools operate. In Mordovia and Karelia, respondents from civil society as well as school employees in most instances had little awareness or knowledge of the amendments. The situation was dramatically different in Tatarstan. Here, the respondents in most cases expressed clear concern about the amendments and their swift adoption. An education specialist at Kazan's Institute of History[36] – who, he said, in the past had been consulted in the formulation of federal education standards – perceived the new regulations as an imposition, given the absence of debate preceding their adoption [2.7]. He believed that Law 309 would prevent Tatarstan from preserving its diversity, and as such constituted a 'threat' to minority cultures.[37] Another Tatar respondent echoed the opinion that Moscow's actions, particularly through the adoption of Law 309, were 'destructive' rather than supportive of Russia's cultural heritage [4.7]. Interviews also revealed confusion and alarm due to hearsay around potential further centralisation, and possible supplementary amendments of the Law 'On Education' – which between 2000 and the end of 2011 was amended 68 times. An education specialist in Moscow spoke about an 'education vertical' [4.14]. The exclusion of regional authorities and minority representatives from decision-making on education reform led these respondents to resent the imposition of new regulations 'from above', and caused uncertainty about their practical consequences.

The discrepancy between the reactions of respondents in the three republics – with more pronounced concerns over Law 309 in Tatarstan than in Mordovia and Karelia – can be explained by a number of factors. Among these are: the much greater size of the Tatar minority[38] compared to the other two, which likely contributes to a more marked ethnic consciousness; the public discourse around the amendments within Tatarstan, more prominent than in other regions; and, in particular, Tatarstan's higher stakes, compared to other republics, in a possible loss of regional autonomy in decision-making in the sphere of education. This last factor is linked to the significantly higher number of schools teaching, or providing instruction in, Tatar language compared to Moksha, Erzya or Karelian, and to the concern in Tatarstan that the amendments would undermine a 2004 ruling of the Russian Constitutional Court (RCC)[39] (Shnirelman 2010: 59–60). This landmark judgement had found the Republic of Tatarstan to be acting within its powers by requiring Tatar and Russian to be studied 'in equal measure' within the republic.[40] Tatarstan had also been affected by two other centralising measures: the rejection by the federal authorities of Tatarstan's initiative to restore the use of the Latin alphabet for the Tatar language;[41] and the introduction of the 'unified state examination' (*Edinyi Gosudarstvennyi Ekzamen* – *EGE*), the final secondary school examination, in all regions of Russia – a process completed in 2009. The examination is conducted entirely in Russian, while previously students from Tatar-medium schools had had the option to take the examination in the language of instruction.[42] Russian language, together with mathematics, is also an *EGE* compulsory subject; the issuing of secondary school diplomas and access to higher education depend on satisfactory results in these two disciplines. Meanwhile, the RCC and the Russian Supreme Court have ruled that basic minimum standards for the study of Russian have to be uniform across all schools in the country, including those operating in minority languages, and that the teaching of other languages should not be to the detriment of the teaching of Russian.[43]

Ultimately, following debate and Parliamentary hearings in February 2009, some (relatively modest) compromises were negotiated. The republics' authorities were enabled to participate in decision-making on minority-language education (on the number of hours and list of subjects) within the boundaries of the Federal State Education Standards (Shnirelman 2010; Yamskov 2010: 203–204; Zamyatin 2012c).[44] The republics were further authorised to require the study of official languages of the republics as compulsory subjects[45] – although their study as 'native languages' (a more intensive type of language teaching),[46] or their use as languages of instruction, was made contingent upon the approval of schools, students and parents. These concessions did not prevent the hearings from ending with numerous question marks as to the reform's exact repercussions and ramifications, including with regard to new divisions of responsibilities between the federal centre and the regions, and respective rights and duties (Shnirelman 2010: 61).

The Russian authorities have emphasised that the motivating factor behind education reform was not the imposition of a new educational or cultural straitjacket upon the regions, but the creation of an overarching, general framework that could be flexibly applied by individual schools, following consideration of the needs of students and their parents.[47] This position can be contrasted with that of a respondent from Tatarstan [2.7], involved in the republic's education system, who argued that discussions took place *ex post facto*, on modalities of implementation of the new provisions rather than on their adoption and content. Moreover, despite the government's assurances, diversity in minority language education has in fact decreased.

Dwindling minority-language education

Two modes of teaching exist in the ethnic republics for the study of titular languages: as 'official languages' of the republics and as 'native languages' – a distinction that has come to be crucially significant. In the first case, a titular language is taught (to all students) by virtue of the fact that it is recognised as an official language within a republic. In this case teaching generally amounts to between one and three hours per week. Instead, the study of a language as 'native' – designed for students of the relevant ethno-linguistic group, for whom the language is 'native'[48] – involves more intensive language training, for up to six hours a week. Despite the ethno-linguistic revival of the 1990s, Finno-Ugric schools never succeeded in extending the teaching of titular languages as 'native' to all students of titular ethnic background. Likewise, post-Soviet Tatarstan, despite its intense ethnic renaissance, did not manage to guarantee to all Tatar students an education through the medium of Tatar (Gorenburg 2005; Zamyatin 2012b: 93). Thus, even before the new regulations introduced by Law 309, levels of titular-language education were low: according to Musina (2011: 16) only 4 per cent of Russia's students were enrolled in national schools in the academic year 2006–2007. One should further note that, despite their name, 'national schools' in some instances have provided only limited minority-language education (and at times even function primarily or exclusively in Russian). This means that the percentage of Russia's students receiving an education through the medium of a minority language was in fact *lower* than 4 per cent in 2006–2007.

Up-to-date statistics on the number of schools and their students, and on language of instruction, are not easy to obtain – and existing data should be treated with caution. Yet what is apparent is an overall tendency towards a reduction of minority-language education: after rapidly rising in the 1990s, it decelerated and stopped in the 2000s, and in some instances reversed (Zamyatin 2012b). According to local surveys, in Tatarstan the percentage[49] of Tatar pupils receiving an education in Tatar was 47 per cent in 1998; it increased until 2007 (52.7 per cent), and then decreased to 46.13 per cent in 2010 (Musina *et al.* 2011b: 145). Data from the Tatastani authorities[50] indicate that the number of schools with instruction in Tatar decreased from 712 in 2004 to 490 in 2009.[51]

According to data provided by Zamyatin (2012b: 83–84),[52] in Mordovia the percentage of students who had Moksha or Erzya as language of instruction went from 11 per cent (in the academic year 1990–1991), to 8.7 per cent (1999–2000), and then to 6.1 per cent (2009–2010). The share of students who studied Moksha or Erzya as 'native' went from 38.6 per cent (1991), to 39.2 per cent (2000), and then to 27.8 per cent (2010). By contrast, students learning Moksha or Erzya as an 'official language' of the republic increased, going from 0 per cent (1991) to 2.5 per cent (2000), to 22.4 per cent (2010). The data indicate a shift from the Mordovian languages being employed as languages of instruction and studied as native languages, to their study (less intensively) as official languages – particularly in urban areas.[53] In Karelia, the percentage of students studying Karelian has progressively increased, starting from 3.4 per cent (1989–1990), to 17.6 per cent (2000–2001), to 25 per cent (2009–2010) (Zamyatin 2012b: 83–84; see also Klement'ev 2006, 2010).[54] At the same time, no students received instruction in Karelian, and, as noted, the study of Karelian has not been introduced as a compulsory subject.

These dynamics are at least partially linked to the standardisation and centralisation of the education system. Thus, for example, after the introduction in 2001 of the federal programme 'Russian Language' for the years 2002–2005, Tatarstan also adopted the programme 'Russian Language in Tatarstan' for the same period, with the objective of actively promoting Russian by expanding the network of Russian schools, and introducing a more intensive teaching of the state language of the Federation. These developments have been referred to as a 'corrective ethnocultural policy' (Makarova 2011b: 14) inasmuch as they reverse linguistic priorities at the regional level, by enhancing the role of the Russian language while simultaneously downgrading titular languages.

Schools and localities: local autonomy or atomisation?

The role of regional decision-making having been reduced through Law 309, the schools have acquired greater autonomy to self-organise with regard to the 'variable' part of the curriculum. In light of this, a respondent (a Moscow-based academic and analyst) considered Law 309 to be an 'achievement', inasmuch as it provided increased autonomy to individual schools [2.23]. Another analyst saw it as a step towards the implementation of the 1985 (Council of Europe) European Charter of Local Self-Government, which was ratified by Russia in 1998 [2.15]. Indeed, cultural diversity tends to be better catered for through decentralisation, as it enhances participation at the local level and facilitates a greater focus on local needs (Grin 2003: 152–153). Through Law 309, the supply of minority-language education has been linked to demand; at the same time, the Law introduced both new responsibilities and new opportunities for schools. Existing circumstances, particularly with reference to federal funding for minority-language education and general socio-economic conditions, impair the fulfilment of responsibilities and the enjoyment of opportunities available to schools. And, in addition to restricting schools' scope of action, they influence the choices of students and their parents.

In order to maximise federal funding, schools have an interest in accommodating the needs of students, as they are allocated funds in a measure that is proportional to the number of enrolled students (Stepanov 2010: 6). Denial of the opportunity to learn a minority language by a school might lead to students transferring to another institution, thereby decreasing the school's financing. Similarly, students who are uninterested in minority languages, even if themselves of ethnic minority background, will prompt schools to reduce minority-language education [2.15; 2.22]. This system is conducive to schools being driven principally by financial considerations rather than the aim of promoting diversity, through a form of monetisation of culture. Indeed, respondents working in the area of education invariably referred to tight budgets, even before the reform. Thus, while schools have been given new rights, they have scarce means to exercise them, particularly in rural and economically deprived areas.[55]

Closely related to the issue of school budgets is the socio-economic environment that minorities inhabit together with the majority. Socio-economic conditions can, in practice, restrict the options available to minorities. The introduction of the *EGE* across the country, with a central role for the Russian language, illustrates this: parents and students might decide, as a consequence, not to avail themselves of their legal right to choose the language of instruction provided by Russian law,[56] as minority languages do not tend to be linked to prospects for professional achievement and financial prosperity. Respondents from a variety of backgrounds made frequent allusions to an increasing number of parents opting for Russian-language education for their children, in light of *EGE* regulations – not only because the examination has to be taken fully in Russian, but due to the fact that Russian and mathematics are its two primary subjects. Research indicates that the *EGE* has had an even greater impact on parents and schools' choices on minority-language education than the introduction of Federal State Education Standards (Alòs i Font 2014; Chevalier 2012).[57]

Russia's linguistic environment has been modified by another new development: the growing importance of English as a global language. For example, although employment in the administration of the Republic of Tatarstan necessitates knowledge of both the titular language and Russian, university education and employment prospects in international organisations and firms require the knowledge of foreign languages (Musina *et al.* 2011b: 3). This adds a new layer a complexity compared to the linguistic environment of the Soviet Union, and it particularly affects (upwardly mobile) young people. Although Tatar enjoys the status of official language within Tatarstan, the general economic environment adversely affects its ability to compete with stronger languages, decreasing its significance within a market economy (Sagitova 2011: 73). These tendencies are even more pronounced in the case of Moksha, Erzya and Karelian. The Karelian language further suffers from competition with another prominent language at the regional level: Finnish. The latter offers better financial prospects than Karelian, and is linked to business and trade opportunities with neighbouring Finland. Indeed, data from the Ministry of Education of the Republic of Karelia show that, in October 2008, Karelian was studied as a subject by 1,559 students, while Finnish courses were taken by 5,573 students[58] – despite the fact that in Karelia there were 45,570 ethnic Karelians compared to 8,577 ethnic Finns (2010 census).

Schools and minority-language education

Schools' new competencies with regard to the 'variable part' of the curriculum have created a need for a new set of skills and for information on their new responsibilities. Following the adoption of Law 309, schools had only minimal knowledge of its provisions and what they entailed (Stepanov 2010). The interviews exposed much confusion: even specialists in Kazan and Moscow had limited information, and were cautious in their predictions as to how the amendments would affect the teaching of minority languages and cultures. A respondent, an academic working on inter-cultural education in Moscow, said:

> Moscow has given more power to individual schools, so they should decide [what to teach] on the basis of [the preferences of] the local population, but it's not clear *how*.... So the regions are suspicious, and they have full right to be suspicious.
>
> [2.22]

Another academic in Moscow – a specialist on minority languages in Russia – observed that the confusion over how to comply with federal standards had led schools to simply prolong previous practices, by continuing to seek guidance from regional regulatory bodies [2.23]. In fact, no substantive changes had been made in minority education in the three republics by 2010–2011, when the interviews took place. The rights of parents and responsibilities of schools remained undefined, which, *inter alia*, caused a lack of formal redress in cases of dissatisfaction.

In addition to a need for new expertise, the activities of schools are constricted by limited resources – both human and financial. The number of qualified minority-language teachers tends to be low: for example, according to some respondents, Karelian speakers (who can also understand Finnish) are more attracted to Finnish firms' high salaries than to the modest income paid to teachers [1.2.2; 1.2.8; 2.3]. The number of Karelian teachers reportedly halved between 2007 and 2011 in Karelia, for a mix of reasons: unfavourable conditions for teachers (low pay and low standards of living in villages where schools are located); the closure of village schools, where Karelian was taught; and the limited interest in the Karelian language of some parents of Karelian ethnic background, particularly when they have themselves spent their lives in a primarily monolingual (Russian) environment (Kovaleva 2010: 316). Meanwhile, demographic shifts (due to low birth rates),[59] financial constraints and migration from rural to urban areas for better employment prospects, have led to the closure of schools. This has particularly affected small village schools (*malokomplektnye shkoly*), in which the language of instruction is more likely to be the language of a minority, as villages tend to be more densely populated by minorities than urban areas.[60] In 2011, an average of 700 village schools were reported to have been closed each year in Russia.[61] In Mordovia, between 2007 and 2010, small rural schools went from 68 per cent to 60 per cent of all schools.[62] These schools are not considered financially viable; they are therefore shut down as part of modernisation plans and the 'optimisation' of the education system.[63] When there is no other minority-language school in the vicinity, students are left with no alternative but to enrol in Russian-language schools. The closure of village schools can also affect minorities in other ways: for example, a Tver Karelian respondent noted that the closure of a Karelian village school near Tver – where Karelian was taught – had meant that a museum devoted to Karelian culture, located within the school, had also been closed [1.1.4].

The reformed education system requires that decisions concerning minority-language education be taken by schools in consultation with parents and students. Interview data[64] indicate that schools interact with parents and students and, in some cases, accommodate them. At the same time, all schools are responsible for fulfilling federal education standards: thus, schools that provide (or may provide) minority-language education have a finite number of hours to comply both with parents' requests (if they are advanced) to teach titular languages under the 'variable part' of the curriculum, *and* with the requirement to prepare students for the *EGE* under the 'obligatory part'. According to an education expert from Tatarstan, ensuring that titular languages and cultures are allocated an adequate number of hours necessitates a strong motivation on the part of schools, given the parallel, and more compelling, responsibilities vis-à-vis federal standards, and the limited resources and materials available to them.[65] Moreover, decision-making on language of instruction is generally based on the wishes of the *majority* of parents, meaning that individual parents' preferences can remain unaccounted for. An alternative option is to divide students into groups operating along different linguistic priorities, yet this requires additional resources which may not be available to schools. In this context, the previously noted shift from the teaching of titular languages as 'native' to their teaching as 'official languages', implying less intensive language training, feeds into homogenising processes by exacerbating a trend towards a superficial study of languages other than Russian (Zamyatin 2012b: 97).

These factors explain the discrepancy between studies pointing to a decrease in minority-language education,[66] and the reports of the Russian government to the ACFC pointing to the opposite. In its Third Report (2010), the Russian authorities stated that 33 languages were used as languages of tuition and 47 additional languages were studied as subjects.[67] The figures had increased from, respectively, 30 and 45 languages in 2005, referred to in the Second Report (for the period 2001–2004).[68] The Third Report added that: 'In recent years, a number of the subjects of the Russian Federation have significantly increased their networks of general education institutions that hold tuition in native languages.'[69]

In its reports to the ACFC, the Russian government supplies data on the number of languages taught, the number of schools with minority-language education and the number of students; but it does not provide comprehensive information on the overall amount of hours devoted to minority-language education. The Russian authorities' data can in fact obfuscate existing trends: the number of schools is particularly deceiving, as rural schools tend have much fewer students than urban ones (Zamyatin 2012c: 22). Moreover, some schools are classified as institutions of titular language-medium instruction, when in reality they operate predominantly in Russian, or are increasingly switching to the use of Russian. For example, in Tatarstan, some Tatar-medium schools have reduced the number of courses taught in Tatar, confining the titular language to the teaching of Tatar literature and history, while using Russian for other subjects (Suleymanova 2011).[70] At times, schools seem to have been wrongly classified as titular language-medium schools: this appears to be linked to a 'conceptual confusion' between schools that employ a titular language as their medium of instruction, and those that have a 'national school programme' – meaning schools that simply teach a minority language (as 'native'), but otherwise provide instruction in Russian (Alòs i Font 2014: 73). Other variables that affect the fortunes of minority languages in the education system are, clearly, the quality of teaching and materials. Hence, what may be perceived as positive outcomes (e.g. the increase in the number of languages taught as subjects) can hide developments inimical to minority-language proficiency (e.g. a decrease in the quality of teaching or the number of hours devoted to it). A factor that seems to have played a role in these dynamics is the tendency to switch from the teaching of minority languages as 'native' to their teaching as 'official languages' – the latter mode of teaching having been labelled as 'formal and ineffective' (Zamyatin 2012b: 95; see also Strogal'shikova 2009b).[71] Even in the case of 'native' language teaching, titular languages sometimes lose out in their competition with Russian: although the teaching of titular languages as 'native' can be for up to six hours a week in schools otherwise operating in Russian, it is frequently restricted to between three and five hours (Zamyatin 2012c: 38).

Parents and students

According to surveys carried out between 2005 and 2008 in the Republic of Tatarstan,[72] 80.5 per cent of ethnic Tatar students considered Tatar lessons to be 'positive', and 13.9 per cent to be 'quite positive' – against 40.9 per cent and 29.9 per cent (repectively) of Russians (Gabdrakhmanova 2011: 84). Thus, despite the lower percentage of Russians favouring the study of Tatar, by no means were they overwhelmingly opposed to it,[73] although they more frequently believed that the study of Tatar ought to be an optional rather than a compulsory subject (ibid.; Musina 2011: 28). Among the motives for wishing to study Tatar were: a belief that one ought to know the official language of the republic where one resides; the view that it is important to know one's native language (for students of Tatar origins); a wish to use Tatar to communicate with friends and family; and personal interest (Sagitova 2011: 62–63).

Despite this, various factors relating to minority-language education can act as deterrents for the 'participants in the education process' – parents in particular – when they consider this option. Respondents (from civil society and academia, and school employees) referred to: poor facilities for the teaching of minority languages [1.2.1; 1.2.2; 1.2.8; 2.5; 2.13; 5.1]; a lack of professional prospects for bilingual teachers and scholars [1.2.9; 1.2.2; 2.2; 2.3; 2.5], or those who are fluent in minority languages [1.1.3; 1.2.1; 2.2; 2.7]; and barriers to taking the state examination in minority languages [2.6; 2.7; 5.2].[74] Such problems persist even in Tatarstan, despite its strong position – compared to Mordovia and Karelia, and other ethnic republics in general – inasmuch as Tatar is spoken by a large part of the student population.[75] Parents in Tatarstan tend to be concerned about the insufficient number of fluent Tatar speakers qualified to teach complex subjects such as advanced mathematics, particularly at the level of secondary and tertiary education. The limited use of Tatar in urban areas is an additional factor that can lead parents to opt for Russian schools for their children (Musina *et al.* 2011b: 5; Sagitova 2011: 71). With reference to the Republic of Karelia, it has been argued that much of what has been achieved in the teaching of Karelian to children stems from the 'enthusiasm of teachers' – who have developed their own materials when textbooks were insufficiently available[76] – in the presence of unfavourable conditions for language transmission (Kovaleva 2010: 309).

Parents of Tatarstan's students, both of Tatar and Russian origin, have further indicated that the amount of time being devoted to the teaching of foreign languages ought to be increased. Indeed, a local survey[77] indicates that they consider foreign European languages, particularly English, to be certainly more important than Tatar, and even Russian, for social mobility (Sagitova 2011: 71–72). Even at the local level, including rural areas, Tatar tends to be seen as of very limited usefulness, as virtually all residents can communicate in Russian (Sagitova 2011: 74–75).[78] A Karelian parent interviewed noted that, despite her emotional attachment to the Karelian language, existing socio-economic conditions meant that she preferred that her children mastered English rather than Karelian [1.1.4]. Similarly, local studies indicate that Karelian students tend to regard Karelian as having an insignificant role not only in the public sphere (with reference to social prestige and business opportunities) but also in the private sphere (communication with friends and family) (Kovaleva 2010: 314–315). And, as noted, in Karelia Finnish competes against the titular language in addition to Russian (and English). Karelian itself can be used as a stepping stone towards knowledge of Finnish given the proximity of the two languages and their mutual intelligibility, along with the marketability of Finnish. In Mordovia opinions on the study of Moksha or Erzya tend to be split along ethnic lines, with persons belonging to the titular nationality more often favouring the teaching of these languages compared to persons belonging to other groups (particularly ethnic Russians and Tatars residing in Mordovia). The main argument against the study of titular languages in Mordovia, as for other ethnic republics, relates to the heavy academic burden placed on students, and the preference given to the study of languages considered to be conducive to financial well-being, such as Russian and English (Martynenko 2010: 62–63).

Against this background, linking the supply of minority-language education to demand (parental choice) can only lead to a downward spiral of both demand and supply. Demand is likely to plummet unless measures are adopted to stimulate it; for this reason, Zamyatin (2012b, 2012c) links the education reform of the 2000s to the reform of the Soviet education system of 1958–1959,[79] when the obligation to learn one's native language was lifted. This move led to a reduction of the teaching of, and through the medium of, titular languages, particularly in urban areas of the RSFSR (Kreindler 1989). As in 1958–1959, parents are interested in their children's opportunities for social mobility; *EGE* regulations tend to discourage parents to enrol their children in schools with titular languages as languages of instruction, given concerns over examination results.[80] In all schools, *EGE* requirements trigger a drive for more hours to be devoted to the study of Russian as a path towards higher academic achievement, even when this implies reducing the hours for minority-language tuition.

As a consequence, despite the options for minority-language education formally available at the local level, the decisions of schools and parents are constrained by federal requirements, to which decisions on the teaching of minority languages and cultures are effectively secondary. The combined effect of Law 309 and *EGE* regulations has been a partial but steady decrease in minority-language education. The new education system seems to be more conducive to the atomisation of efforts to promote minority languages than the accommodation of local interests. To this has to be added that schools operate in an environment fraught with adverse socio-economic conditions, impairing efforts to preserve minority languages and cultures. This is when the federal centre needs to step in, providing legal and procedural clarity for the actors involved in the education process, as well as coherent and sustainable policies that help students, parents and schools to withstand the socio-economic pressures threatening the cultural heritage of minorities.

The federal centre: centralism or laissez-faire*?*

As shown in Chapter 5, Putin's centralising, de-federalising policies have been a fundamental feature of Russian politics since the early 2000s. In the area of education, common *federal* education standards similarly strive to enhance the role of the federal centre. At the same time, certain areas, such as minority-language education, lack central planning, supervision and support. Two aspects of the education system are analysed here in relation to the federal centre: *laissez-faire* tendencies in the sphere of minority-language education and the phenomenon of 'cultural vertical'.

Minority-language education: laissez-faire *(or not?)*

Russian legislation guarantees the right to choose the language of education.[81] International standards provide further guidance in this area, although the state parties to the FCNM are afforded a wide margin of discretion in establishing the rules for its implementation. The FCNM provisions themselves, such as Article 14(2) (education in a minority language), are worded flexibly, in light of the 'financial, administrative and technical difficulties' that may arise in the teaching of, or through the medium of, minority languages.[82] On the basis of the resources available and in the presence of 'sufficient demand', the state parties have to act 'as far as possible' to provide minority-language education.[83] Some flexibility allows for the accommodation of local needs,[84] yet it has to coexist with solid guarantees of a legal and financial nature for cultural diversity to be preserved.[85] Legal guarantees should fit within an 'active and coherent educational policy',[86] which ideally ought to be coordinated with a wider language policy (Council of Europe 2007), in order to withstand the 'inevitably standardising influence' of globalisation.[87]

Russia needs effective language policies to preserve its diversity. Its linguistic landscape is, overall, not conducive to multilingualism, as minorities inhabit an overwhelmingly Russian-speaking environment. Even in Tatarstan, most of the media and forms of public communication are in Russian, while in Karelia the titular language has virtually disappeared from public places; the exception in Karelia is villages densely populated by Karelians, yet the younger generation has tended to leave these localities for cities in search of better employment prospects.[88] The teaching of the Karelian language, amounting only to between one and three hours per week, was not considered by the respondents from minority organisations and a school teacher to be conducive to fluency in the language [1.2.1; 1.2.2; 5.1] (see also Kovaleva 2010: 312). Any progress made towards Karelian proficiency often ends with the last year of school, and subsequently language skills tend to regress, as students have limited opportunities to practice them (ibid.: 313). Even following years of study, levels of fluency in titular languages have been found to be low in republics. An explanation may be that, in those republics in which the study of the titular language is compulsory, schools might make do with low standards of achievement in order to facilitate non-titulars' acceptance of the obligation to attend titular-language classes (Alòs i

Font 2014). Overall, efforts towards the teaching of titular languages have been judged inadequate to ensure inter-generational transmission, thereby paving the way for rising levels of linguistic assimilation (Zamyatin 2012b).

In the absence of a functioning language policy, efforts towards the promotion of minority languages and cultures typically become fragmented, usually consisting of a succession of isolated initiatives.[89] It is in this context that I use the expression *laissez-faire* – with reference to the fact that schools are left to resolve their own issues pertaining to minority-language education (with a paucity of resources), rather than receiving coordinated support.[90] The absence of a comprehensive, strategic plan for the promotion of minority languages was captured by a Karelian activist in Petrozavodsk, who noted that: 'Some work is done for languages – a bit here, a bit there – but there is no comprehensive policy' [1.2.2].

Planning involves strategic choices, which are even more crucial when limited resources exist for the promotion of a very high number of minority (and vulnerable) languages. Without specific guidelines, the Law 'On Education' (both pre- and post-309) has been interpreted and applied differently in various regions and in different schools across the Russian Federation (Stepanov 2010) – not only in response to local needs, but because modalities of implementation are left undetermined rather than being part of a coherent whole. While schools might strive to provide minority-language education even in the absence of specific federal regulations, linguistic rights are not buttressed by clear guarantees.[91] The consequence is wide discretionary powers being vested in individual schools, through a *laissez-faire* approach, by which the preservation of Russia's linguistic wealth seems left to chance.

Language revitalisation is not an easy process. It involves moving up the scale from a condition of vulnerability to a level in which a language is fully functioning and being transmitted to future generations.[92] In some cases reversing the language shift necessitates undoing a process of erosion of its prestige that has occurred over decades or centuries. Grin and Moring (2002) argue that the linguistic environment can be altered – so as to revitalise marginalised languages – in the presence of three conditions: (1) the *capacity* to use a language (achieved through language tuition and education); (2) *opportunities* to use it (particularly through the provision of public services in the relevant language);[93] and (3) a *desire* to use it (linked to efforts to raise the prestige of a language) (ibid.: 74). Of these, Russia provides primarily the first condition,[94] and to a limited extent, as shown in this chapter. It is noteworthy that, according to research conducted in Tatarstan,[95] Tatars have listed among measures likely to stimulate the use of Tatar the same conditions outlined by Grin and Moring: providing opportunities to use the language, including in their future work, and raising the prestige of the language (Sagitova 2011: 76–77). The ACFC has similarly recommended to the Russian government 'the establishment of a climate conducive to the use of minority languages in daily life'.[96] Indeed, success in language revival programmes is generally linked to raising the *status* of the language in question: when it remains subordinate to a stronger language, linguistic behaviour is unlikely to be altered (Gorenburg 2005).

Transferring decision-making on minority-language education to schools and individuals, without however creating an environment conducive to the *use* of such languages, leads to a decrease of both demand and supply. While the issue of low demand was raised repeatedly during interviews, with reference to parents' preferences, a state's positive responsibilities in the area of minority education include the *stimulation* of demand – as well as the provision of supply – through awareness-raising,[97] and a coherent long-term strategy in education. The latter may involve bilingual education in both secondary and tertiary education, so as to enable students to consolidate their language skills throughout the entire education process.[98] As instruction *in* a language is exceedingly important in order to master it (Skutnabb-Kangas 2000), a shift to the study of minority languages as subjects, decreasing their use as languages of instruction, is likely to accelerate assimilation. In language revitalisation processes, Grin and Moring further stress the vital role of impact assessment through the evaluation of language policies. Their effectiveness can be measured on the basis of any possible increase in the amount of time during which a language is used (Grin and Moring 2002: 84–88). Impact assessment, then, requires much more sophisticated monitoring than the simple collection of data on the number of minority-language schools and their students.

Rather than an active promotion of minority languages, the Russian authorities have introduced measures that in practice curtail their use. In addition to a general decrease of minority-language education outlined above, a Karelian activist noted in an interview (held in 2010) that two nurseries operating exclusively in Karelian, under the 'language nest' programme, had been closed by the Russian authorities [1.2.2]. The Russian government argued, in its Third Report to the ACFC, that the 'language nest' method – consisting of full immersion into a minority language by pre-school children – was undesirable as it created a 'closed language environment', which in the 'multinational environment of Russia … would significantly reduce [children's] socialization opportunities'.[99] Such a multinational environment, Putin himself has argued, calls for the 'unifying role of Russian culture, history and language' to be taken into account when devising state policies, including in the area of education.[100] The ACFC has recognised that the promotion of minority languages should not jeopardise the knowledge of a state's official language;[101] at the same time, the protection of minority languages through the education system can coexist with 'equipping the members of minorities with sufficient language skills to succeed in the broader society', as de Varennes and Thornberry (2005: 419) put it: bilingual education can expand, rather than limit, one's horizons in a plurilingual society. By contrast, restricting Karelian-language, pre-school education in Karelia – an overwhelmingly Russian-speaking region, with a declining use of Karelian – could indicate a drive for Russian monolingualism rather than for functioning bilingualism. In this context, the limited efforts to promote minority languages described in this chapter might not just be construed as a form of 'benign neglect' (through *laissez-faire* attitudes), in the presence of more pressing priorities and limited funding; they might hide a drive to further the increasing marginalisation of minority languages, through what can be regarded as 'malign neglect'. The containment of diversity is further evident in the promotion of a 'cultural vertical', described below.

A 'cultural vertical': moving towards uniformity

Alongside forms of *laissez-faire*, and the transfer of some responsibilities from the federal centre to individual schools, there has been a tendency towards the re-centralisation of the education system since the 1990s, with reference to patriotic education and the presentation of particular versions of history in textbooks. In addition to the promotion of the Russian language, various initiatives have advanced the standardisation of education, through a strong emphasis on 'unity' and patriotism. A significant development has been the adoption of the state programme 'Patriotic Education of Citizens of the Russian Federation for 2001–2005'.[102] Following this, the education system has been employed to facilitate the dissemination of patriotic messages in schools – with an overlapping of religiosity, patriotism and militarism. Patriotism and love of the country have become an important part of civic education (Vaillant 2005: 239); but not the only aspect: patriotism has been included in new courses, first introduced in 2009,[103] on 'Foundations of Religious Cultures and Secular Ethics' (FRCSE). The course comprises six modules, from which schools, in consultation with parents, can choose. These are: 'Foundations of Orthodox Culture' (and three other versions of this course on Islamic, Jewish and Buddhist cultures), 'Foundations of the Cultures of World Religions', and 'Foundations of Secular Ethics'.

The standardisation of religious education through the FRCSE course, in its intersection with patriotism, has placed an emphasis on principles such as societal welfare, labour, family and love for the motherland. Thus, this type of education revitalises traditional Communist values, while also promoting the strengthening of the Russian state; textbooks for religious courses stress the paramount role of state institutions and their drive for modernisation (Willems 2012: 34). Religious education can further aid the containment of social ills such as alcoholism and low birth rates, by soliciting a spirit of sacrifice to the benefit of societal welfare, which should take precedence over rampant individualism. As Putin noted in the 2012 state of the nation address: 'Being a patriot means not only to treat one's national history with love and respect ... but first and foremost to serve one's country and society'.[104] One year later, he stated: 'We need schools that do more than just teach; teaching is very important – most important, in fact – but we also need schools to help our nation's citizens form their identity, absorbing the nation's values, history and traditions.'[105]

Despite the variations between different textbooks for the six FRCSE modules, the first and last lessons are identical. The first lesson is entitled 'Russia is our Motherland': the principal message is that even in the presence of a multiplicity of languages and traditions in Russia, its population as a whole forms a 'family of the peoples of Russia'. The last lesson places an emphasis on love for the family and for Russia, on serving society and on patriotism (Willems

2012). The streamlining of religious education, and its incorporation of patriotic principles, can contribute towards counteracting possible state fragmentation on a religious basis: patriotism can act as minimum common denominator for Russia's disparate ethnic and religious groups. The interests of Church and state further converge in the Russian Orthodox Church's condemnation of religious extremism, and its call for the education of 'patriots, good keepers of the family's hearth, and law-abiding citizens', as stated by Patriarch Kirill in 2013.[106] The type of religion promoted in the FRCSE is one that is moderate and can withstand a possible transition to fundamentalism by marrying religious codes with love for the motherland. Textbooks, particularly for 'Foundations of Secular Ethics', integrate militaristic messages on the imperative need to defend the motherland,[107] with the promotion of patriotic values through the education system and beyond (Sperling 2009).

While the FRCSE envisages the option for students to choose between the six modules – with students separating into different groups, if needed, to attend the chosen courses – in order to avoid the impracticality of multiple, simultaneous lessons, as well as to contain costs, the actual choice has been restricted in practice. In some cases entire classes are taught the same module, regardless of individual preferences:[108] according to a 2010 study by the Public Chamber of the Russian Federation, in half the cases recorded students were unable to choose religious courses fully independently, and, in a fifth, decisions on courses were taken unilaterally by the directors of schools and public officials.[109] It was in reference to this that a respondent, the representative of a Jewish organisation, whose son attended a school in Moscow, said: 'I don't like a member of the [Russian Orthodox] clergy to go to my son's school, and my son to tell me that a priest has been there [to talk to the students about Russian Orthodoxy]' [1.2.5].

In the respondent's experience, the choice of module was made on the basis of the views of the majority of parents, while the individual preferences of some parents and students remained unaccounted for. The same respondent pointed to a tendency towards the prevalence of Orthodox Christianity by default, at least in regions where persons affiliated to other religions were not present in substantial numbers:

> In schools there are textbooks on the foundations of Orthodox culture…. Music lessons have traditional Russian songs – Russian Orthodox songs. It is not for any particular policy [of Russian nationalism] but it's because that's what they [the teachers] know. There are no professionals in schools who have received training to deal with inter-religious issues.
>
> [1.2.5]

Similarly, in 2009 Mordovia saw protests by Muslims (mostly Tatars residing in Mordovia) following instances of Muslim children being taught Orthodox poems, songs and prayers without their parents' consent, as well as attempts to involve them in classes of 'Foundations of Orthodox Culture'. Although schools in Mordovia teach this course as elective, some teachers have seemingly tended to display little sensitivity to religious diversity (Martynenko 2010: 64–66).

A movement towards a 'cultural vertical' has been furthered by history textbooks. Overall, the reformist tendencies of history teaching during the 1990s – accompanied by a relaxation of central controls – were replaced by counter-reformist moves in the following decade, as the federal Ministry of Education reaffirmed its central role in education policy (Kaplan 2005: 261–265). The resulting standardisation of education means that, in textbooks, liberal versions of history have tended to be substituted by more conservative ones. The process of devising education standards since the 2000s has oscillated between the affirmation of Russianness *and* efforts to contain xenophobia and chauvinism by promoting multicultural tolerance – with countless debates between historians, centre–periphery tensions and multiple versions of education standards in between. Some politicians have called for the censoring of textbooks, while historians have protested against state interference in their preparation (Shnirelman 2006b). Historical accounts have been influenced by a civilisational approach to Russian history: Soviet textbooks' references to national liberation have, in post-Soviet Russia, been replaced by references to 'cultural identity' of an exclusivist type, creating a discourse akin to Huntington's (1996) 'clash of civilizations'. 'Culture' has tended to be associated with ethnic, race-specific characteristics; and, although textbooks talk about, for example, a 'Slavic-Turkic dialogue', they also include alarmist narratives as to the country's possible fragmentation into parallel 'civilisational systems'. References to Russia as a unique type of civilisation are not infrequent, and ascribe a unified consciousness to its members (Shnirelman 2006a: 189–190).[110] In 2004, new standards for the teaching of history were introduced, although textbooks on the history of titular groups compiled in the regions at first continued to be used therein (Shnirelman 2010: 59). However, a second decree, also adopted in 2004,[111] restricted the autonomy of the regional authorities in this sphere, by mandating that schools are to select their textbooks from a federal list compiled by the Department of State Policy and Education of the Ministry of Education. This approach was reaffirmed through the 2012 Law 'On Education in the Russian Federation', pursuant to which schools select their textbooks from a federal list of recommended materials (Articles 18(4)(1) and 28(3)(9)).[112] The issue of history textbooks was raised by two respondents in Tatarstan, who were involved in their preparation [2.7; 2.8]; the respondents noted an increasing tendency of the federal centre to interfere in the development of textbooks for use at the regional level, accompanied by a growing concern with federal approval of texts on the part of publishing houses.

Conclusion

Following the adoption of Law 309, the republics have been stripped of many of their decision-making powers concerning language of instruction and the teaching of titular languages – although some of the likely repercussions were partially reined in through compromises. Yet while some basic guarantees have been established for the teaching of languages as official languages in the republics, overall the use of minority languages in the education system has decreased, and can be expected to continue to dwindle. A decline has been observed even in Tatarstan, despite the republic's much greater opportunities, compared to other ethnic republics, to create a favourable linguistic environment for the titular language. Meanwhile, in a republic like Karelia, where Karelian speakers are a small numerical minority, the use of the titular language continues to rapidly decrease. While Tatarstan has been particularly vocal in protests against the standardisation of education compared to Finno-Ugric republics, a decline in minority-language education, and a tendency towards cultural and linguistic homogenisation, can be detected across the Federation. It goes without saying that the conditions of minority-language education are more precarious outside the ethnic republics, in regions that do not benefit from the (albeit feeble) legal guarantees afforded to the republics' official languages and the (albeit limited) availability of resources.

The reform of the Russian education system has led to the role of the regions being diminished, with the federal and local levels concurrently acquiring greater prominence. The decreased legal guarantees have caused alarm in some regions, which are faced with a sense of unpredictability at the lack of clarity on the practical consequences of the reform. At the same time, centralising tendencies act to raise the status and financial viability of the Russian language: of crucial significance in these dynamics is the requirement to take the final secondary school examination (*EGE*) in Russian, and the fact that Russian is one of the two compulsory subjects on which students are tested. These regulations were introduced on the basis of legal reform set into motion by the federal authorities, with virtually no consultation with regions and minority groups. In addition to these centralising moves, there are simultaneous localising impulses that place new rights and responsibilities on individual schools by expanding the segment of the curriculum which they can, at least nominally, independently devise. At the same time, schools are confronted with a range of restrictions on their freedom of action, particularly with regard to the scarcity of resources, while parents are influenced in their choices by the often precarious conditions of individual schools and the wider socio-economic environment. This form of localism results in a tendency towards the atomisation of the Russian educational space, which is broken down to individual schools operating along loose federal guarantees for minority-language education, and devoid of language planning (and resources) that can sustain multilingualism. The federal authorities seem to fluctuate between the two poles of centralism, with the imposition of regulations without consultation in some areas and *laissez-faire* attitudes in others. Meanwhile, the rights of minorities remain opaque, exacerbating the difficulties in solidifying guarantees around them.

A form of inter-culturalism is promoted when representatives of all groups, including the majority, are required to study the official languages of the republics in which they reside: the study of minority languages by members of the majority can create opportunities for greater exposure to minority cultures as well as languages, thereby facilitating inter-cultural understanding. However, the study of titular languages as republics' official languages tends to provide students with only rudimentary notions, without the in-depth tuition that can halt (and reverse) moves towards linguistic assimilation. The increased marginalisation of minority languages in the education sphere, and the use of the school environment for patriotic indoctrination, suggest a type of education that is more akin to acculturation than inter-culturalism. Rather than an equilibrium between the identification of common values and diversity, the education system heavily tips the balance towards uniformity. Centralising moves further suggest a drive for the levelling of difference, perceived as a shortcut to social equality.[113] Uniformity is then pursued through standardised education, which relies on the Russian language, patriotism and Russia's traditional values.[114]

If we accept the notion that minority participation is furthered through decentralised arrangements (Grin 2003: 152–153), localism represents a means towards meeting the needs and wishes of minorities. And, in post-Soviet Russia, schools to some extent accommodate parents. However, devolution is insufficient to protect vulnerable languages. The tendency for minority languages to decline mirrors ongoing socio-economic patterns which see the Russian language and culture as the pathway to financial viability. Additionally, in the presence of globalising impulses, minority languages in Russia find themselves competing not only against Russian, but also English and other foreign languages. The prestige and the allure of social mobility are significant motivators in the study of Russian and foreign languages, often to the detriment of minority languages. Thus, the preservation of minority languages and cultures through the education system can only be guaranteed with tailor-made efforts by the state to reverse language shifts through a coherent language and education policy, complete with targets. By contrast, the Russian-language *EGE* and the new Federal Education Standards encourage assimilation as an instrument for full integration into society. Neither is there a systematic assessment of the outcomes of minority-language education; rather, official data tend to obfuscate the decline of minority-language use in the education system (and beyond). These and other developments outlined in this chapter are likely to offset efforts to promote minority languages; in line with this, a Tatar respondent argued that the situation in which persons belonging to minorities find themselves causes them to have 'no real choice' as to whether to preserve their cultural distinctiveness [2.7]. Indeed, while parents, students and schools are nominally given choices on minority-language education, their decisions are made in a socio-economic and political environment that is, overall, adverse to multilingualism.

In conclusion, the preservation of Russia's linguistic and cultural diversity requires the state to embrace its positive responsibilities under domestic and international law, in key areas such as education, transcending forms of *laissez-faire* and benign (or malign) neglect, and facilitating minority participation in decision-making and in policy implementation. In light of this, minority participation is the focus of this book's final chapters.

Notes

1 Sections of this chapter were included in an article published in the *Cambrian Law Review* ('Localism or Centralism? Education Reform in Russia and Its Impact on the Rights of National Minorities', 42, 2011: 113–130).

2 See also the OSCE High Commissioner on National Minorities (HCNM), 1996 Hague Recommendations Regarding the Education Rights of National Minorities; and Article 8 ECRML (education in regional or minority languages).

3 Diversity can be promoted through the education system and also through the media, which plays a crucial role in shaping societal attitudes. The media, however, is outside the scope of this study.

4 No. 3266–1, 10 July 1992 (on the amendments, see pp. 127ff.).

5 In this chapter I use 'minority-language education' to designate the teaching of minority languages as subjects, and instruction through the medium of minority languages. 'Minority education' is broader: in addition to minority languages, it can encompass the teaching of minority cultures, history and religions.

6 Of the interviews conducted, 22 were particularly relevant to this chapter because of the respondents' direct involvement in minority and/or inter-cultural education. These respondents belonged to the following categories: minority NGO (4 respondents), human rights NGO (3), academia (10), public official (3) and school employee (2). The category 'academia' includes analysts from research institutions and academics directly involved in programmes for the preservation of minority languages and cultures.

7 In this chapter I concentrate on the three focal ethnic republics. Schools teaching minority languages also exist outside the ethnic republics, in localities densely populated by members of minority groups. The provision of minority-language education in these cases is subject to demand and availability of resources.

8 One should note that the effects of the reform varied across the Soviet Union (Grenoble 2003: 57–58). Kolstø (2013: 39–40) argues that the number of students who continued to receive an education in their native languages following the reform is higher than is normally acknowledged. Yet in some regions parental choice was restricted. For example, in Chuvashia a 1960 resolution discontinued all instruction in Chuvash from the fifth grade onwards, switching to Russian for all subjects (Resolution of the Council of Ministers of the Chuvash ASSR 'On the Transition to the Teaching in Russian in 5th to 7th Grades and Measures to Improve the Learning of the Russian Language and Literature in Chuvash Schools', 26 July 1960).

9 The report was submitted in 2010. ACFC, (Third) Report submitted by the Russian Federation, 9 April 2010, ACFC/SR/III(2010)005. However, it contains the same data supplied for the previous (second) monitoring cycle (2005), with statistics on minority language education for the period 2001–2004.

10 Until the fourth grade in most cases; in grades five to nine only 90 students had Erzya as language of instruction, and none received Moksha-language instruction (ibid.).

11 As noted, Karelian is not recognised in Karelia as official (as the 'state language' of the republic). However, various programmes have been initiated by the republican authorities to support the Karelian language, as well as the Finnish and Veps languages.

12 This point was stressed in an interview by a representative of the Ministry of Culture in Kazan – although the respondent also expressed disappointment that the ultimate outcomes had not been as far-reaching as the stakeholders had hoped [4.9]. Tatarstan is one of only three republics (with Bashkortostan and Sakha/Yakutia) in which minority-language education is available at the tertiary level (Musina 2011: 17), although university courses in Tatar have been restricted to a limited number of faculties (Gorenburg 2005: 10).

13　Very few pupils study Karelian throughout secondary education. The Third Report to the ACFC (2010) gives the following figures: 1,186 pupils studied Karelian from grades one to four; 615 from grades five to nine; and 32 in grades 11 and 12. ACFC, (Third) Report submitted by the Russian Federation (see note 9) (the figures are in Appendix 6, Table 1 of the Third Report).

14　The 'Concept of Development of Finno-Ugric Schools', adopted in 1997 by the Republic of Karelia, states that the number of hours for the study of languages of Karelia's autochthonous groups (Karelians, Finns and Veps) should be no less than four hours a week. However, the curriculum developed in 2006 by Karelia's Ministry of Education had fewer hours: two or three hours for grades two to nine, and one hour for grades one, ten and 11 (Kovaleva 2010: 310–312).

15　See Resolution of the Government of the Russian Federation 'On the National Doctrine of Education in the Russian Federation' (No. 751, 4 October 2000).

16　See also Chapter 5.

17　Kuz'min is also the author of the explanatory document of the 2001 draft Concept of State Ethno-National Education Policy, cited above.

18　Adopted by Decree of the Ministry of Education and Science of the Russian Federation (No. 201, 3 August 2006).

19　Law 'On the Amendment of Legal Acts of the Russian Federation Modifying the Concept and Structure of State Education Standards' (No. 309-FZ, 1 December 2007).

20　Article 7(3)(1).

21　Such as a nationality's history, traditions and literature.

22　Decree of the Ministry of Education and Science of the Russian Federation 'On the Approval of Federal State Education Standards of General Education' (No. 1897, 17 December 2010).

23　Resolution of the Government of the Russian Federation 'On the Approval of Model Provisions for Institutions of General Education' (No. 196, 18 March 2001) §44. The document states that the 'participants in the education process' are 'students, the teaching staff, and the students' parents'. See also Russia's Third Report to the ACFC, stating that decisions on the variable parts of the curriculum are to be made 'primarily by educational institutions with consideration of the needs of students and their parents, as well as by education regulatory bodies'. ACFC, (Third) Report submitted by the Russian Federation (see note 9), p. 45.

24　No. 273-FZ, 29 December 2012. It came into force on 1 September 2013, when the 1992 Law 'On Education' was repealed.

25　Article 14(1).

26　These are referred to in the Russian Constitution (Article 68(2)) as 'state languages' of the republics. However, for simplicity I use the expression 'official languages', while referring to Russian as the 'state language' for the entire Russian Federation.

27　Article 14(3).

28　Instead, the Russian Constitution declares that Russian is the state language of the Russian Federation (Article 68(1)) and education standards are to be established by the Russian federal government (Article 43(5)). Kuz'min and Artemenko further referred to Article 71(c) of the Constitution, providing that federal jurisdiction encompasses the regulation and protection of the rights and freedoms of citizens, as well as the protection of the rights of national minorities. They argue that, consequently, the rights of citizens in the area of education and culture cannot be exclusively regulated by the subjects of the Federation (Kuz'min and Artemenko 2010: 45).

29　State Council of the Russian Federation, Report 'On the Measures to Strengthen Inter-Ethnic Accord in Russian Society', 29 March 2011, p. 44.

30　See also the 1999 OSCE/HCNM Lund Recommendations on the Effective Participation of National Minorities in Public Life, Point 19.

31 One should note that neither centralism nor localism is per se 'positive' or 'negative', as approaches to them and modes of application vary; nor are local autonomy and democracy indissolubly linked (Elander 1997).

32 Gordeev, I. 22 May 2009. 'Parad Suverenitetov na Shkolnom Urovne' [The Parade of Sovereignties at the School Level], *Nezavisimaya Gazeta*.

33 Article 26 of the Russian Constitution.

34 The expression was used in an interview by an advisor to the Minister of Culture of the Republic of Tatarstan [4.9].

35 These tensions have, however, decreased over time, given the slow and uncertain steps towards the actual implementation of the new provisions.

36 Part of the Academy of Sciences of Republic of Tatarstan.

37 Referring specifically to Law 309, the respondent argued that the federal centre prevented the Republic of Tatarstan from fulfilling the principles enshrined in the FCNM.

38 Both in relation to the ethnic republic and Russia as a whole.

39 RCC, Judgement No. 16-P, 16 November 2004. See Chapter 4.

40 However, in the same judgement it was held that the teaching of titular languages should not be to the detriment of the federal component of the curriculum and to the teaching of the Russian language.

41 See Chapter 5.

42 The change was sanctioned by Decree of the Ministry of Education and Science of the Russian Federation 'On the Approval of Regulations on the Methods and Procedures for the State (Final) Certification of Students Having Completed the Main General Education Programmes of Full Secondary Education' (No. 362, 28 November 2008).

43 See RCC, Judgement No. 16-P (see note 39); and RSC, Appeals Chamber, Judgement No. KAS09–295, 2 July 2009.

44 Rules on the Development and Approval of the Federal State Education Standards, adopted through Resolution of the Government of the Russian Federation No. 142, 24 February 2009. Point 3 states that the Ministry of Education and Science 'guarantees the development of standards with the involvement of organs of executive powers concerned' and with the public institutions participating in the system of education. Draft standards are to be made available to the public, and comments by interested parties reviewed by the Ministry of Education.

45 This is in line with RCC Judgement No. 16-P (see note 39), according to which the compulsory teaching of official languages of the republics is not unconstitutional although it must be in line with federal education standards.

46 See below (same page) on this ('Dwindling minority-language education').

47 ACFC, (Third) Report submitted by the Russian Federation (see note 9), p. 46.

48 Or simply the language of one's ethnic group, even in case of greater fluency in Russian. See also Chapter 2.

49 I focus on percentages rather than actual numbers because the number of students per se has tended to decrease due to a demographic decline, particularly in the case of Finno-Ugric peoples (Strogal'shikova 2009a). As a result, percentages provide a more accurate picture of the situation.

50 Reported in ACFC, (Third) Opinion on the Russian Federation, GVT/COM/III(2012)004, 25 July 2012), §192 (fn. 50).

51 Different figures are provided by Musina *et al.* (2011b), possibly due to a different system of classification of Tatar-language schools. Nevertheless, these authors also refer to a decrease in the number of Tatar schools, from 1,061 (2009) to 997 (2010).

52 Zamyatin's data are based on official statistics of the Mordovian Ministry of Education and on research by local academic institutions.

53 Similar data on the decrease of minority-language education have also been recorded for the Republic of Chuvashia (Alòs i Font 2014).

54 According to data by Kovaleva, the teaching of Karelian started in 11 schools in 1989–1990, and rose to 60 schools in 1995–1996; in the period between the 1996–1997 and 2005–2006 academic years the number of schools was between 49 and 57, but it dropped to 33 in 2009–2010. The number of students learning Karelian rose from 301 (1989–1990) to 2,522 (1995–1996), and dropped to 1,581 (2008–2009). It then rose slightly again to 1,774 in 2011–2012. The highest point was in 2001–2002, with 2,596 students (Kovaleva 2010: 313–314). As noted above, the use of percentages provides a more accurate account of the state of minority-language education, in light of Russia's demographic decline.

55 Private communication with an education expert from Tatarstan, February 2014.

56 Article 26(2) of the Russian Constitution, Article 9 of the Law 'On the Languages of the Peoples of the Russian Federation' (No. 1807-I, 25 October 1991), and Article 14 of the 2012 Law 'On Education in the Russian Federation' (see note 24). However, Article 14 of the Law 'On Education in the Russian Federation' states that instruction in the language of one's choice is realised 'within the limits of the opportunities provided by the system of education'.

57 With regard to the Republics of Altai and Tyva, Chevalier notes that: 'Since the introduction [of the *EGE*] community enthusiasm for local language school programs has been replaced by calls to devote more school resources to Russian language instruction' (Chevalier 2012: 12).

58 These data were provided to the author by Institute of Ethnology and Anthropology, Russian Academy of Sciences (private communication, May 2014).

59 The population of the Russian Federation declined from 148.7 million in 1991 to 145.1 million (2002 census), and then to 142.9 million (2010 census). See also Strogal'shikova (2009a).

60 With regard to Tatarstan and Tatar schools, see Simonova, I. 3 February 2007. 'Kuda Idti Sel'skoy Shkole' [What to Do with the Village School], *Respublika Tatarstan*. Post-Soviet regional education policies attempted to address the urban–rural divide in the sphere of minority-language education that was common in the Soviet period. Thus, in Tatarstan, language revival policies have focused on establishing Tatar-language schools in cities. Yet, as in the Soviet period, Tatar (like the Mordovian languages and Karelian) tends to be employed more in the rural areas, given the greater concentration of speakers and of national schools (Sagitova 2011: 73).

61 Sokolova, V. 1 April 2011. 'Serye Kardinaly Obrazovaniya' [The *Eminences Grises* of Education], *Sovershenno Sekretno*, www.sovsekretno.ru/magazines/article/2758 (accessed 15 October 2014).

62 Ministry of Education of the Republic of Mordovia, 2010. 'Statistical Data and Indicators on the Situation and Dynamics of Development in the Economic, Social and Other Spheres within the Competences of [the] Ministry of Education', cited in Zamyatin (2012b: 94).

63 See Resolution of the Government of the Russian Federation 'On the Restructuring of the Network of Education Institutions Situated in the Rural Areas' (No. 871, 17 December 2001). Government documents on modernisation in the sphere of education include: Decree of the Ministry of Education of the Russian Federation 'On the Concepts of Modernisation of Russian Education until 2010' (No. 393, 11 February 2002), and Resolution of the Government of the Russian Federation 'On the National Doctrine of Education in the Russian Federation' (No. 751, 4 October 2000). On this issue, see also ACFC, (Third) Opinion on the Russian Federation (see note 50), §192.

64 Particularly from interviews with school employees in Petrozavodsk and Kazan [5.1; 5.2].

65 Private communication with an education expert from Tatarstan, February 2014. In order to gain extra hours, schools might decide to operate on a six-day week, with additional lessons on Saturday.

66 Referred to in this chapter (Alòs i Font 2014; Chevalier 2012; Zamyatin 2012b, 2012c).
67 ACFC, (Third) Report submitted by the Russian Federation (see note 9), p. 101. Two years later, the figures had once again increased: the Russian government stated that there were 39 languages of instruction in schools and 50 were taught as subjects in Russian schools. 'Comments of the Government of the Russian Federation on the Third Opinion of the Advisory Committee on the Implementation of the Framework Convention for the Protection of National Minorities by the Russian Federation', 25 July 2012, GVT/COM/III(2012)004, p. 6.
68 ACFC, (Second) Report submitted by the Russian Federation Second, 26 April 2005, ACFC/SR/II(2005)003, p. 30.
69 ACFC, (Third) Report submitted by the Russian Federation (see note 9), p. 101.
70 See also Alòs i Font (2014), in relation to the Chuvash language in Chuvashia's education system.
71 The teaching of titular languages as 'official languages' is commonly confined to only one or two hours per week (Zamyatin 2012c: 37–38).
72 The surveys were conducted by the Centre of Ethno-Sociological Studies of the Institute of History of the Russian Academy of Sciences of the Republic of Tatarstan, as part of the research project 'Official Languages in the System of School Education of the Republic of Tatarstan'. The surveys' participants were 995 students in the tenth to eleventh grades (360 in Kazan, 650 in other localities within the republic), 473 students' parents (158 and 315 respectively) and 330 teachers (142 and 188 respectively). The study included schools with Russian as the language of instruction, Tatar-medium schools, schools with a Russian ethnocultural component, and special schools with a humanities or science orientation (Musina *et al.* 2011a: 6–7).
73 However, some Russian (and Tatar) parents do consider it an unnecessary burden. For example, in early 2011, 600 parents of Tatarstan's schoolchildren, including ethnic Tatars, submitted an appeal to the federal Minister of Education to reduce or end the obligatory study of Tatar. Goble, P. 14 April 2011. 'Kazan Parents' Call for Studying Russian not Tatar Sparks Conflicts about More than Language', *The Kazan Herald*. See also RCC, Judgement No. 16-P (see note 39).
74 This last issue was only raised by respondents in Tatarstan, as other regions visited had never had such an option.
75 Local data for 2008 (see note 72) suggest that approximately three-quarters of students of Tatar origin and nearly one-fifth of students of Russian origin are conversant in Tatar (Makarova 2011a: 31).
76 Schools are supplied materials – textbooks on minority languages and cultures – free-of-charge, although these were at times found by the respondents to be insufficient to meet existing needs [e.g. 1.2.1; 5.1].
77 See note 72.
78 According to the same survey, among the students who were in favour of studying Tatar, 46 per cent thought Tatar would be useful in their future work, although a much higher percentage thought that Russian (90 per cent) and foreign languages (82 per cent) would be useful for the same reason (Gabdrakhmanova 2011: 85).
79 See p. 125 ('From Soviet to post-Soviet minority-language education').
80 At the same time, the ACFC also refers to instances in which parents wished to enrol their children in schools with minority-language education, yet spaces were unavailable. ACFC, (Third) Opinion on the Russian Federation (see note 50), §197.
81 See note 56.
82 FCNM, Explanatory Report, §75.
83 Ibid; Article 14(2) FCNM.
84 ACFC, 'Commentary on Education under the Framework Convention for the Protection of National Minorities', 2 March 2006, ACFC/25DOC(2006), p. 6.
85 On the need for strong legal guarantees, see for example ACFC, (Second) Opinion on Switzerland, 2 September 2008, ACFC/OP/II(2008)002, §67; 80. The Opinion

recommends regular dialogue between regional and federal authorities in implementing the relevant legal provisions (§17).

86 ACFC, Commentary on Education (see note 84), p. 10.

87 Particularly due to the frequent marginalisation of minority languages – and the prevalent use of dominant languages – in the media. ECRML, Explanatory Report, §2.

88 This issue was noted by Karelian respondents as one of the main reasons for the withering use of their language [1.4.1; 2.1; 2.2].

89 Generally on the need for a coordinated programme for the teaching of minority languages, see for example ACFC, (First) Opinion on Italy, 4 September 2001, ACFC/INF/OP/I(2002)007, §58.

90 I do not refer to a *laissez-faire* approach with regard to language policy *generally*. An overall *laissez-faire* approach with regard to language policy is hardly possible, as language is inseparable from language management, implying continuous choices by the state as to what languages ought to be used in public life. And, in some instances, as emphasised in this chapter, the Russian government has introduced regulations that considerably impact upon language use in the education system, such as the obligation to take examinations in Russian. I am grateful to Hèctor Alòs i Font for his comments with reference to this particular point.

91 The ACFC in 2007 further referred to a 'poorly defined' division of responsibilities between the local, regional and federal bodies in the sphere of education. ACFC, (Second) Opinion on the Russian Federation, 2 May 2007, ACFC/OP/II(2006)004, §251.

92 For example, see Fishman's Graded Intergenerational Disruption Scale, ranging from stage 8 (moribund language) to stage 1, where a language is fully functioning and inter-generational transmission is secured (Fishman 1991). Other scales include the Ethnologue's 'Expanded Graded Intergenerational Disruption Scale' (www.ethnologue.com/about/language-status, accessed 2 February 2015) and UNESCO's 'Language Vitality and Endangerment' (www.unesco.org/new/en/culture/themes/endangered-languages/language-vitality/, accessed 2 February 2015).

93 In light of this, the ECRML includes provisions for the safeguard of minority languages that encompass multiple spheres of language usage – education, judiciary, administrative authorities, media, cultural activities, economic and social life – reflecting a need to approach language preservation policies holistically for them to be successful.

94 Some opportunities to use titular languages in Russia are provided through legislation stipulating that public services are to be made available in these languages in particular regions. For example, Tatarstan's Law 'On the Use of the Tatar Language as a State Language of the Republic of Tatarstan' (No. 1-ZRT, 12 January 2013) guarantees the right of citizens to receive information in Tatar from administrative authorities (Article 2).

95 See note 72.

96 ACFC, (Third) Opinion on the Russian Federation (see note 50), §196.

97 ACFC, (Second) Opinion on the Russian Federation (see note 91), §250. On this, see also, for example, ACFC, (First) Opinion on the United Kingdom, 30 November 2001, ACFC/INF/OP/I(2002)006, §91. The ACFC encouraged the British government to be more proactive in facilitating minority-language education in localities densely populated by minorities. Awareness-raising has been linked to creating an expectation that the relevant rights will be realised if claimed (de Varennes and Thornberry 2005: 419).

98 ACFC, (First) Opinion on the Russian Federation, 13 September 2002, ACFC/INF/OP/I(2003)005, §97. See also, for example, ACFC, (First) Opinion on Albania, 12 September 2002, ACFC/INF/OP/I(2003)004, §105; ACFC, (First) Opinion on Cyprus, 6 April 2001, ACFC/INF/OP/I(2002)004, §39; ACFC, (First) Opinion on the United Kingdom (ibid.), §92.

99 ACFC, (Third) Report submitted by the Russian Federation (see note 9), pp. 103–104. See also Chapter 4.

100 President of Russia, Address to the National Assembly of the Russian Federation, 12 December 2013, http://eng.kremlin.ru/news/6402 (accessed 25 September 2014).

101 The ACFC has acknowledged that the majority language should be an integral part of the curriculum even in minority-language schools. See for example ACFC, (First) Opinion on Serbia and Montenegro, 27 November 2003, ACFC/INF/OP/I(2004)002, §98.

102 Adopted through Resolution of the Government of the Russian Federation No. 122, 16 February 2001.

103 From the 1990s, the Russian Orthodox Church had lobbied for the teaching of religious education as an optional course. 'Foundations of Orthodox Culture' was introduced as an optional course in Smolensk oblast in 1991, and in 34 other regions between 1996 and 2006. Instructions to commence the teaching of the new subject elsewhere were issued in 2009 by (then) President Medvedev, first in selected regions, and subsequently in all schools.

104 President of Russia, Address to the National Assembly of the Russian Federation, 12 December 2012, http://eng.kremlin.ru/transcripts/4739 (accessed 24 September 2014).

105 Address to the National Assembly, 12 December 2013 (see note 100).

106 'Doklad Svyateishego Patriarkha Kirilla na Otkrytii XXI Mezhdunarodnykh Rozhdestvenskikh Chtenii' [Report of the Holy Patriarch Kirill at the Opening of the XXI International Christmas Readings], 13 January 2013, www.patriarchia.ru/db/text/2746897.html (accessed 2 September 2014).

107 While the six modules conform to the same patriotic framework, there are also variations between them. The textbook for 'Foundations of Secular Ethnics' goes further in its patriotic messages with a militaristic slant than the textbook for 'Foundations of Orthodox Culture'. The 'Foundations of Secular Ethics' module presents an exclusively positive view of Russian history, of which Russian citizens should be proud, and stresses the need for Russians to defend their country (Willems 2012: 37).

108 Demidova, E. 18 August 2010. 'Uchit'sya, Uchit'sya i Uchit'sya … Dolzhny Uchitelya' [Teachers Should … Learn, Learn, Learn], *Nezavisimaya Gazeta*, www.ng.ru/ng_religii/2010–08–18/4_study.html (accessed 3 October 2014).

109 Turovskii, D. 1 December 2010. 'Shkol'nikam ne Dayut Vozmozhnost' Vybrat' Religiosnyi Kurs' [Schoolchildren Have No Option to Choose their Religious Course], *Kommersant*, www.kommersant.ru/doc/1549580 (accessed 3 October 2014). The study examined pilot religious courses in 19 regions of Russia between April and December 2010.

110 On nationalism in textbooks see also Shevyrev (2005: 284–287).

111 Decree of the Ministry of Education 'On the Approval of Federal Lists of Textbooks, Recommended (Admitted) for Use in the Education Process …' (No. 03–410, 21 October 2004).

112 These textbooks were included in the federal list of recommended textbooks following an assessment carried out with the participation of the relevant organs of the subjects of the Federation (Article 18(6)); however, the procedure for compiling the list is established at the federal level (Article 17).

113 See also Chapter 4.

114 In 2012 Putin stressed 'the enormous significance of high-quality education in the Russian language, history, literature, the foundations of secular ethics and traditional religions. These subjects have a special role: they form a personality, an individual'(Address to the National Assembly, 12 December 2012 (see note 104)).

7 Participation through cooperation?

Minority associations and state institutions[1]

Participatory rights are essential in the formulation of effective minority policies for the protection of distinctive cultures, reflecting their beneficiaries' needs and interests, but they are probably the most complex rights to delineate and regulate. Difficulties in implementing participatory rights exist in all countries: international standards are so flexible as to sometimes seem ephemeral, and there are logistical difficulties in the establishment of effective mechanisms to channel stakeholders' needs to higher, decision-making levels. These difficulties are due to an interplay of factors, including possible majority–minority tensions, in-group differences and the issue of accountability of representation. At the same time, the benefits of participation are manifold. The inclusion of the various societal groups in the political and cultural life of a country facilitates a sense of 'joint ownership' of the state and its policies. It lessens possible feelings by minority groups of being subdued by a dominant group, and helps maintain peace and stability, by furthering the conditions for harmonious majority–minority relations. Ultimately, participation facilitates the social integration of all groups, by promoting their genuine equality (Hofmann 2006). Conversely, the absence of representation of minority interests can lead to disillusionment and disengagement. The opportunistic manipulation of the political sphere by political entrepreneurs (themselves influenced by specific institutional contexts) can lead to disaffection among the electorate,[2] and their withdrawal from the political system – a form of 'political *malaise*' (Offe 2006: 23). This phenomenon has been linked to, among other things, difficulties in holding representatives accountable for their actions (Offe 2006).

This and the next two chapters examine the participatory rights of minorities in the formulation and implementation of policies affecting languages and cultures. I differentiate between participation through general cooperation between state organs and civil society[3] (Chapter 7) *and* official (or semi-official) mechanisms of participation, such as national cultural autonomy, advisory councils and elected bodies (Chapters 8 and 9). Data from interviews are used to illustrate the dynamics of civil society activity with reference to cooperation with the authorities, and potential impact upon decision-making affecting the exercise of minorities' cultural rights. In examining the relationship between civil society and public officials, two elements are particularly relevant: informal practices present in official and unofficial systems of representation; and patterns of loyalty that often emerge in majority–minority relations. Chapters 7, 8 and 9 combined show that minorities in Russia are excluded from most processes of policy-making and policy implementation, and generally remain disempowered with regard to the future of their cultural distinctiveness.

Russia is bound to promote the right to participation of minorities by Article 15 FCNM,[4] and to guarantee the right to freedom of association by Article 7 FCNM[5] and Article 11 ECHR.[6] Freedom of association refers to an organisation's right to 'exist', through the recognition of its legal personality, and to freely operate. It enables minorities to exercise their rights *as a group*. Machnyikova writes:

> The right to freedom of assembly and association is one of the central rights, whose free enjoyment is essential for the preservation of the identity of persons belonging to national minorities, since it is geared towards persons uniting and associating to express and protect their common characteristics and interests. In fact, the right to associate is a precondition for the existence of a group.
>
> (Machnyikova 2005: 204)

By uniting, minorities gather strength to more forcefully call for their rights. The right to association and participation overlap and form a continuum: in line with the FCNM, minority groups have the right to self-organise without interference from the government; and, in turn, the government must involve minority groups in decision-making processes.

In addition to the FCNM provisions already cited, of relevance to participation is Article 8 FCNM (the right to manifest one's religion or belief, including by establishing religious associations), and Article 7(4) ECRML, which states: 'In determining their policy with regard to regional or minority languages, the Parties shall take into consideration the needs and wishes expressed by the groups which use such languages.'[7]

The implementation of these provisions requires special mechanisms such as advisory councils – institutionalised points of contact between the authorities and stakeholders[8] – as well as a favourable environment for inclusive decision-making. The latter, in turn, implies a common civil society, even in the presence of multiple ethnic communities (Klinke and Renn 1997: 257), or a 'civic culture' (Almond and Verba 1989) accompanied by mutual respect and recognition (Shils 1991) and the appreciation of pluralism (Ghai 2000: 16). An additional crucial ingredient for participation is the opportunity for civil society to express and advance its interests in an autonomous way, so as to keep potential oligarchic impulses at bay; without such freedom of action, state authoritarianism might prevail over, or even manoeuvre, grass-roots activism (Rueschemeyer 1998).

In Eastern European countries the Communist legacy has led to an inherent weakness of civil society, with citizens often reluctant to become involved with activism. This disinclination has been linked to two factors among others: a memory of compulsory participation in state-sponsored public activities, combined with the vibrancy of private networks (Howard 2003); and limited exposure to democratic politics. The latter can lead to apolitical tendencies among some citizens of post-Communist countries, with clientelistic networks and personalistic interests more commonly dictating voters' choices than candidates' proposed policies. Institutions inherited from the Communist period themselves display a legacy of oligarchic monopoly and control from above (Barnes 2006: 77–78). Besides these general (post-Communist) trends, interview data (and secondary sources) point to three main reasons that cause Russian civil society to operate in an environment that is unfavourable to its input in decision-making in the sphere of minority rights. First, the public discourse on minority issues – and dialogue between the state and civil society in this sphere – is primarily confined to themes that do not overstep pre-established boundaries, remaining in the realm of 'culture' per se, rather than 'cultural rights' or 'minority rights'. Second, the state's approach to civil society rests on a limited receptiveness of civil society initiatives, and on precarious modalities of cooperation. Informal practices and political considerations are variable factors affecting the fortunes of civil society, in an environment in which windows of opportunity appear and vanish ad hoc. Third, Russia's civil society finds itself in a position of vulnerability, due to legal restrictions on its activities – with occasional direct infringements of the right to association – and a paucity of available funds. Hence, depending on the circumstances, the Russian authorities may respond to civil society's initiatives for the promotion of minority cultures in any of the following ways: through cooperation and support; with indifference and disinterest; or by erecting walls around civil society activity.

One has to add that Russian public officials can use their discretion in applying (and thereby operationalising) formal rules and legislation. While this is the case in many countries, including Western democracies, Solomon (2008b) stresses the leeway that public officials enjoy in Russia, with few constraints to limit the potential manipulation of formal rules to pursue self-interest, or to accommodate their cultural predispositions and views. A crucial role is being played, again, by informal institutions and practices, including clientelistic networks. These dynamics fit into a form of *laissez-faire* at the micro-level, outlined in previous chapters, by which the actions of individual public officials can deviate from formal rules and policies; civil servants can, then, resort to 'non-compliance, virtual or creative compliance, and partial or fully manipulated compliance' (ibid.: 131). Yet non-compliance is not only confined to state structures: Osipov (2012) points to a 'systemic hypocrisy' which may be embraced by public officials and civil society alike, and that manifests itself when: 'deliberate avoidance of implementing certain normative provisions generates no criticism in the given society and goes in combination with the overall silent consent on this state of affairs of all the stakeholders, including minority activists themselves' (ibid.: 425).

This scenario translates into a reliance on *symbolic* policies, which provide a non-controversial form of interaction between state officials and minority groups (through superficial 'communication'), and which can take the place of *instrumental* policies (ibid.).

The boundaries of public discourse

As noted, three factors impair cooperation between minority associations and state institutions, which *inter alia* affect minority participation in shaping policy-making on matters impacting upon their cultural rights: a superficial discourse on minority issues; the discretion of public officials in their cooperation (or non-cooperation) with civil society; and civil society's vulnerability. In the first case, boundaries are placed around the public discourse on minority rights: the interviews revealed a disinclination in the authorities to engage in 'hard talk' – discussion on politically sensitive matters not fully aligned to the official position – *or* to deviate from consolidated patterns of approaching nationality issues. This situation has led to a public discourse on *cultural development* of ethnic groups, rather than their *rights*. A report to the Parliamentary Assembly of the Council of Europe refers to the 'folklorisation' of minorities – or minorities' linguistic and cultural rights being approached as folklore;[9] indeed, a focus on (folkloristic) festivals can be seen in Russia's reports to the ACFC, in which lengthy lists feature prominently.[10] A legacy of folklore can be traced back to the Soviet period: the rationale for this approach can be found in the Soviets' treatment of folklore as politically harmless, linked to (non-militant) pride in one's nationality, as opposed to rampant nationalism.[11] Writing about Mordovia, Abramov criticises the 'folklorisation' of the Soviet period. In the 1960s, he argues, the teaching of the Mordovian languages in schools was abolished – with an adverse effect on national culture in education, journalism and literature – while folklore was upgraded: '[T]he national aspect, in essence, was limited only to folklore, which strengthened its primitive character and precluded the development into modern forms' (Abramov 2010: 121).

A respondent from Karelia, an activist seeking to promote Karelian-language education, echoed this, saying that 'language issues are mixed with folklore' [1.2.2]; their disaggregation, she suggested, would likely lead to more nuanced (and effective) state policies on Karelian-language teaching. Some respondents (from civil society and academia) believed that the celebration of minority cultures through festivals was superficial – a palliative failing to reach down to underlying minority concerns [1.2.1; 1.2.2; 1.2.9; 1.5.7; 4.14; 2.16]. Indeed, in Russia the specificities of cultural and linguistic rights tend to be left at the periphery of the minority rights discourse, and circumscribed to narratives on the coexistence of cultures and 'tolerance'. At the opposite end of the spectrum is the flip-side of 'tolerance' – 'extremism', which also enters the public discourse through official pronouncements featured in the Russian media. For example, in his 2013 state of the nation address, Putin argued that 'the most important topic requiring frank discussion in our society today is interethnic relations'.[12] Yet he linked this primarily to extreme positions, rather than pervasive discrimination and stereotyping. Persons who fuel inter-ethnic tensions were considered to be:

'insolent people from certain southern Russian regions, corrupt law enforcement officials who cover for ethnic mafias, so-called Russian nationalists, various kinds of separatists who are ready to turn any common tragedy into an excuse for vandalism and bloody rampage.'[13]

The binary nature of the discourse around diversity (tolerance and 'harmless' folklore versus extremism) oversimplifies a complex set of issues relating to social integration and discrimination. It further acts to reinforce stereotypes, by ascribing specific (folklore-based) traits to certain groups. It singles out a few problematic elements in society (the 'extremists') rather than highlighting patterns of racism and discrimination across Russian society (see Osipov 2013c: 66–67). It is in this context that one can understand the Russian authorities' rejection of the findings of a 2006 report by the UN Special Rapporteur on Contemporary Forms of Racism, Racial Discrimination, Xenophobia and Related Intolerance. The report had found widespread discrimination against, and harassment of, particularly disadvantaged, minorities, principally non-Slavic, darker-skinned groups, such as Central Asians, Caucasians and African immigrants.[14] A representative of the Russian authorities condemned the report and its 'far-reaching conclusions ... based on unproven data and falsifications'.[15] Yet levels of racism in Russia remain high.[16] They are fed by fears of Russians being harmed by 'aliens', themselves fuelled by references to a declining Russian population combined with waves of immigration (mostly from Central Asia), and the growth of the Muslim population (primarily in the North Caucasus) (Shnirelman 2009a). It is not unusual for these issues to be taken up by politicians to construe populist messages, amplified through the media.

Other respondents were more positive about members of minority groups expressing themselves though festivals and folklore. For example, Karelians from Petrozavodsk and Tver who had lived through the Soviet period noted that, after (what they judged as) the Soviets' repression of their ethno-linguistic distinctiveness,[17] they overcame feelings of shame in their origins – and found pride in their ethnic belonging – through festivals [2.4; 2.5]. Indeed, festivals provided a much-welcomed opportunity to freely celebrate their culture. Tatar respondents similarly noted the importance of celebrating traditional Tatar national holidays and festivals [1.1.5; 1.3.6; 1.4.2]. The representative of an NGO, and academic in Moscow, believed that Russia's support of festivals indicated the Russian government's symbolic acceptance of and respect for minorities [1.5.1]. Another respondent, the director of a minority NGO in Karelia, saw festivals as occasions for members of minority associations to bond and attract new recruits [1.2.1]. As such, these modes of minority expression are often not challenged by minorities themselves, possibly due to their familiarity with them, having long inhabited this (folkloristic) milieu. Similarly, during *perestroika* many minorities did not question the existing system of diversity management, but strived to improve their position *within* it (Gorenburg 2003); in post-Soviet Russia representatives of minorities similarly seek room for manoeuvre through options that are available to them, making use of institutions and practices that have survived the transition from the Soviet to post-Soviet period, including those that are predominantly folkore-based. A possible downside of this approach is that the Russian authorities might be instrumentalising folkloristic events and cultural programmes to channel nationalistic sentiments in a purely cultural direction, while also promoting Russian patriotism (and, ultimately, a strong state). For example, in one Mordovian ethnic festival (observed by the author in 2010),[18] in addition to the celebration of the Mordovian culture, an emphasis was placed on good inter-ethnic relations, and a form of patriotism that mixed elements of the 'Great Patriotic War' – through references to the 65th anniversary of the victory – with those of United Russia. The ruling party's flags were scattered around the festival area.[19]

The same director of an NGO in Karelia, cited above [1.2.1], commented on what she perceived to be, overall, the superficial approach of post-Soviet nationalities policy:

> The [Karelian] Ministry on Nationality Policy[20] doesn't look for solutions to serious problems.... When you want to talk about things that are serious, they just don't want to.... For example, about the publication of children's books [in minority languages]: already for years we have said that if we have a Finnish magazine for children, let's also have one for Karelians and Veps, or otherwise divide the money available in equal parts. Nothing happened. One starts getting tired by how difficult it is. But the money is there for events [festivals] ... [these events] are empty of meaning ... They [the authorities] need to go much deeper.
>
> [1.2.1]

Issues such as the one raised by this respondent (minority-language publications) relate to non-political, cultural matters, but they may be susceptible to marginalisation if they do not correspond to the local authorities' priorities and consolidated modalities of approaching nationality issues. The respondents (civil society and academia) referred to other issues that do not tend to be discussed publicly – despite their being closely linked to minority rights – such as the low salaries of language teachers [1.2.2; 2.7], and the closure of national schools on the grounds that they are not financially viable [1.2.2; 1.1.4; 2.5].[21] A Mordovian academic and activist observed that those benefits that do arise from ethnic festivals could be achieved with fewer events, while this downsizing would allow for other types of initiatives to be more adequately funded [2.14].[22] He further suggested that the Russian authorities had made festivals the centrepiece of their nationality programmes, as these events indicated a commitment to a multi-ethnic country without however engaging in complex, wide-ranging reforms. This interpretation is consistent with the view of Russia pursuing stability through an all-encompassing Russian patriotic idea, while also projecting the image of a multi-ethnic and multi-faith country.[23] Meanwhile, the tendency to folklorisation and the superficiality of the minority discourse was found by some respondents to hamper their activities and cooperation with the authorities. Restricting the scope of debate to an emollient language on cultural programmes limits the options for minority concerns (as *rights*) to be articulated and taken into account in policy-making. A respondent from a minority NGO in St Petersburg said:

> I must say that they [the authorities] prefer to make beautiful things. Like different folkloristic festivals for example. Something you can show. We did something good [that fits into this framework]: an [itinerant] museum, moving from place to place, for Finno-Ugric peoples from the region. But I think the main problem for us is losing our national identity and most importantly losing our language.
>
> [1.2.8]

This respondent implied that the state's preconceptions over the formats of cultural programmes for national minorities forced his organisation to reformulate its priorities. While overall satisfied with the itinerant museum, this initiative had not assisted the minority NGO with what it had identified as the ethnic group's primary concern: the loss of its linguistic identity.

At the same time, another respondent, from a minority NGO in St Petersburg, referred to recent efforts to contain folklorisation, combined with an increase in opportunities for education and inter-ethnic dialogue [1.2.9]. She believed that activities to promote minority cultures in her city had become more outward-looking by involving inter-group dynamics. Earlier, she said, activities had been 'internal':

> Now it is two directions: it's for the nationality [itself], but there is also the dissemination of information [outside the group]. [Activities] are not done with the *balalaika* but with education, with seminars. Before there was a certain closure, the [ethnic] groups were separated from the rest of society. Now there are people who come to our [Finno-Ugric] organisation who are Tatars or from other groups, but they are interested in other nationalities.... Some of the activities are shown on television. We want to stop national separatism, because nobody is 100% of a particular nationality, we are all mixed.
>
> [1.2.9]

In welcoming a new effort towards education and inter-group exchanges, the respondent implicitly criticised the folkloristic slant of some cultural programmes.

Civil society and the state: working together, sometimes

A second hindrance to minority participation was linked by the respondents to the over-reliance on personal networks that characterises cooperation between the Russian authorities and civil society. While these networks may benefit minorities, their regulation remains undefined, impeding the application of formal standards. In principle, civil society and the state can be mutually reinforcing.

Respondents from civil society saw support from and cooperation with the authorities as a fundamental vehicle for the success of their activities. One specialist on minority education in Moscow described the importance of cooperation by arguing: 'there is no point in producing educational materials that will not be institutionalised [and therefore remain unused]' [4.14]. In turn, the state, given its finite resources, can benefit from civil society, when the latter complements, and sometimes substitutes, state programmes. In the ethnic republics visited, the state had outsourced grammar books for the teaching of minority languages and financed Sunday schools and adult education classes on minority languages, as well as the organisation of events such as the traditional Tatar festival *Sabantui*. Among the respondents were representatives of organisations that: acted as focal points for other minority organisations and groups, facilitating joint activities; engaged in capacity-building of newly established organisations; provided training for activists (on minority rights in Russian and international law); trained law-enforcement officers or public officials on minority issues; provided legal advice and representation in court to minorities, particularly in discrimination cases; and provided fora for discussion for representatives of government and civil society, including minority groups, to promote dialogue and joint problem-solving. Respondents from civil society (in Petrozavodsk, Saransk and Voronezh) noted that in some cases they had forged fruitful cooperation with the authorities, primarily at the local level – perhaps due to the distance from the 'core' policies formulated in Moscow – allowing them to promote their interests [1.1.1; 1.1.2; 1.2.6; 1.2.9; 1.3.1; 1.3.2; 1.4.3]. The respondents further referred to instances in which the Russian authorities had solicited input from civil society specialists and academics in the formulation of minority-related policies. An example from Tatarstan concerned an active exchange in the preparation of federal educational standards for primary schools:[24] a representative of the Institute of History of Tatarstan's Academy of Sciences noted in an interview that the Institute had been consulted by the federal Ministry of Education and Science throughout the entire process [2.7]. In Karelia, one of the respondents, an academic in Petrozavodsk, was among the drafters of the republic's nationalities policy [2.4].

Analysts interviewed saw as an essential ingredient for cooperation between civil society and the authorities – and for furthering minority rights generally – the maintenance of good relations between the two groups [1.5.1; 2.14; 2.15; 2.17; 2.19]. Indeed, most respondents of the 'civil society' category had sought cooperation rather than confrontation, and had relied on personal networks to pursue their goals. The drawback of such informal arrangements is that much is left to the discretion of the local authorities, or even individual public officials – whose commitment to cultural diversity was at times found to be wanting by the respondents. They cited varying levels of commitment and support in different cities or regions, or even at different times in the same region, as a supportive public official's position could be left vacant, through personnel cuts or internal restructuring, or occupied by a person with different priorities and interests. The director of a minority NGO in Karelia said that 'all authorities have their own priorities', and saw as particularly problematic what she believed was an attitude of indifference often displayed by the authorities [1.2.1]. With regard to the teaching of minority language, she added:

> If there wasn't a group of activists nobody would do anything. The state doesn't take the initiative. [An NGO] started to prepare materials [for schools]. Then they distribute them. And the authorities never admitted that this type of materials has to be provided [by the state] by law. Instead [the NGO] takes the materials to schools, and, if the local authorities are not against, they can be used.... The federal authorities are completely uninterested.
>
> [1.2.1][25]

An academic and Tatar activist in Kazan summarised the situation as follows: 'The authorities have things that they absolutely must do, and things that they can do if they wish to. Nationality issues are in the second category, they are optional' [2.6].

Similarly, another respondent, the director of an NGO working on inter-ethnic relations in Moscow, believed that interest in and commitment depended on individual public officials and institutions, and their interests and priorities [1.2.3]. Even allowing for possible exaggeration by some of the respondents, the absence of precise programmes for the preservation of minority cultures and languages point to a volatility of these initiatives. According to Russian civil society organisations that authored the 2006 FCNM Shadow Report to the ACFC in the period 2004–2006, contacts between minority NGOs and federal ministries were only sporadic, and there was 'no overall cooperation'.[26]

While establishing optimal mechanisms for inclusive decision-making is a widespread challenge, Russia is affected by a legacy of Soviet centralism, and by Putin's own 'power vertical', which, by streamlining decision-making and favouring appointments over elections,[27] sustains a system that limits entry points for civil society in decision-making.[28] Various achievements in the area of minority rights – such as the expansion of minority-language education and the recognition of titular languages as co-official alongside Russian in ethnic republics – were secured immediately following the Soviet Union's collapse. In some, more recent, cases, the federal centre has been less responsive to demands from the regions – for example with regard to education reform and its impact on minority languages and cultures.[29] With activists restricted in their scope of action, a highly centralised political system has discouraged grass-roots initiatives, which, Kuzivanova argues, has led to inertia:

> The leading role of the state shaping virtually all life aspects of ethnicities has, possibly, formed a paternalistic and latent model of interaction. This paternalistic pattern of interaction brings inertia ... constraints a search for new forms of interaction between people and authorities.
>
> (Kuzivanova 2009: 93)

Interview data as well as other sources[30] indicate that the marginalisation and limited impact of civil society in the area of minority rights is not commonly linked to the direct repression of organisations, although intimidation may also play a role in state–civil society relations.[31] Rather, problems cited by the respondents included the frequent indifference by the authorities towards minority issues, and approaches to nationality issues that rely on obsolete, Soviet models. In the latter case, cultural programmes for minorities, at both the federal and regional levels, continue to reproduce existing blueprints. This results in the already noted perpetuation of nationality programmes with a strong folkloristic slant. Whether new approaches are introduced appears circumstantial, and dependent on individual public officials. A respondent in St Petersburg, from a minority NGO, referred to a shift towards education-based cultural programmes, which local public officials had enabled:

> Two years ago nationality issues were seen as just festivals. Now there are new public officials [in St Petersburg] and with them we work on a different level. The discussion is not only on the preservation of [minority] cultures, but also on ethnic identity.... It's good that these public officials came, it all depends on them.... Before national issues only meant music groups [playing traditional music], but now it's also education, publications, etc. This new situation has created new conflicts [between the public officials with a more traditional outlook and civil society] ... [The former] try to get their festivals, civil society wants to have conferences, education.
>
> But I am happy that things have changed. Before nationalities were like exotic animals in a zoo. Some public officials just say: 'I love Veps – beautiful costumes, tasty pies', and nationalities only mean this to them. They don't realise that nationalities have their own unique mythology and much else.
>
> [1.2.9][32]

The respondent placed the St Petersburg House of Nationalities[33] among the more traditional institutions for the promotion of cultural programmes for minorities:

> The [St Petersburg] House of Nationalities is the typical Soviet institution ... it's Soviet in style. They mostly focus on festivals. The House wants to have festivals with a lot of different nationalities. Their message with these events is: 'Look how many nationalities we have!'
>
> [1.2.9]

Another respondent from St Petersburg, a representative of a different minority, displayed similar views:

> A: The House of Nationalities tries [to be helpful] but [its approach] is losing touch with the times.[34] It's not the work [they do], but the format of

their work. Mostly it is the way it was in the past. There is a certain
conservatism.
Q: Is it 'Soviet' in style?
A: Something like that.

[1.2.11]

Thus, these respondents complained of a trivialisation of their status as national
minorities, and of a simplification of the nationality discourse – with institutions
such as the House of Nationalities unable to meet existing (and evolving) challenges.[35] They saw a tendency by the authorities to rely, by default, on pre-
established modalities of interaction with civil society. Transcending, by
modernising, these dynamics was linked to public officials themselves, given
that state policies amount to a general set of principles devoid of concrete
targets. The open-endedness of nationalities policy can facilitate flexible arrangements, meeting the particular needs of minorities, but also exempt public officials from specific responsibilities. It can only result in varied (and unpredictable)
forms of consultation.

Consultation: varied outcomes

Respondents (academia and civil society) referred to Law 309, amending the
Law 'On Education',[36] as the principal example of reform affecting the cultural
and linguistic rights of minorities that had failed to involve them in consultation.
Those respondents who believed they had been excluded from public debate on
legal reform encompassed representatives of minorities working for specialised
bodies: a section of the Ministry of Education [4.14], the Institute of History of
the Academy of Sciences of the Republic of Tatarstan [2.7], and a federal
national cultural autonomy [1.1.6]. The adoption of Law 309 had led to an extra-
ordinary response, with numerous nationalities and their representative bodies
protesting in unison.[37] Former President of Tatarstan Mintimer Shaimiev had
been among the most influential figures opposed to the new provisions. Yet the
results were not what the campaigners had hoped for:

> At first we thought that Law 309 might be repealed quickly, or at least that
> there could be amendments, but it hasn't happened ... All agree that the law
> is bad and there was a lot of noise, but there was no positive response from
> the authorities.

[2.7]

The absence of public discussions and the swiftness of the law's adoption, noted
by respondents working in the area of minority education [2.7; 4.7; 4.14] generated widespread concern among many persons belonging to minorities.[38]

Other specialists (academics and members of advisory committees on nationality issues) similarly noted difficulties in inputting into decision-making. Only
one respondent in Karelia said that the local authorities took the opinions of

persons belonging to minorities into account in decision-making – the represent-ative of a quasi-state institution, the Centre of National Cultures in Petrozavodsk [1.3.2]. Other civil society representatives generally noted that the discussions were 'useful', without however referring to a possible tangible impact on decision-making [1.1.1; 1.1.5; 1.2.5; 1.2.6; 1.2.7] – with a few exceptions out-lined below. The disparity between respondents who felt excluded and those who felt included might be explained through the respondents' differing inter-pretations of participation in decision-making and the format of stakeholders' input. The civil society representatives who saw impediments to their participa-tion mentioned specific issues, such as minority education [1.2.1; 1.2.2]; those who found discussions satisfactory, or partially so, referred to the promotion of minority cultures and tolerance generally. While both aims correspond to FCNM principles, the latter is more closely aligned to the official Russian discourse on nationality issues, based on general notions of 'tolerance' and 'cultural develop-ment'. In sum, the more satisfied minority representatives might be those who do not hit the invisible boundaries of minority activism.

Despite this, respondents provided some examples of minorities' participation in decision-making on matters affecting them. In Karelia, respondents cited the opening of Karelian-language nurseries, following a petition organised by local civil society activists [1.3.2]. A respondent from the Centre of National Cultures in Petrozavodsk stated that the institution had itself been opened as a result of public calls for it, which had won the support of the Karelian authorities [1.3.1]. A representative of the House of Nationalities in Moscow had a similar story over the establishment of his institution [1.3.4]. Another example from Karelia was the recognition, in 2006, of the Veps minority as one of Russia's 'small-in-number indigenous peoples', following a long and somewhat tortuous journey that had lasted 20 years [1.2.1]. At the same time, none of these claims was of a political, controversial nature (with the exception, perhaps, of the status of indi-genous peoples for the Veps minority). None of them required wide-ranging reforms, while there have been no cases[39] of successful campaigns for adminis-trative or legal reform.[40] Additionally, results might not be long-lasting: a respondent referred the closure of two Karelian-language nurseries that had only briefly operated under the 'language nest' programme.[41] Newly established insti-tutions might also function poorly: in the case of new schools or courses teach-ing minority languages, a respondent complained of scarce resources in terms of materials and teachers [1.4.2].[42] In the case of Houses of Nationalities, respond-ents (representatives of minorities and NGOs), while valuing their existence and support, noted their limited impact [1.2.4; 1.2.5; 1.2.11].

Opportunities for minorities to input into decision-making can be further reduced, in some cases, by the fragmentation of minority associations. Two ana-lysts (academics in Moscow) commented on the fact that minority groups rarely build bridges for concerted action [2.17; 2.18]. At the same time, minority associations proliferate. Although some groups with ethnocultural affinity do join forces – as in the case of the Association of Finno-Ugric Peoples or the World Congress of Tatars – competition and collision are not uncommon.[43]

During interviews respondents, both observers (analysts and academics) and representatives of minority organisations themselves, made countless references to these tensions. The latter at times expressed hostility towards other stakeholders, including persons belonging to the same minority. In some cases tensions were observed between members of organisations that cultivated good relations with the authorities and those that distanced themselves from the government and were more or less openly critical of it. Some respondents further referred to what they considered as instances of opportunism on the part of some individuals belonging to minorities. For example, the representative of a minority organisation in Moscow referred contemptuously to another organisation working for the same minority in the same city, whose head had substantial business interests. In the opinion of the respondent, his counterpart used the minority organisation simply as a means to achieving his personal promotion [1.2.4].[44] Fragmentation resulting from in-group tensions can only complicate any consideration of the needs of minorities by the authorities, due to the proliferation of interlocutors.

According to some respondents, written appeals to the authorities were the principal means for civil society to articulate their claims [1.2.1; 2.6; 4.14]. The prime minister and president of Russia, seen as the true holders of power, were the primary targets. A respondent summarised the situation as such: decisions[45] are taken by the presidential administration; writing to the president is, therefore, 'the only hope that something will change' [4.14]. This attitude reveals an absence of trust in consultation, or in institutions that could in principle offer lobbying opportunities such as the Committee of the State Duma on Nationality Affairs, as, in this respondent's view, it had no influence. The highest echelons of power are seen as the only hope, albeit a very remote hope given that the respondents had received no replies to their appeals. Yet Putin has promoted such an approach, for example by establishing a channel of communication with members of the public during his annual (since 2000) televised question-and-answer session, 'Direct Line with Vladimir Putin', broadcast by the main television channels.[46] He has provided an immediate resolution of, or final say on, the issues raised during the programme. This is an informal practice, and a way of circumventing ordinary systems *par excellence*. It consolidates the perception that *networks* are the way forward, while *systems* are unreliable. In line with this, the respondents saw contacts and networks as prerequisites for impact – although the fact that some well-connected minority activists also complained of the minimal impact of their efforts indicates that networks are a necessary, but not sufficient, condition for it.

Civil society's vulnerability

One last obstacle to minority participation is the vulnerability of civil society – including minority associations – vis-à-vis the authorities. Two main factors result in the fragility of civil society: direct interference in the right to freedom of association, and the limited resources available to organisations. The right to free association, like other international legal principles, has been applied selectively in

Russia. This right, protected by Articles 7 FCNM and 11 ECHR, is itself not absolute: state parties have a margin of appreciation in ECHR implementation,[47] and a state can develop its own *modus operandi* to guarantee the right to association. At the same time, in line with Article 11(2) ECHR, restrictions must be 'necessary in a democratic society', and proportional to a legitimate aim pursued.[48] Selective implementation occurs when a state oversteps the boundaries of these legitimate restrictions and disproportionately limits the right of free association.

While in many instances Russian law in the area of minority rights does not come into direct conflict with international standards – rather, it tends to be vague and declarative, and to be enforced to a limited extent – in the case of the right of association such a conflict does arise. General guarantees of freedom of association can be found in the Russian Constitution's Article 30, but legislation on NGOs, particularly following amendments introduced in 2006,[49] permits wide-ranging controls on the activities of civil society and their receipt of foreign funds. Furthermore, Russia's regulations on registration have been applied selectively, for example in cases of arbitrary non-registration of organisations.[50] Civil society representatives who authored the 2006 Shadow Report to the ACFC argued that obstacles to registration arose when the 'authorities [we]re not comfortable with an association'.[51] On some occasions, registration was denied for administrative reasons – minutiae such as imprecisions in 'founding documents'.[52] The law permits the suspension of activities or closure of an NGO by court order when it repeatedly violates the law or its activities are 'contrary to the charter goals'.[53] In these cases, Russian courts assess whether an organisation's activities fully correspond to what is stated in the objectives of the organisation's charter, rather than examining the potential threat to society of the organisation's activities themselves, and whether banning them is 'necessary in a democratic society' (as per Article 11(2) ECHR). Meanwhile, Russian legislation includes vague, opaque provisions left open to elastic interpretation which might be used to threaten organisations.[54] A respondent – a public official and Tatar activist in Kazan – commented on the authorities' powers on civil society: 'They can always find something wrong with you [your organisation] if they want. It could just be something like fire regulations. In Russia you don't violate the law only if you're dead' [4.7].

Since the interviews were conducted, a major development has taken place: the adoption, in 2012, of legislation that has come to be known as the 'Foreign Agents' Law.[55] The new regulations stipulate that any organisation in receipt of foreign funding and carrying out 'political activities' must register as an 'organisation performing the functions of a foreign agent'. The expression 'foreign agent' conjures up associations with international espionage, and such labelling implicitly discredits organisations. The law further imposes numerous and cumbersome obligations relating to reporting and auditing of civil society activity as 'foreign agents', in addition to those that already exist for all NGOs.

Overall, issues of registration, arbitrary closure and obstacles to free association have rarely affected minority associations,[56] and most such organisations have maintained amicable relations with the authorities. The fact that minority organisations have generally not aroused the authorities' suspicions is likely due to their activities remaining confined to the cultural sphere, and their refraining from raising controversial subjects. There may be various explanations for these organisations' near-exclusive focus on culture: a genuine lack of interest in becoming politically involved; the existence of a (government-supported) gulf between the cultural and political spheres in the activities of minority groups; a possible 'chilling effect' on minority organisations due to the mere existence of punishing provisions; and the preference for informal practices in raising claims, rather than direct confrontation or even open and frank debate.

A respondent, the leader of a minority institution in Kazan, referred to another possible means to eliminate minority organisations' political threats, involving informal, covert practices. He believed that Russia's Federal Security Service (FSB) was 'very active' in scrutinising minority organisations' operations [1.4.2]. Similarly, the Shadow Report to the ACFC documented the FSB's 'warnings' designed to intimidate organisations, including minority groups.[57] The representative of a minority in St Petersburg alluded to a different type of surveillance:

> There is some freedom in working on nationality issues, but in this freedom one is also under control. There is a feeling that one needs to *regulate* nationalities. This is why there are institutions like the Houses of Nationalities. If all [nationalities] worked separately it would be difficult [to monitor them], but if you gather them all in the same place, then all is in front of your eyes, all can be seen.
>
> [1.2.11]

In conclusion, civil society's scope of action is restricted by a need to maintain good relations with the authorities, and by the menace of the latter's possible abuse of legal provisions. The last two cited respondents also believed that there was a governmental effort to control (regulate) minority organisations, through overt or covert means. Institutions that should supposedly aid pluralism and participation, such as Houses of Nationality, might partially contribute to a form of control. A final source of vulnerability relates to funding.

Funding pains

> 'The adoption of the Law on national cultural autonomy raised expectations of state financial support [for minority organisations]. We quickly came to the understanding that there would be no such support.'[58]
>
> [1.2.4]

Programmes to preserve a country's cultural and linguistic diversity require investment on the part of the state. In its reports to the ACFC, Russia has emphasised that substantial funds have been made available for national minorities' cultural programmes.[59] Despite this, respondents of the various 'civil society' categories reported operational difficulties linked to limited funding.

The issues raised by the respondents can be grouped into two main areas: funds originating from the Russian *state*, and *non-state* funds. In the case of state funds, respondents referred to their scarcity, and to the limited autonomy in the management of funds. In the case of non-state funds, respondents primarily raised concerns about obstacles to their free use, particularly with regard to foreign grants.

With reference to state funding, the ACFC has recommended that representatives of national minorities participate in decision-making over the allocation of financial resources, including through a 'greater portion' of the available funds being 'managed directly' by national cultural autonomies (NCAs) and other minority associations.[60] The issue of limited finances was noted by numerous respondents. In the case of NCAs, only miniscule resources are allocated to them by the state, and in an intermittent manner, while only very rarely do such organisations own property or have the means for a steady income (Osipov 2004: 186–187; 198–205). Respondents from the bigger NCAs stated that they operated primarily through funds from private sponsors rather than from the government.[61] Other respondents reported working as unpaid volunteers [1.2.3; 1.2.4], and developing strategies to minimise costs. For example, a respondent in Moscow described the containment of expenditure in this way: the members of his organisation were volunteers, thereby incurring no salary costs; a rent-free venue for events was normally supplied by the Moscow House of Nationalities; the House of Nationalities further provided some financial help for events; other costs (such as printing costs for publications and some expenditure for events) were covered by the organisers' own funds and by ad hoc sponsors. He added that 'the rest is taken care of by our enthusiasm' [1.2.4]. Yet the ACFC has recommended not a greater *amount* of funds to be made available for programmes promoting minority rights, but rather greater minority *participation* in decision-making on funding allocation, as well as *autonomy* in the management of funds.

State funds can be subdivided into three categories. The first category includes funds managed by the authorities themselves, for centrally-conceived and centrally-managed programmes. Among these are events organised by the (former) federal Ministry of Regional Development[62] – for example, 65 events in 2008, including youth forums, youth camps, festivals and conferences – and sociological studies on inter-ethnic relations and extremism.[63] Second, funds are allocated to selected institutions in receipt of regular state contributions, primarily through the budgets of the republics. The main beneficiaries of federal funds have been cultural institutions: the already-cited Centres of National Cultures, Houses of Nationalities, or similar.[64] These are effectively semi-official institutions, affiliated to, as well as funded by, regional or local government. Their function is to coordinate local activities, provide fora for discussions, and often serve as venues for events or other initiatives (e.g. language classes) organised by minority associations.[65] Other organisations in receipt of federal funds, whose representatives were interviewed, included the Inter-Regional Social Movement of Mordovian (Moksha and Erzya) Peoples [1.4.3], and regional minority media, such as Moksha- and Erzya-language newspapers published in Saransk [3.3; 3.5]. These respondents indicated that they had continued to receive state support, even though in modest amounts, despite the global financial crisis from 2008 onwards.

Third, alongside those institutions in receipt of regular funding are other organisations that apply for funding from the authorities for individual projects – at the local, regional or federal levels. The modalities of funding allocation vary from region to region in the case of local and regional funds. Respondents in the position of grantees in some cases reported continuity in the inflow of funds – with regular funding applications followed by regular grants [1.3.5; 1.1.2]. This suggests the building of a relationship based on cooperation between the authorities and minority associations. It could simultaneously mean the marginalisation of organisations that have not developed the contacts and networks they need to thrive. In Tver, for example, a public official in the local administration stated that, on the one hand, the selection of successful projects was made by assessing the quality of the planned projects themselves, rather than the organisations proposing them; on the other, organisations registered for less than a year were automatically excluded from competition. This was justified by the need to eliminate from the selection process those organisations that existed only on paper [4.6]. Indeed, respondents across different categories noted the volatility of organisations – many of which appeared and, shortly after, disappeared, for reasons including both external factors (paucity of funds and bureaucratic difficulties) and the organisations' internal weaknesses (inadequate management skills and human resources). At the same time, in Tver, the representative of an (established) organisation commented that the exclusion of recently established organisations from competition would prevent them from developing [2.5].

Even in the case of sustained financial support, the respondents referred to bureaucratic hurdles that impeded the smooth unfolding of civil society programmes. I provide three examples to show how cases can vary: from Tver, Mordovia and St Petersburg. In Tver, a respondent described the local funding cycle thus:[66] a funding application is submitted at the beginning of the year; in May–June the applicant learns the outcome of the funding proposal; if successful, the funds become available no earlier than July; the grant's financial report has to be prepared in December, before compiling and submitting another application early in the following year [2.5]. There was no option of fundraising for a multiple-phase project, running over a year. The respondent, who managed a newspaper in Karelian language, said in May 2010:

> We got a grant this year but we still don't have the money. We used to get a salary automatically every year for the newspaper, now we have to apply every year for a grant. [With the old system] the newspaper used to come out six times a year, now only twice a year, because we have fewer funds and they are not regular. [This system] is fine for festivals, they can be organised any time [of the year]. But it's harder for the newspaper, which has to come out at regular intervals.... The money has to be spent in just a

few months. We try to have a newspaper come out in the summer, which is prepared very quickly, and another around November.

[2.5]

A public official responsible for the management of grants in Tver explained in an interview that the regional authorities, in providing funds, were required to follow the calendar year (January to December): administrative procedures, as well as project implementation, have to be completed within this time frame [4.6]. The regions with fewer human and administrative resources are then likely to be more susceptible to delays that constrain the grantees' activities. In Mordovia, greater expediency was reported by a grantee, with a call for proposals in September and results in mid-December, making it possible to start a project in January [1.3.5]. In St Petersburg, a respondent from a minority organisation noted a relaxation of bureaucratic requirements which led to her organisation's receipt, in early 2010, of a long-term (two-year) grant. Increased flexibility, with the removal of the rigid one-year time frame, she said, allowed the organisation to expand its activities, and publish books for dissemination among local schools – which she saw as an organisational priority. However, she noted that financial uncertainties would re-emerge when the two years elapsed [1.2.9]. Thus, the interview data indicate a prevailing tendency to provide discreet funding for self-contained, short-term initiatives, whereas civil society organisations do not have the security of continuity of funding for other structural needs, such as administrative costs and the rent of premises (see also Osipov 2004: 198–205).

In another case, a Karelian (civil society) respondent talked about funds that were promised but never delivered:

> We worked on the preparation of a programme.... The [Karelian] Ministry agreed that a budget would be allocated to the project ... but didn't try to actually get the money, because they had other priorities, for other projects.... For three years we didn't get the three millions roubles [promised].... We wrote many times, met many times, but never received the money.
>
> [1.2.1][67]

The figures provided in Russia's reports to the ACFC, on funding allocated to minority programmes, are not accompanied by a detailed breakdown of expenses. Governmental data are insufficient to: quantify the financial support to minority groups; analyse what groups are awarded grants; and show what types of projects are funded. What the data, including reports to the ACFC, clearly indicate is a recurring prominence of cultural programmes including festivals and 'programmes on tolerance', reflecting a centrally-conceived notion of cultural programmes for nationalities. In addition, a respondent from a minority NGO in St Petersburg believed that the awarding of grants was linked to a certain type of performance, rather than simply the organisations' levels of professionalism:

> There is no obligation on the authorities to finance our activities, and if we are good, if we are quiet, maybe they will give something … maybe. The state has no obligation, they decide. If we try to criticise them too much I'm not sure that we will get anything.
>
> [1.2.8]

The respondent was of the opinion that his organisation had managed to forge a good working relationship with the city authorities and thus had been awarded grants. He was generally satisfied with the local authorities' receptive attitude towards his organisation's needs and objectives. He noted, however, that the local authorities expressed preferences as to the projects they wished to fund, in practice requiring organisations to tailor their projects accordingly if they wished to maximise their chances of being funded. The authorities had been providing funding 'according to their own criteria':

> In all the projects one of the criteria [set by the authorities] was to organise training for young people, to involve youth. In this case sometimes they demand things that are very strange, that we have to involve other national communities in our activities. They declare ideas of tolerance, which is good in some ways but sometimes it's difficult, because we want to have our own festivals…. We don't necessarily want to involve Lithuanians, or Poles. This [type of joint festivals] is very good but it's something different.
>
> [1.2.8]

Another area in which officialdom might have a degree of control over civil society's activities is in the linkages between networks and funding. One example was provided by a representative of the (Saransk-based) Association of Finno-Ugric Peoples of Russia (AFUN): the nomination of Mordovia's Minister of Culture, Petr Tultaev, as leader of AFUN in September 2009 had reportedly coincided with the start of a regular inflow of funds to the institution [1.4.3]. In another case from Tver, a public official stated that, in the case of application for federal funding, a letter of support by the local authorities was required by the federal authorities [2.5], with clear implications of potential vetting. Respondents further pointed to favouritism of loyal groups [1.4.2] and lack of transparency in decision-making on financing [2.19]. One analyst observed that, with regard to funding, 'all is negotiable' [2.15]. The ACFC has further referred to 'a lack of support for activities other than cultural in a narrow sense', as well as an absence of transparency in the procedures and criteria for the allocation of financial support.[68]

It is due to this governmental control over funds that the ACFC recommended that minorities be enabled to directly manage the funds that are earmarked for the preservation of minority cultures and languages. In its Third Report, in response to the ACFC's recommendation to '[t]ake steps in order to ensure the balance between the financing provided to cultural activities and the needs of the national minorities concerned', the Russian government simply referred to the Law 'On National Cultural Autonomy' (NCA Law), whose Article 16 concerns funding from federal, regional and local authorities.[69] A public official who was interviewed similarly answered a question on the limited funds for NCAs by referring to the same legal provisions [4.15]. These are not, however, matched by a concurring obligation for the authorities to provide funding in practice.[70] Legal provisions themselves are vague, with a different formulation used in Article 16 for three levels of authorities: the article states that the federal authorities '*can* provide support' to NCAs from the federal budget; Russia's subjects 'provide support' from the subjects' budgets; and the organs of local self-government '*have the right* to provide support' [italics added]. Additionally, Article 9 of the NCA Law was amended in 2004,[71] modifying the provision that federal and regional authorities 'assist' NCAs, to the stipulation that they 'can support' NCAs in their activities in the sphere of education and the media. A respondent linked this type of provision to a Russian joke, on the exchange between an ordinary citizen and one in a position of authority:

'I have the right ...'
'Yes, you have the right.'
'I didn't finish, I have the right ...'
'Yes, you have the right.'
'...Then I can ...'
'No, you can't!'

[1.2.9]

The respondent considered the law's formulation (the authorities '*can* provide support') as symptomatic of the Russian state's approach to nationality issues, which in her opinion, was encapsulated in this joke. It made existing systems simply 'declarative':

The authorities *can* do something, but they also can *not* do it. [Equally] people have a right [to receive funding] but they still in practice cannot do anything. There are no mechanisms.... You can request that your child receive an education in a [particular] language, but not find a [suitable] school. I can do something but at the same time I can't do it.

[1.2.9]

The absence of specific responsibilities also means that networks and good relations with the authorities are not necessarily a recipe for financial security – for example, if the local authorities (even if generally sympathetic to the needs of minorities) have other (more pressing) priorities, or insufficient funds to implement minority-friendly policies.

An alternative source of funds is represented by non-state donors, both international donors and those based in Russia. In the case of international donors, the respondents referred to funding from Finland and other Finno-Ugric countries (for Finno-Ugric nationalities), Canada and the United States. As part of the programme 'Minorities in Russia',[72] the Council of Europe had also financed four small projects in Mordovia on the preservation and development of the Mordovian languages. However, (civil society) respondents referred to bureaucratic hurdles and financial disincentives over the receipt of foreign funds, particularly following 2006 legal amendments, which increased the level of state scrutiny over the inflow of foreign funds to NGOs registered in Russia.[73] The first notable disincentive is high taxation for the receipt of funds originating from abroad, with the exceptions of foreign institutions that are on a list of accredited donors whose grants are not taxable. The number of donors on this list was reduced from 101 to 12 in June 2008.[74] Moreover, bank checks and tax inspections are routinely carried out, while NGOs are required to submit reports to the local authorities four times a year for fiscal purposes.[75] These regulations, with the exception of the list of accredited donors, affect all institutions and not only NGOs. The director of a human rights NGO, however, linked human rights activities to enhanced control by the authorities [1.5.5]. Meanwhile, international organisations with a presence in Russia have themselves been subjected to pressure (sometimes resulting in the closure of their local offices),[76] which can clearly affect their ability to provide financial support to, and cooperate with, Russian NGOs.

One last source of funds for minority organisations is private sponsors – usually wealthy business people belonging to national minorities. While these donations provide release from dependency on state funds and a break from the red tape, the boundaries between businesses and the state are often blurred – with networks encompassing the private financial and political spheres. At a minimum, people who own businesses do not wish to antagonise politicians and civil servants – particularly where they use informal networks to protect their interests. Hence, private sponsorship of minority activities might not necessarily signify freedom to engage in forms of activism that may be unpalatable to the authorities; rather, they generally result in cultural events not dissimilar to those sponsored by the Russian state. Some of the respondents who were leaders of minority groups were themselves business people who used their own private funds to support minority organisations. In these cases minority associations might have the dual function of promoting individuals and their interests as well as minority cultures per se.[77]

Conclusion

Civil society is confronted with numerous obstacles to its activities. Local authorities shy away from debate on minority issues that cross into the political sphere. State-sponsored minority programmes tend to skim the surface, dealing with symptoms rather than causes. In turn, civil society's frequent condition of dependency on the state for funding, coupled with its administrative and financial vulnerability, typically makes it reluctant to challenge the authorities. Indeed, good relations with the authorities were perceived by civil society respondents as the most effective tool for advancing minority interests; and in some cases civil society has been able to cooperate quite fruitfully with the authorities, primarily at the local level, also thanks to the high levels of activism and commitment of some organisations. At the same time, cooperation is generally contingent upon public officials' discretion. This causes an unreliability of systems for cooperation, the volatility of public officials' support, and high levels of reliance on personal and local circumstances. The institutions that are points of contact between the authorities and civil society, such as Houses of Nationalities, were often found to have limited effectiveness by the respondents, and potentially even harbour informal practices that could be harmful to minority groups. Finally, the state has the power to intervene to undermine the activities of civil society, including through abuse of the law and procedures such as tax inspections.[78] Similar issues emerged in interviews in all regions – in the three ethnic republics, as well as in Moscow and St Petersburg.

Centralised control of funding greatly restricts opportunities for minorities to distance themselves, if they so wish, from Soviet-inspired approaches to nationality programmes. This is exacerbated by the absence of detailed programmes to promote minority rights, with precise targets, and their relatively low priority in contemporary Russian politics – compared, for example, to the state's objective to fight extremism and popularise a Russian patriotic discourse. Euphemistically confining the discourse on diversity to 'culture', to the detriment of 'minority rights', has a strategic value in containing minority claims; yet the enjoyment of cultural rights requires not only cultural programmes, but also participation in decision-making. Meanwhile, the vertical structure of executive power, and minorities' dependence on public officials' discretion, has created a tension between centralism and localism; core policies (e.g. the Russian patriotic discourse) coexist with a form of *laissez-faire*, as individual public officials are exempt from well-defined responsibilities in the area of nationalities policy. Civil society is caught between these two poles: on one side, it finds inflexible, centrally-conceived regulations (e.g. exceedingly burdensome taxation and registration requirements); on the other, loose regulations for the upholding of minority rights, with public officials free to take arbitrary decisions. In an environment afflicted by 'symbolic politics' and a democratic deficit, it becomes hardly possible for minority representatives to challenge existing institutions and practices; rather, the actions of minority representatives are, to varying degrees – and willingly or unwillingly – shaped by the same institutions and practices.

Notes

1 Some sections of this and the next two chapters were included in an article published in the *Netherlands Quarterly of Human Rights* ('Power, Politics and Participation: The Russian Federation's National Minorities and their Participatory Rights', 30(1) 2012: 66–96).
2 On 'disaffection' of citizens, see Pharr *et al.* (2000).
3 The expression 'civil society' is employed here to designate Russia-based, non-profit organisations – many of which are run by minorities themselves – that promote minority rights in Russia. I also take into account institutes working on minority

issues, both at the federal and regional levels. Consideration of national cultural autonomies is excluded from this chapter and they are analysed in Chapter 8 instead; reference to national cultural autonomies is made in this chapter only with regard to funding. The main interviews that provided data for this and the next two chapters were held with representatives of: minority NGOs (9 respondents), cultural associations (4), peoples' congresses (3), national cultural autonomies (2), human rights NGOs (7), academics (14) and public officials (7).

4 Article 15 FCNM states: 'The Parties shall create the conditions necessary for the effective participation of persons belonging to national minorities in *cultural*, social and economic life and in public affairs, in particular those affecting them' [italics added].

5 Article 7 FCNM reads: 'The Parties shall ensure respect for the right of every person belonging to a national minority to freedom of peaceful assembly, freedom of association, freedom of expression, and freedom of thought, conscience and religion.'

6 Article 11(1) ECHR states: 'Everyone has the right to freedom of peaceful assembly and to freedom of association with others.'

7 See also Article 12(1)(f) ECRML on participation in 'cultural activities and facilities', and the OSCE/HCNM Lund Recommendations on the Effective Participation of National Minorities in Public Life.

8 These are analysed in Chapters 8 and 9.

9 PACE, 'Situation of Finno-Ugric and Samoyed Peoples', 26 October 2006, Doc. 11087.

10 For example, see ACFC, (Third) Report submitted by the Russian Federation, 9 April 2010, ACFC/SR/III(2010)005, pp. 30–43.

11 As noted (Chapter 2), nationalism per se has been linked to aggressiveness and instability, and to attempts by one ethnic group to prevail over others.

12 President of Russia, Address to the National Assembly of the Russian Federation, 12 December 2013, http://eng.kremlin.ru/news/6402 (accessed 25 September 2014).

13 Ibid.

14 Report by the Special Rapporteur on Contemporary Forms of Racism, Racial Discrimination, Xenophobia and Related Intolerance, Doudou Diène, 'Mission to the Russian Federation', 20 May 2007, A/HRC/4/19/Add.3.

15 Statement by Ambassador Valerii Loshchinin, reported in: 'Open Letter to the UN High Commissioner for Human Rights Louise Arbour', 10 September 2007, www. sova-center.ru/en/xenophobia/news-releases/2007/09/d11531/ (accessed 10 September 2014). See also Chapter 3.

16 See also Chapter 2.

17 The word 'repression' was used by Karelian respondents (academics) in Petrozavodsk and Tver [2.4; 2.5].

18 A Mordovian festival held in a Mordovian village in Chuvashia, June 2010.

19 On United Russia, see Chapter 9.

20 The full name is Ministry of the Republic of Karelia on Issues of Nationalities Policy and Relations with Religious Associations.

21 See Chapter 6.

22 None of the respondents from civil society had been involved in decision-making on the use of government funds, or participated in targeted discussions on this issue. Minority organisations may however submit project proposals to the authorities. See p. 168 ('Funding pains').

23 See also Osipov (2012, 2013c), on the Russian authorities' promotion of non-controversial forms of communication in relation to nationalities policy.

24 Prior to the education reform initiated in 2007, described in Chapter 6.

25 The Republic of Karelia does provide materials for the study of minority languages free of charge, but these were deemed to be insufficient by the respondent. Similarly, a school employee in Karelia [5.1] noted that her school had to make do with the limited resources available. See also Chapter 6.

26 NGO Shadow Report 'On the Implementation of the Framework Convention for the Protection of National Minorities by the Russian Federation', February 2006, §348. In its Second Opinion on the Russian Federation, the ACFC similarly expressed concern at the fact that advisory councils 'are expected to implement rather than contribute to the preparation of minority-relevant legislation'. ACFC, (Second) Opinion on the Russian Federation, 2 May 2007, ACFC/OP/II(2006)004, §90.

27 See Chapter 5.

28 This was particularly emphasised by an activist from Karelia [1.2.1], who believed that opportunities for campaigning and consultation had decreased in tandem with the consolidation of Putin's power.

29 See Chapter 6.

30 ACFC Opinions and the 2006 NGO Shadow Report submitted to the ACFC (see note 26). See also Osipov (2004: 170).

31 One such cases concerns the Anti-Discrimination Centre (ADC) Memorial in St Petersburg, an NGO that has monitored and exposed instances of harassment and discrimination against Roma and immigrants. On 23 December 2013, the Leninsky District Court ruled that ADC Memorial's work amounted to 'the activity of an NGO fulfilling the functions of a foreign agent'. The NGO closed down in April 2014. See ACD Memorial, 26 April 2014. 'ACD "Memorial" Received Notice of its Liquidation', http://adcmemorial.org/www/9248.html/?lang=en (accessed 25 May 2014).

32 See also a related statement by the same respondent, on p. 157 ('The boundaries of public discourse'). This respondent was the only one who spoke about a new emphasis on education rather than folklore on the part of public officials.

33 Houses of Nationalities, which exist in several Russian cities (including Moscow and St Petersburg), are venues providing office space to specialists and some representatives of minority associations engaging in activities relating to nationalities policy and the preservation of minority cultures. They further provide conference rooms and concert halls for events.

34 The respondent used the expression 'it is getting old' [*staraetsiya*].

35 Despite this, the respondent also saw a positive role for the House of Nationalities: its events provided opportunities for exchanges between persons belonging to different nationalities, and for the coordination of activities.

36 See Chapter 6.

37 See for example Lobjakas, A. 23 April 2009. 'Apparently Russia Needs Just One "National Component"', *Radio Free Europe/Radio Liberty*, www.rferl.org/content/Apparently_Russia_Needs_Just_One_National_Component/1614655.html (accessed 15 February 2014).

38 See Chapter 6.

39 Cited by the respondents or known to the author.

40 As noted, protests against Law 309 did not lead to the amendment of the relevant provisions. See Chapter 6.

41 See Chapters 4 and 6.

42 See also Chapter 6.

43 In at least one case mentioned by respondents from Tatarstan a splinter organisation had separated from the 'mother' organisation. See also Chapter 8 on the fragmentation of minority institutions.

44 See also Chapter 8.

45 The respondent was talking about decisions in the sphere of minority education.

46 See President of Russia, 'Direct Line with Vladimir Putin', 17 April 2014, http://eng.kremlin.ru/news/7034 (accessed 12 June 2014).

47 A margin with regard to ECHR implementation, to reflect the cultural and historical differences between the Council of Europe member states.

48 According to Article 11(2) ECHR, the right to free association can be limited by restrictions that are:

prescribed by law and are necessary in a democratic society in the interests of national security or public safety, for the prevention of disorder or crime, for the protection of health or morals or for the protection of the rights and freedoms of others.

49 Law 'On the Amendment of Certain Legislative Acts of the Russian Federation' (No. 18-FZ, 10 January 2006). Among others, it amended the Law 'On Public Organisations' (No. 82-FZ, 19 May 1995). The Law 'On Public Organisations' was amended 17 times between 1997 and 2014. See also note 55 on the Law 'Foreign Agents' Law.

50 Relevant case-law of the European Court of Human Rights on Russia includes: *Presidential Party of Mordovia* v. *Russia* (Application No. 65659/01, 4 October 2004); *Vatan* v. *Russia* (Application No. 47978/99, 7 October 2004); and three cases in which re-registration of religious organisations was denied: *Moscow Branch of the Salvation Army* v. *Russia* (Application No. 72881/01, 5 October 2006), *Church of Scientology Moscow* v. *Russia* (Application No. 18147/02, 5 April 2007), and *Jehovah's Witnesses of Moscow* v. *Russia* (Application No. 302/02, 10 June 2010).

51 NGO Shadow Report submitted to the ACFC, 2006 (see note 26), §197.

52 I.e. data on the organisation's founders, Ibid.

53 Articles 42 and 44, Law No. 82-FZ (note 49). The charter is a document (outlining its mandate) that an NGO is required to submit at the time of registration.

54 The ACFC has argued that the Law 'On Public Organisations' leaves 'a large amount of discretion to the competent authorities to deny registration and to interfere with the activities of associations, especially those receiving foreign funding', many provisions being left 'open to interpretation'. ACFC, (Second) Opinion on the Russian Federation (see note 26), §159.

55 The full name is Law 'On the Amendment of Certain Legislative Acts of the Russian Federation in the Regulation of Activities of Non-Commercial Organizations Fulfilling the Functions of Foreign Agents' (No. 121-FZ, 20 June 2012).

56 See Shadow Report submitted to the ACFC (note 26), §195–197. See also ACFC, (Third) Opinion on the Russian Federation, 24 November 2011, ACFC/OP/III(2011)010, §133.

57 The Shadow Report cites the case of representatives of the Khemshil minority in Krasnodar krai, who, between 2001 and 2005, were 'warned' not to establish an organisation to promote their interests. Ibid., §199.

58 Interview with the representative of a minority organisation in Moscow [1.2.4].

59 240 million roubles per year (approximately 5.7 million euro) for 'events for the realisation of the national policy'. ACFC, (Third) Report submitted by the Russian Federation (see note 10), p. 82.

60 ACFC, (Second) Opinion on the Russian Federation (see note 26), §85. See also ACFC, (Third) Opinion on the Russian Federation (note 56), §20; 65–70.

61 Russia-based sponsors in the case of the Tatar federal NCA; international sponsors in the case of another federal NCA whose representatives were interviewed, and who benefited from international contacts with co-ethnics.

62 The Ministry was abolished in September 2014. See Chapter 4 (note 39).

63 ACFC, (Third) Report submitted by the Russian Federation (see note 10), p. 33.

64 ACFC, (Second) Opinion on the Russian Federation (see note 26), §80.

65 Some of them have provided small sums of money (to fund events) to groups loosely affiliated to them – mostly minority NGOs and NCAs.

66 The information related to the year 2010, when the interview took place.

67 The respondent, the director of a minority NGO in Petrozavodsk, sat on Karelian and Russia-wide advisory bodies for the protection of Finno-Ugric cultures, and regularly participated in events organised by the local authorities. She was therefore well-placed to cultivate good relations with the regional authorities.

68 ACFC, (Third) Opinion on the Russian Federation (see note 56), §20; 68.

69 ACFC, (Third) Report submitted by the Russian Federation (see note 10), p. 104. On NCA, see Chapter 8. The provision contained in Article 16 was added in 2009, through Law 'On the Amendment of Article 16 of the Federal Law "On National Cultural Autonomy"' (No. 11-FZ, 9 February 2009).

70 ACFC, (Third) Opinion on the Russian Federation (see note 56), §20; see also Osipov 2004 (198–205).

71 Law 'On the Amendment of Legal Acts of the Russian Federation ...' (No. 122-FZ, 22 August 2004), Article 76.

72 See Chapter 1.

73 See note 49.

74 Resolution of the Government of the Russian Federation 'On the List of International Organisations ... that are not Liable to Taxation for Financial Assistance to Russian Organisations' (No. 485, 28 June 2008). The list includes the European Commission and various UN agencies. The original list, with 69 donors, was contained in Resolution No. 165, 5 March 2001. More donors were added in subsequent years, until the list reached 101 donors in 2007 (Resolution No. 159, 15 March 2007), before being drastically cut.

75 Article 29 of the Law 'On Public Organisations', amended in 2006 (see note 49).

76 For example, in December 2007 the British Council was required by the Russian authorities to close its offices in St Petersburg and Ekaterinburg by January 2008. The request was justified on the grounds of alleged irregularities, including tax evasion. The allegations were denied by the British Council. See BBC News, 12 December 2007. 'Russia to Limit British Council', http://news.bbc.co.uk/2/hi/europe/7139959. stm (accessed 12 February 2014).

77 See Chapter 8. This was also the opinion of an academic from Moscow [2.19].

78 For example, The European Court of Human Rights acknowledged that tax inspections can be abused in Russia to intimidate applicants to the European Court (see *Fedotova* v. *Russia*, Application No. 73225/01, 13 April 2006).

8 National cultural autonomy

Real or fictitious participation?

The participatory rights of minorities can be upheld through special mechanisms, encompassing consultation through advisory bodies and representation in elected organs. This chapter examines the form of consultation championed by the Russian authorities: national cultural autonomy (NCA).[1] The expression designates a form of autonomy for national minorities that is based on ethnic affiliation rather than territory. In Russia the notion of NCA has been reworked into a mechanism for minority groups to form associations (national cultural autonomies – NCAs), with a view to their becoming involved in public affairs, thereby exercising their cultural rights. The Russian authorities have described the NCA system, together with other forms of ethnicity-based public associations, as 'the major direction of implementation' of the FCNM.[2] They have outlined the activities of NCAs in their reports to the ACFC, yet the ACFC has raised concerns in relation to their effectiveness.[3] Indeed, nearly 20 years since the enactment of the 1996 federal Law 'On National Cultural Autonomy' (NCA Law),[4] it was apparent that the system it created has no real 'autonomy' to minority groups, despite the Russian government's assertion that the institution is based on the principles of 'self-organization and self-government'.[5] Similarly, a considerable body of academic research has shown that the Russian NCA system is largely ineffective (Bowring 2005, 2007; Filippova and Filippov 2008; Osipov 2004, 2012).[6] One respondent referred to NCAs as a 'palliative', rather than a mechanism that could provide practical solutions to minorities' concerns [1.4.2].[7]

In this chapter I assess the reasons for the limited effectiveness of NCAs in upholding minorities' participatory rights – which, in turn, affects the exercise of their cultural rights. I argue that hindrances to effective participation come from two directions: from within the minority organisations themselves, and from the conditions surrounding cultural 'autonomy'. In the first case, NCAs offer no guarantees that the concerns of 'ordinary' persons belonging to national minorities will be represented at higher levels by NCA leaders. From the top down, established mechanisms for consultation (consultative councils at various governmental levels) equally offer few opportunities for concrete impact. The NCA system, therefore, displays complexities both in its bottom-up and top-down dynamics, with issues of *internal* democracy, and a stultified process for input into state policies. Given the NCAs' shortcomings, many minority representatives among the interviewees continued to associate the enjoyment of cultural rights to territoriality rather than an ephemeral 'cultural autonomy'. The former was seen as furthering (some) autonomy in decision-making over cultural rights, while the 'participation' offered by NCAs was regarded by various respondents as little more than 'fiction'.[8]

NCAs are multi-layered bodies, conceived as a vertically integrated system of representation. Local NCAs can choose to merge to form regional NCAs, which can, in turn, unite to establish federal NCAs. Thus, the NCA system was envisioned as naturally developing from the bottom up (Osipov 2004: 121) – with its various building blocks interacting with the state authorities at the local, regional and federal levels. As NCAs move higher towards the apex of the NCA system, culminating with the establishment of a federal NCA for a particular national minority, bureaucratic responsibilities grow accordingly. Thus, of the three case studies, only Tatars had a functioning federal NCA, while Mordovians and Karelians had only registered local and regional NCAs. Additionally, the NCA Law stipulates that NCAs can be formed by groups 'in a situation of national minority in a particular territory'.[9] The rationale for this legal requirement[10] is that the NCA system was conceived by the law's authors as a mechanism for the representation of minorities in a disadvantaged position, rather than those benefiting from territoriality.[11] Generally the provision has been interpreted as prescribing that NCAs may exclusively be established by non-titular minority groups (minorities without a territory), or by members of titular nationalities located *outside* 'their' ethnic republics.[12] As a result of this prevailing interpretation of 'situation of national minority' as equivalent to 'non-titularity', Karelian NCAs have not been established in Karelia – nor Mordovian NCAs in Mordovia, nor Tatar NCAs in Tatarstan.[13] Consequently, of the three case studies, this chapter only includes data from interviews with representatives of a Tatar NCA (in Moscow) and a Karelian NCA (in Tver). I supplement these data with that from interviews with representatives of NCAs of nationalities other than the three focus minorities, as well as with academics and public officials, who offered insight on NCAs' structures, functions and operations. Findings relating to the complexities of translating NCA activity into effective participation were consistent across all ethnic groups represented by the respondents. The observed differences in perceptions of NCAs were primarily by category of respondents – NCA, non-NCA civil society, public officials and academics – rather than revealing variance based on ethnicity. After an introduction on the meaning of *effective* participation, I briefly outline the rationale for the establishment of NCAs in post-Soviet Russia. I then examine the reasons for the limited guarantee of participation provided by this system: first focusing on NCAs' internal structure, and subsequently on the environment in which NCAs operate.

From territorial to cultural autonomy

The right to participation of national minorities is upheld by Article 15 FCNM, which states: 'The Parties shall create the conditions necessary for the effective participation of persons belonging to national minorities in cultural, social and economic life and in public affairs, in particular those affecting them.' State obligations in the area of participatory rights further arise from Article 27 of the 1966 UN International Covenant on Civil and Political Rights (ICCPR), in light of General Comment 23 of the UN Human Rights Committee, stating that the exercise of cultural rights 'may require ... measures to ensure the effective participation of members of minority communities in decisions which affect them'.[14] The 1992 UN Declaration on the Rights of Persons Belonging to National or Ethnic, Religious and Linguistic Minorities makes reference to 'participation' in the context of cultural, religious, social, economic and public life, as well as decision-making affecting minorities.[15] The 1965 UN Convention on the Elimination of All Forms of Racial Discrimination includes provisions on participation in elections and public affairs (Article 5(c)), and on the right to equal participation in cultural activities (Article 5(e)(6)). Soft law standards on participation are also contained in the OSCE Lund Recommendations.[16]

The adjective 'effective', in relation to participation, is employed, *inter alia*, in Articles 2(2) and 2(3) of the UN Declaration on the Rights of Persons Belonging to National or Ethnic, Religious and Linguistic Minorities, with the importance of effectiveness further stressed in the Declaration's Commentary (de Varennes 2005: §38). Effectiveness is linked in the Commentary to the involvement of minorities in all stages of decision-making affecting them – at the local, national and international levels. The expression 'effective participation' is also found in the Lund Recommendations, where it is described as an 'essential component of a peaceful and democratic society' (Point 1.1). 'Effectiveness' of participation relates to the 'impact on the situation of the persons concerned and on the society as a whole' resulting from the participatory process.[17] Hence, the Lund Recommendations further note:

> [I]t is not sufficient for State Parties to formally provide for the participation of persons belonging to national minorities. They should also ensure that their participation has a *substantial influence on decisions* which are taken, and that there is, as far as possible, a shared ownership of the decisions taken [italics added].[18]

This means that the voice of minorities should not only be heard but also be taken seriously (Henrard 2005). Thus, the *presence* of minorities in consultative and elected bodies has to be matched by their actual *influence* on decision-making (Verstichel 2008: 452–453).[19] ACFC Opinions have further indicated that effective participation is closely linked to the achievement of full and effective equality (Marko 2006: 3; Verstichel 2008: 454; Weller 2005: 435). The adoption of 'special measures' in the form of affirmative action may be required to achieve real equality, so as to concretely level opportunities for minorities and the majority. Moreover, while minorities have a clear right to effective participation in matters that affect them,[20] such as linguistic and education policies, it is now recognised that such rights should extend to other areas, such as the social and economic spheres.[21] This signals that the state also 'belongs to' minorities, their being an integral part of the country where they reside (Hofmann 2006: 6–7).

International standards afford states considerable latitude in devising programmes to uphold minorities' participatory rights. Special measures tend to combine two forms of participation, which should act in unison and be mutually supporting (Marko 2006: 9): representation in elected bodies and consultation through consultative mechanisms.[22] In the first case, in Russia no special measures exist to guarantee the presence of minorities in elected bodies.[23] In the case of consultation, Russia has chosen national cultural autonomy as its principal mechanism. The NCA model, described by Karl Renner in his article *State and Nation* (2005 [1899]), is based on the 'personality principle' – the idea that communities may be autonomous and sovereign within a multinational state, regardless of whether they have, or identify with, a particular territory (ibid.).[24] The concept has been taken up by modern scholars (Kymlicka 2007b; Nimni 2005, 2007), and there has been experimentation with NCA in countries other than Russia.[25]

The appeal of NCAs in post-Soviet Russia was exactly the disassociation of nationality and territoriality – a departure from the territoriality-centred Soviet approach to the national question, which had rested on the forging of a link between ethnicity and territory.[26] Placing territoriality at the heart of Soviet nationalities policy had, in many ways, not proved to be a viable arrangement. First, this system did not accommodate non-titular nationalities, or titular nationalities residing outside 'their' territories: data from 1989 (also cited in Chapter 5) reveal that only ten million of the 27 million non-Russians in the RSFSR benefited from territoriality (Codagnone and Filippov 2000: 266). Second, ethnic federalism provided the foundations for post-Soviet ethnic mobilisation, with republics claiming sovereignty *en masse* between 1990 and 1992.[27] At this stage the intelligentsia started to distance itself from the territoriality principle, which had become associated with ethnic claims (Codagnone and Filippov 2000), by shifting the emphasis of nationalities policy from the national-territorial to the national-cultural principle (Osipov 2004: 66). In 1992 the (then) Minister for Nationalities Valerii Tishkov first proposed introducing NCAs: these would not displace existing territorial autonomies – which titular nationalities were unlikely to relinquish – but act as complementary institutions, moulding themselves around the existing structures (Codagnone and Filippov 2000; Filippova and Filippov 2008). At the same time, those ethic communities that did not have a territorial formation, or those groups residing outside such formations, could self-organise in the cultural sphere, autonomously creating the conditions for the expression of their cultural and linguistic distinctiveness (Osipov 2004: 68).

NCA is defined in Article 1 of the 1996 NCA Law as:

> [A] form of national and cultural self-determination constituting a public association of citizens of the Russian Federation, identifying with a particular ethnic community, finding themselves in a situation of national minority in a particular territory, based on their voluntary chosen identity

for the purpose of independently regulating the issues of their identity preservation   and   their   linguistic,   educational   and   national   cultural
development.[28]

That NCAs would not modify the existing ethnicity-based territorial arrange-
ments, and were to remain confined to the cultural sphere, was made clear by the
NCA Law itself.[29] In line with this, a respondent, a scholar and former advisor to
Yeltsin on nationality issues, said in an interview:

> I never thought that [the NCA system] was realistic. Never. When ethnic
> federalism was strong NCAs were not needed. Nowadays that the problems
> of migrants and diasporas are growing there could be some opportunities for
> NCAs, but as an *addition* to ethnic federalism.
>
> [2.18]

The Russian authorities have further stressed that NCAs can benefit non-
territorial minorities. In its first report to the ACFC, the Russian government
noted, with reference to NCAs: '[T]his practical form of self-determination and
realization of the rights of national minorities is of special importance for those
ethoses that do not enjoy territorial autonomy in view of their geographical
dispersion.'[30]

Theorists accept that the concept of NCAs, although in principle transcending
territory, can coexist with it (Nimni 2007: 356). Tishkov's (1996) theoretical
approach certainly seems a sensible one: while not stripping titular nationalities
of their acquired rights to territorial autonomy, it introduces an additional mechanism to accommodate those minority groups that Soviet ethnic federalism had
neglected. According to Russia's Third Report to the ACFC, 18 federal, 208
regional and 501 local NCAs were registered in Russia at the end of 2008.[31] In
2012 the numbers were 15 federal, 241 regional and 643 local NCAs.[32] Yet these
institutions remain largely ineffective in upholding the participatory rights of
minorities in the sphere of culture. This is shown, in the remainder of the
chapter, from two points of view: 'from below' (NCAs' internal shortcomings),
and 'from above' (conditions created by the Russian authorities).

NCAs: what type of representation?

NCAs' internal shortcomings relate to the absence of guarantees of a wide representative base for minorities, which can reflect the multiplicity of the group's
views and concerns. There are two primary reasons: first, a presumption of group
homogeneity inherent in the NCA system; and, second, a tenuous link of
accountability between the representatives (leaders of NCAs) and the represented ('ordinary' persons belonging to national minorities).

As noted, the NCA system was meant to create a pyramidal structure of
representation, with local, regional and federal NCAs. The system would carry
the concerns of minorities from the local sections up to the highest political

institutions. It would act as the main form of exchange between authorities and minorities, condensing the various messages from minority institutions into manageable 'bites', to which the government could respond. It was envisaged that each minority as a group would effectively speak with one voice, reducing redundant or contradictory messages, and distilling 'core' messages that should lay the foundations of nationalities policy. The drive to streamline the system of consultation is evident in a 2004 judgement of the Russian Constitution Court, which ruled that no more than *one* regional NCA per nationality could be established in the same subject of the Russian Federation.[33]

This approach indicates an assumption of homogeneity in groups, as it fundamentally presupposes one institution (one 'autonomy') per nationality per subject. It is reminiscent of Brubaker's 'groupism', defined as: '[T]he tendency to take discrete, sharply differentiated, internally homogeneous and externally bounded groups as basic constituents of social life, chief protagonists of social conflict, and fundamental units of social analysis'(Brubaker 2002: 164).

Such a tendency further reflects the Soviet essentialist approach to ethnicity, which links specific, 'core' traits to each ethnic group. The internal complexity behind the homogenising façade of minority groups is one of the reasons why the idea of a consultative system with a neat pyramidal structure has not been translated into a mechanism guaranteeing effective minority participation. Some of the respondents linked this failing to rivalries between competing leaders of minority organisations. For example, a respondent from a cultural association in Moscow said:

> NCAs were established because they [the authorities] wanted to have a system that was like a pyramid. There would be local, regional and federal NCAs. At the top there would be the federal consultative council on NCAs,[34] that would bring groups together. But not all [groups] have formed a federal NCA. The reason is that people have their own ambitions. Two people would want to be leaders of the federal NCA, and the people supporting one would not support the other, so it just didn't happen. The reason why there are NCAs and *also* public organisations [NGOs] is this, because of personal ambitions, and more than one person wants to be leader.
>
> [1.3.4]

Besides possible conflicts between leaders of minority organisations (including NCAs), complexities linked to representativeness stem from a group's heterogeneity – given its members' different traits (gender, age, profession etc.), as well as variegated allegiances, affiliations and opinions. Clearly, an individual's identity is not shaped solely by his/her ethnic background. Given these multiple layers of identity, one could argue for an attempt to engage with diversity by widening the potential for participation, enabling different segments of the minority population to become involved (Phillips 2002: 21). Similarly, Palermo (2008: 411) asserts that 'the benchmark of the effectiveness of participation is its degree of pluralism'. While minorities should be allowed to develop a 'group-oriented dimension' through the right of association (Marko 2006: 4), a group's internal differences also need to be recognised through a system of representation that allows a broad range of voices to receive attention during consultation. Thus, there also needs to be space for internal dissent within the group's collective persona (Nimni 2007: 360).[35]

A missing link of accountability

The NCA's hierarchical structure rests on the assumption that local concerns will be elevated to the federal level, and represented in the federal consultative council on national cultural autonomy.[36] However, this seemingly inclusive system does not provide for the election of delegates, or other means to facilitate broad representation, while it is effectively based on self-appointment.[37] Hence, the NCA system operates on the basis of communication channels whose trajectory is from a narrow local elite to the federal, via the regional, elite. Two respondents expressed the opinion that ethnic leaders belong to minority groups' 'intelligentsia', while 'ordinary' minority members tend to be marginalised, particularly in the case of disadvantaged minorities, such as Roma and persons originating from Central Asia. In the case of ethnic groups from Central Asia, the first respondent, an academic in Moscow, noted:

> There is a gap between the minority leaders and the rest of the group, and not even communication between them.... The leaders represent the intelligentsia, people who have lived in Russia for a long time, have status and work.
>
> [2.19][38]

The second respondent, an activist on Roma rights in St Petersburg (herself an ethnic Russian) said:

> There was a roundtable I attended, where there was a discussion on [Roma] settlements of the town of [X].[39] There was a conflict between the Roma and the administration, on houses that were built without permission, and some were destroyed by a decision of the court. At the roundtable there was nobody from the community, only a representative of the Roma federal NCA, a famous singer and actor. He is the picture of Roma life that corresponds to the stereotype, not to reality. He didn't defend the Roma, he said that the authorities were right.
>
> [1.5.8]

The Russian NCA system is based on a 'descriptive', rather than 'substantial', form of representation – the former guided by a presumption that belonging to a certain (ethnic) group will automatically lead to the representation of the group's interests. Yet more important than ethnic affiliation, Verstichel (2008: 459) argues, is a 'link of accountability' between representatives and the represented.[40] This link is tenuous in Russia, in the absence of procedures to elect or remove delegates. Similarly, the motivations for establishing NCAs do not always appear to be linked to ethnic leaders' concerns over the interests of the group they represent. Once the NCA Law was adopted, an 'offer' was implicitly made to minority groups to organise themselves into NCAs. Osipov (2004) argues those who accepted the 'offer' did so for reasons that are not necessarily (or solely) linked to cultural preservation, but (also) to calculations of potential material benefits (with expectations of government support), and possibly to ingratiate themselves with the authorities (by demonstrating loyalty). Finally, persons belonging to minorities in some instances have established NCAs to fill an existing niche, thereby preventing other (potentially rival) organisations from benefiting from this opportunity (ibid.: 179).

These motivating factors indicate a preoccupation with relations with state organs rather than the minority group per se. Registering as an NCA, in particular, signals to the authorities that an organisation wishes to focus on culture in its activities, distancing itself from politics and thus refraining from challenging the status quo. While some respondents referred to forms of cooperation with the local authorities that assisted them in promoting minority cultures,[41] one respondent, an academic in Moscow, voiced the opinion that cooperation came with a 'contract' of loyalty [2.21]. Daucé (2015) similarly argues that the Tatar NCAs in Moscow oblast were established under the auspices of the regional authorities in order to promote a joint loyalty in the various groups comprising the Tatar community.

In practice, NCAs are not necessarily given preference compared to other minority organisations, and financial and other government support is scarce (Osipov 2004: 198–205).[42] Yet NCAs continue to be established. According to one respondent, an academic belonging to a national minority in Moscow, leadership of an NCA is sometimes seen as a step towards a political career [2.20].[43] Another respondent, head of a minority association in Kazan, expressed the opinion that the flexibility and non-transparency in the management of NCAs meant that these institutions might give access to opportunities for their leaders to enrich themselves through illicit means [1.4.2]. Some noted other potential benefits of loyalty to the authorities: speaking about a NCA in Petrozavodsk, the director of an NGO in the same city said: '[The representatives of this NCA] are not interested in the *kopeks* that they might get from the government. They have their own festivals. What they need is visas and work permits for their relatives and friends [fellow minority members]' [1.2.1].

In this case, NCAs may become an instrument to facilitate amicable relations with the authorities, and the resulting networks may be used to benefit other members of the same minority. In an environment where unpredictability is the norm and informal practices abound (Ledeneva 2006b), these networks may in practice be necessary. The same leader of the NCA in Petrozavodsk referred to by respondent 1.2.1, noted (in another interview) that, for members of his minority – some of whom were recent immigrants from a former USSR republic – citizenship was the priority in seeing one's rights respected [1.1.1].

If NCAs' networks are indeed (indirectly) employed to obtain work permits and citizenship rights, NCAs might enable the resolution of some very real concerns for persons belonging to minorities, including immigrants – yet in a circuitous and opaque manner, through behind-the-scenes negotiations and informal networks.[44]

Respondents of both civil society and academia argued that ethnic leaders might be driven more by self-interest than altruism. Approximately half of the minority leaders interviewed were wealthy business people: informal networks might help protect their businesses from the unpredictability of the Russian economic and legal environment, where, again, informal practices are ubiquitous. The reality is likely to be an amalgam of motivations. Helping fellow minorities will reconfirm one's position as the group's leader and ultimately serve his/her interests. For the cultivation of good relations with the authorities, membership in bodies such as Public Chambers[45] and Parliamentary assemblies are of additional benefit to one's status.[46] This form of 'representation' might in practice be beneficial to minority members, even when it originates from self-interest. The leaders of minority organisations may use their informal networks with the local authorities to help fellow minorities – for example, if the latter are harassed by law-enforcement officials. One respondent, the leader of a minority group in a city (not in an ethnic republic), and the head of a Public Chamber advising the local authorities on nationality issues, said: 'When people [persons belonging to minorities] get stopped by the police they call me. They ask me to go and speak to the police' [1.2.6].

Interestingly, the respondent added that police officers might similarly ask him to intervene to assist in resolving issues of law-enforcement that concern persons belonging to minorities. At the same time, the potential benefits of this system come with the risk of bestowing excessive discretionary powers on minority groups' leaders. As noted by a respondent, an academic in Moscow:

> For the elites [the NCA system] is an instrument of self-realisation. They [the leaders] do represent the interests of the group, but they have the right to [the control of] the point of contact between the group and the authorities. This unique channel is monopolised by these leaders. The majority of them are good, they want to help. But the system is built in a way that even good people become corrupted by it.... They have to show their loyalty.
>
> [2.21]

An excessive reliance on informal practices can further mean that those who cannot penetrate the existing networks may remain without support from both the authorities and the minority group to which they belong. Limited accountability and uncertain responsiveness to the needs of minority members point to the questionable internal democracy of NCAs.[47] Ultimately, NCAs' minority leaders can be complicit in perpetuating the (government's) unwritten rules for the regulation of nationality issues. This can lead to 'symbolic', in lieu of 'instrumental' law and policy (Osipov 2013a; Malakhov and Osipov 2006). As Osipov puts it, the situation thus created is one of:

'governmentality' (*gouvernementalité*) in Foucault's terms, in the sense that power means general acknowledgement of certain ideas and rules as part of the natural and unavoidable order. Power functions as a wide range of control and disciplinary techniques embedded in society itself, and it remains invisible, being literally kept out of politics in the narrow sense. Thus, the Russian system of diversity governance looks stable and rests on a silent agreement between the government and the citizenry.

(Osipov 2013a: 79)

Such a stultified system of representation fails to involve any but the (self-appointed) leaders of minority institutions. Even in the case of minority leaders, participation can remain at a superficial level, and be devoid of effectiveness in the sense of Article 15 FCNM. Thus, the NCA system in practice consists of a loose arrangement for the 'consultation' of the few, rather than an institutionalised form of participation encompassing a minority group's many diverse segments. It can favour forms of co-optation of ethnic entrepreneurs by state structures rather than the accountability of leaders to the group vis-à-vis the represented.

A framework 'from above'

In addition to internal shortcomings, the environment in which NCAs operate does not provide favourable conditions for effective participation. It has been argued that NCAs are structures that originate 'from above', having been established by law by the Russian government, with minorities having no co-ownership of them (Filippova and Filippov 2008). In addition to this, the NCAs' scope of action is restricted, with various inhibitors to effective participation, including: NCAs' limited autonomy and opportunities for consultation; the unrepresentativeness of the federal NCA consultative body; the fragmentation of minority representative institutions; and an inadequate legal entrenchment of NCAs.

In principle the NCA system can facilitate the realisation of minorities' participatory rights in two ways: by ensuring autonomy in decision-making on matters affecting minorities, and by guaranteeing participation in governmental decision-making through consultative mechanisms. The NCA Law opens up opportunities for autonomy, stipulating, at Article 1, that NCAs are established to 'independently regulate the issues of their identity preservation'. This form of autonomy can transcend the constrains of ethnic federalism and the territoriality principle. This point was made by an academic from Moscow, who argued in an interview that NCAs can benefit dispersed minorities by upholding the rights of minorities 'regardless of where they are' [2.17]. And, if true autonomy is attained, the need for 'special measures' to accommodate minorities is virtually eliminated, as minorities are equipped with the authority and resources to manage their cultural distinctiveness independently (Nimni 2007: 360). Despite autonomy being guaranteed in the NCA Law, in practice NCAs have no authority to make decisions on matters linked to minority concerns, such as the teaching of minority languages in schools. In light of this, a Russian scholar in Moscow observed in an interview that, of the three words in the expression 'national cultural autonomy', the first two may be accurate but 'autonomy' is 'unfortunate' as not reflecting the reality on the ground [2.21]. In addition to the absence of autonomous decision-making, the dependence upon (precarious) financial support – from the government or other sources – means that NCAs have no true autonomy of action (Filippova and Filippov 2008).[48]

The NCA Law also carves out a role for NCAs as advisors of governmental bodies.[49] In practice, the Russian NCA system is only at the periphery of commonly endorsed mechanisms for minority consultation foreseen by international standards for minority protection. These include mechanisms for co-decision, which may be divided into 'soft' and 'hard powers of co-decision'. 'Soft powers of co-decision' designate arrangements by which the views of minorities must be heard before decisions are taken or laws adopted on matters concerning them; 'hard powers of co-decision' are those by which minorities have the right of legislative initiative and veto powers in the case of legislation affecting their interests. Mechanisms of minority participation further encompass fully independent decision-making in specific areas, including through forms of self-government. In these cases the government provides a 'general framework' on minority policies, but decision-making in specific areas, such as minority education, and on the use of funds allocated to minority programmes, are left to minorities themselves (Weller 2008: 430–431). Set against these models, the Russian NCA system is only a feeble mechanism of participation. As the ACFC put it, consultative councils in Russia 'are expected to implement rather than contribute to the preparation of minority-relevant legislation'.[50] A respondent from a minority NGO in Moscow, who had taken part in public discussions on minority issues, commented on their overly general nature, followed by 'no outcome' [1.2.5]. No specific provision is made to hear minorities' views prior to decisions or the adoption of laws affecting them; and, in 2004, amendments to the NCA Law[51] removed the legal obligation for the Russian authorities to take into account proposals from NCAs in the formulation and realisation of federal programmes on the development of minority cultures.[52]

Despite the scarcity of opportunities for impact, the respondents referred to examples of fruitful cooperation between the authorities and the NCAs or other minority associations, for example in the case of the NCA of Tver Karelians [1.1.2; 2.5].[53] With reference to the Mordovian NCA in Ul'yanovsk, Abramov writes that 'a mutual understanding was established with the leadership of the Ul'yanovsk oblast' (Abramov 2010: 173).[54] Other positive examples cited by Abramov are the Mordovian NCA for Tatarstan, and NCAs in cities with Mordovian settlements such as Penz and Samara (Abramov 2010:173–175). The activities undertaken by NCAs mentioned in interviews – and carried out with the cooperation or approval of the local authorities – included: the publication of newspapers in minority languages; the teaching of minority languages; the celebration of 'days of national languages'; the organisation of festivals, concerts and cultural programmes; and the establishment and running of cultural centres for

minorities. The NCAs' objectives encompassed the raising of ethnic consciousness in members of minorities: for example, a representative of the Tatar NCA
of Moscow oblast reported engaging in activities aiming at encouraging ethnic
Tatars to self-identify as Tatars in the 2010 census, rather than as ethnic Russians [1.1.5].

At the same time, as seen in Chapter 7, some respondents noted a tendency
by the authorities to limit exchanges with civil society to a discourse confined to
pre-existing boundaries, centring around general policies and cultural programmes, such as ethnic festivals – with a disinclination to discuss, for example,
the intricacies of educational policies.[55] A representative of a federal NCA noted
that he wished NCAs to have a more meaningful role (by becoming 'partners'
with law-makers) and thereby have some input into legislation [1.1.6]. The
respondent further denounced the 'alarming tendencies' to place inter-ethnic dialogue on a superficial level, by 'trying to revive the hypocritical form of "friendship of peoples" [*druzhba narodov*] of the Soviet period'.[56] The ACFC has
similarly expressed concern that the activities of NCAs are confined to 'culture
in the narrow sense', particularly in light of the fact that Russian law does not
allow the establishment of political parties on ethnic grounds.[57] The ACFC
added:

> [T]he concepts of 'culture' and the 'preservation of the essential elements of
> identity', contained in Article 5 of the Framework Convention, are quite
> broad and include an engagement with issues of general relevance within
> the community, such as youth work, religious activities, the promotion of
> research, or issues connected to participation in public affairs. Against this
> background and given the restrictive interpretation of the term 'culture' in
> [the NCA Law] ... the Advisory Committee regrets the explicit limitation of
> national-cultural autonomies to cultural activities. ... the preoccupation of
> national-cultural autonomies with the organisation of folklore events and
> Sunday schools could discourage minority communities from engaging in
> broader political discourse in society and thereby inhibit their effective
> participation in public life generally.[58]

Along these lines, Osipov has argued that narratives linked to notions of 'cultural dialogue' and the 'development of ethnic groups', when combined with
'cultural autonomy', contribute to excluding from public agendas controversial
issues such as discrimination on ethnic grounds (Osipov 2013a: 79). A respondent, an academic in Moscow, believed that NCAs, having been prevented from
acquiring a meaningful function, have tended to become inward-looking, focusing on their own short-term projects, rather than fulfilling the functions outlined
in the NCA Law. He said: 'As a rule they [NCAs] don't solve problems. They
have no influence at higher levels. They only solve their own issues, such as
getting their own grants' [2.20].

In some areas the scope of the debate might be broader. For example, the
(former) Ministry of Regional Development reported that the themes discussed

at a meeting of the federal consultative council on national cultural autonomy – held in June 2014 under the auspices of the Ministry – included issues concerning formerly deported people of Crimea.[59] Other (more typical) themes on the agenda comprised the 'linguistic, ethnocultural and educational needs of the peoples of Crimea', as well as planned activities in the area of 'harmonisation of inter-ethnic relations' in Crimea, albeit in the context of 'unity of the Russian nation [*rossiiskaya natsiya*]'. The meeting further involved presentations by representatives of the Ministry itself on the measures adopted by the state, at the federal and regional level, in specific priority areas: the creation of a system of monitoring and early warning of ethnic conflict; an information campaign on the promotion of the idea of a 'Russian nation' [*rossiiskaya natsiya*]; prevention of extremism and xenophobia; and financial support for initiatives aiming at fostering civic unity and harmonious inter-ethnic relations. In planning future sessions, it was agreed that one of the subsequent sessions of the consultative council would be within the framework of the youth-educational forum 'Patriot', scheduled for September 2014 in Crimea.[60] Thus, the activities of the consultative council seem to adapt to the Russian government's pursuits in the strengthening of patriotism and national cohesion.

Despite a rigid framework constraining NCA activism, NCAs (and other minority institutions) can play a significant role in the lives of persons belonging to minorities. Many NCA members are motivated volunteers who wish to preserve their traditions and assist others in pursuing the same goal, for example by organising, and sometimes teaching, language classes.[61] Some respondents indicated that these activities were essential to the preservation of their cultural uniqueness and ethnic consciousness. Similarly, Popov (2008) argues that cultural autonomies fulfil a social function by creating an internal support system for minority communities – which had once been provided by Soviet institutions – as well as, in the case he examines, a system of moral values.[62] Despite this, the NCA system remains insufficient to fully uphold the participatory rights of minorities in Russia: as Osipov (2004) contends, NCAs are virtually indistinguishable from NGOs, and are devoid of specific rights and guarantees. It is indicative that NCAs were offered no opportunity to debate the adoption of Law 309 and the reform of the education system, despite their likely impact on the teaching of minority languages, history and cultures.[63] Even the very ratification of the FCNM by Russia in 1998 was not discussed in the Council: its members were simply informed of it (Osipov 2004: 193).

The Consultative Council: exclusive consultation

The second obstacle to participation facing NCAs is the 'exclusive consultation' system found at the apex of the NCA structure: the federal consultative council on National Cultural Autonomy. The Council has undergone various transformations, with its last incarnation established in 2006 under the (former) Ministry of Regional Development.[64] Although a plethora of consultative councils exists in Russia – with multiple institutions at the local and regional levels – the consultative council is the only consultative body at the *federal* level. It consists of representatives of federal NCAs (FNCA),[65] who through the Council can raise their concerns with high-ranking public officials. However, two problems have continued to surface. First, actual meetings have taken place intermittently, sometimes with yearly gaps between them (Osipov 2004: 194). Second, although the Council is envisaged as a forum for discussion and consultation for representatives of the various minorities in Russia, the number of registered FNCAs has been between 15 and 18 in the period 2008–2014,[66] out of the over 170 nationalities recognised Russia. A re-organisation of the Council was carried out in October 2013,[67] nominally to raise its status within the Ministry of Regional Development and to initiate the holding of regular sessions[68] – although the abolition of the Ministry in September 2014[69] is likely to aggravate the precariousness of the conditions in which the Council operates. The first meeting of 2014 saw the participation of only 14 representatives of FNCAs. The Council's representative deficiency is primarily linked to the bureaucratic effort that an FNCA entails, both for its establishment and maintenance [1.1.5; 1.1.6; 3.2].[70]

A complicating factor in creating a wide representative base for minorities through NCAs is that by law NCAs can only be established in localities where a group is in a 'situation of national minority'.[71] Hence, there are, for example, no Mordovian NCAs in Mordovia: the main organisation promoting Mordovian interests in the Republic of Mordovia is, instead, the Inter-Regional Social Movement of Mordovian (Moksha and Erzya) Peoples (hereinafter Mordovian Movement). The Mordovian Movement's members, however, are unable to access the federal consultative council, being outside the federal NCA system, and not having established a Mordovian FNCA. The Tatar minority has been represented by a Tatar FNCA, which brings together the Tatar NCAs from outside the Republic of Tatarstan. At the same time, alternative institutions have been established *within* the republic, primarily the World Congress of Tatars. Similarly, in Petrozavodsk the main institution uniting Karelian activists is the Congress of Karelians. Thus, NCA regulations effectively cause the fragmentation and asymmetry of the system of minority representation. Ultimately, alternative (and at times informal) channels of communication between non-NCA structures and the authorities have been forged. For example, the Mordovian Movement approaches the Russian authorities to further Mordovian interests, as this is its *raison d'être*. NCA and non-NCA structures are not necessarily placed antagonistically to each other: for example, the NCA of Ul'yanovsk oblast was registered in 2000 following the third Congress of Mordovian Peoples (Abramov 2010: 173). The same members can sometimes be found in Tatar NCAs and also in the World Congress of Tatars.[72] Yet with the said plurality of communication channels the opportunities for bilateral, informal negotiations multiply, with a proliferation of parallel minority institutions.

Proliferation and fragmentation of minority representative institutions

The foregoing takes us to the third obstacle to effective participation: the proliferation and fragmentation of minority representative institutions. In addition to the institutions already cited (such as the Mordovian Movement), a complex web of consultative bodies can be found below the federal consultative council. Article 7 of the NCA Law stipulates that government bodies are to form 'advisory councils on national-cultural autonomy'. A number of advisory councils have in fact been established,[73] although they do not represent an integral and distinct feature of the NCA system: in the councils no distinction is made between members of NCAs, NGOs and other ethnicity-based organisations. Indeed, in reports to the ACFC, the Russian authorities, in listing Russia's mechanisms of consultation, refer not only to NCA-based consultative bodies but to various institutions including Public Chambers;[74] this reveals that NCAs do not serve as the main channel of communication and cooperation between authorities and minorities. Some incoherencies thus emerge: on the one hand, there is an attempt to maintain a unified structure of representation – by precluding the establishment of more than one NCA per region per minority. On the other hand, the system displays considerable elasticity, in the absence of membership rules for consultative councils; meanwhile, the exclusivity rule of one NCA per minority per region is immaterial if alternative (non-NCA) institutions may be established for the same minority, whose treatment is indistinguishable from the treatment of an NCA.

In principle a plurality of voices is conducive to a vibrant democratic society.[75] In line with this, ACFC recommendations have focused on inclusiveness, urging Russia to promote 'high levels of representativeness' of NCAs, while also involving other groups in consultation processes alongside them, so as to 'ensure pluralism among the state's interlocutors'.[76] Certainly, in addition to more formal systems of representation there is space for pressure groups and campaign organisations. These may operate and lobby alongside more formal, institutionalised structures, which enjoy specific constitutional guarantees. At the same time, ACFC's Opinions include two principal recommendations with regard to consultative bodies: that they be 'institutionalised' and in 'permanent dialogue' with the authorities (Marko 2006: 7). Responsibilities may be distributed among several bodies (Weller 2008: 439),[77] yet these ought to be part of the same cohesive structure. Constituent bodies should be interlocking and multi-layered,[78] rather than duplicating each other's functions. The Council of Europe favours 'a comprehensive and integrated design of minority consultative structures', with '[a]n overall minority consultative council operating at the national level, and including all minorities'.[79] Various institutions should radiate from this focal point. Weller (2008: 443) suggests that, when there is no one single institution recognised by different minorities (or by different groups within the same minority) as a single umbrella organisation representing their interests, the state might encourage minorities to reach consensus on a single representative body.[80] In this way, institutions can converge into a single interlocutor, thereby simplifying consultation processes.

International standards do not delineate precise regulations to translate these guidelines into practice, which have instead to be devised by individual states. To be sure, it is not easy to strike a balance between creating a coherent, effective system for minority participation and guaranteeing minorities independence of action as to their own systems of representation. Even in the presence of adequate mechanisms, minorities might encounter difficulties in effectively representing their interests through these bodies (Marko 2006: 8; Weller 2008: 443), due to the potentially diverging viewpoints of different members of minority groups. These complexities are multiplied in the case of Russia, given the extremely high number of minorities residing within its boundaries, and the fragmentation created by the various existing structures of representation. Moreover, the Russian system is simultaneously exclusive and inclusive: it strips NCAs of their special function in the nationality discourse, by failing to effectively institutionalise their role, and it involves other institutions in discussions that have little practical impact. Rather than ensuring pluralism in decision-making, this ostensibly inclusive system muffles voices that are already feeble.

Participation without legal guarantees

The fourth obstacle to NCAs' effective participation is the inadequate legal guarantees provided to them as consultative bodies. Such institutions cannot function in a vacuum, but only as part of a system that provides legal guarantees and judicial remedies. NCA theorists argue that NCAs should have exclusive decision-making in spheres of culture – in the form of constitutionally-enshrined rights (Nimni 2007: 347). Similarly, international standards relating to the participation of minorities foresee the legal entrenchment of mechanisms for consultation.[81] Thus, the shedding of the territoriality principle through cultural autonomy does not imply an overly flexible, amorphous system devoid of rights for its participants. Russian law and practice on NCAs distance themselves from the relevant international standards in two ways. First, there has been no sustained effort to implement the provisions contained in the NCA Law (Osipov 2013a). Second, the vagueness of the Law's provisions means that the rights of NCAs tend to be ambiguous and open to interpretation (Osipov 2004: 163–167). In particular, respondents (civil society) pointed to the NCA Law's vague provisions on funding, and the absence of an unequivocal obligation on state organs to provide financial support [1.1.6; 1.2.8; 1.2.9].[82] The fact that the NCA Law lacks detailed provisions for relations between NCAs and the authorities, as well as for financing, precludes long-term and fruitful cooperation. At the other end of the spectrum, legal vagueness exempts public structures from specific responsibilities to follow advice and recommendations originating from NCAs and advisory councils.

Hence, the environment in which NCAs operate offers scarce opportunities for the effective participation of minorities in decision-making. This might be the reason why some respondents emphasised what they saw as the crucially important nexus between nationality and territoriality [2.20; 4.14].[83] They believed that territoriality provided more substantial powers of decision-making and autonomy than NCAs in the cultural sphere. Indeed, during the Soviet era territoriality had advanced the right of education, facilitated the establishment of cultural institutions and promoted minority languages (Harris 1993). In post-Soviet Russia, several ethnic republics – including Tatarstan and Mordovia – have introduced the compulsory study of titular languages even for ethnic Russians.[84] Titular languages are recognised as official by the republics' laws of languages.[85] Although the respondents referred to instances of limited implementation of these legal guarantees, the said provisions unequivocally signal that titular languages enjoy a special status in the ethnic republics.[86]

Perceptions as to the importance of territory are illustrated in the following excerpts from interviews. The first is from an interview with a scholar from Moscow's Russian Academy of Sciences:

> People see that with territorial autonomy much more can be achieved [than with NCAs]. [In an ethnic republic] you can have a national theatre, and regular financing. In schools there is education, students have to learn the [titular] language, there are textbooks, there are strong ethnological institutions, culture. People can see the difference, the type of guarantees that are there for ethnic groups. NCAs don't give the opportunity to print textbooks and disseminate them – or maybe they can disseminate them but they can't do anything else with them.[87]
>
> [2.20]

An employee of the Ministry of Education, who worked to promote the education rights of ethnic minorities, strongly criticised the NCA system, asserting that cultural autonomy merely amounted to 'fiction' [4.14]. She referred to the case of Roma, a particularly disadvantaged minority: the cultural and educational needs of Roma, she argued, could not be met by an NCA. She believed that those nationalities benefiting from territoriality have the freedom and concrete opportunities to formulate and implement their own cultural and education projects in their own regions:

> Other nationalities, like Tatars and Bashkirs, have their own territorial administrative divisions and own budgets, through which they realise their cultural policies. Those [nationalities] that have no territory ... have no opportunity to realise their rights and develop their native culture and language.
>
> [4.14]

While territoriality is not synonymous with autonomy and access to resources,[88] these statements display little faith in the ability of NCAs to influence the conditions surrounding minorities' enjoyment of their cultural rights.

Conclusion

The NCA system is unequipped to satisfy the participatory rights of minorities in Russia, and, as such, to provide the means for minorities to effectively exercise their cultural rights. NCAs offer no guarantees that the concerns of 'ordinary' persons belonging to national minorities will be represented at higher levels. NCA leaders are unelected members of minority groups, and, in some cases, appear to promote their own interests in addition to, or rather than, those of their fellow members. The NCA system is mono-dimensional – with one NCA per minority per region – yet it also coexists with an (uncoordinated) proliferation of consultative bodies, leading to the fragmentation and dilution of minorities' voices, as well as potentially aggravating the rivalry between minority leaders. International standards on participatory rights arising from the ACFC's Opinions are not guaranteed in the Russian system, for a combination of reasons, namely: the absence of legal entrenchment of the status, role and functions of advisory bodies; the lack of systematic and effective consultation on matters that affect minorities; and the failure to provide justifications when minorities' concerns are not taken into account in policy-making. Moreover, the NCA system seems to be employed to promote a particular interpretation of minority issues (such as the 'cultural development' of minority groups), itself immersed in an overarching patriotic framework.

Informal networks radiating from NCAs may benefit minorities in some instances. The downside of an over-reliance on informal networks is the lack of transparency and the absence of a direct 'link of accountability' between leaders and 'ordinary' members of minority groups. Without strong guarantees and a clear role for NCAs, their leaders and government structures alike are exempted from specific responsibilities. Ultimately, what happens is ad hoc: NCA leaders might help their co-ethnics, but they also might not. Public officials might cooperate with minority groups, but they also might not. Rather than a pluralistic, coherent and institutionalised system, the Russian NCA system brings together a few individuals at the apex of multiple organisations, whose activities are generally uncoordinated as well as entangled in a web of informal networks. The paucity of opportunities provided by NCAs as institutions greatly restricts the scope of action of minorities, and, arguably, contributes to the shaping of a cognitive frame that reflects a near-exclusive link between minority issues and cultural issues. The focus on 'cultural development' is also a characteristic of other (non-NCA) consultative mechanisms, and ultimately leads to an apolitical system of representation; these issues are explored in Chapter 9.

Notes

1 Other forms of participation are analysed in the next chapter.
2 ACFC, (Second) Report submitted by the Russian Federation, 26 April 2005, ACFC/SR/II(2005)003, p. 17.
3 ACFC, (Second) Opinion on the Russian Federation, 2 May 2007, ACFC/OP/II(2006)004, §14; 88–95.
4 Law 'On National Cultural Autonomy' (No. 74-FZ, 17 June 1996). See also Chapter 7.
5 ACFC, (Second) Report submitted by the Russian Federation (see note 2), p. 8.
6 Reasons range from financial constraints to the lack of implementation of the NCA Law, as outlined below.

7 The respondent was a representative of the World Congress of Tatars in Kazan.

8 The expression was used by two respondents [2.20; 4.14].

9 Article 1, NCA Law.

10 The provision was introduced through amendments in 2003 (Law 'On the Amendment of the Federal Law on National Cultural Autonomy, No. 136-FZ, 10 November 2003).

11 Titular nationalities do not tend to be regarded as 'minorities' in 'their own' republics, despite the fact that they often number less than the local Russian population.

12 This interpretation has been supported by official pronouncements that NCAs should add to, but not replace, ethnic federalism. From this follows that NCAs can be established by persons belonging to minorities who do not have (or reside in) their own state formations (Osipov 2004: 230). At the same time, the provision has remained open to interpretation, resulting in variations in its application across regions.

13 For example, in December 2014 Karelia had no Karelian NCA, but Jewish, Azerbaijani, Belarusian, Kyrgyz, Polish, Uzbek, Ukrainian, Roma, Lithuanian, Polish, German local NCAs; and Kyrgyz, Lithuanian, Armenian, Polish and Jewish regional NCAs (see the website of the Russian Ministry of Justice, http://unro.minjust.ru/NKAs.aspx, accessed 15 December 2014).

14 UN Human Rights Committee, 'CCPR General Comment No. 23: Article 27 (Rights of Minorities)', 8 April 1994, CCPR/C/21/Rev.1/Add 5, §7.

15 Articles 2(2), 4(5) and 5.

16 OSCE/HCNM Lund Recommendations on the Effective Participation of National Minorities in Public Life. See Drzewicki (2010).

17 ACFC, 'Commentary on the Effective Participation of Persons Belonging to National Minorities in Cultural, Social and Economic Life and in Public Affairs', 27 February 2008, ACFC/31DOC(2008)001, §18.

18 Ibid., §19.

19 See for example ACFC, (Second) Opinion on Finland, 20 April 2006, ACFC/OP/II(2006)003, §156. The Opinion states that the views of minorities (the Sami Parliament in this case) should be 'fully taken into account in decision-making affecting the protection of the Sami'.

20 Article 15 FCNM; Lund Recommendations (see note 16), Points 13, 16 and 19.

21 See ACFC, Commentary on the Effective Participation (note 17). See also Palermo (2008).

22 See, for example, ACFC, (First) Opinion on Albania, 12 September 2002, ACFC/INF/OP/I(2003)004, §72.

23 This regulatory vacuum is examined in the next chapter.

24 The other author who elaborated the concept is Otto Bauer, in *The Question of Nationalities and Social Democracy* (*Die Nationalitätenfrage und die Sozialdemokratie*), published in 1907. Renner and Bauer, who were among the leading Austro-Marxist intellectuals, developed their theory during the final stages of the Austro-Hungarian Empire (see Bottomore and Goode 1978).

25 For example, in Hungary and Estonia. See Nimni *et al.* (2013).

26 See Chapter 2.

27 A phenomenon known as the 'parade of sovereignties'. See Hale (2000).

28 Article 1, NCA Law.

29 Article 4 states that : 'The right to national cultural autonomy does not correspond to the right to national territorial self-determination.'

30 ACFC, (First) Report submitted by the Russian Federation, 8 March 2000, ACFC/SR(1999)015, p. 12.

31 ACFC, (Third) Report submitted by the Russian Federation, 9 April 2010, ACFC/SR/III(2010)005, p. 24.

32 State Duma, 2012. 'Gosudarstvennyi Yazyk i Mnogoobrazie Rossiiskoi Federatsii' [State Language and Cultural Diversity of the Russian Federation], http://pda.iam.duma.gov.ru/node/8/4911/19836 (accessed 10 December 2014).

33 RCC, Judgement No. 5, 3 March 2004. The case followed the registration of two German regional NCAs in Altai krai.The Court justified its decision on the basis that NCAs not only provide rights to minority groups, but they also create corresponding responsibilities for state bodies, including in relation to the provision of state support to NCAs. The NCA system could not, therefore, sustain more than one institution per region. However, in practice the rules for NCA registration have at times been applied arbitrarily by local judicial authorities, resulting in their being interpreted and implemented differently in different regions (Osipov 2004: 161–164).

34 See p. 192 on this ('The Consultative Council: exclusive consultation').

35 The expectation, within and outside the group, of general consent, can cause a stultified debate and even self-censorship. See also Chapter 9.

36 See p. 192 on this ('The Consultative Council: exclusive consultation').

37 Article 6 of the NCA Law includes the vaguely-worded provision that a local NCA is established by 'a general gathering of citizens of the Russian Federation, who consider themselves to be part of a specific ethnic community and reside permanently in the territory of the respective municipality'. By contrast, in the case of Peoples' Congresses, another form of minority institutions (see Chapter 9 and Osipov 2011), representatives are elected by members (e.g. the Congress of Karelians and the Inter-Regional Movement of Mordovian (Moksha and Erzya) Peoples). However, Abramov (2010) argues, with reference to the Mordovian case, that voting results might be influenced by the Russian authorities.

38 Many Central Asians, instead, are migrants living in extremely precarious conditions.

39 Not specified in the interests of confidentiality.

40 The issue of descriptive representation and the 'link of accountability' are further discussed in Chapter 9. On 'descriptive' and 'substantive' representation, see Pitkin (1967).

41 See p. 189 ('A framework "from above"').

42 At the same time, a small amount of financial or logistic support can make a significant difference to institutions operating with very limited resources.

43 Osipov (2004: 177) believes that such cases are however rare. More common is for members of NCAs to be persons belonging to the group's intelligentsia (as some respondents [2.19; 1.5.8] similarly argued), with an interest in promoting minority language and cultures; or, at times, business people, for whom participation in an NCA can be a means towards self-realisation (Osipov 2004: 176–177).

44 Osipov (2004: 184) similarly argues that NCAs provide 'informal' protection for some of their members.

45 Public Chambers are another type of consultative body. See Chapter 9.

46 Some of the minority leaders interviewed had passes to access the state Duma by virtue of their leadership roles within minority groups in their regions.

47 See also Chapter 9 on the issue of internal democracy.

48 See Chapter 7 on the funding of NCAs.

49 Article 7 provides for the creation of a Consultative Council on National Cultural Autonomy at the level of the government of the Russian Federation. However, paragraph 4 of Article 7, stating that similar advisory councils 'can be' established at the regional and local levels, was repealed in 2004 (Article 38, Law 'On the Amendment of Various Legislative Acts of the Russian Federation ...', No. 58-FZ, 29 June 2004).

50 ACFC, (Second) Opinion on the Russian Federation (see note 3), §90. Overall, these consultative councils have been viewed by the ACFC as ineffective in advising the authorities on matters concerning minority interests (§14).

51 Article 76, Law 'On the Amendment of Legal Acts of the Russian Federation ...' (No. 122-FZ, 22 August 2004).

52 The requirement to take such proposals into account was only preserved with regard to regional programmes (Article 14, NCA Law). Even in this case, there is no obligation to act upon the proposals.

53 The ACFC similarly referred to the NCA of Tver Karelians as a positive example of cooperation. ACFC, (Second) Opinion on the Russian Federation (note 3), §89.
54 To promote Mordovians' 'survival', in the sense of retention of Mordovian ethnic identity, as opposed to assimilation into the Russian majority.
55 See Chapter 7. However, interestingly Putin noted that he would favour expanding the powers and financing of NCAs to implement programmes for the integration of immigrants. President of Russia, Address to the National Assembly of the Russian Federation, 12 December 2012, http://eng.kremlin.ru/transcripts/4739 (accessed 24 September 2014).
56 The citation is from a speech delivered at a conference on national cultural autonomies in Kazan in 2009 (unpublished). 'Friendship of peoples' was a Soviet-sponsored discourse based on general notions of multi-ethnic tolerance.
57 ACFC, (Third) Opinion on the Russian Federation, 24 November 2011, ACFC/OP/III(2011)010, §26.
58 Ibid., §74.
59 The meeting followed Crimea's annexation by Russia in 2014.
60 Ministry of Regional Development, 19 June 2014. 'Sostoyalos' Pervoe Zasedanie Konsul'tativnogo Soveta po Delam National'no-kul'turnyx Avtonomii pri Minregione Rossii' [First Meeting of the Consultative Council on NCA under the Ministry of Regional Development], www.minregion.ru/news_items/4613?locale=ru (accessed 2 October 2014).
61 For example, this was the case in Tver, in the youth branch of the NCA of Tver Karelians [1.1.3].
62 Popov examined the case of Greek communities in Southern Russia.
63 This information was provided in an interview by a member of the federal Consultative Council [1.1.6].
64 Decree of the Government of the Russian Federation 'On the Establishment of the Consultative Council on National Cultural Autonomy under the Ministry of Regional Development' (No. 527-r, 17 April 2006). The first Consultative Council was established in 1996, through the Decree 'On the Consultative Council on Affairs of National Cultural Autonomies under the Government of the Russian Federation' (No, 1517, 18 December 1996).
65 As noted, FNCAs are formed when regional NCAs converge to form a FNCA; in turn, regional NCAs are established through the union of local NCAs (for other – less common – options to form regional NCAs and FNCAs see Osipov 2004: 168–172, and Article 5 of the NCA Law).
66 Only 18 FNCAs were registered at the end of 2008 (ACFC, (Third) Report submitted by the Russian Federation, note 31, p. 24), and 15 FNCAs in 2012 (State Duma, note 32). The Ministry of Justice in December 2014 listed 16 registered FNCAs: Azerbaijani, Kurdish, Jewish, German, Roma, Lezgian, Tatar, Chuvash, Belarusian, Polish, Lithuanian, Assyrian, Kazakh, Greek, Armenian and Ukrainian FNCAs. The Karachai FNCA (registered in 2002), Armenian FNCA (2002), Korean FNCA (2003) and Ukrainian FNCA (2003) were reported as no longer operating. A second Armenian FNCA and a second Ukrainian FNCA were registered in 2012 and 2011 respectively (see the website of the Ministry of Justice, http://unro.minjust.ru/NKAs.aspx, accessed 15 December 2014). On the difficulties experienced by some FNCAs, see ACFC, (Third) Opinion on the Russian Federation (note 57), §145.
67 Decree of the Ministry of Regional Development No. 449 (17 October 2013).
68 Ministry of Regional Development (see note 60).
69 See Chapter 4 (note 39).
70 The respondents who provided this information were, or had been, active in FNCAs.
71 Article 1, NCA Law.
72 This information was provided by a respondent from the Tatar NCA of Moscow oblast [1.1.5]. See also Osipov (2004: 179).

73 However, this has not happened consistently across the country (Osipov 2004: 195).
74 See, for example, ACFC, (Third) Report submitted by the Russian Federation (note 31). On Public Chambers, see Chapter 9.
75 See for example, *Handyside* v. *the United Kingdom*, European Court of Human Rights, Application No. 5493/72, 7 December 1976, §49.
76 ACFC, (Second) Opinion on the Russian Federation (see note 3), §164.
77 Institutionalised consultative bodies need to fulfil numerous functions, which one consultative body, on its own, is unlikely to encompass. These functions include participation in the sphere of minority issues, with regard to: needs assessment, devising policy priorities, decision-making on funding, monitoring and evaluation of programmes, and devising legislative and other proposals (Weller 2008: 438; see also the Lund Recommendations, note 16, Point 13). One can find consultative bodies with both a vertical, multi-layered structure (from local to nationwide bodies), or a horizontal one (specialised bodies). Specialised bodies might be thematic and/or focus on specific minorities (Weller 2008: 434–5). See Council of Europe, Committee of Experts on Issues relating to the Protection of National Minorities, 'Handbook on Minority Consultative Mechanisms', 20 October 2006, DH-MIN(2006)012, §25.
78 Council of Europe (ibid.).
79 Ibid., §33.
80 The state, however, needs to avoid preferential treatment of an organisation over another. See, for example, ACFC, (First) Opinion on Romania, 6 April 2001 ACFC/INF/OP/I(2002)001, §67.
81 Among other things, the ACFC has stressed that 'it is important to ensure that consultative bodies have a clear legal status'. ACFC, Commentary on Participation (see note 21), §107.
82 See Chapter 7. See also ACFC, (Third) Opinion on the Russian Federation (note 57), §72. The ACFC recommended 'more clarity on the legal status and competencies of national-cultural autonomies and to establish clear and transparent criteria and procedures for the allocation of funding' (§75).
83 These respondents are cited on p. 196.
84 See Chapter 6.
85 The only exception in Russia's 21 ethnic republics is Karelia.
86 See also the judgement of the Russian Constitutional Court on the constitutionality of the obligation to study Tatar and Russian 'in equal measure' in the Republic of Tatarstan (RCC, Judgement No. 16-P, 16 November 2004: see also Chapter 4.
87 Such as ensuring that they are used in schools.
88 See Chapter 5; see also Alexander (2004).

9 Minorities' voices

Ad hoc consultation and (a)political participation

Obstacles to the participation of minorities in decision-making have led to the formulation of minority policies that tend to be centrally-defined and top down. This approach reveals a tendency, already present in the Soviet period, to *manage* rather than *engage* with diversity. In post-Soviet Russia, although some basic provisions for minority participation exist, they are not buttressed by guarantees that bottom-up initiatives will be effectively elevated to decision-making levels. The prevalence of informal practices in Russian society means that mechanisms that ought to enable minority participation are themselves immersed in such practices and thus lack institutionalisation. The ad hoc nature of informal practices fails to guarantee the accountability of the main actors in majority–minority relations: public officials and institutions, *and* leaders of minority groups themselves. The use of informal networks to advance minority interests does not necessarily signify a disregard or direct violation of the law, but rather it represents a (perhaps inevitable) response to the lack of clear, legally-entrenched guarantees for minority groups. The absence of guarantees for effective participation is shown in this chapter with reference to (non-NCA) mechanisms for consultation and political representation in elected bodies.

In addition to national cultural autonomies (NCAs), described in the previous chapter, a plethora of consultative and coordination bodies exist in Russia. The types of bodies vary geographically as well as in format. They can be nationality-specific and focus on minority concerns, or they can cover a wider range of issues. To the first category belong advisory bodies devoted to nationality issues in city or regional governments, such as the consultative council on Nationality Issues of Moscow oblast and the National Chamber of Voronezh oblast. To the second category belong institutions such as Public Chambers (*obshchestvennye palaty*): despite not being specialised bodies specifically addressing minority concerns, they at times count among their members representatives of minorities pursuing minority interests. For example, in Mordovia, the republic's Public Chamber has served as an instrument for minority participation, with de facto reserved seats for the three autochthonous nationalities – Mordovians (both Moksha and Erzya speakers), Russians and Tatars. Other, smaller advisory bodies have also been established, for example at the level of city mayors' offices. Debates on matters of relevance to minorities are further conducted in institutions such as Houses of Nationalities (in Moscow and St Petersburg among the regions visited), and in Peoples' Congresses. The latter are structures established by minorities themselves, primarily for their internal management; they can be institutions for specific minority groups (e.g. the Congress of Karelians), or encompass a combination of groups united by ethnocultural affinity (e.g. the Association of Finno-Ugric Peoples of Russia).[1]

In addition, the Russian authorities have established what are generally known as 'mechanisms for coordination'.[2] These differ from minority consultative bodies in that they are *state* bodies for the coordination of activities on minority issues across governmental structures. In Russia the epicentre of this activity was, until September 2014, the Ministry of Regional Development, and its Department of Inter-Ethnic Relations – and subsequently the Ministry of Culture.[3] Ministries on nationality issues are also found at the level of the republics,[4] and ethnic republics are represented at the presidential level.[5] Although these organs can facilitate the expression of regional minority interests vis-à-vis the federal authorities, they are part of the executive apparatus rather than consultative bodies *stricto sensu*.

Consultative mechanisms: cooperation or infiltration?

The blurring of the distinction between minority consultative mechanisms and the executive – with the same persons involved in both – appears to be a frequent feature at the federal and regional[6] levels. For example, in 2010 the head of the federal consultative council on national cultural autonomy was also the deputy minister in the Ministry of Regional Development; in 2011, the head of the National Council of Voronezh oblast, which advises the governor on nationalities policy, was the governor himself;[7] and the speaker of the Tatar Duma in 2011 was also a member of the Assembly of Peoples of Tatarstan – itself a semi-official body, financially supported by the Republic of Tatarstan. Joint consultative bodies, formed by minority representatives and public officials, can in principle further dialogue, and elevate the concerns of minorities to policy- and law-making bodies. The circumstances of each case will determine whether these mixed consultative institutions function as genuine consultative bodies, or effectively just as 'mechanisms of coordination', driven primarily by state interests.

Respondents of ethnic minority background made reference to public officials attending meetings or being members of minority associations themselves. For example, the Minister of Culture of Mordovia in 2011 was also the head of the Association of Finno-Ugric Peoples of Russia. A member of the Assembly of Peoples of Tatarstan noted that 'several representatives of ministries' attended their sessions [4.8]. A member of the Congress of Karelians – one of the Peoples' Congresses – argued that the presence of public officials at their meetings did not result in servility, but rather it meant that issues of concern could be brought directly to their attention; he added that he did not refrain from criticising decisions by public officials at these meetings [1.4.1]. At the same time, the presence of public officials could mutate into monitoring activity, and consultative bodies and minority associations might become vulnerable to co-optation by the authorities. Abramov (2010) suggests this scenario in the case of Mordovia's Peoples' Congress, the Inter-Regional Social Movement of Mordovian (Moksha and Erzya) Peoples Movement (hereinafter the Mordovian Movement). This movement operates through a voting system to elect its representatives, and has a vertical structure – at district, regional and federal levels. Abramov (2010: 164) argues that the Mordovian Movement holds 'joint meetings' with the participation of the state structures of power, and that elections to the institution's executive committee have been manipulated in support of candidates favoured by the authorities.

Similarly, a respondent, the director of a human rights NGO in Voronezh, expressed the following view on the National Chamber of Voronezh oblast, which gathers members of minority groups residing in the city:

> Our regional National Chamber was established by governmental decree. And the governor is the head of this body, which shows that it's not totally independent and more of a way for representatives of [national] diasporas to be close to the authorities. They don't raise their voices. They try to deal with issues using personal contacts and avoiding media coverage. That explains a lot.
>
> [1.5.5]

An example external to the case studies is indicative of possible behind-the-scenes manipulation of minority associations. In 2009, when a United Russia MP of the Republic of Buryatia became the head of the All-Buryat Association for the Development of Culture, it was described as a case of 'infiltration'.[8] The MP, Vladimir Buldayev, was allegedly handpicked as a Putin loyalist to support the merger of Buryat regions with predominantly Russian ones,[9] which the Association had strongly opposed. The appointment, it was suggested, aimed at de-politicising the activity of the Association, transforming it into a loyal body.[10] Interview data suggest the presence, in some cases, of similar dynamics in the activities of Public Chambers.

Public Chambers: serving the public?

Some of the characteristics of Public Chambers[11] are exemplified by the interview with a representative of the Public Chamber for her city (not in an ethnic republic), as well as in another Public Chamber specifically for the city's Police Department. The respondent had also been invited to join the *regional* Public Chamber, but she had declined, as discussed below. Neither the respondent's work nor the Public Chambers she had joined focused specifically on minority issues, but the interview provides a clear illustration of the dynamics behind Public Chambers, given the details provided by this respondent, and her openness in discussing controversial subjects.[12]

Q: How do you find the [city] Public Chamber [PC]?

A: It's not very efficient in my mind. In general PCs are not really effective, probably because they are not formed out of *active* members of civil society. They are formed out of *respected* members of society, like the deans of universities, writers or artists, or actors ...

Q: Have you felt any pressure in the PC?

A: Well, sometimes they sort of push us to agree with certain decisions. It might not be that serious but still I don't like it when it happens. Like the last time we voted on the 'honoured citizens' of our town.... This year we all received the portfolios of seven people who were nominated, and basically I was told who had to be picked. I said: 'what if I don't want this particular person?' And it was explained to me that the mayor and the head of the PC had already met and decided that those two would be preferable, so [they said] 'we kindly ask you to vote for these people'. They have their own games that are not transparent and democratic. Maybe these two are good people – in fact I wanted to vote for one of them. But I don't like it when I'm being told what to do. Or once last year ... we were invited to an event to plant trees in the city, initiated by the members of the PC. I went and I found a lot of people with signs of United Russia [UR]. And I didn't like it, I don't want to be associated with UR, if it's an event to plant trees. So they exploited that as well, because the head of the PC is a [public] official from UR, so he probably decided to combine the two things to show that he is also doing something for UR.

Q: Do you feel that certain decisions that concern the PC are being made at the top (as in the 'honoured citizens' episode)? Are instructions handed down?

A: I can't say for sure, because those instructions would mostly be given to the chairperson, and then he would be promoting certain ideas, when discussing things with us. Then another question is whether the members of the PC themselves want to be independent. I feel that they are quite passive, I don't see any active initiative, something substantial ... [besides the] little things that they would also do within their NGOs or institutes, universities, or legal clinics. [What they do] is so small and irrelevant, and if they wished to do something major, I think they could, but they don't raise the issues that are uncomfortable for the authorities.

[1.5.5]

In a follow-up interview, the respondent added:

The PC is a small step towards more transparency. The police PC is more effective than the regional PC, there are more possibilities. It's an individual thing, the head of the police [in our town] is quite charismatic, and [instead] the administration is more closed than the police. In other regions it could be the opposite, like in [Town X],[13] where there is a better administration.

To raise an issue you don't need to be a member of the [regional] PC. But if you are a member they will use you 10 times more than you benefit from them. They will say that a decision has been approved after discussion with the PC, and they will not even tell you the details of the decision. But your name will be there. They will abuse your name, your good reputation. That's why I did not want to get involved. At least in the city PC and in the police PC we have some control.

If you are everywhere [in many different official bodies] and you try to sell yourself you can get many advantages ... I have a special [identification] card because I'm a member of the police PC but I never showed it to anybody. I could show it to people when I need to.... Some of the members of the PC are there only to have this police ID and avoid possible conflicts – for example, if they are stopped by the police when they drive. Or otherwise [being on these bodies] can be useful if you have a business. Normally the authorities can put pressure on you through tax inspections and fire regulations. If you have an affiliation with the authorities you don't have these problems. It has nothing to do with law and democracy. The system is abused by both the authorities and civil society, who try to get personal gain. The PC is more a platform for people to raise their profile, and it's not independent.

[1.5.5]

Hence, this respondent believed that: membership of a PC can be sought for opportunistic reasons; a PC can be exploited by its members and the authorities alike to further their interests; where PC membership is not abused, its members might tend towards passivity; and the benefits that a PC may provide to society are variable, and depend on individuals and regions. In the particular circumstances of her region, the respondent believed that the PC members had more freedom in the city and police PCs, and less so in the regional PC, headed by the governor.

Another respondent, working for the Russian human rights ombudsman in Moscow came to similar conclusions. He believed that the function of the PC system, which should be that of a 'social Parliament',[14] remained unfulfilled. He identified two reasons: first, he said, PCs' members often were 'not experts' in human rights or social issues; second, they had only limited, and variable, influence:

The PCs' members can get the authorities' attention [on particular issues] but they can't change the *system*. Sometimes they can raise some issues, complain vigorously.... If there is a very bad draft law they might be able to stop it.... When issues are raised there can be exposure through the media.... But with regard to the effectiveness of PCs, it depends. Mostly they only amount to discussions.... Their role is purely consultative and there is no obligation to follow their recommendations. It's important to what extent the leader [of a PC] is authoritative. Some PCs are very servile.

In some cases it's possible to have some influence, in others it's just a beautiful façade.

[1.5.3]

Another respondent, the representative of a minority and member of St Petersburg's city PC, similarly noted that 'the PC can only make recommendations'. The authorities could simply respond to these recommendations by pointing to the lack of funds to translate them into action [1.2.9].[15] At the same time, the respondent noted, when some funds had become available in 2010, and the PC proposed to use them for a two-year project to promote minority cultures in the city, the local authorities had given their consent.

Hence, interview data with respondents involved in PCs indicate, first, that there are no formal or informal safeguards, such as rules on conflicts of interest, to guarantee that those who join these bodies do not abuse their networks and influence for personal advantage. Second, the members tend to be 'respected' persons, but they might not have a specialisation in (or any knowledge of) human or minority rights. Only two-thirds of the members are nominated and appointed by civil society (including minority groups), and those involved in the process of nomination or appointment may well be immersed in the same web of informal networks described in previous chapters, raising issues of representativeness. Some exceptions were also recorded, with reference to appointments as PC members of persons known for their political independence [1.5.2]. Yet overall, the views of the respondents diverge greatly from Putin's pronouncements on the functions of PCs. In the 2013 state of the nation address the president argued: '[Public] councils should not be formal or decorative structures. On the contrary, they should act as expert groups, and sometimes as the government's constructive opponents, and be active participants in anti-corruption efforts.'[16]

Respondents referred to another type of semi-state structure, specifically focusing on nationality issues: Houses of Nationalities.[17] The representatives of Houses of Nationalities who were interviewed argued that they would welcome any group that wished to cooperate with them [1.3.6; 1.3.7]. The interviews with persons belonging to minorities did not expose cases in which the opposite was true. At the same time, there are few benefits to be reaped from these systems being fully inclusive, since the outcomes of their activities are dependent upon variable socio-political circumstances, and the attitudes of individual public officials. A respondent, the representative of a minority NGO in St Petersburg, expressed the following views on meetings held in the House of Nationalities in her city:

A: Sometimes the discussions are important because you meet other people, colleagues. It's good to know that there is a place where people can meet. The discussions sometimes are constructive, sometimes they haven't been well prepared – they are too spontaneous.

Q: At these meetings can you provide feedback on events [organised by the House], and recommendations for future events?

A: This feedback hasn't been requested. Usually the approach is: the event took place, all was good, and who was there.

[1.2.11][18]

Thus, interview data indicate that obstacles to participation are linked to the ineffectiveness of the existing mechanisms; as for the case of the NCAs, the weakness of the relevant institutions stems from an absence of guarantees that the interests of minorities will reach decision-making levels and be acted upon. A question then arises as to possible forms of *direct* representation of minorities in the political life of the country, through their involvement in political parties and elected bodies. In this context, of paramount importance is the role played by United Russia, and the way persons belonging to minorities position themselves around and, crucially, *in* the party.

(A)political minority participation

It has already been noted that minority issues have been linked principally to cultural programmes rather than to civil and political rights, while also perpetuating the Soviet legacy of actively promoting *patriotism* and containing ethnic *nationalism*. Yet it is also the specific characteristics of Russian politics and society that contribute to largely excluding minority concerns from the political sphere. Most notable is the fact that Russian law prevents the establishment of political parties on the basis of ethnicity.[19] The constitutionality of this restriction was confirmed by the Russian Constitutional Court on the grounds that the existence of ethnic parties could exacerbate ethnic or religious tensions.[20] The potential scope of the legal provision in question goes even further than prohibiting ethnicity-based political parties: if broadly interpreted, it could be used to ban political parties simply for including in their platforms advocacy designed to further the interests of national minorities.[21] These regulations are hardly needed to exclude minority interests from politics: in 1995, before the ban was introduced, the 5 per cent threshold for Parliamentary access was insurmountable for any single ethnicity- or religion-based political group; for example, the Muslim bloc 'Nur' had less than 1 per cent of votes. Additionally, the fact that most minorities are dispersed and numerically small means that there is no wooing of their representatives by the main parties to attract ethnic votes (Moser 2000: 83).

Legal reform under Putin has introduced new conditions for political parties to be legally registered, and thereby access the Duma. Through amendments introduced in 2004,[22] parties were required to have: a minimum of 50,000 members (raised from 10,000); regional branches with at least 500 members each in no less than half of Russia's federal subjects, and at least 250 members in the remaining regional branches.[23] The following year, a 7 per cent threshold (up from 5 per cent) was introduced, along with a prohibition on the formation of electoral blocs.[24] These changes have diluted the influence of the regions as political players (Hashim 2005: 36), and thus advanced centralisation.[25] In 2012, the required minimum membership for each party was reduced to 500,[26] and in

2014 electoral barriers for Parliamentary representation were lowered from 7 per cent to the (pre-2005) 5 per cent threshold. While these last modifications ostensibly create a more liberal system, parties and independent candidates are still required to prove their popularity in order to access the Duma: parties need to gather at least 200,000 signatures from supporters across the country, and independent candidates have to demonstrate the support of at least 3 per cent of their constituents.[27] The collection of signatures is not required of parties that gained at least 3 per cent of votes in the preceding elections, or that have a seat in the legislature of at least one of Russia's subjects: thus, the electoral system has continued to privilege existing dominant parties and to disadvantage new parties and independent candidates. Finally, the electoral system has seen shifts from a mixed to a fully proportional system (2007), and then back to a mixed system (2014).[28] The pace and reach of these alterations bear witness to a volatile electoral system, which is subject to frequent and centre-driven reform.

Even without their own political parties, persons belonging to minorities can still reach elected bodies.[29] This may happen through regular electoral processes, or through special measures guaranteeing minority representation in elected bodies. As the Lund Recommendations' Explanatory Note clarifies, states should devise electoral systems that 'would result in the most representative government in their specific situation', so as to facilitate adequate representation of national minorities.[30] Representation in elected bodies has been regarded as a *sine qua non* for the effective participation of minorities. As Hofmann writes:

> [A] seat in elected bodies is seen as a necessary requirement for effective political participation. In my opinion, this means that there are good arguments to consider the mere existence of *consultative mechanisms* ... as *not sufficient* for effective political participation [italics added].
>
> (Hofmann 2006: 13)

Special measures for minority representation might involve proportional representation systems, preference voting (with voters ranking candidates in order of choice) and the lowering of threshold requirements for minority parties to more easily access legislative bodies.[31] This type of special measures has not been incorporated into the Russian electoral system.[32] The resulting absence of guarantees of minority representation affects primarily smaller, non-titular minorities – and particularly dispersed, non-territorial ones:[33] while representatives of minorities that are geographically concentrated have tended to be elected by their co-ethnics, this is not the case for those minorities that are more scattered. Persons belonging to these minorities have entered the state Duma through 'support from the Russian majority' and through 'assimilation' (Moser 2008). This deficiency is captured in the statement of a public official (who worked in the area of minority, particularly Roma, education), who stated: 'The Roma [in Russia] are nationalities without status.... The situation of Tatars, for example, is very different. Tatars are represented in Ministries. They have their own Ministry of Education in Tatarstan' [4.14].

The point is borne out by the comments of a Tatar activist and member of a Tatar NCA: 'The head of the federal Tatar NCA is also an MP. I can call him any time. I can also go to the Duma any time' [1.1.5]. Indeed, unlike more disadvantaged and vulnerable minorities, Tatars can benefit from territoriality, resources and, seemingly, high-ranking contacts. Moreover, despite the exclusion of smaller groups, in practice there have been, overall, high levels of representation of minorities in both federal and regional elected bodies. Yet by looking more closely at the type of representation, an additional caveat comes into focus: the representation offered to minorities is *descriptive* in Pitkin's (1967) sense of the expression – meaning that representatives 'resemble' the represented, in this case by sharing the same ethnic background. This however does not guarantee a *substantive* form of representation, by which minority interests are effectively represented.[34]

Thus, Russia's patterns of diversity and assimilation are affected not only by policies that may, say, reduce the use of minority languages, but also by political uniformity. This is a general trend affecting all groups that deviate from the Kremlin-backed political orientation, but it also signifies the absorption of persons belonging to national minorities into the 'political majority'. These dynamics are situated in a general framework of de-ethnification and marginalisation of minority concerns – including through the exploitation of patterns of loyalty in minority representatives, which may result in their co-optation. In particular, a significant development under the Putin leadership, which has acted to further advance political uniformity, has been the consolidation of United Russia as the party of power – a party strongly associated with Putin himself.

United Russia has proved to be a successful and durable party. The percentage of its seats in the state Duma rose from 37.6 per cent in 2003 to 64.3 per cent in 2007, although it subsequently decreased to 49.3 per cent (in 2011). In March 2014, ratings were at their highest in five years (56.2 per cent): in February 2014 they had been 43.2 per cent, and, over the preceding two years, they had averaged 45 per cent.[35] Putin's own approval ratings have followed a similar trajectory: his ratings went from 54 per cent in December 2011 (a low point amidst public protests and accusations of vote rigging during the 2011 Parliamentary elections) to 68.8 per cent in May 2012 (at the time of the inauguration of Putin's third term as president). They continued on an upward path in 2014: from 60.6 per cent in January to 74.4 per cent in March (with the success of the Sochi Olympics and the political crisis in Ukraine), and up to 82.3 per cent at the end of March 2014[36] (with Russia's annexation of Crimea), thus reaching their highest point in six years.[37]

Even more crucially, while approval ratings have fluctuated United Russia has remained unchallenged by other political parties. Gel'man (2008) classifies United Russia as a 'dominant party', which he defines as:

> a party that is established by and closely tied to the rulers of an authoritarian regime; freely employing state power and resources to maintain its dominance; and uses extra-constitutional means to control the outcomes of politics during elections and beyond.
>
> (Ibid.: 915)

While the political system under Putin is not entirely authoritarian – given that it is not completely devoid of democratic elements (Sakwa 2011b; White 2012) – it displays the attributes of both personalist and party-based authoritarianism (Gel'man 2008). Indeed, it is characterised by a strong personalism, having been built around the figure of Putin as an indispensable leader (Isaacs and Whitmore 2014: 709); and it sustains a 'mini cult of personality', with Putin's portraits hanging in offices of the presidential administration and governmental departments (Sakwa 2004: 76). Moreover, while political parties went from being underdeveloped in the 1990s to emerge as major political actors in the 2000s, party competition has virtually been eliminated (White 2012; Gel'man 2006, 2008; Ross 2011; Sakwa 2011b). A combination of formal means (e.g. amendments of electoral legislation to favour incumbents)[38] and informal practices (e.g. the inconsistent application of electoral legislation)[39] have been employed to minimise electoral competition and neutralise challenges to the party of power (Isaacs and Whitmore 2014: 709). After the introduction of more stringent regulations for political party registration, referred to above, the number of parties dropped drastically: from 44 to seven in the period 2003–2009 (Ross 2011: 438). And, while opposition parties articulate criticism of the ruling elite, they also 'self-limit' themselves in practice: informal 'rules of the game' prevent them from translating rhetoric into action (March 2012).[40]

United Russia serves practical purposes: it is used for elite cohesion and management (Reuter 2010), and especially to strengthen the unity of the political leadership. It is a polymorphous party: it formally encompasses a multitude of ideologies, positions and factions, as well as combining liberal and statist – and anti-Western and pro-Western – elements (Laruelle 2009a: 149; 151). United Russia contributes to the creation of a 'reconciliatory dynamic' through the presidential apparatus, which is made possible by maintaining an imprecise patriotic doctrine, so as to avoid internal ruptures (ibid.: 136). Thus, while the party incorporates various political views, it fully upholds none: its vagueness results in its flexibility, enabling it to adjust to the needs of its top leaders, (partially) accommodating their differences for the sake of strength through unity. United Russia provides incentives for the ruling elite to make use of the opportunities it offers them (Gel'man 2006: 554), thereby feeding a form of mutual dependency, and continuously consolidating existing systems of loyalty: party membership has become a prerequisite for access to public life, the administration and the economy (Laruelle, 2009a: 151–152).[41] United Russia can thus be described as a 'mechanism' aiming at guaranteeing the loyalty of the political elite – particularly so in the case of governors (White 2012: 217). Indeed, one of the reasons for United Russia's ubiquity across the country is the fact that most regional governors joined its ranks in the mid-2000s (Reuter 2010),[42] a trend that also became common among civil servants. By the end of 2007, 78 of Russia's 83 (president-appointed) governors were members of United Russia (Reuter 2011: 3). Moreover, while until 2003 the members of the regional assemblies were mostly independent members of regional parties or electoral blocs,[43] in 2010 United Russia held 73 per cent of the seats of the assemblies in Russia's 83 subjects (Ross 2011). Regional leaders have benefited from career prospects and other advantages provided by their allegiance to United Russia; in turn, United Russia has gained from the financial and administrative support harnessed by governors to broaden the party's electoral base across the country (Reuter 2011),[44] using networks that envelop local administration bodies and private companies. These networks are mobilised by governors to assure votes for the ruling party (albeit with some variations between regions) – at times by resorting to illicit practices, including the falsification of results (Golosov 2011: 637).[45] The system thus created is one of inter-dependency between the president and the governors (Reuter 2010).

United Russia's pervasiveness is further linked to its involvement in countless and diverse activities, such as supporting road infrastructures, libraries and the restoration of historic buildings (Laruelle 2009a: 137). United Russia flags are a frequent sight at all kinds of public events, including ethnic minority festivals. According to Gel'man (2008: 917), the long-term stability of the political system rests on a threefold strategy pursued by the Putin administration: control over the political and policy agenda; elimination or co-optation of independent actors (including parties, NGOs and the media); and the elites' loyalty to the existing regime. At the same time, United Russia is not omnipotent, but rather displays a form of '"weak" dominance' (Roberts 2012b). The role of United Russia as a dominant party is in fact limited, given that, as Sakwa asserts, parties in Russia only amount to 'accessories to processes taking place within the regime'; United Russia is, then, 'at best a party *of* power, but not a party *in* power' [emphasis in original] (Sakwa 2012: 318). Moreover, United Russia's focus on minimising elite fragmentation through a strong leadership clearly reduces the role of the party as an autonomous policy-making actor, and causes its virtual subservience to the political regime (Isaacs and Whitmore 2014; Slider 2010; Sakwa 2011b). Its personalism and close association to Putin can weaken the party in the long-term, as shown by the plummeting of its popularity in 2011–2012: thus, the party's reliance on loyalty is, simultaneously, its strength and weakness.[46] These complexities have been exacerbated by difficulties in controlling intra-elite struggles in some regions, where support for the party has not been consolidated, and in less authoritarian regions, particularly since the 2011 protests. The fact that governors and civil servants joined the party did not always pre-empt the emergence of divisive regional interests, and, while various regional leaders were integrated into the 'vertical', some retained influence at the regional level (Isaacs and Whitmore 2014).[47] Finally, Putin himself has had an ambiguous approach to United Russia: he officially became the party's leader only in March 2008, and he later distanced himself from it, particularly with the fall of its popularity in 2011, including by forming the All-Russian Popular Front so as to expand his support base (Isaacs and Whitmore 2014: 709). Putin ceded the leadership of the party to Medvedev in May 2012. At the same time, the absence of real political competition, and the virtual elimination of multipartism, means that United Russia remains the party of power.

Russia's political system is further characterised by the predominance of the executive over the legislature, combined with United Russia's own links with the executive power. United Russia is not the manifestation of 'dominant-power politics' typical of many modern ruling parties, but is rather the agent of a mighty executive – a party actively and principally employed by non-party power-holders (Roberts 2012a). Legislative decisions have been taken by the executive, mostly outside the legislature itself. Thus, Chaisty writes:

> The legislative work of the Parliament and the government became much more closely integrated [under Putin] than had been the case in the previous Dumas: conflicts on legislation were effectively reconciled before bills received their official 'readings' in the assembly. These informal arrangements for resolving disputes before legislation was introduced ... means that the lobbying opportunities for distributive amendments afforded by the previous regime were restricted.
>
> (Chaisty 2006: 195)

What does such a political system mean to minorities? First, ethnic issues continue to be kept firmly outside the political sphere – with the exception of a simplistic rhetoric revolving around inter-ethnic tolerance and cultural development. A respondent, the director of a human rights NGO, emphasised the utilitarian and managerial nature of United Russia. She called it a 'party of bureaucrats', in which the interests of national minorities, ethnicity, even forms of Russian nationalism, are unimportant. What matters, she argued, are the particularistic interests of those in power, closely associated with the Putin–Medvedev duo. She put it this way:

> In Chechnya for instance there are no ethnic Russians among the authorities[48] but they are all members of United Russia and when Chechnya organises elections the entire population votes for United Russia....[49] Bureaucracy is all that people care about, and if you are a member of United Russia you can become a public official, a functionary, you have privileges, you have good cars, you have businesses, nobody will touch you. People who are in power are all members of United Russia. I feel they just created this kingdom of United Russia, of pro-Putin bureaucrats.... In all regions the governor is also the head of United Russia.... Regional leaders are not fighting for their right to be independent, they want to be 'the same', part of the network and matrix of power.
>
> [1.5.5]

In line with this, Moser (2013) notes that, while in the 1990s ethnic federalism tended to further minority representation, Putin's centralising policies have resulted in a marked increase in clientelism and voting manipulation, with vote rigging becoming more common in the ethnic regions than in the Russian ones.

Second, the ban on ethnic and regional parties results in party politics being largely confined to the federal level, and in its being incorporated into Putin's centralising project (White 2012: 214). State control on political narratives means that the voices of minorities can be marginalised; this can be seen as part of a general democratic deficit, which implies low levels of representation of citizens' interests, including those of persons belonging to minorities. Third, the personalised politics typical of United Russia is a breeding ground for informal practices. On the basis of such practices, the numerous minority leaders who have joined United Russia might further the interests of their fellow minorities – but equally they might simply refrain from doing so. They sit in elected bodies *not* by virtue of their minority status, and to provide substantive representation on the basis of a political platform incorporating minority interests, but as members of United Russia. Thus, they have no specific obligations vis-à-vis their co-ethnics, while persons belonging to minorities as 'minority representatives' can only sit on consultative bodies. The ACFC has advanced the opinion that those minority representatives who engage in mainstream politics are generally 'unwilling to represent the interests of their minority community', and that 'mainstream political parties are, reportedly, not very sensitive to minority-related issues and to involving persons advocating for minority rights in their ranks'.[50]

Fourth, the dominance of the executive over the legislature – with the state Duma shaping its performance to accommodate the demands of the executive (Chaisty 2006) – contributes to reducing the salience of ethnicity (Giuliano and Gurenberg 2012). Ethnicity has played a minor role in post-Soviet Russian politics, with the exception of a short period of ethnic revival in the 1990s.[51] Since then, ethnicity has rarely been politicised despite the fact that ethnic identities are felt – albeit to a varying degree – among the members of national minorities, and in the presence of an ethnicity-based form of federalism. There has been a shift since the 1990s: while in the second (1996–1999) and third (2000–2003) Dumas there was at least some substantive representation of minority interests, this was much reduced by the United Russia party predominance in the fourth Duma (2004–2007).[52] At this stage numerous minority leaders joined its ranks (Chaisty 2013), with non-Russian elites seeking integration into Russian power politics. Similarly, the 2006 NGO Shadow Report to the ACFC on Russia argues that '[e]thnic activists wishing to stand in elections become totally dependent on federal political parties'.[53] Thus, United Russia has created a web of connections whose common feature is loyalty to the federal centre; rather than representing the interests of citizens and regions, the prevalence of United Russia has created a mechanism for the management of the loyalties of 'bureaucrats' at various levels of the executive (Goode 2010: 242).

Ineffective participation

Despite the foregoing, the ACFC has commended the (descriptive) minority representation in the Duma, referring in its Second Opinion (2007) to 30 national minorities being represented therein.[54] Persons belonging to minorities can vote in the Duma, being themselves MPs, meaning that they ostensibly have the wherewithal to exercise influence on law-making. However, as we have seen in this chapter, the mere presence of minorities in elected and consultative bodies is not sufficient to ensure their *effective* participation. The ability of minority representatives to influence decision-making is key, as is the representation of minority interests to enable the exercise of their cultural (and other) rights. The Russian Duma, having no parties or individual MPs devoted specifically to minority interests, lessens the chances of minority concerns being genuinely represented. In addition, the Duma is an ineffective body where dominant political forces prevail, marginalising concerns that are not aligned with the Kremlin's priorities, including those of minorities. The Duma does not serve as an effective counterbalance to the executive, including in the areas of federalism and nationalities policy.

One last complexity linked to representativeness is the issue of the internal democracy of minority associations. The freedom of minorities to self-organise risks the monopolisation of resources by ethnic entrepreneurs,[55] when minority 'leaders' choose to prioritise their own interests over the group's. In all countries, minority groups' commitment to social inclusion reflects their degree of responsiveness to the concerns of group members (Protsyk 2008: 472–473) – which clearly vary from case to case. When low levels of representation of national minorities have been observed in the Parliaments of the member states, the ACFC has encouraged the adoption of measures by the state to rectify this,[56] so as to facilitate an inclusive decision-making process.[57] In the case of advisory councils, the state must guarantee continuous and constructive exchanges.[58] Yet international standards do not venture so far as to regulate relations between the members of a group and its leaders. Indeed, while the state parties to the FCNM must guarantee the effective participation of minorities in decision-making, ECHR ratifying states are also under an obligation to ensure the right to free association, meaning that, among other things, they ought to refrain from interfering with the activities of minority groups.[59] Thus, international law cannot reach down to the complexities posited by the relationships between leaders and 'ordinary' members of minority groups, and eradicate hindrances to broad and accountable representation. It cannot assure that a strong 'link of accountability' is established between the representatives and the represented – often resulting in a truncated form of (descriptive) representation, by which minority interests at the grass-roots level do not reach elected bodies at the state or regional level. In practice, representativeness depends on both the state and minority organisations themselves, with the two sharing an 'equal burden of responsibility'.[60] In sum, difficulties in assuring minority representation come from two directions: from the top down – through a centralised system furthering political uniformity, and the exploitation of patterns of loyalty by the political leadership; and from the bottom up – through issues linked to internal democracy of minority institutions, by which personalistic interests can prevail over the accountability of representatives vis-à-vis the represented.

Conclusion

Minorities are confronted with multiple challenges as they seek to exercise their participatory rights in Russia. Ethnic political parties may not be established and there is no *substantive* minority representation in the state Duma. In the absence of guarantees for the representation of minority interests in elected bodies, consultative mechanisms automatically acquire an even greater significance, having to compensate for the absence of the other building block to participation. Yet Russia's consultative mechanisms are devoid of legal guarantees which would enable minorities to impact upon decision-making in matters that directly affect them. Meanwhile, the flexibility of international standards in the sphere of minority participation, and limits to their reach – particularly with reference to issues of internal democracy of minority institutions – means that they provide few incentives or guidance to induce or facilitate minorities' effective participation.

Members of minorities are not utterly excluded from decision-making on issues affecting their cultural rights, but inclusion depends on circumstances rather than on formal systems guaranteeing representation and participation. Political centralism and the 'power vertical', routinely relying on non-democratic appointment processes, reinforces arrangements that see many leaders of minority groups directing their allegiance to the federal authorities rather than the ethnic groups they supposedly represent. For national minorities United Russia's predominance in the Duma has consolidated the overwhelmingly *descriptive* nature of minority representation. United Russia has not fully eliminated regional and ethnic interests, which instead continue to surface, but it directs the political system towards uniformity. If specialised political parties were established by minorities, in practice the conditions of minorities might not see concrete improvement due to the Duma's own ineffectiveness, as well as a plethora of existing options to marginalise non-dominant parties; at the same time, the presence of these parties, and the freedom to establish them, would carry some symbolic weight, as it would provide formal processes for minorities' entry into politics.

Exchanges between the state authorities and minority groups for the purposes of consultation are sporadic, lack institutionalisation and are often inconclusive. While challenges to participation particularly affect small and dispersed minorities, issues of representation tended to bear similarities across the three case studies, particularly with regard to the ineffectiveness of consultative mechanisms. Examples of fruitful cooperation between minorities and the authorities, contributing to programmes to preserve minorities' cultural heritage, seem to be ad hoc and fortuitous. Recommendations that may arise from consultative bodies tend not to produce concrete responses by the authorities, in the absence of obligations to follow such recommendations, or to provide justifications for not complying with them. Ultimately, there is no marked distinction between general and informal cooperation between civil society and the authorities (described in Chapter 7), and 'official' mechanisms for consultation. They replicate the same patterns, with an analogous precariousness resulting from dependence on circumstances and individuals. To conclude, ethnic institutions continue to operate, as they did in the Soviet period, through apolitical means, remaining confined to cultural (and symbolic) policies. The ineffectiveness of systems of participation means that minorities remain disempowered, unable to affect circumstances that influence patterns of diversity and assimilation.

Notes

1 The workings of Peoples' Congresses and their impact is an area that remains under-researched. See Osipov (2011; 2013b).
2 Council of Europe, Committee of Experts on Issues relating to the Protection of National Minorities, 'Handbook on Minority Consultative Mechanisms', 20 October 2006, DH-MIN(2006)012, §19.
3 Following the abolition of the Ministry of Regional Development in September 2014. See Chapter 4 (note 39).
4 Of the three focus republics, special ministries existed in Karelia and Mordovia: the Ministry of the Republic of Karelia on Issues of Nationalities Policy and Relations with Religious Associations; and the Ministry on Nationalities Policy of the Republic of Mordovia. In Tatarstan nationality issues are incorporated into the programmes of various ministries, such as the Ministry of Culture and the Ministry of Education and Science, as well as the Cabinet of Ministers itself.
5 For example, the Permanent Representation of the Republic of Karelia under the President of the Russian Federation, established by presidential Decree No. 318, 26 December 1991.
6 In the regions visited during the fieldwork.
7 The National Chamber in Voronezh was established by the governor through Decree 'On the Establishment of the National Chamber of the Governor of Voronezh oblast' (No. 300, 7 September 2010). The Chamber is a permanent consultative organ whose goal is to 'improve ... the realisation of national policy in the territory of Voronezh oblast' (Part 1, Point 2.1), and its head is the governor of Voronezh oblast (Part 2, Point 1.1).
8 Berezin, S. 2 June 2009. 'Buryatskoi Intelligentsii Podobrali Partiinogo Lidera' [A Party Leader was Chosen for the Buryat Intelligentsia], *Nezavisimaya Gazeta*.
9 See Chapter 5.
10 Berezin (see note 8).
11 The federal Public Chamber was established by the Law 'On the Public Chamber of the Russian Federation' (No. 32-FZ, 4 April 2005) to facilitate consultation between the state and civil society. One-third of its 126 members are appointed by presidential decree, the others by 'public associations'. Other Public Chambers, with similar responsibilities and procedures, have also been established at the regional level.
12 Other respondents who were asked about discussions in advisory bodies and Houses of Nationalities said that they dealt with 'current issues' [e.g. 1.3.6] (or similar expressions) affecting minorities, without however isolating specific cases and providing examples. The reason for this vagueness might be that discussions themselves were general, and failed to identify specific concerns or corresponding solutions. Generalisations may have also been used as a screen to protect respondents from scrutiny by a foreign researcher.
13 Not specified in the interests of confidentiality.
14 The respondent's expression.
15 The respondent added that the PC in St Petersburg had only existed for a few months at the time of the interview, thus complicating its assessment.

16 President of Russia, Address to the National Assembly of the Russian Federation, 12 December 2013, http://eng.kremlin.ru/news/6402 (accessed 25 September 2014).

17 See also Chapter 7 on Houses of Nationalities.

18 The respondent added that most meetings were held in the afternoon, meaning that minority representatives in full-time employment could attend only with difficulty. She had not been given the option of feeding into the discussion by email.

19 As well as professional affiliation and religious identity. Article 9(3) of Law 'On Political Parties' (No. 95-FZ, 11 July 2001).

20 RCC, Judgement No. 18-P, 15 December 2004. The ACFC has criticised the excessive breadth of this form of pre-emptive measure by stating that:

> [The ACFC] regrets that the federal legislation prohibiting the creation of political parties established 'on the grounds of professional, racial, national or religious belonging' has not been amended ... this law is restricting the scope for persons belonging to national minorities to set up political parties representing their legitimate interests. Bearing in mind that the competence of national-cultural autonomies is restricted to the field of cultural affairs ... such parties could make it possible for the concerns and interests of persons belonging to national minorities, particularly in the regions where they live in substantial numbers, to be better represented and possibly better taken into account in elected bodies at local and central level.

ACFC, (Third) Opinion on the Russian Federation, 24 November 2011, ACFC/OP/III(2011)010, §136; see also §206. The ban is also incompatible with the 1999 OSCE/HCNM Lund Recommendations on the Effective Participation of National Minorities in Public Life, which states that the principle of freedom of association 'includes the freedom to establish political parties based on communal identities' (Point 8). See also Weller (2005: 440).

21 NGO Shadow Report 'On the Implementation of the Framework Convention for the Protection of National Minorities by the Russian Federation', February 2006, §341.

22 Law 'On the Amendment of Federal Law "On Political Parties"' (No. 168-FZ, 20 December 2004).

23 The Russian Constitutional Court has confirmed the constitutionality of this provision (RCC, Judgement No. 1-P, 1 February 2005). By contrast, the ACFC has argued that the requirement to have regional branches in at least half the subjects of the Federation impairs the ability of minorities concentrated in a particular territory to form political parties. ACFC, (Third) Opinion on the Russian Federation (note 20), §206. These and other amendments to electoral legislation were further criticised by the Committee of Ministers of the Council of Europe, in the Resolution 'On the Implementation of the Framework Convention for the Protection of National Minorities by the Russian Federation', 2 May 2007, CM/ResCMN(2007)7, Point 1(b).

24 Law 'On the Amendment of Laws of the Russian Federation on Elections and Referenda and Other Legal Acts of the Russian Federation' (No. 93-FZ, 21 July 2005).

25 The ACFC recommended a revision of the electoral system, with a view to introducing modifications to enhance the effective participation of persons belonging to minorities. ACFC, (Third) Opinion on the Russian Federation (see note 20), §209.

26 Law 'On the Amendment of Federal Law "On Political Parties"' (No 28-FZ, 2 April 2012). The number had also been previously reduced from 50,000 to 45,000 (2012) and then to 40,000 (2010).

27 Law 'On the Elections of the Deputies of the State Duma of the Federal Assembly of the Russian Federation' (No. 20-FZ, 22 February 2014). No more than 7,000 signatures can come from any one region: this ensures that support comes from across the country, but it also makes signature collection particularly onerous.

28 Prior to 2007, half of the Duma seats were allocated through a party-list proportional system, and half through single-member electoral districts; this was replaced by a fully proportional party-list system, before reverting back, in 2014, to a mixed system

(half deputies running on party lists and half on single-mandate districts). On election regulations see also http://eng.kremlin.ru/acts/6732 (accessed 12 November 2014).

29 On minorities and elections, see also the 2001 OSCE Warsaw Guidelines to Assist National Minority Participation in the Electoral Process.

30 OSCE/HCNM Lund Recommendations on the Effective Participation of National Minorities in Public Life, Explanatory Note, Point 7.

31 Ibid., Point 9. See also Weller (2005).

32 Quotas for indigenous peoples existed for the dumas of Russia's federal subjects, but were removed in 2004. The ACFC criticised this move, referring to it as a 'step backwards' in the implementation of the FCNM's Article 15. ACFC, (Second) Opinion on the Russian Federation, 2 May 2007, ACFC/OP/II(2006)004, §260. See also ACFC, (Third) Opinion on the Russian Federation (note 20), §207. The original provision (Article 13 of Law 'On the Guarantees of the Rights of Small-in-Number Indigenous Peoples', No. 82-FZ, 30 April 1999) was repealed by the Law 'On the Amendment of Legal Acts of the Russian Federation .' (No. 122-FZ of 22 August 2004).

33 The ACFC has stressed the need for small, non-territorial minorities to also be guaranteed representation. See for example, ACFC, (First) Opinion on Switzerland, 20 February 2003, ACFC/INF/OP/I(2003)007, §76.

34 See also Chapter 8.

35 Russian Public Opinion Research Center (VTsIOM), 27 March 2014. 'Reiting Putina: Novaya Vysota' [Putin's Ratings: New Highs], http://wciom.ru/index.php?id=268&uid=114759 (accessed 10 September 2014).

36 Ibid. The survey was conducted on 22–23 March 2014; 1,600 persons participated in it, in 130 centres in 46 subjects of the Federation.

37 Since February 2008, when the ratings were 82.9 per cent.

38 Outlined on pp. 208–209.

39 So as to favour a party over the others. See OSCE/ODIHR Election Observation Mission. 'Russian Federation, State Duma Elections, 4 December 2011: Final Report', January 2012, www.osce.org/odihr/86959 (accessed 10 October 2014).

40 March argues that: '[M]ore attention should be devoted to informal factors, above all patronage relations within the elite and party self-censorship at the ideological and strategic level: these are 'opposition' parties that are neither willing nor able really to oppose' (March 2012: 243).

41 Generally on patterns of loyalty and informal practices, see also Ledeneva (2013).

42 Reuter (2010) shows that governors joined the party incrementally from the beginning to the mid-2000s, starting with those with fewer resources then including those in a stronger position politically and economically.

43 Only 18.4% of the members of regional assemblies were also members of national political parties (Ross 2011).

44 With regard to the December 2003 Parliamentary elections, Clem writes: 'United Russia enjoyed an almost nationwide constituency … but did exceptionally well in terms of vote percentages in West and East Siberia, the North Caucasus, some parts of the Urals, and in Tatarstan' (Clem 2006: 392).

45 According to OSCE election monitoring, the 2011 Parliamentary elections 'were marked by the convergence of the state and the governing party'. OSCE/ODIHR (see note 39), p. 1. Among the problems recorded by OSCE/ODIHR were: the arbitrary denial of registration of some parties, media partiality (favouring the ruling party), procedural violations and manipulation such as ballot box stuffing, obstructions in the activities of election observers, and abuse of office by state and local officials.

46 The effectiveness of the electoral machine, which has relied on governors' networks, was compromised with the abolishment of governors' direct elections in 2004 (see Chapter 5), as it resulted in unpopular governors in some regions or weak local networks. The systems came to rest on even more shaky foundations following the 2011 elections (Isaacs and Whitmore 2014: 709).

47 At the same time, tensions between regional elites, and the resulting inability to form strong regional institutions, might in fact be the Kremlin's desired outcome, as Slider (2010) suggests.

48 According to the 2010 census, ethnic Russians in Chechnya only amounted to 1.9 per cent of the population (against 95.3 per cent Chechens). In 1989, 24.8 per cent of the population had been made up by Russians and 60 per cent by Chechens (1989 census data).

49 United Russia gained over 99 per cent of votes in Chechnya in the 2007 and 2011 Parliamentary elections. See *RIA Novosti*, 3 December 2007. 'United Russia Wins Over 99% of the Vote in Chechnya – Preliminary Data', http://en.ria.ru/russia/20071203/90609389.html (accessed 15 February 2014); and *RIA Novosti*, 5 December 2011. 'United Russia Gets Over 99% of Votes in Chechnya, http://en.ria.ru/society/20111205/169358392.html, (accessed 15 February 2014).

50 ACFC, (Third) Opinion on the Russian Federation (see note 20), §206.

51 Even violence in the North Caucasus following the Chechen conflicts erupted primarily due to religious, rather than ethnic, causes: membership of Islamic groups has transcended ethnicity (Giuliano and Gorenburg 2012).

52 Chaisty (2013) shows this through the analysis of the legislation adopted by successive legislatures.

53 NGO Shadow Report submitted to the ACFC, 2006 (see note 21), §342.

54 ACFC, (Second) Opinion on the Russian Federation (note 32), §258; see also (Third) Opinion on the Russian Federation (note 20), §206.

55 In some cases mechanisms for minority representation can be abused. For example, in Hungary the creation of local minority councils led to the 'cuckoo phenomenon', or the running for elections to these councils of persons *not* belonging to minorities and occupying seats reserved for minority representatives. These candidates engaged in 'ethnobusiness' – an expression designating the abuse of opportunities for minority representation to pursue personal political or economic ambitions (Carstocea 2011). The ACFC called upon Hungary to intervene to guarantee the 'credibility of the system' of minority representation in Hungary's mechanisms for elections to local self-government. See ACFC, (First) Opinion on Hungary, 22 September 2000, ACFC/INF/OP/I(2001) 004, §52.

56 For example, ACFC, (First) Opinion on the United Kingdom, 20 November 2001, ACFC/INF/OP/I(2002)006, §126.

57 For example, ACFC, (First) Opinion on the Czech Republic, 6 April 2001, ACFC/INF/OP/I(2002)002, §70.

58 Some of the advisory councils may be hybrid institutions – counting among their members both minority representatives and public officials. Weller (2005:450) argues that if the government retains its influence on consultative councils ('a practice not to be encouraged'), then the government is responsible for their effective functioning. He refers to the ACFC's First Opinion on Croatia, where the Croatian government was urged to review the 'appointment procedures, structures and working methods' of bodies working on minority issues. ACFC, (First) Opinion on Croatia, 6 April 2001, ACFC/INF/OP/I(2002)003, §63.

59 Article 11 ECHR and Article 22 ICCPR.

60 Committee of Experts on Issues relating to the Protection of National Minorities, 'Handbook on Minority Consultative Mechanisms' (see note 2), §63.

Conclusion

Russia is, and has always been, a multicultural, multi-ethnic country. Its schools teach a myriad of minority languages and in some cases provide instruction through the medium of these languages. Governmental institutions, both at the federal and regional levels, promote minority cultures and languages. These efforts are the continuation of a long tradition of attention to diversity – made imperative by the coexistence of a plurality of ethnicities in Russia. And, admittedly, the upholding of minority rights is extremely complex: the state needs to promote a form of integration that does not tip the balance over to assimilation, and further the preservation of cultural and linguistic wealth while avoiding state fragmentation or minority groups' ghettoisation.

This book has argued that despite Russia's lingering diversity, it is experiencing moves towards cultural homogenisation. These dynamics are influenced by three main processes: the selective implementation of domestic and international norms for the protection of minorities and their cultural distinctiveness (with formal norms becoming entangled with informal practices); the presence of discourses and policies promoting uniformity; and the marginalisation of minority concerns due to an ineffective form of participation. Underlying these processes are ideological underpinnings and perceptions that originate from historical (particularly Soviet) institutional legacies. The traditional essentialist approach to ethnicity, typical of Soviet nationalities policy, shaped a perception of rigid demarcations between groups – and potentially of exclusive forms of nationalism in perennial conflict – as opposed to transient and fluid forms of belonging. A preoccupation with state fragmentation is particularly acute given Russia's territorial vastness, combined with extremely high levels of hetereogeneity. Perceived tensions between national unity and diversity reflect a widespread belief in the mutual exclusivity of the two, and of a causal relation between 'excessive' diversity and disunity. The existing institutional framework contributes to minorities' (self-)perceptions and delimits their scope of action, as well as presenting a plethora of structural shortcomings, particularly linked to the ineffectiveness of such a framework in upholding minority rights; these deficiencies are often addressed (or exacerbated) through a reliance on informal practices.

Of particular significance in devising and implementing minority policies has been the role played by the Putin leadership since 2000. The Putin administration has furthered: the projection of the view of Russia as a 'great power', which impacts upon the fulfilment of its international commitments, including in the sphere of minority rights; an overall movement towards (cultural) homogenisation and the reduction of the saliency of ethnic diversity in Russia, while promoting Russian patriotism; and a widening democratic deficit, which affects the participatory rights of minorities. These dynamics impact upon processes of assimilation versus diversity preservation. While not predicated by classic nation-state narratives, but rather by a general discourse on Russian (*rossiiskii*) patriotism, Russia is gravitating towards increased cultural homogenisation, where the dilution of diversity, if not an objective, has certainly resulted in a degree of collateral damage.

The general move towards uniformity is reflected in the analysis of the national minorities selected as case studies: the Tatars, Mordovians and Karelians. Despite the differences between the them – in terms of population size, resources and levels of ethnic consciousness, among others – the concerns of the three groups tended to resemble one another. In all three cases, the teaching of minority languages, or teaching through the medium of these languages, has lessened, either through the decrease of the number of schools devoted to minority-language education, or through a reduction of the number of hours for language courses. All three cases displayed limited autonomy in policy-making concerning the cultural rights of the titular groups within 'their' republics, as well as ineffective forms of representation of minorities at the local, regional and federal levels. These commonalities emerged despite the fact that respondents of Tatar origins generally displayed a stronger ethnic consciousness than representatives of the two other groups, which at times resulted in more pronounced activism and greater awareness of nationality issues.[1] By contrast, the diverging opinions and interpretations of respondents seemed to more commonly emanate from their profession and type of relations with the (local or regional) authorities, rather than ethnic affiliation. The frequent convergence of views among representatives of various minorities may be explained by the fact that even the presence of favourable conditions (in terms of numerical size and resources of titular groups in 'their' republics) have provided no guarantee of autonomy or effective participation in decision-making in relation to cultural matters. Given Russia's high levels of centralism, all its national minorities are at risk of being affected by homogenising impulses, while state support of initiatives for the preservation of minorities' cultural distinctiveness remains scattered. Not only are tendencies towards uniformity a reality in all three case studies, but so is the use of informal practices as well as an alternation of centralism in some areas and *laissez-faire* in others. These factors affect the implementation of minority policies and standards, and patterns of diversity and assimilation.

Domestic and international law and minorities: selective implementation and informal practices

In exploring the application of minority policies in the area of cultural rights, one needs to consider both endogenous (domestic standards) and exogenous (international standards that are binding upon Russia) elements. The application of international standards stems from processes of legal transplantation, or the incorporation of external norms into the domestic sphere. The types of legal transfer analysed in this book involve a set of international legal commitments, voluntarily entered into, that are integrated into domestic law in an attempt to incorporate international and domestic legal principles into one functioning mechanism. Processes of domestic transformation through international norms are often unpredictable, and adaptational pressure is not always effective – particularly when, as in the case of the Council of Europe, one can rely on little more than the 'mobilisation of shame' (Keck and Sikkink 1999: 97) when a member state refuses to comply with its obligations. Despite this, legal reform has been undertaken by Russia since it joined the Council of Europe in 1996, and Russia has acceded to the FCNM and the ECHR. The increasing application of the ECHR in Russian courts, and Russia's participation in FCNM monitoring processes, reveal incremental steps towards the implementation of the standards contained in these instruments.

At the same time, the fluidity and flexibility of international minority rights law, together with the practices and attitudes of Russian officials, have generally prevented these rights from being translated into a comprehensive and functioning domestic legal framework. The elastic nature of international minority rights law means that it is unable to reach down to resolve the complexities posited by informal practices and centralised decision-making combined with *laissez-faire* attitudes. The relative scarcity of European Court of Human Rights judgements on issues relating to minority rights means that, until a set of pre-packaged legal principles is crystallised by the Court, the onus remains on Council of Europe member states to solidify modalities of application of international standards in this area. Yet, thus far, international standards have exerted little influence over the advancement of minority rights in Russia: its government maintains a balance between sufficient engagement in order to reap some benefits (trade-related, political or other) from adherence to the international human rights system, without fully immersing itself in it. This is the situation when a country, for example, adopts legislation upholding the rights of minorities, but de facto abuses this same legislation, and refuses to bend to the pressure of international bodies in selected cases. This book's findings point to the conclusion that the success of legal transplants cannot be found solely in external influence imposed on a vaguely compliant but reluctant state, but rather in internal factors, and in a government's perception of (some) benefits resulting from being a member of the international community.

Interview data indicate that attitudes to minority rights, and to relevant international standards, have been primarily shaped by the environment within which individual respondents operate, and their legal and institutional cultures, instead of, or jointly with, personal inclinations. Thus, public officials and civil society representatives closer to the establishment and its institutions tended to espouse traditional views of minority issues (with such issues being perceived as closely linked to 'culture' rather than 'rights'). They further saw Russia as 'different' from other Council of Europe member states, resulting in a perceived mismatch between Russia's characteristics *and* international standards. At the same time, Russian legal history is littered with borrowings from Western Europe, revealing legal and cultural traditions that have not proceeded on two parallel, separate trajectories. The framing of Russia as 'different' by some respondents might be linked principally to a *perception* of difference, and/or represent a means for the Russian authorities to justify a refusal to undergo unwanted and wide-ranging reforms. While part of Russia's civil society has embraced the international minority rights system, the Russian government is resisting international pressure and selected aspects of its international obligations in order to preserve its own (Russian) way of dealing with its internal diversity. This approach is linked to a self-perception as a 'great power', and also to a complex relationship with the Council of Europe and other IGOs. Such factors impair the ability of international standards to influence processes of diversity or assimilation.

Despite this, minorities in Russia can draw some benefits from the international mechanisms for the protection of minority rights. The Council of Europe has introduced an additional, regulatory layer above the Russian domestic sphere – that of a supranational body, which offers everyone in Russia the opportunity to submit cases to the European Court of Human Rights. Similarly, the Council of Europe's ACFC Opinions and Committee of Ministers Resolutions provide an alternative interpretation to the Russian government's nationality discourse, counteracting the over-simplification of the nationality question as filtered through a dual narrative of 'tolerance' and 'extremism': the ACFC focuses on minority *rights*, rather than generally, or solely, on the preservation of national cultures and languages. The Council of Europe further involves Russian civil society in FCNM monitoring processes, through the consideration of NGOs' shadow reports, and in Council of Europe-sponsored events, such as those promoting the FCNM's implementation and the ECRLM's ratification. Even when these events do not lead to tangible, immediate results, they may contribute to the shifting of political processes to a more open system, somewhat more amenable to dialogue with domestic and international actors alike.

Russia is, clearly, not a unitary, internally homogeneous, polity. Some of the respondents stated that they firmly believed in the principles underpinning international standards on minority rights – although an essentialist, folkloristic approach to minorities tended to prevail in public discourse and government-supported programmes. Members of all three case study minorities have developed what Keck and Sikkink (1998, 1999) call 'transnational advocacy networks', through their members' participation in international institutions such as the World Congress of Tatars and the World Congress of Finno-Ugric Peoples. In addition, Russian NGOs have forged networks with IGOs, for example through programmes and activities on human (minority) rights.

With regard to domestic law and practice, I have argued that the absence of a precise, comprehensive legal framework for the promotion of cultural rights of minorities has compounded a shift towards cultural homogenisation in Russian society. The absence of legal entrenchment of mechanisms for the realisation of minority rights results in difficulties in pinning down what constitutes a 'violation' of such rights. There are no clear obligations on Russian public officials, nor have precise targets been set, while Russian jurisprudence in this area is still miniscule. I have further referred to 'localism' to designate the phenomenon by which nationalities policy becomes fragmented and lacks coherence. While localism can provide the flexibility to develop ad hoc, targeted policies at the local level, much is left to the goodwill of individual actors. This is when informal practices and networks come into play: as they are highly dependent on individual public officials and minority leaders, and their own particularistic needs and wishes, any 'special measures' to promote minority cultures become further atomised. At the same time, localism has alternated with centralised, federal-level law- and policy-making initiatives, from which localities and regions have been routinely excluded.

Russo-centric homogenisation

With limited legal guarantees, minorities have few means at their disposal to contain the dilution of diversity. While Russia has inherited both ethnic pluralism and Soviet methods to regulate it – particularly in the form of ethnic federalism – Putin's leadership has seen a departure from earlier nationalities policy towards new forms of homogenisation which command greater uniformity. Putinite policies have promoted the development of a common loyalty, a joint identity unifying the country's nationalities through patriotism, which acts to simultaneously downgrade (non-Russian) ethnicity and reassert Russianness. Although presented as a form of civic, rather than ethnic, nationalism, the general Russian (*rossiiskii*) patriotic discourse borrows from Russian (*russkii*) cultural themes. The resulting homogenising measures do not seem to emanate from a quasi-imperialistic desire to Russianise ethnic minorities per se, but from a drive to strengthen and politically streamline the state. Thus, the leadership's approach to ethnicity is complex: the ruling party, United Russia, is devoid of a discernible ethnic dimension and is rather seen as a 'party of bureaucrats';[2] at the same time, the leadership makes use of patriotic narratives to convey the image of a strong Russia, with an conflation of *russkii* and *rossiiskii* elements. This scenario leads to various tensions: first, between the leadership's attempts to reconcile Russia's historical legacy as a multinational state and a (Russian) patriotic idea; second, between the official position on Russia's multinationality and a longing by some ethnic Russians for a Herderian nation that can satisfy the yearning for identity validation; and, third, between the official patriotic (Russian) project and the resentment felt by some minority representatives witnessing the construction of a post-Soviet identity around a core Russian culture, in tandem with the increasing erosion of (non-Russian) ethnic attributes.

In the area of education, uniformising trends are similarly discernible. To adverse socio-economic circumstances one has to add the introduction of new regulations on minority-language education, which have effectively elevated the

Russian language to the *condition sine qua non* for (economic, social and political) success. This has simultaneously acted to lower the marketability, and with it the prestige, of titular languages. With the exception of committed activists, interviews revealed a perceived need for an either-or choice by persons belonging to minorities: full integration into the Russian cultural sphere was frequently equated with economic and social welfare, while a decision to maintain one's original identity implied a possible sacrifice in status. Uniformity is further promoted through a ubiquitous patriotic discourse in schools, including in the shape of 'militarised patriotism'.

Ongoing efforts to preserve minority cultures take place primarily within small oases for minorities, rather than being incorporated into country-wide programmes. This points to a situation in which minority cultures are 'tolerated', in Žižek's interpretation of the word (2011: 46),[3] rather than being fully valued and respected. At the other end of the spectrum, patriotism is being produced and disseminated for mass consumption, including through the federal media. Some respondents discerned a pattern by which the authorities, while to some extent accommodating minorities, and certainly not directly repressing them, prevented alternative ethnic identities from flourishing – thus confining them to marginal roles in Russian society, including through the 'management' of diversity. Indeed, homogenising moves can derive both from an active (assimilationist) state policy, but also from negligence: it is not only what the government does, and but also what it *refrains* from doing; and, in sone instances, 'benign neglect' can morph into a form of 'malign neglect', depending on the attitudes of individual public officials. While one cannot be sure about the motivations of the upper (or lower) echelons of power, failure to intervene to preserve cultural and linguistic pluralism results in a loss of diversity, to which public officials can implicitly acquiesce. Whether blaming homogenising tendencies on the government or on socio-economic conditions, some respondents belonging to minorities had become resigned to the fact that advancing Russianisation, or even globalisation, could no longer be stopped.

Fictitious participation

This type of pessimism is likely to be exacerbated by the fact that Russia offers no special measures to guarantee the enjoyment of the participatory rights of minorities, causing them to remain disempowered in the exercise of their cultural (as well as other) rights. Ethnicity-based parties are prohibited by law, and concerns of minorities remain generally unrepresented in elected bodies; consultative bodies can only produce recommendations, with no obligation on the authorities to act upon them. The activism of persons belonging to minorities, as *minorities*, is largely confined to the cultural sphere, although these same persons are not discouraged from entering politics as United Russia representatives – essentially, if they are politically streamlined. Indeed, through United Russia many regional (and ethnic) leaders have been absorbed into the 'power vertical'. Even general cooperation between civil society and the authorities is impaired, as civil society operates in an unfavourable environment, given the burdensome bureaucratic requirements and a paucity of resources. Although some respondents provided examples of consultation, the policies examined in this book, impacting upon the cultural rights of minorities, were predominantly centrally-conceived. These included policies on: minority education (marginalising minority languages and cultures); de-federalisation (merging predominantly Russian with ethnic regions); and de-ethnification (favouring a Russian patriotic rather than a genuinely multi-ethnic discourse). More broadly, centralising measures have involved a widening democratic deficit through a general movement towards the replacement of elections to key positions with appointments. This has simultaneously downgraded ethnicity, and resulted in the Russian authorities effectively retreating from obligations under international and domestic law to protect minorities and their cultural distinctiveness.

Generally, minority concerns do not tend reach the public discourse, with the exception of a simplified discourse of 'tolerance' versus 'extremism', which does not reflect the depth and multiple layers of minorities' variegated opinions and concerns. Interviews further pointed to a restricted scope for consultation and lobbying as a result of Putin's undemocratic reforms and 'power vertical'. Attempts to decouple ethnicity and territory with the formation of national cultural autonomies (NCAs) have not yielded positive results: NCAs, which should *inter alia* uphold the participatory rights of minorities, are afflicted by the same malaise as numerous other institutions in Russia: a clan mentality and a loyalty to the centres of power. While 'special relationships' are forged between some NCA leaders and the authorities, other persons belonging to minorities can remain marginalised and voiceless, with no access to genuine political representation. Although persons belonging to minorities might themselves benefit from personal networks, their arbitrariness denies the guarantees of a fully functioning legal system. Legality is replaced by pervasive informal (often opportunistic) practices of the elites; this can lead to symbolic politics, by which minority representatives themselves can be complicit in promoting the establishment's unwritten rules, whether on the basis of self-interest or simply because no other option is in sight. Among minority leaders there are of course varying degrees of professionalism, commitment, and differing priorities, and the way in which minority leaders choose to use their networks is circumstantial. For some minority leaders the main drive is the genuine representation of the group's interests; others (more or less evenly) juggle private interests with those of the group; for a third category of minority leaders private interests prevail over group interests. Yet in all cases the dominant role of informal practices and networks reduces the independence and assertiveness of civil society vis-à-vis the organs of power, with ethnicity-based organisations often shaping their programmes around government priorities, so as to access funding and other opportunities.

International standards on minorities' participatory rights are unable to break through barriers, thus excluding minorities (and civil society generally) from mainstream politics and policy-making. They are also unequipped to address one of the main inhibitors of effective participation: the missing 'link of account-ability' between representatives and represented in elected and non-elected bodies. Finally, the Russian system of diversity management favours a form of groupism which glosses over multidimensionality *within* a group. The Russian government is not only refraining from *interfering* with internal decision-making in minority groups, but rather *facilitating* a system that favours negotiations with particular individuals. It does so by refraining from institutionalising the rela-tionship between the state and minority organisations, and from implementing possible recommendations developed by minority-based advisory councils, while replacing such processes with 'discussions' with a narrow elite. These arrangements impact on the cultural rights of minority groups by affecting policy-making on areas such as minority-language education and measures to promote cultural diversity.

What next?

The situation described above is one that moves inexorably towards rising levels of cultural absorption. These tendencies, furthered through education (and the media), can lead to a societal transformation that might be imperceptible to many, given the relatively slow pace of change and the frequent use of a 'banal' form of nationalism, itself normalised and often eclipsed by various ills plaguing Russian society, such as economic hardship. In reality, initiatives for the preser-vation of minority cultures and languages are continuously undermined by coun-tervailing assimilatory tendencies. The resultant effect is minorities' disempowerment with regard to policies affecting their cultural distinctiveness, and, if we accept that one's cultural identity is linked to one's dignity, a scenario that raises questions as to the long-term implications of a system that chips away at individuals' cultural rights. Alongside considerations grounded in a human rights perspective, there is a further argument for the preservation of cultures and languages by virtue of their own 'intrinsic value' (Musschenga 1998). Similarly, Crystal (2000) contends that all people, not only persons belonging to linguistic minorities, should be concerned when a language dies (see also Krauss 1992: 8). Mithum writes in a similar vein: 'The loss of languages is tragic precisely because they are not interchangeable, precisely because they represent the distil-lation of the thoughts and communication of a people over their entire history' (Mithum 1998: 189).

Yet among the effects of centralisation (in politics, education and the media) is not only the dilution of diversity, but also an increased risk of inter-ethnic ten-sions. Declining levels of linguistic, cultural and ethnic diversity can aggravate a situation in which multiple groups in Russian society simultaneously experience a sense of alienation. This can only be exacerbated by the ineffective mecha-nisms which should enable members of minorities (as well as civil society as a whole) to contribute to decision-making. Moreover, it is not only 'benign' patri-otism that has spread throughout Russian society, but also, as byproducts, its more extreme forms. Despite an attempt to control extreme nationalism, and a state interest in containing its de-stabilising elements, it has not been eradicated. In fact extremism, in small doses, could even further some governmental aims: it enhances the cohesiveness of the majority population, and promotes the image of the Russian state protecting its citizens against (internal as well as external) enemies. At the same time, these dynamics can impair the peaceful coexistence of Russia's multiple groups.

While this book has not focused on the media, in considering the future of ethnocultural and linguistic diversity in Russia one cannot but note that the evolving media environment is likely to increasingly supply a range of new forms of expression to minorities, and new means to preserve their languages and cultures. Technological advancements and new media, and their effect on minorities and their languages, call for more research. Yet new media also tends to fragment the media environment along its multiple users (who are simultaneously its audience and contributors), while it is the larger media outlets – particularly state, nation-wide television – that popularise messages and shape social attitudes to diversity. The federal media has promoted the predominance of the Russian language and culture, and Russian nation-building itself (Hutchings and Miazhevich 2010; Hutchings and Rulyova 2009; Novikova 2010), while also frequently reinforcing negative stereotypes about minorities.[4] Thus, new communicative channels are needed, not only as forms of expression for minority groups, but also to stimulate *inter-cultural* understanding.

International standards of minority rights might acquire a greater role in the coming years, with the opening up of new opportunities to reduce or even reverse the movement towards homogenisation. Indeed, the limited role of international standards in Russia thus far ought not to be attributed to their 'incompatibility' with the Russian socio-political system, or to the Russian authorities' being oblivious of international scrutiny. A full, rather than selective, implementation of international human rights law is very much dependent on changing political circumstances. And, despite the seeming strength of the Putin administration and political machine, one should not assume a perpetual 'power vertical'. Personalistic political parties such as United Russia rely on the belief of the 'indispensability and inevitability of the leadership' (Isaacs and Whitmore 2014: 709); but their source of strength can also be their Achilles' heel, exposing their fragility during politically turbulent times.

International standards can advance an alternative view to that which equates a diverse society with a potential threat – all too often 'resolved' by keeping minorities trapped within a controlled essentialist (and folkloristic) approach. This alternative discourse may coexist with, and potentially ultimately penetrate and revitalise, existing narratives on minority issues. Among other things, the Advisory Committee on the FCNM has promoted among the state parties the principle that minority groups are entitled to benefit not only from the right to participate in public and Parliamentary debates, but also to *influence* policy-making. The crystallisation of more principles relating to minority rights in international jurisprudence through the European Court, if it occurs, could contribute to further concretising state responsibilities in this sphere.

Additional ingredients for a more effective implementation of minority rights law and policies are their *bona fide* application in a favourable environment, and the respect and appreciation of diversity. In the first case, legal provisions are a necessary but *in*sufficient condition for the enjoyment of minority rights: other factors have to be present, which may not be amenable to legal codification. Marko argues:

> [T]he best legal instruments for 'effective participation' cannot 'ensure' this goal if there is not a political climate and *willingness of inter-ethnic dialogue* and co-operation to give the members of national minorities a voice which is also 'taken seriously' [italics added].
>
> (Marko 2006: 9)

In the second case, a respondent, a representative of a minority organisation, noted in an interview: 'Many things have to be changed before the voices of minorities will be needed. They might be heard now but they are not needed' [1.2.5]. The respondent believed that minorities' opinions might be voiced during public discussions, but their input is not *used* (as it is not *needed*) to formulate policies on minorities' cultural rights. Thus, these voices are tolerated, but they are treated as a superfluous addition to existing policy-making processes. For minority voices to become influential, the respondent argued, fundamental, wide-spread perceptions of national minorities will have to alter. Should this not happen, we will continue to witness the shrinking of Russia's rich cultural and linguistic landscape. This would not only be an enormous loss for the minority groups concerned, but for Russian society as a whole.

Notes

1 There were few differences between Mordovians and Karelians. Some structural differences were recorded, such as the greater use of the Mordovian languages in education compared to Karelian, but no major dissimilarities were detected in the answers of the respondents of the two groups that belonged to the same category.
2 The expression was used by a respondent – the director of a human rights organisation [1.5.5].
3 See Chapter 5.
4 See for example, the ACFC, (Third) Opinion on the Russian Federation, 24 November 2011, ACFC/OP/III(2011)010, §96–105.

Appendix

Respondents

Abbreviations

Ethnic group			*Cities*	
KAR	Karelian		KAZ	Kazan
MOR	Mordovian		MOS	Moscow
RUS	Russian		PETR	Petrozavodsk
TAT	Tatar		SAR	Saransk
TKAR	Tver Karelian		STPB	St Petersburg
MIN	Minority (other than the three case studies)		VOR	Voronezh

Cities where the interviews took place

Petrozavodsk	Tver	Saransk	St Petersburg
Moscow	Kazan	Voronezh	

Respondents

1 Civil society

1.1 Civil society – (national cultural autonomy – NCAs) (six respondents)

Table A1.1 Minority associations

Code	Respondent	City	M/F	Ethnic group	Interview date
1.1.1	Leader of the NCA of a minority in Petrozavodsk	PETR	M	MIN[1]	21/05/10
1.1.2	Leader of the NCA of Tver Karelians	TVER	F	TKAR	03/06/10
1.1.3	Representative of the youth branch of the NCA of Tver Karelians	TVER	F	TKAR	04/06/10
1.1.4	Representative of the youth branch of the NCA of Tver Karelians	TVER	F	TKAR	04/06/10
1.1.5	Representative of the Tatar NCA for Moscow oblast	MOS	M	TAT	01/06/10
1.1.6	Leader of a federal NCA	MOS	M	MIN	18/10/10

Note
1 Indicating a minority other than the case studies.

1.2 Civil society – minority NGOs (11 respondents)

Table A1.2 Minority NGOs

Code	Respondent	City	M/F	Ethnic group	Interview date
1.2.1	Director of a minority NGO, activist for a Finno-Ugric minority (NGO #1)	PETR	F	MIN[1]	21/05/10
1.2.2	Activist in an NGO promoting Karelian language through projects in the area of education (NGO #2)	PETR	F	KAR	24/05/10
1.2.3	Director of an NGO promoting inter-ethnic tolerance (NGO #3)	MOS	M	MIN	25/05/10
1.2.4	Representative of an NGO promoting a minority culture (NGO #4)	MOS	M	MIN	13/10/10
1.2.5	Representative of an NGO promoting inter-ethnic tolerance (NGO #5)	MOS	M	MIN	21/02/11
1.2.6	Leader of a minority association (NGO #6)	VOR	M	MIN	14/10/10
1.2.7	Leader of a minority association (NGO #7)	VOR	M	MIN	14/10/10
1.2.8	Representative of an NGO promoting a minority culture (NGO #8)	STPB	F	MIN	22/10/10
1.2.9	Representative of an NGO promoting a minority culture (NGO #8)	STPB	M	MIN	23/10/10
1.2.10	Representative of an NGO promoting a minority culture (NGO #9)	STPB	F	MIN	24/10/10
1.2.11	Representative of an NGO promoting a minority culture (NGO #10)	STPB	F	MIN	25/10/10

Note
1 Indicating a minority other than the case studies.

1.3 Civil society – cultural associations (seven respondents)

Table A1.3 Cultural associations

Code	Respondent	City	M/F	Ethnic group	Interview date
1.3.1	Director of a Centre of National Cultures, Petrozavodsk	PETR	F	MIN[1]	19/05/10
1.3.2	Deputy Director of a Centre of National Cultures, Petrozavodsk	PETR	F	KAR	19/05/10
1.3.3	Project Manager of a Centre of National Cultures, Petrozavodsk	PETR	F	KAR	20/05/10
1.3.4	Representative of the Moscow House of Nationalities	MOS	M	MIN	11/10/10
1.3.5	Representative of a Centre of Cultures of Finno-Ugric Peoples, Saransk	SAR	M	MOR	21/06/10
1.3.6	Representative of the St Petersburg House of Nationalities	STPB	M	TAT	22/10/10
1.3.7	Representative of the St Petersburg House of Nationalities	STPB	F	RUS	22/10/10

Note
1 Indicating a minority other than the case studies.

1.4 Civil society – peoples' congresses (three respondents)

Table A1.4 Peoples' congresses

Code	Respondent	City	M/F	Ethnic group	Interview date
1.4.1	Representative of the Congress of Karelians	PETR	M	KAR	20/05/10
1.4.2	Representative of the World Congress of Tatars	KAZ	M	TAT	11/06/10
1.4.3	Leader of the Inter-Regional Social Movement of Mordovian (Moksha and Erzya) Peoples; academic	SAR	M	MOR	17/06/10

1.5 Civil society – human rights NGOs (11 respondents)

Table A1.5 Human rights NGOs

Code	Respondent	City	M/F	Ethnic group	Interview date
1.5.1	Lawyer for a human rights NGO (NGO #11); academic specialising in minority issues	MOS	M	RUS	25/05/10
1.5.2	Director of a human rights NGO (NGO #12); academic	MOS	F	RUS	11/10/10
1.5.3	Representative of a human rights NGO (NGO #13), also working for Russia's human rights ombudsman	MOS	M	RUS	20/10/10
1.5.4	Representative of an human rights NGO, working on financial and fiscal matters (NGO #14)	VOR	F	RUS	13/10/10
1.5.5	Director of a human rights NGO (NGO #14)	VOR	F	RUS	16/10/10
1.5.6	Representative of a human rights NGO (NGO #15)	STPB	F	MIN[1]	25/10/10
1.5.7	Representative of a human rights NGO, working on minority issues, with a focus on Roma (NGO #15)	STPB	F	RUS	25/10/10
1.5.8	Representative of a human rights NGO, working on minority issues, with a focus on Roma (NGO #15)	STPB	F	RUS	25/10/10
1.5.9	Specialist on inter-ethnic tolerance in schools, cooperating with a human rights NGO (NGO #15)	STPB	M	RUS	25/10/10
1.5.10	Representative of a human rights NGO (NGO #16)	STPB	F	RUS	25/10/10
1.5.11	Director of a human rights NGO (NGO #17)	STPB	M	RUS	26/10/10

Note
1 Indicating a minority other than the case studies.

2 *Academia (23 respondents)*

Table A2.1 Academia

Code	Respondent	City	M/F	Ethnic group	Interview date
2.1	Representative of the Pedagogical Academy, Petrozavosk, and of the Congress of Karelians	PETR	F	KAR	19/05/10
2.2	Karelian language expert; member of Orthographic Commission for the Karelian language	PETR	F	KAR	19/05/10
2.3	Professor of Karelian and Veps languages, Faculty of Philology, Petrozavodsk State University	PETR	M	KAR	20/05/10
2.4	Sociologist at the Karelian Research Centre, Russian Academy of Sciences	PETR	M	TKAR	20/05/10
2.5	Professor at the Department of Russian, Tver State University; member of the NCA of Tver Karelians	TVER	F	TKAR	04/06/10
2.6	Researcher, Institute of History of the Academy of Sciences of Tatarstan (ASRT); Tatar activist	KAZ	M	TAT	09/06/10
2.7	Researcher, Institute of History, ASRT, Department of Tatar Education	KAZ	M	TAT	09/06/10
2.8	Sociologist, Institute of History, ASRT, Department of Ethnology	KAZ	F	TAT	09/06/10
2.9	Sociologist, Institute of History, ASRT, Department of Ethnology	KAZ	F	TAT	09/06/10
2.10	Academic, Russian Islamic University of Kazan	KAZ	M	TAT	10/06/10
2.11	Language teacher, Kazan State University, working on methodologies for minority languages education	KAZ	F	RUS	14/06/10
2.12	Director of Institute for the Development of Education of Tatarstan	KAZ	M	TAT	14/06/10
2.13	Academic, Kazan State University; Tatar activist	KAZ	M	TAT	15/06/10

continued

Table A2.1 Continued

Code	Respondent	City	M/F	Ethnic group	Interview date
2.14	Academic, Dept of History of Peoples of Russia, Mordovian State University; Mordovian activist	SAR	M	MOR	20/06/10
2.15	Academic, Institute Ethnology and Anthropology, Russian Academy of Sciences (IEA–RAS)	MOS	M	RUS	26/05/10
2.16	Academic, IEA–RAS	MOS	F	RUS	26/05/10
2.17	Analyst, Canergie Moscow Center	MOS	M	RUS	28/05/10
2.18	Scholar; former presidential advisor (under Yeltsin) on nationality issues	MOS	M	MIN[1]	21/09/10
2.19	Researcher, IEA–RAS	MOS	F	RUS	12/10/10
2.20	Researcher, IEA–RAS; specialist on the North Caucasus	MOS	M	MIN	12/10/10
2.21	Researcher, Institute of Geography, RAS	MOS	F	RUS	21/02/11
2.22	Researcher, IEA–RAS; specialist on minority education	MOS	M	RUS	22/02/11
2.23	Researcher, IEA–RAS; specialist on minority languages	MOS	M	RUS	24/02/11

Note
1 Indicating a minority other than the case studies.

3 Media (11 respondents)

Table A3.1 Media

Code	Respondent	City	M/F	Ethnic group	Interview date
3.1	Journalist covering minority issues in the media in Karelia	PETR	F	RUS	20/05/10
3.2	Journalist at Radio Free Europe; former representative of the Federal Tatar NCA	KAZ	M	TAT	10/06/10
3.3	Editor of the (Moksha-language) newspaper *Moksha Pravda*	SAR	M	MOR	18/06/10
3.4	Editor of the (Erzya-language) newspaper *Erzya Pravda*	SAR	M	MOR	18/06/10
3.5	Editor of the (Moksha-language) magazine *Moskha*	SAR	M	MOR	18/06/10
3.6	Editor of a Tatar-language newspaper in Saransk	SAR	F	TAT	18/06/10
3.7	Journalist at the magazine *Finno-Ugorskii Mir*	SAR	M	MIN[1]	18/06/10
3.8	Broadcaster for a programme in Mordovian languages	SAR	F	MOR	21/06/10
3.9	Journalist; director of a media freedom organisation	MOS	M	RUS	21/02/11
3.10	Journalist; representative of a media freedom NGO; member of the Russian Union of Journalists	MOS	F	RUS	24/02/11
3.11	Journalist specialising in media ethics and diversity	STPB	F	RUS	24/10/10

Note
1 Indicating a minority other than the case studies.

4   Public officials (18 respondents)

Table A4.1 Public officials

Code	Respondent	City	M/F	Ethnic group	Interview date
4.1	Public official, Ministry on Nationality Policy, Karelia (programmes on Finno-Ugric peoples)	PETR	F	KAR	18/05/10
4.2	Public official, Ministry on Nationality Policy, Karelia (programme on indigenous peoples)	PETR	F	MIN[1]	18/05/10
4.3	External relations officer, office of Petrozavodsk Mayor (also working on minority issues)	PETR	F	TAT	18/05/10
4.4	Specialist on education, Ministry of Education, Karelia	PETR	F	KAR	19/05/10
4.5	Local MP	PETR	F	MIN	20/05/10
4.6	Public official, Tver administration	TVER	M	TKAR	04/06/10
4.7	Public official, city department on national (Tatar) education	KAZ	M	TAT	09/06/10
4.8	Representative of the Assembly of Peoples of Tatarstan	KAZ	M	MIN	10/06/10
4.9	Advisor, Ministry of Culture; part-time journalist	KAZ	F	TAT	12/06/10
4.10	Representative of the Cabinet of Ministers, working on nationality issues	KAZ	M	TAT	14/06/10
4.11	Representative of the Committee on National Policy, government of the Republic of Mordovia	SAR	M	MOR	17/06/10
4.12	Representative of the Research Institute of Humanitarian Sciences, government of Mordovia	SAR	M	MOR	21/06/10
4.13	Former high-ranking public official in the area of nationalities; manager at IEA–RAS	MOS	M	RUS	02/06/10
4.14	Specialist on minority education (focusing on Roma), Russian Ministry of Education	MOS	F	MIN	31/05/10

continued

Table A4.1 Continued

Code	Respondent	City	M/F	Ethnic group	Interview date
4.15	Representative of the State Committee on Nationality Affairs, State Duma	MOS	M	MOR	01/06/10
4.16	Public official, Russian Ministry of Regional Development	MOS	M	RUS	23/06/10
4.17	Employee of the Voronezh police department (also working on minority issues)	VOR	F	RUS	15/10/10
4.18	MP, St Petersburg Legislative Assembly, working on relations with religious confessions	STPB	M	RUS	25/10/10

Note
1 Indicating a minority other than the case studies.

5 School employees (two respondents)

Table A5.1 School employees

Code	Respondent	City	M/F	Ethnic group	Interview date
5.1	Teacher, Finno-Ugric school	PETR	F	KAR	19/05/10
5.2	Director, Tatar gymnasium	KAZ	F	TAT	15/06/10

Bibliography

Abramov, V.K., 2010. *Mordovskoe Natsional'noe Dvizhenie [Mordovian National Movement]*. 2nd edn. Saransk, Russia: Mordovian State University 'Ogareva'.

Agarin, T., 2013. The Dead Weight of the Past? Institutional Change, Policy Dynamics and the Communist Legacy in Minority Protection. In: K. Cordell, T. Agarin and A. Osipov, eds. *Institutional Legacies of Communism: Change and Continuities in Minority Protection*. Abingdon and New York: Routledge, 14–30.

Ajani, G., 1995. By Chance and Prestige: Legal Transplant in Russia and Eastern Europe. *The American Journal of Comparative Law*, 43 (1), 93–117.

Alexander, J., 2004. Federal Reforms in Russia: Putin's Challenge to the Republics. *Demokratizatsiya*, 12 (2), 233–263.

Almond, G.A. and Verba, S., 1989. *The Civic Culture: Political Attitudes and Democracy in Five Nations*. London: Sage.

Alòs i Font, H., 2014. Chuvash Language in Chuvashia's Instruction System: An Example of Educational Language Policies in Post-Soviet Russia. *Journal of Ethnopolitics and Minority Issues in Europe*, 13 (4), 52–84.

Anderson, B., 1991. *Imagined Communities: Reflections on the Origin and Spread of Nationalism*. London: Verso.

Anderson, B.A. and Silver, B.D., 1984. Equality, Efficiency, and Politics in Soviet Bilingual Education Policy, 1934–1980. *The American Political Science Review*, 78 (4), 1019–1039.

Arel, D., 2002. Demography and Politics in the First Post-Soviet Censuses: Mistrusted State, Contested Identities. *Population (English edition)*, 57 (6), 801–827.

Arias, A.K. and Gurses, M., 2012. The Complexities of Minority Rights in the European Union. *The International Journal of Human Rights*, 16 (2), 321–336.

Artobolevskii, C.C., Vendina, O.I., Gontmakher, E.S., Zubarevich, N.V. and Kynev, A.V., 2010. *Ob'edinenie Sub'ektov Rossiiskoi Federatsii: Za i Protiv [Merging the Subjects of the Russian Federation: For and Against]*. Moscow: INSOR.

Aukerman, M.J., 2000. Definitions and Justifications: Minority and Indigenous Rights in a Central/East European Context. *Human Rights Quarterly*, 22 (4), 1011–1050.

Bache, I., Bulmer, S. and Gunai, D., 2012. Europeanization: A Critical Realistic Perspective. In: T. Exadaktylos and C.M. Radaelli, eds. *Research Design in European Studies: Establishing Causality in Europeanization*. Basingstoke: Palgrave Macmillan, 64–84.

Baev, P.K., 2005. Counter-Terrorism as a Building Block for Putin's Regime. In: J. Hedenskog, V. Konnander, B. Nygren, I. Oldberg and C. Pursiainen, eds. *Russia as a Great Power*. London: Routledge, 323–344.

Banks, M., 1996. *Ethnicity: Anthropological Constructions*. London: Routledge.

Baranovsky, V., 2000. Russia: A Part of Europe or Apart from Europe? *International Affairs*, 76 (3), 443–458.

Barnes, S.H., 2006. The Changing Political Participation of Postcommunist Citizens. *International Journal of Sociology*, 36 (2), 76–98.

Barry, B., 2001. *Culture and Equality: An Egalitarian Critique of Multiculturalism*. Cambridge: Polity.

Barsh, R.L., 1996. Indigenous Peoples and the UN Commission on Human Rights: A Case of the Immovable Object and the Irresistible Force. *Human Rights Quarterly*, 18 (4), 782–813.

Bassin, M., 2007. Lev Gumilev and Russian National Identity During and After the Soviet Era. In: A. Leoussi and S. Grosby, eds. *Nationalism and Ethnosymbolism: History, Culture and Ethnicity in the Formation of Nations*. Edinburgh: Edinburgh University Press, 143–160.

Bauer, M.W., Knill, C. and Pitschel, D., 2007. Differential Europeanization in Eastern Europe: The Impact of Diverse EU Regulatory Governance Patterns. *Journal of European Integration*, 29 (4), 405–423.

Bauer, O., 2000 [1907]. *The Question of Nationalities and Social Democracy*. Minneapolis: University of Minnesota Press.

Beissinger, M., 2002. *Nationalist Mobilisation and the Collapse of the Soviet State*. Cambridge: Cambridge University Press.

Bilinsky, Y., 1962. The Soviet Education Laws of 1958–9 and Soviet Nationality Policy. *Soviet Studies*, 14 (2), 138–157.

Billig, M., 2004. *Banal Nationalism*. London: Sage.

Bonnett, A., 2002. Communists Like Us: Ethnicized Modernity and the Idea of 'the West' in the Soviet Union. *Ethnicities*, 2 (4), 435–467.

Börzel, T.A. and Risse, T., 2003. Conceptualizing the Domestic Impact of Europe. In: K. Featherstone and C.M. Radaelli, eds. *The Politics of Europeanization*. Oxford: Oxford University Press, 57–82.

Börzel, T.A. and Risse, T., 2012. From Europeanization to Diffusion. *West European Politics*, 35 (1), 1–19.

Bottomore, T. and Goode, P., eds., 1978. *Austro-Marxism*. Oxford: Clarendon.

Bourdieu, P., 1991. *Language and Symbolic Power*. Cambridge, MA: Harvard University Press.

Bowring, B., 2002. Austro-Marxism's Last Laugh? The Struggle for Recognition of National-Cultural Autonomy for Rossians and Russians. *Europe-Asia Studies*, 54 (2), 229–250.

Bowring, B., 2003. Rejected Organs? The Efficacy of Legal Transplantation, and the Ends of Human Rights in the Russian Federation. In: E. Örücü, ed. *Judicial Comparativism in Human Rights Cases*. London: British Institute of International and Comparative Law, 159–181.

Bowring, B., 2005. Burial and Resurrection: Karl Renner's Controversial Influence on the 'National Question' in Russia. In: E. Nimni, ed. *National-Cultural Autonomy and its Contemporary Critics*. Abingdon: Routledge, 191–206.

Bowring, B., 2007. The Tatars of the Russian Federation and National-Cultural Autonomy: A Contradiction in Terms? *Ethnopolitics*, 6 (3), 417–435.

Bowring, B., 2008. *The Degradation of the International Legal Order? The Rehabilitation of Law and the Possibility of Politics*. Abingdon: Routledge.

Bowring, B., 2010a. Enhanced Local Self-Government as a Means of Enhancing Minority

Governance. In: M. Weller and K. Nobbs, eds. *Political Participation of Minorities: A Commentary on International Standards and Practice*. Oxford: Oxford University Press, 661–681.

Bowring, B., 2010b. The Russian Constitutional System: Complexities and Asymmetry. In: M. Weller, ed. *Asymmetrical State Design as a Tool in Ethnopolitical Conflict Resolution*. Philadelphia: University of Pennsylvania Press, 48–74.

Bowring, B., 2013a. *Law, Rights and Ideology in Russia: Landmarks in the Destiny of a Great Power*. Abingdon: Routledge.

Bowring, B., 2013b. Minority Protection in Russia: Is there a Communist Legacy? In: K. Cordell, T. Agarin and A. Osipov, eds. *Institutional Legacies of Communism: Change and Continuities in Minority Protection*. Abingdon and New York: Routledge, 45–59.

Bowring, B., 2013c. Russian Legislation in the Area of Minority Rights. In: O. Protsyk and B. Harzl, eds. *Managing Ethnic Diversity in Russia*. Abingdon: Routledge, 15–36.

Bowring, B., 2015. Case-Law of the European Court of Human Rights Concerning the Protection of Minorities, July 2012 to August 2014. *European Yearbook of Minority Issues*, 12.

Bromley, J., 1983. *Ocherki Teorii Etnosa [Essays on the Theory of Ethnos]*. Moscow: Nauka.

Bromley, J. and Kozlov, V., 1989. The Theory of Ethnos and Ethnic Processes in Soviet Social Sciences. *Comparative Studies in Society and History*, 31 (3), 425–438.

Brubaker, R., 1994. Nationhood and the National Question in the Soviet Union and post-Soviet Eurasia: An Institutionalist Account. *Theory and Society*, 23 (1), 47–78.

Brubaker, R., 1996. *Nationalism Reframed: Nationhood and the National Question in the New Europe*. Cambridge: Cambridge University Press.

Brubaker, R., 1999. The Manichean Myth: Rethinking the Distinction between 'Civic' and 'Ethnic'. In: H. Kriesi, K. Armingeon, H. Siegrist and A. Wimmer, eds. *Nation and National Identity: The European Experience in Perspective*. Zurich: Ruegger, 55–71.

Brubaker, R., 2002. Ethnicity without Groups. *European Journal of Sociology*, 43 (3), 163–189.

Brubaker, R., 2004. 'Civic' and 'Ethnic' Nationalism. In: *Ethnicity without Groups*. Cambridge, MA: Harvard University Press, 132–146.

Brubaker, R., 2011. Nationalizing States Revisited: Projects and Processes of Nationalization in Post-Soviet States. *Ethnic and Racial Studies*, 34 (11), 1785–1814.

Brysk, A., 1994. *The Politics of Human Rights in Argentina: Protest, Change, and Democratization*. Stanford: Stanford University Press.

Bunce, V., 1999. *Subversive Institutions: The Design and the Destruction of Socialism and the State*. Cambridge: Cambridge University Press.

Burkov, A., 2007. *The Impact of the European Convention on Human Rights on Russian Law: Legislation and Application in 1996–2006*. Stuttgart: Ibidem-Verlag.

Capotorti, F., 1979. *Study on the Rights of Persons Belonging to Ethnic, Linguistic and Religious Minorities*. New York: UN Publications.

Carstocea, A., 2011. Ethno-Business: The Manipulation of Minority Rights in Romania and Hungary. In: T. Bhambry, C. Griffin, T. Hjelm, C. Nicholson and O. Voronina, eds. *Perpetual Motion? Transformation and Transition in Central and Eastern Europe and Russia*. London: UCL SSEES, 16–28.

Cashaback, D., 2003. Risky Strategies? Putin's Federal Reforms and the Accommodation of Difference in Russia. *Journal of Ethnopolitics and Minority Issues in Europe*, 3, 1–31.

Chaisty, P., 2006. *Legislative Politics and Economic Power in Russia*. Basingstoke: Palgrave Macmillan.

Chaisty, P., 2013. The Descriptive and Substantive Representation of Ethnic Minorities in the Russian Parliament. In: O. Protsyk and B. Harzl, eds. *Managing Ethnic Diversity in Russia*. Abingdon: Routledge, 238–262.

Chandler, D., 1999. The OSCE and the Internationalisation of National Minority Rights. In: K. Cordell, ed. *Ethnicity and Democratisation in the New Europe*. London: Routledge, 61–73.

Chebankova, E., 2007. Putin's Struggle for Federalism: Structures, Operation and the Commitment Problem. *Europe-Asia Studies*, 59 (2), 279–302.

Chebankova, E., 2012. Contemporary Russian Multiculturalism. *Post-Soviet Affairs*, 28 (3), 319–345.

Chevalier, J.F., 2012. Multilingual Education in South Siberia: National Schools in the Republics of Altai and Tyva. *Heritage Language Journal*, 9 (2), 1–17.

Choltaev, Z., 2003. A New Nationality Policy or a New Setback for Russia. *Russian and Eurasia Review*, 2 (2), 5–9.

Clem, R.S., 2006. Russia's Electoral Geography: A Review. *Eurasian Geography and Economics*, 47 (4), 381–406.

Codagnone, C. and Filippov, V., 2000. Equity, Exit and National Identity in a Multicultural Federation: The 'Multicultural Constitutional Patriotism' Project in Russia. *Journal of Ethnic and Migration Studies*, 26 (2), 263–288.

Colton, T.J. and Hale, H.E., 2009. The Putin Vote: Presidential Electorates in a Hybrid Regime. *Slavic Review*, 68 (3), 473–503.

Connor, W., 1984. *The National Question in Marxist-Leninist Theory and Strategy*. Princeton, NJ: Princeton University Press.

Cordell, K., 2013. The Ideology of Minority Protection during the Post-Communist Transition in Europe. In: K. Cordell, T. Agarin and A. Osipov, eds. *Institutional Legacies of Communism: Change and Continuities in Minority Protection*. Abingdon and New York: Routledge, 77–89.

Council of Europe, 2007. *From Linguistic Diversity to Plurilingual Education: Guide for the Development of Language Education Policies in Europe*. Strasbourg: Council of Europe.

Crews, R., 2006. *For Prophet and Tsar: Islam and Empire in Russia and Central Asia*. Cambridge, MA: Harvard University Press.

Crystal, D., 2000. *Language Death*. Cambridge: Cambridge University Press.

Danilenko, G., 1999. Implementation of International Law in CIS States: Theory and Practice. *European Journal of International Law*, 10 (1), 51–69.

Daucé, F., 2015. Patriotic Unity and Ethnic Diversity at Odds: The Example of Tatar Organisations in Moscow. *Europe-Asia Studies*, 67 (1), 68–83.

Daucé, F., Désert, M., Laruelle, M., Le Huérou, A. and Rousselet, K., 2010. Les Usages Pratiques du Patriotisme en Russie. *Questions de Recherche*, 32, 1–31.

de Swann, A., 2001. *Words of the World: The Global Language System*. Cambridge: Polity.

de Varennes, F., 2000. *Minority Rights and the Prevention of Ethnic Conflict*. UN Working Group on Minorities, Sub-Commission on Promotion and Protection of Human Rights, Commission of Human Rights, 6th session, 22–26 May 2000.

de Varennes, F., 2005. *Commentary of the Working Group on Minorities to the United Nations Declaration on the Rights of Persons Belonging to National or Ethnic, Religious and Linguistic Minorities, UN Doc. E/CN.4/Sub.2/AC.5/2005/2*.

de Varennes, F. and Thornberry, P., 2005. Article 14. In: M. Weller, ed. *The Rights of Minorities in Europe: A Commentary on the European Framework Convention on the Protection of National Minorities*. Oxford: Oxford University Press, 407–428.

Donnelly, J., 1986. International Human Rights: A Regime Analysis. *International Organization*, 40 (3), 599–642.

Drzewicki, K., 2010. OSCE Lund Recommendations in the Practice of the High Commissioner on National Minorities. In: M. Weller and K. Nobbs, eds. *Political Participation of Minorities: A Commentary on International Standards and Practice*. Oxford: Oxford University Press, 256–284.

Duncan, P., 1999. Russia: Accommodating Ethnic Minorities. In: D. MacIver, ed. *The Politics of Multinational States*. London: Macmillan, 63–83.

Duncan, P., 2000. *Russian Messianism: Third Rome, Holy Revolution, Communism and After*. London and New York: Routledge.

Duncan, P., 2004. Westernism, Eurasianism and Pragmatism: The Foreign Policies of the Post-Soviet States 1991–2001. In: W. Slater and A. Wilson, eds. *The Legacy of the Soviet Union*. Basingstoke and New York: Palgrave Macmillan, 228–253.

Duncan, P., 2007. Regime and Ideology in Putin's Russia. In: P. Duncan, ed. *Convergence and Divergence: Russia and Eastern Europe into the Twenty-First Century*. London: UCL SSEES, 139–158.

Elander, I., 1997. Between Centralism and Localism: On the Development of Local Self-Government in Postsocialist Europe. *Environment and Planning C: Government and Policy*, 15 (2), 143–159.

Ellickson, R.C., 1991. *Order without Law: How Neighbors Settle Disputes*. Cambridge, MA: Harvard University Press.

Estébanez, M.A.M., 2005. Council of Europe Policies Concerning the Protection of Linguistic Minorities and the Justiciability of Minority Rights. In: N. Ghanea and A. Xanthaki, eds. *Minorities, Peoples and Self-Determination*. Leiden: Martinus Nijhoff, 269–298.

Ewald, W., 1995. Comparative Jurisprudence (II): The Logic of Legal Transplants. *The American Journal of Comparative Law*, 43 (4), 489–510.

Exadactylos, T. and Radaelli, C.M., 2012. Lessons Learned: Beyond Causality. In: T. Exadactylos and C.M. Radaelli, eds. *Research Design in European Studies: Establishing Causality in Europeanization*. Basingstoke: Palgrave Macmillan, 255–264.

Featherstone, K., 2003. Introduction: In the Name of 'Europe'. In: K. Featherstone and C.M. Radaelli, eds. *The Politics of Europeanization*. Oxford: Oxford University Press, 3–26.

Feldbrugge, F., 1993. *Russian Law: The End of the Soviet System and the Role of Law*. Dordrecht: Martinus Nijhoff.

Feldbrugge, F., 2007. *Russia, Europe and the Rule of Law*. Leiden: Martinus Nijhoff.

Figes, O., 2003. *Natasha's Dance: A Cultural History of Russia*. London: Penguin.

Filippova, E. and Filippov, Y., 2008. National-Cultural Autonomies in Post-Soviet Russia: A Dead-End Political Project. Paper presented at the ASN Sciences Po Conference 'Empire and Nations', Paris, France, 3–5 July 2008.

Fishman, J., 1991. *Reversing Language Shift: Theoretical and Empirical Foundations of Assistance to Threatened Languages*. Clevedon: Multilingual Matters.

Friedrich, C., 1968. *Trends of Federalism in Theory and Practice*. London: Pall Mall.

Gabdrakhmanova, G.F., 2011. Uchitel'skii Korpus i Uchebno-Metodicheskii Kompleks po Tatarskomu Yazyku i Literature dlya Srednei Shkoly [Teaching and Methodology for Tatar Language and Literature in Secondary School]. In: R.N. Musina, G.F. Gabdrakhmanova and L.V. Sagitova, eds. *Yazyki v Sisteme Obrazovaniya Respubliki Tatarstan [Languages in the System of Education of the Republic of Tatarstan].* Kazan: Tatarskoe Knizhnoe Izdatel'stvo, 78–103.

Garipov, Y.G. and Faller, H.M., 2003. The Politics of Language Reform and Bilingualism in Tatarstan. In: F. Daftary and F. Grin, eds. *Nation-Building, Ethnicity and Language Politics in Transition Countries.* Budapest: Open Society Institute, 163–183.

Gel'man, V., 2004. The Unrule of Law in the Making: The Politics of Informal Institutional Building in Russia. *Europe-Asia Studies*, 56 (7), 1021–1058.

Gel'man, V., 2006. From 'Feckless Pluralism' to 'Dominant Power Politics'? The Transformation of Russia's Party System. *Democratization*, 13 (4), 545–561.

Gel'man, V., 2008. Party Politics in Russia: From Competition to Hierarchy. *Europe-Asia Studies*, 60 (6), 913–930.

Ghai, Y., 2000. Ethnicity and Autonomy: A Framework for Analysis. In: Y. Ghai, ed. *Autonomy and Ethnicity: Negotiating Competing Claims in Multi-Ethnic States.* Cambridge: Cambridge University Press, 1–26.

Ghanea, N. and Xanthaki, A., eds., 2005. *Minorities, Peoples and Self-Determination.* Leiden: Martinus Nijhoff.

Gibatdinov, M., 2010. Cross-Referencing Images of Muslims and Islam in Russian and Tatar Textbooks (1747–2007). In: G. Jonker and S. Thobani, eds. *Narrating Islam: Interpretations of the Muslim Worlds in European Texts.* London: Tauris, 62–93.

Gilbert, G., 1996. The Council of Europe and Minority Rights. *Human Rights Quarterly*, 18 (1), 160–189.

Gilbert, G., 2002. The Burgeoning Minority Rights Jurisprudence of the European Court of Human Rights. *Human Rights Quarterly*, 24 (3), 736–780.

Giuliano, E., 2011. *Constructing Grievance: Ethnic Nationalism in Russia's Republics.* Ithaca, NY: Cornell University Press.

Giuliano, E. and Gorenburg, D.P., 2012. The Unexpectedly Underwhelming Role of Ethnicity in Russian Politics, 1991–2011. *Demokratizatsiya*, 20 (2), 175–188.

Goetz, K.H., 2000. European Integration and National Executives: A Cause in Search of An Effect? *West European Politics*, 23 (4), 211–231.

Golosov, G.V., 2011. The Regional Roots of Electoral Authoritarianism in Russia. *Europe-Asia Studies*, 63 (4), 623–639.

Goode, P., 2010. The Fall and Rise of Regionalism? *Journal of Communist Studies and Transition Politics*, 26 (2), 233–256.

Gorenburg, D.P., 2003. *Minority Ethnic Mobilization in the Russian Federation.* Cambridge: Cambridge University Press.

Gorenburg, D.P., 2005. Tatar Language Policies in Comparative Perspective: Why Some Revivals Fail and Some Succeed. *Ab Imperio*, 1, 1–28.

Grabbe, H., 2001. How does Europeanization Affect CEE Governance? Conditionality, Diffusion and Diversity. *Journal of European Public Policy*, 8 (6), 1013–1031.

Graney, K.E., 1999. Education Reform in Tatarstan and Bashkortostan: Sovereignty Projects in Post-Soviet Russia. *Europe-Asia Studies*, 51 (4), 611–632.

Green Cowles, M. and Risse, T., 2001. Transforming Europe: Conclusions. In: M. Green Cowles, J. Caporaso and T. Risse, eds. *Transforming Europe: Europeanization and Domestic Change.* Ithaca, NY: Cornell University Press, 217–237.

Grenoble, L.A., 2003. *Language Policy in the Soviet Union.* Dordrecht: Kluwer.

Grin, F., 2003. *Language Policy Evaluation and the European Charter for Regional or Minority Languages.* Basingstoke: Palgrave Macmillan.

Grin, F. and Moring, T., 2002. *Support for Minority Languages in Europe: Final Report*. European Bureau for Lesser-Used Languages/European Centre for Minority Issues.

Gumilev, L., 2007. *Etnogenez i Biosfera Zemli [Ethnogenesis and the Earth Biosphere]*. Moscow: Airis-Press.

Haarmann, H., 1998. Multilingual Russia and its Soviet Heritage. In: C.B. Paulston, ed. *Linguistic Minorities in Central and Eastern Europe*. Philadelphia: Clevedon, 224–254.

Hagendoom, L., Poppe, E. and Minescu, A., 2008. Support for Separatism in Ethnic Republics of the Russian Federation. *Europe-Asia Studies*, 60 (3), 353–373.

Hahn, G.M., 2001. Putin's 'Federal Revolution': The Administrative and Judicial Reform of Russian Federalism. *East European Constitutional Review*, 10 (1), 68–75.

Hahn, G.M., 2003. The Impact of Putin's Federative Reforms on Democratization in Russia. *Post-Soviet Affairs*, 19 (2), 114–153.

Hahn, G.M., 2010. 'Medvedev, Putin, and Perestroika 2.0', *Demokratizatsiya*, 18 (3), 228–259.

Hahn, J., 2008. Have Putin's Policies on Local Government Changed the Way Yaroslavl is Governed? *Demokratizatsiya*, 16 (4), 383–389.

Hale, H.E., 2000. The Parade of Sovereignties: Testing Theories of Secession in the Soviet Setting. *British Journal of Political Science*, 30 (1), 31–56.

Hanson, P., 2005. Federalism with a Russian Face: Regional Inequality and Regional Budgets in Russia. In: P. Reddaway and R. Orttung, eds. *The Dynamics of Russian Politics: Putin's Reforms of Federal-Regional Relations. Volume II*. Lanham, MD: Rowman & Littlefield, 295–318.

Harris, C.D., 1993. The New Russian Minorities: A Statistical Overview. *Post-Soviet Geography*, 34 (1), 1–27.

Hasan, R., 2010. *Multiculturalism: Some Inconvenient Truths*. London: Politico's.

Hashim, S.M., 2005. Putin's Etatization Project and Limits to Democratic Reforms in Russia. *Communist and Post-Communist Studies*, 38, 25–48.

Haukkala, H., 2008. A Norm-Maker or a Norm-Taker? The Changing Normative Parameters of Russia's Place in Europe. In: T. Hopf, ed. *Russia's European Choice*. New York: Palgrave Macmillan, 35–56.

Heim, S.G., 1996. Predicting Legal Transplants: The Case of Servitudes in the Russian Federation. *Transnational Law and Contemporary Problems*, 6, 187–223.

Helmke, G. and Levitsky, S., 2004. Informal Institutions and Comparative Politics: A Research Agenda. *Perspectives on Politics*, 2 (4), 725–740.

Hendley, K., 2007. Are Russia's Judges Still Soviet? *Post-Soviet Affairs*, 23 (3), 240–274.

Henrard, K., 2000. *Devising an Adequate System of Minority Protection: Individual Human Rights, Minority Rights and the Right to Self-Determination*. The Hague: Martinus Nijhoff.

Henrard, K., 2005. 'Participation', 'Representation' and 'Autonomy' in the Lund Recommendations and the Reflections in the Supervision of the FCNM and Several Human Rights Conventions. *International Journal on Minority and Group Rights*, 12, 133–168.

Héritier, A., 2001. *Differential Europe: The European Union Impact on National Policy-making*. Lanham, MD: Rowman & Littlefield.

Hirsch, F., 2005. *Empire of Nations: Ethnographic Knowledge and the Making of the Soviet Union*. Ithaca, NY: Cornell University Press.

Hofmann, R., 2006. Political Participation of Minorities. *European Yearbook of Minority Issues*, 6, 5–17.

Hofmann, R., 2008. The Future of Minority Issues in the Council of Europe and the Organization for Security and Cooperation in Europe. In: M. Weller, D. Blacklock and K. Nobbs, eds. *The Protection of Minorities in the Wider Europe*. New York: Palgrave Macmillan, 171–205.

Hosking, G., 1990. *The Awakening of the Soviet Union*. London: Heinemann.

Hosking, G., 1998. *Russia: People and Empire, 1552–1917*. London: Harper Collins.

Hosking, G., 2005. The State and Russian National Identity. In: L. Scales and O. Zimmer, eds. *Power and the Nation in European History*. Cambridge: Cambridge University Press, 195–211.

Howard, M.M., 2003. *The Weakness of Civil Society in Post-Communist Europe*. Cambridge: Cambridge University Press.

Hughes, J., Sasse, G. and Gordon, C., 2004. *Europeanization and Regionalization in the EU's Enlargement to Central and Eastern Europe: The Myth of Conditionality*. Basingstoke: Palgrave Macmillan.

Huntington, S., 1996. *The Clash of Civilizations and the Remaking of World Order*. New York: Simon and Schuster.

Hutchings, S. and Miazhevich, G., 2010. Television, Nation Building and the Everyday in Contemporary Russia. *Russian Journal of Communication*, 3 (3–4), 173–184.

Hutchings, S. and Rulyova, N., 2009. *Television and Culture in Putin's Russia: Remote Control*. London: Routledge.

Hyde, M., 2001. Putin's Federal Reforms and their Implications for Presidential Power in Russia. *Europe-Asia Studies*, 53 (5), 719–753.

Ilyukha, O.P., 2009. *Finskii Faktor v Istorii i Kul'ture Karelii XX Veka [The Finnish Factor in the History and Culture of Karelia in the 20th Century]*. Petrozavodsk: Russian Academy of Sciences.

Isaacs, R. and Whitmore, S., 2014. The Limited Agency and Lifecycles of Personalized Dominant Parties in the Post-Soviet Space: The Cases of United Russia and Nur Otan. *Democratization*, 21 (4), 699–721.

Jackson-Preece, J., 2014. Beyond the (Non) Definition of Minority. *ECMI Issue Brief No. 30*. Flensburg: European Centre for Minority Issues.

Janis, M., 1997. Russia and the 'Legality' of the Strasbourg Law. *European Journal of International Law*, 8 (1), 93–99.

Jordan, P., 2003. Russia's Accession to the Council of Europe and Compliance with European Human Rights Norms. *Demokratizatsiya*, 11 (2), 281–296.

Kahn-Freund, O., 1974. On Uses and Misuses of Comparative Law. *The Modern Law Review*, 37 (1), 1–27.

Kangaspuro, M. and Lassila, J., 2012. Naming the War and Framing the Nation in Russian Public Discussion. *Canadian Slavonic Papers/Revue Canadienne des Slavistes*, 54 (3–4), 377–399.

Kaplan, V., 2005. History Teaching in Post-Soviet Russia: Coping with Antitethical Tradition. In: B. Eklof, L.E. Holmes and V. Kaplan, eds. *Education Reform in Post-Soviet Russia: Legacies and Prospects*. Abingdon: Frank Cass, 247–271.

Kappeler, A., 2001. *The Russian Empire: A Multiethnic History*. Harlow: Longman.

Keck, M.E. and Sikkink, K., 1998. *Activists Beyond Borders: Advocacy Networks in International Politics*. Ithaca, NY: Cornell University Press.

Keck, M.E. and Sikkink, K., 1999. Transnational Advocacy Networks in International and Regional Politics. *International Social Science Journal*, 51 (159), 89–101.

Khakimov, R., 1993. *Sumerki Imperii: K Voprosu o Natsii i Gosudarstve [The Twilight of the Empire: Towards the Issue of Nation and State]*. Kazan: Tatarskoe Knizhnoe Izdatel'stvo.

Kharlamova, Y., 2009. Voploshchenie Evropeyskoy Konventsii po Pravam Chekoveka: Pochemu eto Nevozmozhno v Usloviakh Rossii [The Realisation of the European Convention of Human Rights: Why it is Impossible in Russia]. In: A. Umland, ed. *The Implementation of the European Convention on Human Rights in Russia: Philosophical, Legal and Empirical Studies.* Stuttgart: Ibidem-Verlag, 51–62.

Kirkow, P., 1995. Regional Warlordism in Russia: The Case of Primorskii Krai. *Europe-Asia Studies*, 47 (6), 923–946.

Kirkow, P., 1998. *Russia's Provinces: Authoritarian Transformation versus Local Autonomy?* Basingstoke: Palgrave Macmillan.

Kirkwood, M., ed., 1989. *Language Planning in the Soviet Union.* London: Macmillan.

Klement'ev, Y., 2006. Yazykovoe Pravo i Obrazovatelnaya Politika [Language Law and Education Policy]. *Kazanskii Federalist*, 1–2 (17–18), 182–195.

Klement'ev, Y., 2010. Kareliya: Shkola kak Etnokulturnyi Tsentr' [Karelia: The Republic of Karelia: School as an Ethno-Cultural Centre]. In: V.V. Stepanov, ed. *Etnokul'turnoe Obrazovanie: Metody Sotsial'noi Orientatsii Rossiiskoi Shkoly [Ethnocultural Education: Methods of Social Orientation of Russian Schools].* Moscow: Russian Academy of Sciences, 27–44.

Klinke, A. and Renn, O., 1997. Ethnic Cooperation and Coexistence: International Mediation, International Governance, and Civil Society for Ethnically Plural States. In: A. Klinke, O. Renn and J.-P. Lehners, eds. *Ethnic Conflicts and Civil Society: Proposals for a New Era in Eastern Europe.* Aldershot: Ashgate, 251–276.

Knill, C., 1998. European Policies: The Impact of National Administrative Traditions. *Journal of Public Policy*, 18 (1), 1–28.

Kohn, H., 1944. *The Idea of Nationalism: A Study in its Origins and Background.* New York: Collier Books.

Kokko, V.A. and Kon'kova, O.I., 2009. *Ingermanlandskie Finny: Ocherki Istorii i Kul'tury [Ingermanland Finns: Outline of their History and Culture].* St Petersburg: Russian Academy of Sciences.

Kolstø, P., 2013. Faulted for the Wrong Reasons: Soviet Institutionalisation of Ethnic Diversity and Western (Mis)interpretations. In: K. Cordell, T. Agarin and A. Osipov, eds. *Institutional Legacies of Communism: Change and Continuities in Minority Protection.* Abingdon and New York: Routledge, 31–44.

Koroteev, K., 2008. The European Factor in Russian Justice. *Open Democracy*, 26 June 2008.

Koroteev, K. and Golubok, S., 2007. Judgement of the Russian Constitutional Court on Supervisory Review on Civil Proceedings: Denial of Justice, Denial of Europe. *Human Rights Law Review*, 7 (3), 619–632.

Kovaleva, S.V., 2010. Karel'skii Yazyk v Sisteme Obrazovaniya Respubliki Kareliya [The Karelian Language in the Education System of the Republic of Karelia]. In: *Etnokul'turnoe Obrazovanie: Metody Sotsial'noi Orientatsii Rossiiskoi Shkoly [Ethnocultural Education: Methods of Social Orientation of Russian Schools].* Moscow: Russian Academy of Sciences, 309–320.

Krasnov, M., 2004. The Rule of Law. In: M. McFaul, N. Petrov and A. Ryabov, eds. *Between Dictatorship and Democracy: Russian Post-Communist Political Reform.* Washington, DC: Carnegie Endowment for International Peace, 195–212.

Krauss, M., 1992. The World's Languages in Crisis. *Language*, 68 (1), 4–10.

Kreindler, I.T., 1985. The Mordvinians: A Doomed Soviet Nationality? *Cahiers du Monde Russe et Soviétique*, 26 (1), 43–62.

Kreindler, I.T., 1989. Soviet Language Planning since 1953. In: M. Kirkwood, ed. *Language Planning in the Soviet Union.* London: Macmillan, 46–63.

Kryazhkov, V.A., 2010. *Korennye Malochislennye Narody v Rossiiskom Prave [Small-in-Number Indigenous Peoples in Russian Law]*. Moscow: Norma Publishing.

Kutafin, O.E., 2006. *Rossiiskaya Avtonomiya [Russian Autonomy]*. Moscow: Prospekt.

Kuzio, T., 2002. The Myth of the Civic State: A Critical Survey of Hans Kohn's Framework for Understanding Nationalism. *Ethnic and Racial Studies*, 25 (1), 20–39.

Kuzivanova, O.Y., 2009. Finno-Ugric Ethnicities and Power: Problems and Interaction. In: A.K. Konyukhov, ed. *Finno-Ugric Ethnicities in Russia: Yesterday, Today and Tomorrow*. Syktyvkar: 'Finland-Russia' Society, 81–94.

Kuz'min, M.N., 2005. K Voprosu o Razrabotke Kontseptsii Federal'noi Etnonatsional'noi Obrazovatel'noi Politiki Rossiiskoi Federatsii [On Compiling a Concept of Federal Ethnonational Educational Policy of the Russian Federation]. In: *Materials of the Conference 'Realisation of the National Regional Component of History Education in the National Republics of the Volga and Ural Regions: Problems and Perspectives', 26 October 2004*. Kazan: Academy of Sciences of the Republic of Tatarstan, 14–24.

Kuz'min, M.N. and Artemenko, O., 2010. Iazykovaia Politika Rossii v Svete Novykh Pravovykh Norm [Language Policy in Russia in Light of New Legan Norms]. In: V.A. Tishkov and V.V. Stepanov, eds. *Etnopoliticheskaya Situatsiya v Rossii i Sopredel'nykh Gosudarstvakh v 2009 Godu [The Ethnopolitical Situation in Russia and Neighbouring States in 2009]*. Moscow: Russian Academy of Sciences, 44–46.

Kymlicka, W., 1995. *Multicultural Citizenship: A Liberal Theory of Minority Rights*. Oxford: Clarendon Press.

Kymlicka, W., 2007a. *Multicultural Odysseys: Navigating the New International Politics of Diversity*. Oxford: Oxford University Press.

Kymlicka, W., 2007b. National Cultural Autonomy and International Minority Rights Norms. *Ethnopolitics*, 6 (3), 379–393.

Laitin, D.D., 1998. *Identity in Formation: The Russian-Speaking Populations in the Near Abroad*. Ithaca, NY: Cornell University Press.

Landman, T., 2003. *Issues and Methods in Comparative Politics: An Introduction*. London: Routledge.

Lankina, T., 2002. Local Administration and Ethno-Social Consensus in Russia. *Europe-Asia Studies*, 54 (7), 1037–1053.

Lankina, T., 2005. President Putin's Local Government Reforms. In: P. Reddaway and R. Orttung, eds. *The Dynamics of Russian Politics. Putin's Reforms of Federal-Regional Relations. Volume II*. Lanham, MD: Rowman & Littlefield, 145–177.

Laruelle, M., 2009a. *In the Name of the Nation*. New York and Basingstoke: Palgrave Macmillian.

Laruelle, M., 2009b. Introduction. In: M. Laruelle, ed. *Russian Nationalism and the National Reassertion of Russia*. Abingdon: Routledge, 1–10.

Laruelle, M., 2009c. Rethinking Russian Nationalism: Historical Continuity, Political Diversity, and Doctrinal Fragmentation. In: M. Laruelle, ed. *Russian Nationalism and the National Reassertion of Russia*. Abingdon: Routledge, 13–48.

Leatherbarrow, W., 2010. Conservatism in the Age of Alexander I and Nicholas I. In: W. Leatherbarrow and D. Offord, eds. *A History of Russian Thought*. Cambridge: Cambridge University Press, 95–115.

Ledeneva, A., 1998. *Russia's Economy of Favours: Blat, Networking, and Informal Exchange*. Cambridge: Cambridge University Press.

Ledeneva, A., 2006a. Behind the Facade: 'Telephone Justice' in Putin's Russia. In: *Dictatorship or Reforms? The Rule of Law in Russia*. London: The Foreign Policy Centre, 24–36.

Ledeneva, A., 2006b. *How Russia Really Works*. Ithaca, NY: Cornell University Press.

Ledeneva, A., 2008. Telephone Justice in Russia. *Post-Soviet Affairs*, 24 (4), 324–350.

Ledeneva, A., 2013. *Can Russia Modernise? Sistema, Power Networks and Informal Governance*. Cambridge: Cambridge University Press.

Lemaître, R., 2006. The Rollback of Democracy in Russia after Beslan. *Review of Central and East European Law*, 31 (4), 369–411.

Lenin, V.I., 1972 [1913]. Critical Remarks on the National Question. In: *Lenin Collected Works*. Moscow: Progress, 17–51.

Lewis, G., 1972. *Multilingualism in the Soviet Union: Aspects of Language Policy and its Implementation*. The Hague: Mouton.

Liber, G., 1991. Korenizatsiia: Restructuring Soviet Nationality Policy in the 1920s. *Ethnic and Racial Studies*, 14 (1), 15–23.

Lieven, A., 2003. *Empire: The Russian Empire and its Rivals from the Sixteenth Century to the Present*. London: Pimlico.

Lipschutz, R.D., 1992. Reconstructing World Politics: The Emergence of Global Civil Society. *Millenium: Journal of International Studies*, 21 (3), 389–420.

Lipset, H., 1967. The Status of National Minority Languages in Soviet Education. *Soviet Studies*, 19 (2), 181–189.

Lynch, A.C., 2001. The Realism of Russia's Foreign Policy. *Europe-Asia Studies*, 53 (1), 7–31.

Lynggaard, K., 2012. Discoursive Analytical Strategical Studies. In: T. Exadaktylos and C.M. Radaelli, eds. *Research Design in European Studies: Establishing Causality in Europeanization*. Basingstoke: Palgrave Macmillan, 85–104.

Machnyikova, Z., 2005. Article 7. In: M. Weller, ed. *The Rights of Minorities in Europe: A Commentary on the European Framework Convention on the Protection of National Minorities*. Oxford: Oxford University Press, 193–224.

Makarova, G.I., 2011a. Etnoyazykovoe Povedenie Uchashchikhsya Starshikh Klassov [Ethnolinguistic Behaviour of Students of the Higher Classes]. In: R.N. Musina, G.F. Gabdrakhmanova and L.V. Sagitova, eds. *Yazyki v Sisteme Obrazovaniya Respubliki Tatarstan [Languages in the System of Education of the Republic of Tatarstan]*. Kazan: Tatarskoe Knizhnoe Izdatel'stvo, 29–50.

Makarova, G.I., 2011b. Yazykovye Reformy v Sfere Obrazovaniya RT v Kontekste Etnokul'turnoi Politiki Federal'nogo Tsentra i Respubliki Tatarstan [Language Reform in Education in the Republic of Tatarstan in the Context of the Ethnocultural Policy of the Federal Centre and the Republic of Tatarstan]. In: R.N. Musina, G.F. Gabdra-khmanova and L.V. Sagitova, eds. *Yazyki v Sisteme Obrazovaniya Respubliki Tatar-stan [Languages in the System of Education of the Republic of Tatarstan]*. Kazan: Tatarskoe Knizhnoe Izdatel'stvo, 9–15.

Malakhov, V. and Osipov, A., 2006. The Category of Minorities in the Russian Federa-tion: A Reflection on Uses and Misuses. In: S.S. Åkermark, ed. *International Obliga-tions and National Debates: Minorities Around the Baltic Sea*. Marienhamn: The Åland Islands Peace Institute, 497–544.

Malfliet, K. and Parmentier, S., eds., 2010. *Russia and the Council of Europe: 10 Years After*. Basingstoke: Palgrave Macmillan.

Mannens, W., 1999. The International Status of Cultural Rights for National Minorities. In: P. Cumper and S. Wheatley, eds. *Minority Rights in the 'New' Europe*. The Hague: Kluwer, 185–196.

March, L., 2012. The Russian Duma 'Opposition': No Drama Out of Crisis? *East Euro-pean Politics*, 28 (3), 241–255.

Marko, J., 2006. *Effective Participation of National Minorities: A Comment on Conceptual, Legal and Empirical Problems*. Strasbourg: Council of Europe.

Martin, T., 2001. *The Affirmative Action Empire*. Ithaca, NY: Cornell University Press.

Martinsen, D.S., 2012. The Europeanization of Health Care: Processes and Factors. In: T. Exadaktylos and C.M. Radaelli, eds. *Research Design in European Studies: Establishing Causality in Europeanization*. Basingstoke: Palgrave Macmillan, 141–159.

Martynenko, A.V., 2010. Respublika Mordoviya: Polikul'turnoe Obrazovanie [The Republic of Mordovia: Multicultural Education]. In: *Etnokul'turnoe Obrazovanie: Metody Sotsial'noi Orientatsii Rossiiskoi Shkoly [Ethnocultural Education: Methods of Social Orientation of Russian Schools]*. Moscow: Russian Academy of Sciences, 61–67.

Medda-Windischer, R., 2008. *Old and New Minorities: Reconciling Diversity and Cohesion*. Baden Baden: Nomos.

Medda-Windischer, R., 2009. The European Convention on Human Rights and Language Rights: Is the Glass Half Empty or Half Full? *European Yearbook of Minority Issues*, 7, 95–121.

Medda-Windischer, 2014. Integration of New and Old Minorities in Europe: Different or Similar Policies and Indicators? *Integrim Online Papers*, 10.

Medvedev, S., 2008. The Stalemate in EU-Russia Relations: Between 'Sovereignty' and 'Europeanization'. In: T. Hopf, ed. *Russia's European Choice*. New York: Palgrave Macmillan, 215–232.

Melvin, N., 2007. Putin's Reform of the Russian Federation. In: A. Pravda, ed. *Leading Russia: Putin in Perspective*. Oxford: Oxford University Press, 203–227.

Mertus, J., 1999. From Legal Transplants to Transformative Justice: Human Rights and the Promise of Transnational Civil Society. *American University International Law Review*, 14, 1335–1389.

Mirgaleev, I.M., 2001. Istoriya Prinyatiya Islama Tatarskim Narodom [History of the Introduction of Islam among the Tatar People]. *Idel'*, 7, 72–73.

Mithum, M., 1998. The Significance of Diversity in Language Endangerment. In: L. Grenoble and L. Whaley, eds. *Endangered Languages: Language Loss and Community Response*. Cambridge: Cambridge University Press.

Mitin, D., 2008. From Rebellion to Submission: The Evolution of Russian Federalism under Putin. *Problems of Post-Communism*, 55 (5), 49–61.

Moravcsik, A., 1998. *The Choice for Europe: Social Purpose and State Power from Messina to Maastricht*. Ithaca, NY: Cornell University Press.

Moravcsik, A., 2000. The Origins of Human Rights Regimes: Democratic Delegation in Postwar Europe. *International Organization*, 54 (2), 217–252.

Moseley, C., ed., 2010. *Atlas of the World's Languages in Danger*. 3rd edn. Paris: UNESCO.

Moser, R., 2000. *Unexpected Outcomes: Electoral Systems, Political Parties, and Representation in Russia*. Pittsburgh, PA: University of Pittsburgh Press.

Moser, R., 2008. Electoral Systems and the Representation of Ethnic Minorities: Evidence from Russia. *Comparative Politics*, 40 (3), 273–292.

Moser, R., 2013. Ethnic Federalism, Electoral Systems and the Representation of Ethnic Minorities: Evidence from Russia. In: O. Protsyk and B. Harzl, eds. *Managing Ethnic Diversity in Russia*. Abingdon: Routledge, 215–237.

Moucheboeuf, A., 2006. *Minority Rights Jurisprudence Digest*. Strasbourg: Council of Europe.

Munro, N., 2006. Russia's Persistent Communist Legacy: Nostalgia, Reaction, and Reactionary Expectations. *Post-Soviet Affairs*, 22 (4), 289–313.

Musina, R.N., 2011. Natsional'nye Yazyki v Sisteme Shkol'nogo Obrazovaniya [National Languages in the System of School Education]. In: R.N. Musina, G.F. Gabdrakhmanova and L.V. Sagitova, eds. *Yazyki v Sisteme Obrazovaniya Respubliki Tatarstan [Languages in the System of Education of the Republic of Tatarstan].* Kazan: Tatarskoe Knizhnoe Izdatel'stvo, 16–28.

Musina, R.N., Gabdrakhmanova, G.F. and Sagitova, L.V., 2011a. Introduction. In: R.N. Musina, G.F. Gabdrakhmanova and L.V. Sagitova, eds. *Yazyki v Sisteme Obrazovaniya Respubliki Tatarstan [Languages in the System of Education of the Republic of Tatarstan].* Kazan: Tatarskoe Knizhnoe Izdatel'stvo, 3–8.

Musina, R.N., Gabdrakhmanova, G.F. and Sagitova, L.V., 2011b. Statistics. In: R.N. Musina, G.F. Gabdrakhmanova and L.V. Sagitova, eds. *Yazyki v Sisteme Obrazovaniya Respubliki Tatarstan [Languages in the System of Education of the Republic of Tatarstan].* Kazan: Tatarskoe Knizhnoe Izdatel'stvo, 139–152.

Musschenga, A.W., 1998. Intrinsic Value as a Reason for the Preservation of Minority Cultures. *Ethical Theory and Moral Practice*, 1 (2), 201–225.

Nekrich, A.M., 1978. *The Punished Peoples.* New York: Norton.

Neumann, I.B., 2005. Russia as a Great Power. In: J. Hedenskog, V. Konnander, B. Nygren, I. Oldberg and C. Pursiainen, eds. *Russia as a Great Power: Dimensions of Security under Putin.* London: Routledge, 13–28.

Neumann, I.B., 2011. Entry into International Society Reconceptualised. *Review of International Studies*, 37 (2), 463–484.

Nimni, E., 2005. *Natural Cultural Autonomy and its Contemporary Critics.* Abingdon: Routledge.

Nimni, E., 2007. National-Cultural Autonomy as an Alternative to Minority Territorial Nationalism. *Ethnopolitics*, 6 (3), 345–364.

Nimni, E., Osipov, A. and Smith, D.J., eds., 2013. *The Challenge of Non-Territorial Autonomy: Theory and Practice.* Bern: Peter Lang.

Novikova, A., 2010. Myths about Soviet Values and Contemporary Russian Television. *Russian Journal of Communication*, 3 (3/4), 280–295.

Nussberger, A., 2008. The Reception Process in Russia and Ukraine. In: H. Keller and A. Stone Sweet, eds. *A Europe of Rights.* Oxford: Oxford University Press, 603–674.

O'Dwyer, C., 2006. Reforming Regional Governance in East Central Europe: Europeanization or Domestic Politics as Usual? *East European Politics and Societies*, 20 (2), 219–253.

Oeter, S., 2013. International Norms and Legal Status of Minority Languages in Russia. In: O. Protsyk and B. Harzl, eds. *Managing Ethnic Diversity in Russia.* Abingdon: Routledge, 37–61.

Offe, C., 2006. Political Disaffection as an Outcome of Institutional Practices? Some Post-Tocquevillean Speculations. In: M. Torcal and J.R. Montero, eds. *Political Disaffection in Contemporary Democracies: Social Capital, Institutions and Politics.* London: Routledge, 23–45.

Okin, S.M., 1999. *Is Multiculturalism Bad for Women?* Princeton, NJ: Princeton University Press.

Okin, S.M., 2002. 'Mistresses of their Own Destinies': Group Rights, Gender, and Realistic Right of Exit. *Ethics*, 112, 205–230.

Olsen, J., 1996. Europeanization and Non-State Dynamics. In: S. Gustavsson and L. Lewin, eds. *The Future of the Nation State: Essays on Political Pluralism and Political Integration.* Stockholm: Nerenius and Santerus.

Olsen, J., 2002. The Many Faces of Europeanization. *Journal of Common Market Studies*, 40 (5), 921–952.

Opalski, M., 2001. Can Will Kymlicka Be Exported to Russia? Western Political Theory and Ethnic Relations in Eastern Europe. In: W. Kymlicka and O. Oracheva, eds. *Can Liberal Pluralism Be Exported?* Oxford: Oxford University Press, 298–319.

Oracheva, O. and Osipov, A., 2010. Territories of 'Special Status' in Russia: The Ethnic Dimension. *Journal of Communist Studies and Transition Politics*, 26 (2), 212–232.

Örücü, E., 2002. Law as Transposition. *The International and Comparative Law Quarterly*, 51 (2), 205–223.

Osipov, A., 2004. *Natsional'no-Kul'turnaya Avtonomiya: Idei, Resheniya, Instituty [National Cultural Autonomy: Ideas, Decisions, Institutions]*. St. Petersburg: Centre for Independent Sociological Research.

Osipov, A., 2010. National Cultural Autonomy in Russia: A Case of Symbolic Law. *Review of Central and East European Law*, 35, 27–57.

Osipov, A., 2011. The 'Peoples' Congresses' in Russia: Failure or Success? Authenticity and Efficiency of Minority Representation. *Working Paper No. 48*. Flensburg: European Centre for Minority Issues.

Osipov, A., 2012. Implementation Unwanted? Symbolic vs. Instrumental Policies in the Russian Management of Ethnic Diversity. *Perspectives on European Politics and Society*, 13 (4), 425–442.

Osipov, A., 2013a. National-Cultural Autonomy in Russia: A Matter of Legal Regulation or the Symbolic Construction of an Ethnic Mosaic? In: O. Protsyk and B. Harzl, eds. *Managing Ethnic Diversity in Russia*. Abingdon: Routledge, 62–84.

Osipov, A., 2013b. Non-Territorial Autonomy as a Way to Frame Diversity Policies: The Case of Russia. In: E. Nimni, A. Osipov and D.J. Smith, eds. *The Challenges of Non-Territorial Autonomy: Theory and Practice*. Bern: Peter Lang, 133–148.

Osipov, A., 2013c. Soviet Party of Nations or Western Non-Discrimination: Is there a Dilemma for Russia? In: K. Cordell, T. Agarin and A. Osipov, eds. *Institutional Legacies of Communism: Change and Continuity in Minority Protection*. Abingdon and New York: Routledge, 59–73.

Osipov, A., 2014. What do the Crimean Tatars face in Crimea? *ECMI Issue Brief No. 32*. Flensburg: European Centre for Minority Issues.

Oversloot, H., 2007. Reordering the State (without Changing the Constitution): Russia under Putin's Rule, 2000–2008. *Review of Central and East European Law*, 32, 41–64.

Oversloot, H., 2013. The Homogeneity of Russia, or the Remains of an Empire (Federalism and Regionalism). In: O. Protsyk and B. Harzl, eds. *Managing Ethnic Diversity in Russia*. Abingdon: Routledge, 87–110.

Packer, J., 1993. On the Definition of Minorities. In: J. Packer and K. Myntti, eds. *The Protection of Ethnic and Linguistic Minorities in Europe*. Turku: Abo Akademi University, 23–65.

Packer, J., 1999. Problems in Defining Minorities. In: D. Fottrell and B. Bowring, eds. *Minority and Group Rights in the New Millenium*. The Hague: Martinus Nijhoff, 223–273.

Pain, E., 2005. Reforms in the Administration of the Regions and their Influence on Ethnopolitical Processes in Russia, 1999–2003. In: P. Reddaway and R. Orttung, eds. *The Dynamics of Russian Politics: Putin's Reforms of Federal-Regional Relations. Volume II*. Lanham, MD: Rowman & Littlefield, 341–370.

Palermo, F., 2008. The Dual Meaning of Participation: The Advisory Committee's Commentary to Article 15 of the FCNM. *European Yearbook of Minority Issues*, 7, 409–424.

Pavlenko, A., 2008. Multilingualism in Post-Soviet Countries: Language Revival, Language Removal, and Sociolinguistic Theory. In: A. Pavlenko, ed. *Multilingualism in Post-Soviet Countries*. Bristol: Multilingual Matters, 1–40.

Pentassuglia, G., 2003. *Minorities in International Law: An Introductory Study*. Strasbourg: Council of Europe.

Pentassuglia, G., 2009. *Minority Groups and Judiciary Discourse in International Law: A Comparative Perspective*. Leiden: Martinus Nijhoff.

Peroni, L. and Timmer, A., 2013. Vulnerable Groups: The Promise of an Emerging Concept in European Human Rights Convention Law. *International Journal of Constitutional Law*, 11 (4), 1056–1085.

Peters, B., 1998. *Comparative Politics: Theories and Methods*. New York: New York University Press.

Peterson, M.J., 1992. Transnational Activity, International Society and World Politics. *Millenium: Journal of International Studies*, 21 (3), 371–388.

Petrov, N., 2004. Federalism. In: M. McFaul, N. Petrov and A. Ryabov, eds. *Between Dictatorship and Democracy: Russian Post-Communist Political Reform*. Washington, DC: Carnegie Endowment for International Peace, 213–238.

Petrov, N., 2010. Regional Governors under the Dual Power of Medvedev and Putin. *Journal of Communist Studies and Transition Politics*, 26 (2), 276–305.

Petrov, N. and Slider, D., 2010. The Regions under Putin and After. In: S.K. Wegren and D.R. Herspring, eds. *After Putin's Russia: Past Imperfect, Future Uncertain*. Lanham, MD: Rowman & Littlefield, 59–82.

Pharr, S.J., Putnam, R.D. and Dalton, R.J., eds., 2000. *Disaffected Democracies: What's Troubling the Trilateral Countries?* Princeton, NJ: Princeton University Press.

Phillips, A., 1991. *Engendering Democracy*. Cambridge: Polity.

Phillips, A., 2002. *Democracy and Difference*. Cambridge: Polity.

Pilkington, H., Omel'chenk, E. and Garifzianova, A., 2010. *Russia's Skinheads: Exploring and Rethinking Subcultural Lives*. London: Routledge.

Pitkin, H., 1967. *The Concept of Representation*. Berkeley: University of California Press.

Pohl, J.O., 1999. *Ethnic Cleansing in the USSR, 1937–1949*. Westport, CT: Greenwood.

Pomeranz, W., 2009. Supervisory Review and the Finality of Judgements under Russian Law. *Review of Central and East European Law*, 34, 15–36.

Popov, A., 2008. Ethnicity and Civil Society after Socialism: The Politics of Representation among Greek Communities in Southern Russia. In: M. Flynn, R. Kay and J. Oldfield, eds. *Trans-National Issues, Local Concerns and Meanings of Post-Socialism*. Lanham, MD: University Press of America, 195–211.

Popova, M., 2012. *Politicized Justice in Emerging Democracies: A Study of Courts in Russia and Ukraine*. Cambridge: Cambridge University Press.

Powell, W.W. and DiMaggio, P.J., eds., 1991. *The New Institutionalism in Organizational Analysis*. Chicago: University of Chicago Press.

Prina, F., 2011a. Homogenisation and the 'New Russian Citizen': A Road to Stability or Ethnic Tensions? *Journal on Ethnopolitics and Minority Issues in Europe*, 10 (1), 59–93.

Prina, F., 2011b. Linguistic Rights in a Former Empire: Minority Languages and the Russian Higher Courts. *European Yearbook of Minority Issues*, 10, 61–89.

Prina, F., 2011c. Localism or Centralism? Education Reform in Russia and Its Impact on the Rights of National Minorities. *Cambrian Law Review*, 42, 113–130.

Prina, F., 2012. Power, Politics and Participation: The Russian Federation's National Minorities and their Participatory Rights. *Netherlands Quarterly of Human Rights*, 30 (1), 66–96.

Prina, F., 2014. What Next for Moldova's Minorities after Crimea? *ECMI Issue Brief No. 33*. Flensburg: European Centre for Minority Issues.

Protsyk, O., 2008. Accountability within Minority Political Participation. *European Yearbook of Minority Issues*, 7, 467–478.

Pulchalska-Tych, B. and Salter, M., 1996. Comparing Legal Cultures of Eastern Europe: The Need for a Dialectical Analysis. *Legal Studies*, 16 (2), 157–184.

Ramaga, P.V., 1992a. The Bases of Minority Identity. *Human Rights Quarterly*, 14 (3), 409–428.

Ramaga, P.V., 1992b. Relativity of the Minority Concept. *Human Rights Quarterly*, 14 (1), 104–119.

Ram, M.H., 2012. Legacies of EU Conditionality: Explaining Post-Accession Adherence to Pre-Accession Rules on Roma. *Europe-Asia Studies*, 64 (7), 1191–1218.

Rechel, B., ed., 2009. *Minority Rights in Central and Eastern Europe*. Abingdon: Routledge.

Reddaway, P., 2004. Historical and Political Context. In: P. Reddaway and R. Orttung, eds. *The Dynamics of Russian Politics: Putin's Reform of Federal-Regional Relations. Volume I*. Lanham, MD: Rowman & Littlefield, 1–18.

Reidel, L., 2010. What are Cultural Rights? Protecting Groups with Individual Rights. *Journal of Human Rights*, 9, 65–80.

Remington, T., 2003. Majorities without Mandates: The Russian Federation Council since 2000. *Europe-Asia Studies*, 55 (5), 667–691.

Renner, K., 2005 [1899]. State and Nation. In: E. Nimni, ed. *National Cultural Autonomy and its Contemporary Critics*. Abingdon: Routledge, 15–47.

Reuter, O.J., 2010. The Politics of Dominant Party Formation: United Russia and Russia's Governors. *Europe-Asia Studies*, 62 (2), 293–327.

Reuter, O.J., 2011. United Russia and the 2011 Elections. *Russian Analytical Digest*, 102, 2–6, 26 September 2011.

Riasanovsky, N.V., 1985. *The Image of Peter the Great in Russian History and Thought*. Oxford: Oxford University Press.

Risse, T., Green Cowles, M., and Caporaso, J., 2001. Europeanization and Domestic Change: Introduction. In: M. Green Cowles, J. Caporaso and T. Risse, eds. *Transforming Europe*. Ithaca, NY: Cornell University Press, 1–20.

Ritchie, J. and Spencer, L., 1994. Qualitative Data Analysis for Applied Policy Research. In: A. Bryman and R.G. Burgess, eds. *Analyzing Qualitative Data*. Abingdon: Routledge, 173–194.

Roberts, S.P., 2012a. *Putin's United Russia Party*. Abingdon: Routledge.

Roberts, S.P., 2012b. United Russia and the Dominant-Party Framework: Understanding the Russian Party of Power in Comparative Perspective. *East European Politics*, 28 (3), 225–240.

Roeder, P., 1992. Soviet Federalism and Ethnic Mobilisation. In: R. Denber, ed. *The Soviet Nationality Reader*. Boulder: Westview, 147–178.

Ross, C., 2011. The Rise and Fall of Political Parties in Russia's Regional Assemblies. *Europe-Asia Studies*, 63 (3), 429–448.

Rudden, B., 1994. Civil Law, Civil Society, and the Russian Constitution. *The Law Quarterly Review*, 110 (1), 61–83.

Rueschemeyer, D., 1998. The Self-Organization of Society and Democratic Rule. In: D. Rueschemeyer, M. Rueschemeyer and B. Wittrock, eds. *Participation and Democracy: East and West*. Armonk, NY: M.E. Sharpe, 9–25.

Sagitova, L.V., 2011. Motivatsii k Izucheniyu Yazykov sredi Uchashchikhsya Shkol RT i ikh Roditelei [Motivations in the Study of Languages among Students in Schools of the Republic of Tatarstan and their Parents]. In: R.N. Musina, G. Gabdrakhmanova and

L.V. Sagitova, eds. *Yazyki v Sisteme Obrazovaniya Respubliki Tatarstan [Languages in the System of Education of the Republic of Tatarstan]*. Kazan: Tatarskoe Knizhnoe Izdatel'stvo, 51–77.

Sakwa, R., 2004. *Putin: Russia's Choice*. London: Routledge.

Sakwa, R., 2005. Partial Adaptation and Political Culture. In: S. Whitefield, ed. *Political Culture and Post-Communism*. Basingstoke: Palgrave Macmillan.

Sakwa, R., 2008. *Russian Politics and Society*. London and New York: Routledge.

Sakwa, R., 2011a. Russia's Identity: Between the 'Domestic' and the 'International'. *Europe-Asia Studies*, 63 (6), 957–975.

Sakwa, R., 2011b. *The Crisis of Russian Democracy: The Dual State, Factionalism, and the Medvedev Succession*. Cambridge: Cambridge University Press.

Sakwa, R., 2012. Party and Power: Between Representation and Mobilisation in Contemporary Russia. *East European Politics*, 28 (3), 310–327.

Shahin, T., 1989. Ethnicity in the Soviet Union: Analytical Perceptions and Political Strategies. *Comparative Studies in Society and History*, 31 (3), 409–424.

Sharafutdinova, G., 2003. Paradiplomacy in the Russian Regions: Tatarstan's Search for Statehood. *Europe-Asia Studies*, 55 (4), 613–629.

Shevel, O., 2011. Russian Nation-building from Yel'tsin to Medvedev: Ethnic, Civic or Purposefully Ambiguous? *Europe-Asia Studies*, 63 (2), 179–202.

Shevtsova, L., 2003. *Putin's Russia*. Washington DC: Carnegie Endowment for International Peace.

Shevtsova, L., 2007. Vladimir Putin's Political Choice: Towards Bureaucratic Authoritarianism. In: A. Pravda, ed. *Leading Russia: Putin in Perspective*. Oxford: Oxford University Press, 229–253.

Shevyrev, A., 2005. Rewriting the National Past: New Images of Russia in History Textbooks of the 1990s. In: B. Eklof, L.E. Holmes and V. Kaplan, eds. *Education Reform in Post-Soviet Russia: Legacies and Prospects*. Abingdon: Frank Cass, 272–290.

Shils, E., 1991. The Virtue of Civil Society. *Government and Opposition*, 26 (1), 3–20.

Shleifer, A. and Treisman, D., 2004. A Normal Country. *Foreign Affairs*, 83 (1), 20–38.

Shnirelman, V., 1999. In Search of the Prestige Ancestors: Ethno-Nationalism and the School Textbooks. *Information Mitteilungen Communications*, 20 (1), 45–52.

Shnirelman, V., 2006a. 'Nesovmestimost' Kul'tur': Ot Nauchnykh Kontseptsii i Shkol'nogo Obrazovaniya do Real'noy Politiki ['The Incompatibility of Cultures': From National Concepts and School Education to Realpolitik]. In: A. Verkhovsky, ed. *Russkii Natsionalizm: Ideologiya i Nastroenie [Russian Nationalism: Ideology and Tendencies]*. Moscow: SOVA Center for Information and Analysis, 183–222.

Shnirelman, V., 2006b. Rossiiskaya Shkola i Natsional'naya Idea [The Russian School and the National Idea]. *Neprikosnovennyi Zapas*, 6 (50), 232–249.

Shnirelman, V., 2009a. New Racism, 'Clash of Civilisation,' and Russia. In: M. Laruelle, ed. *Russian Nationalism and the National Reassertion of Russia*. Abingdon: Routledge, 125–144.

Shnirelman, V., 2009b. Stigmatized by History or by Historians? The Peoples of Russia in School History Textbooks. *History and Memory*, 21 (2), 110–149.

Shnirelman, V., 2010. Rossiiskaya Shkola na Perelome [The Russian School in Transition]. In: V.A. Tishkov and V.V. Stepanov, eds. *Entopoliticheskaya Situatsiya v Rossii i Sopredel'nykh Gosudarstv v 2009 godu [The Ethnopolitical Situation in Russia and Neighbouring States in 2009]*. Moscow: Russian Academy of Sciences, 59–61.

Shulman, S., 2002. Challenging the Civic/Ethnic and West/East Dichotomies in the Study of Nationalism. *Comparative Political Studies*, 35 (5), 554–585.

Sigler, J., 1983. *Minority Rights: A Comparative Analysis*. London: Greenwood.

Silverman, D., 2000. *Interpreting Quantitative Analysis: Methods for Analysing Talk, Text and Interaction*. London: Sage.

Silverman, D., 2005. *Doing Qualitative Research*. London: Sage.

Simonsen, S.G., 1996. Raising the 'Russian Question': Ethnicity and Statehood – Russkie and Rossiya. *Nationalism and Ethnic Politics*, 2 (1), 91–110.

Skutnabb-Kangas, T., 1994. *Linguistic Human Rights: Overcoming Linguistic Discrimination*. Berlin: Mouton de Gruyter.

Skutnabb-Kangas, T., 2000. *Linguistic Genocide in Education, or Worldwide Diversity and Human Rights?* Mahwah, NJ: Lawrence Erlbaum Associates.

Slezkine, Y., 1994. The USSR as a Communal Apartment, or How a Socialist State Promoted Ethnic Particularism. *Slavic Review*, 53 (2), 413–452.

Slider, D., 2010. How United is United Russia? Regional Sources of Intraparty Conflict. *Journal of Communist Studies and Transition Politics*, 26 (2), 257–275.

Smith, A.D., 1998. *Nationalism and Modernism: A Critical Survey of Recent Theories of Nations and Nationalism*. Abingdon: Routledge.

Smith, M.G., 1998. *Language and Power in the Creation of the USSR, 1917–1953*. Berlin and New York: Mouton de Gruyter.

Sokolovskii, S.V., 2004. *Perspektiva Razvitii Kontseptsii Etnonatsional'noi Politiki v Rossiiskoi Federatsii [Perspectives for the Development of Ethnonational Policy in the Russian Federation]*. Moscow: Privet.

Solomon, P., 2005. Threats of Judicial Counterreform in Putin's Russia. *Demokratizatsiya*, 13 (3), 325–345.

Solomon, P., 2008a. Assessing the Courts in Russia: Parameters of Progress under Putin. *Demokratizatsiya*, 16 (1), 63–74.

Solomon, P., 2008b. Law in Public Administration: How Russia Differs. *Journal of Communist Studies and Transition Politics*, 24 (1), 115–135.

Solvang, O., 2008. Russia and the European Court of Human Rights: The Price of Non-Cooperation. *Human Rights Brief*, 15 (2), 14–17.

Sperling, V., 2009. Making the Public Patriotic: Militarism and Anti-Militarism in Russia. In: M. Laruelle, ed. *Russian Nationalism and the National Reassertion of Russia*. Abingdon: Routledge, 218–271.

Stake, R.E., 1995. *The Art of Case Study Research*. London: Sage.

Stalin, J., 1950 [1913]. *Marksizm i Natsional'nyi Vopros [Maxism and the National Question]*. Moscow: State Political Literature Publishing.

Stalin, J., 1954 [1926]. To Comrade Kaganovich and the Other Members of the Political Bureau of the Central Committee, Ukraine C.P.(B.). In: *Works*. Moscow: Foreign Languages Publishing House/Marxist Internet Archive, 157–163.

Stepan, A., 2000. Russian Federalism in Comparative Perspective. *Post-Soviet Affairs*, 16 (2), 133–176.

Stepanov, V.V., 2010. Sotsial'naya Orientatsiya Rossiiskoi Shkoly [The Social Orientation of Russian Schools]. In: V.V. Stepanov, ed. *Etnokul'turnoe Obrazovanie: Metody Sotsial'noi Orientatsii Rossiiskoi Shkoly [Ethnocultural Education: Methods of Social Orientation of Russian Schools]*. Moscow: Russian Academy of Sciences, 5–13.

Stoner-Weiss, K., 1999. Central Weakness and Provincial Autonomy: Observations on the Devolution Process in Russia. *Post-Soviet Affairs*, 15 (1), 87–106.

Strogal'shikova, Z.I., 2009a. Ethnodemografic Processes among Finno-Ugric Population of the Russian Federation. In: A.K. Konyukhov, ed. *Finno-Ugric Ethnicities in Russia: Yesterday, Today, Tomorrow*. Syktyvkar: 'Finland-Russia' Society, 32–59.

Strogal'shikova, Z.I., 2009b. Finno-Ugric Languages: Current Status and Practices in the System of Education of the Russian Federation. In: A.K. Konyukhov, ed. *Finno-Ugric Ethnicities in Russia: Yesterday, Today, Tomorrow*. Syktyvkar: 'Finland–Russia' Society, 135–153.

Suleymanova, D., 2010. International Language Rights Norms in the Dispute over Latinization Reform in the Republic of Tatarstan. *Caucasian Review of International Affairs*, 4 (1), 43–56.

Suleymanova, D., 2011. Schooling an Ethno-National Personhood: Education Politics in Post-Soviet Tatarstan. Paper presented at the 16th Annual World Conference, Association for the Study of Nationalities, New York, 14–16 April 2011.

Suny, R.G., 1993. *The Revenge of the Past: Nationalism, Revolution, and the Collapse of the Soviet Union*. Stanford, CA: Stanford University Press.

Suny, R.G., 1998. *The Soviet Experiment: Russia, the USSR, and the Successor States*. Oxford: Oxford University Press.

Suny, R.G. and Martin, T., 2002. *A State of Nations: Empire and Nation-Making in the Age of Lenin and Stalin*. Oxford: Oxford University Press.

Surkov, V., 2006. Natsionalizatsiya Budushchego [The Nationalisation of the Future]. In: *Suverennaya Demokratiya: Ot Idei k Doktrine [Sovereign Democracy: From Idea to Doctrine]*. Moscow: Evropa.

Taagepera, R., 1999. *The Finno-Ugric Republics and the Russian State*. London: C. Hurst & Co.

Taylor, B., 2005. Russia's Regions and Law Enforcement. In: P. Reddaway and R. Orttung, eds. *The Dynamics of Russian Politics: Putin's Reforms of Federal-Regional Relations. Volume II*. Lanham, MD: Rowman & Littlefield, 65–90.

Thaman, S., 2008. Jury Trial and Adversarial Procedure in Russia: Reform of Soviet Inquisitorial Procedure or Democratic Window-Dressing? In: G. Smith and R. Sharlet, eds. *Russia and its Constitution: Promise and Political Reality*. Leiden: Martinus Nijhoff, 141–180.

Thornberry, P., 1991. *International Law and the Rights of Minorities*. Oxford: Clarendon.

Thornberry, P., 2002. *Indigenous Peoples and Human Rights*. Manchester: Manchester University Press.

Tishkov, V.A., 1993. *Strategiya i Mekhanizmy Natsional'noi Politiki v Rossiiskoi Federatsii: Materialy Nauchno-Prakticheskoi Konferentsii [Strategy and Mechanisms of National Policy in the Russian Federation: Materials of an Academic-Practical Conference], Lipki, 1992*. Moscow: Nauka.

Tishkov, V.A., 1996. *Kontseptual'naya Evolutsiya Natsional'noi Politiki v Rossii [Conceptual Evolution of Nationalities Policy in Russia]*. Moscow: Russian Academy of Sciences.

Tishkov, V.A., 1997. *Ethnicity, Nationalism, and Conflict In and After the Soviet Union: The Mind Aflame*. London: Sage.

Tishkov, V.A., 2011. Rossiiskaya Natsiya i Rossiiskie Natsional'nosti [Russian Nation and Russian Nationality]. In: V.A. Tishkov, ed. *Rossiiskaya Natsiya: Stanovlenie i Etnokul'turnoe Mnogoobrazie [The Russian Nation: Formation and Ethnocultural Diversity]*. Moscow: Russian Academy of Sciences, 13–26.

Tishkov, V.A. and Filippova, E., 2002. *Local Governance and Minority Empowerment in the CIS*. Budapest: Open Society Institute.

Tolz, V., 1998. Forging the Nation: National Identity and Nation-Building in Post-Communist Russia. *Europe-Asia Studies*, 50 (6), 993–1022.

Tolz, V., 2001. *Russia: Inventing the Nation*. London: Arnold.

Trochev, A., 2008. *Judging Russia: Constitutional Court in Russian Politics 1990–2006.* Cambridge: Cambridge University Press.

Trochev, A., 2009. All Appeals Lead to Strasbourg? Unpacking the Impact of the European Court of Human Rights on Russia. *Demokratizatsiya*, 17 (2), 145–178.

Trochev, A. and Solomon, P., 2005. Courts and Federalism in Putin's Russia. In: P. Reddaway and R. Orttung, eds. *The Dynamics of Russian Politics: Putin's Reforms of Federal-Regional Relations. Volume II.* Lahnam: Rowman & Littlefield, 91–121.

Umland, A., 2009. Fascist Tendencies in Russia's Political Establishment: The Rise of the International Eurasian Movement. *Russian Analytical Digest*, 60, 13–17.

Vaillant, J.G., 2005. Civic Education in a Changing Russia. In: B. Eklof, L.E. Holmes and V. Kaplan, eds. *Education Reform in Post-Soviet Russia: Legacies and Prospects.* Abingdon: Frank Cass, 221–246.

Vareikis, I. and Zelenskii, I., 1924. *Natsional'no-Gosudarstvennoe Razmezhevanie Srednei Azii [The National-State Disengagement in Central Asia].* Tashkent: Sredne-Aziatskoe Gosudarstvennoe Izdatel'stvo.

Varlamova, N., 2001. *Sovremenniy Rossiiskii Federalizm: Konstitutsionnaya Model' i Politico-Provovaya Dinamika [Contemporary Russian Federalism: Constitutional Model and Politico-Legal Dynamics].* Moscow: Institute of Law and Public Policy.

Verkhovsky, A., 2009. Future Prospects of Contemporary Russian Nationalism. In: M. Laruelle, ed. *Russian Nationalism and the National Reassertion of Russia.* Abingdon: Routledge, 89–103.

Verstichel, A., 2008. Representation and Identity: The Right of Persons Belonging to Minorities to Effective Participation in Public Affairs. *European Yearbook of Minority Issues*, 7, 449–466.

Vujačič, V., 2009. Stalinism and Russian Nationalism: A Reconceptualization. In: M. Laruelle, ed. *Russian Nationalism and the National Reassertion of Russia.* Abingdon: Routledge, 49–74.

Waltz, K.N., 1979. *Theory of International Politics.* Boston: McGraw Hill.

Watson, A.A., 1974. *Legal Transplants: An Approach to Comparative Law.* Edinburgh: Scottish Academic Press.

Weller, M., 2005. Article 15. In: M. Weller, ed. *The Rights of Minorities in Europe: A Commentary on the European Framework Convention on the Protection of National Minorities.* Oxford: Oxford University Press, 429–461.

Weller, M., ed., 2007. *Universal Minority Rights: A Commentary on the Jurisprudence of International Courts and Treaty Bodies.* Oxford: Oxford University Press.

Weller, M , 2008. Minority Consultative Mechanisms: Towards Best Practices. *European Yearbook of Minority Issues*, 7, 425–445.

White, D., 2012. Re-conceptualising Russian Party Politics. *East European Politics*, 28 (3), 210–224.

Willems, J., 2007. Fundamentals of Orthodox Culture (FOC): A New Subject in Russia's Schools. *British Journal of Religious Education*, 29 (3), 229–243.

Willems, J., 2012. 'Foundations of Orthodox Culture' in Russia: Confessional or Non-Confessional Religious Education? *European Education*, 44 (2), 23–43.

Wolman, H., 1990. Decentralization: What It Is and Why We Should Care. In: R.J. Bennet, ed. *Decentralization, Local Government and Markets.* Oxford: Clarendon, 29–43.

Xanthaki, A., 2004. Indigenous Rights in the Russian Federation: The Case of the Numerically Small Peoples of the Russian North, Siberia and Far East. *Human Rights Quarterly*, 26 (1), 74–105.

Xanthaki, A., 2010. Multiculturalism and International Law: Discussing Universal Standards. *Human Rights Quarterly*, 32 (1), 21–48.

Yamskov, A.N., 2010. Problema Ekspertizy Federal'nykh Obrazovatel'nykh Gosudarstvennykh Standartov [The Problem in the Evaluation of Federal Education Standards]. In: *Etnokul'turnoe Obrazovanie: Metody Sotsial'noi Orientatsii Rossiiskoi Shkoly [Ethnocultural Education: Methods of Social Orientation of Russian Schools]*. Moscow: Russian Academy of Sciences, 193–204.

Zamyatin, K., 2012a. Finno-Ugric Languages in Russian Education: The Changing Legal-Institutional Framework and Falling Access to Native Language Learning. *Études Finno-Ougriennes*, 44, 2–44.

Zamyatin, K., 2012b. From Language Revival to Language Removal? The Teaching of Titular Languages in the National Republics of Post-Soviet Russia. *Journal on Ethnopolitics and Minority Issues in Europe*, 11 (2), 75–102.

Zamyatin, K., 2012c. The Education Reform in Russia and Its Impact on Teaching of the Minority Languages: An Effect of Nation-Building? *Journal on Ethnopolitics and Minority Issues in Europe*, 11 (1), 17–47.

Zamyatin, K., 2014. *An Official Status for Minority Languages? A Study of State Languages in Russia's Finno-Ugric Republics*. Helsinki: Uralica Helsingiensia 6.

Žižek, S., 2011. *Living in the End Times*. London: Verso.

Index